AFTER THE GULAG

AFTER THE GULAG

A HISTORY OF MEMORY IN RUSSIA'S FAR NORTH

TYLER C. KIRK

INDIANA UNIVERSITY PRESS

This book is a publication of

Indiana University Press
Office of Scholarly Publishing
Herman B Wells Library 350
1320 East 10th Street
Bloomington, Indiana 47405 USA

iupress.org

© 2023 by Tyler C. Kirk

All rights reserved
No part of this book may be reproduced or utilized in any form or by any
means, electronic or mechanical, including photocopying and recording,
or by any information storage and retrieval system, without permission in
writing from the publisher. The paper used in this publication meets the
minimum requirements of the American National Standard for Information
Sciences—Permanence of Paper for Printed Library Materials,
ANSI Z39.48–1992.

Manufactured in the United States of America

First printing 2023

Library of Congress Cataloging-in-Publication Data

Names: Kirk, Tyler C., author.
Title: After the gulag : a history of memory in Russia's far north / Tyler
  C. Kirk.
Description: Bloomington, Indiana : Indiana University Press, [2023] |
  Includes bibliographical references and index.
Identifiers: LCCN 2023017100 (print) | LCCN 2023017101 (ebook) | ISBN
  9780253067494 (hardback) | ISBN 9780253067500 (paperback) | ISBN
  9780253067517 (ebook)
Subjects: LCSH: Internment camp inmates—Soviet Union. | Political
  prisoners—Soviet Union—History. | Forced labor—Soviet Union. |
  Memorialization—Russia (Federation) | BISAC: HISTORY / Russia / Soviet
  Era | POLITICAL SCIENCE / World / Russian & Soviet
Classification: LCC HV8964.S65 K57 2023 (print) | LCC HV8964.S65 (ebook)
  | DDC 365/.4509470904—dc23/eng/20230608
LC record available at https://lccn.loc.gov/2023017100
LC ebook record available at https://lccn.loc.gov/2023017101

CONTENTS

Preface vii

Acknowledgments ix

Introduction 1

1. Letters to Syktyvkar Memorial: "Who Will Remember If I Forget?" 23

2. The "Brotherhood of *Zeks*": Constructing Community and Identity through Memoirs 63

3. Alternative Forms of Autobiography: Konstantin Ivanov's Letters and Art 101

4. "How I Remained a Human Being": Elena Markova's Spiritual Resistance Inside and Outside the Gulag 147

5. Local Newspapers and the Production of Cultural Memory in Komi, 1987–2021 174

Epilogue 229

Bibliography 245

Index 273

PREFACE

Georgii Ustilovskii, a Gulag returnee and founder of the Sosnogorsk Memorial Society in the Komi Republic, wrote in a 2002 op-ed in *30 Oktiabria*, "We try to do everything we can so that we do not return to the bloody totalitarian regime. We do not have any weapon other than the truth. And we try to uphold this word and teach the youth, whose understanding of the past is far from the truth."[1] The world has changed since the research for this book was conducted. On December 28, 2021, the Supreme Court of the Russian Federation ordered the closure of the International Memorial Society (Memorial)—one of Russia's oldest human rights and civic organizations. The civil society that Russian citizens built following the collapse of the Soviet Union has been crushed by the state under President Vladimir Putin. The Russian state has silenced the last independent voices in the state-controlled press, clamped down on nongovernmental organizations, and imprisoned protesters and anyone who criticizes the war Russia unleashed on Ukraine on February 24, 2022. The state prevents those who wish to learn the truth about their past by restricting access to archives to only those with repressed relatives and then intimidating those researchers with an opaque and Byzantine bureaucracy despite their legal right to access their relatives' files. The Russian state has passed "memory laws," similar to those enacted in Western Europe to criminalize the denial of the Holocaust and racism, to label the regime's critics as "Nazis" and criminalize interpretations of history that challenge the growing cult of victory of World War II, known by its Soviet-era moniker as the "Great Patriotic War." History in Putin's Russia is being distorted to the point of justifying the largest land invasion in Europe since World War II. Political repression is arguably the worst it

viii   PREFACE

has been in Russia since Stalin. The politics of memory have never been a more pertinent topic or had greater implications than they do today.

This book reveals a lost era when civil society organizations like Memorial existed and served citizens grappling with the painful chapters of their recent history. It explores the legacy of Stalinist repression and how those who survived the brunt of Stalinist violence entered into dialogue with those who had not been repressed. They rewrote the history of their country at a moment of tumultuous change and hope for a democratic future. This history of memory in the Russian Far North informs readers about the effort to come to terms with the crimes of the Soviet regime but also has direct implications for understanding Putin's Russia today. It speaks to how Russian society attempted, and failed, to come to terms with the past. It also shows how ordinary citizens in Russia's regions have resisted the crushing might of the state. They pushed back against the state's attempt to wrest control over the past from those engaged in a memory project of coming to terms with Stalinism and the crimes of the Soviet regime.

Themes: civil society, truth and reconciliation, trauma, memory, authoritarianism, and democratic breakdown

Note

1. Georgii Ustilovskii, "U nas net drugogo oruzhiia krome slova pravdy," *30 Oktiabria*, no. 22 (2002), Soviet and Post-Soviet Independent Publications, box 2, Hoover Institution Library and Archives.

ACKNOWLEDGMENTS

During the decade in which I worked on this project, I amassed a number of personal, professional, and intellectual debts. The research and writing of this book were generously funded by several fellowships and institutions, including the J. William Fulbright US Student Research Program with funds provided by the US Department of State, Bureau of Educational and Cultural Affairs; the Title VIII Research Scholarship provided by the Kennan Institute at the Woodrow Wilson Center for International Scholars; the Hoover Institution at Stanford University; Arizona State University's School of Historical, Philosophical, and Religious Studies, Center for Jewish Studies, and Melikian Center for Russian, Eurasian, and East European Studies; the University of Alaska Fairbanks and the University of Alaska Foundation. I also wish to express special thanks to the following people and institutions for their permission to reproduce the images in this book: Fond Pokaianie, the International Memorial Society, the Vorkuta Museum–Exhibition Center, the Inta Local History Museum, the State Gulag History Museum, A. A. Popov, the National Museum of the Komi Republic, the National Gallery of the Komi Republic, and the National Archive of the Komi Republic. I—and not the organizations listed—am solely responsible for the opinions and content expressed herein.

This work would not have been possible without the personal contributions of numerous extraordinary people who shared their stories and guided me through the research on a particularly difficult subject. I acknowledge the survivors and their children that I met in the course of researching and writing this book. With equal gratitude, I acknowledge those who I did not have the privilege to meet but whose experiences are documented in this work. I also

X ACKNOWLEDGMENTS

acknowledge their allies, who not only were participants in the events described in this book but also made introductions, guided me, and provided me with access to the materials on which this history is based. The late Mikhail Borisovich Rogachev was a mentor and friend throughout the process of researching and writing this book. During my time in Komi and in Moscow, I was also greatly aided by dedicated and passionate researchers, historians, archivists, and teachers. My time there would not have been a success without Marina Klimova, Nikolai Morozov, Liubov' Maksimova, Elena Morozova, Anatolii Popov, Svetlana Khudiaeva, Galina Khudiaeva, Nadezhda Bazhanova, Nadezhda Beliaeva, Galina Trukhina, Tat'iana Zashikhina, Fedor Kolpakov, Evgeniia Zelenskaia, Oskana Gritsenko, Alena Kozlova, Tat'iana Goloven, Natasha Chuprova, Elena Stanislavovna, G. M. Artemenko, Ol'ga Abachieva, Anastasiia Lazareva, Roman Romanov, Alena Kozlova, and many others.

I was fortunate to work with exceptional teachers and mentors during my undergraduate and graduate studies. I built a strong foundation in Russian and Soviet history with Louis Sell at the University of Maine at Farmington and then with Sheila Fitzpatrick at the University of Chicago. I learned Russian at the Komi State Pedagogical Institute in Syktyvkar, Russia and the Kathryn Davis School of Russian at Middlebury College where I made lifelong friends with many teachers, including Evgeny Dengub, who helped me decipher occasionally cryptic handwriting found in the letters I examined in this book. I had the extremely good fortune of working with a number of excellent historians and mentors at Arizona State University. I am eternally grateful to my dissertation cochair, Laurie Manchester, who encouraged me to think outside the box and to pursue nontraditional sources wherever they may lead. I am also grateful to her for teaching me to be a better writer over the course of many drafts of the manuscript. I am likewise grateful to my other dissertation cochair at Arizona State University, Mark von Hagen, who always pushed me to think big while respecting the most minute detail. Our conversations over the years continue to shape my thinking, and I wish you could read this work now.

Anna Holian and Alan Barenberg provided me with excellent training and thoughtful insights at every stage of this project. I am equally grateful to many colleagues who provided me with guidance as I researched and wrote this book. I greatly benefited from the advice and encouragement that I received over the years from many others who read drafts of chapters, reviewed the entire manuscript, or provided me with fresh insight. They include Kathleen Smith, Jeff Hardy, Philip Skorokhodov, Mikhail Nakonechnyi, Golfo Alexopoulos, Steve Barnes, John Romero, Peter Winsky, Mehmet Volkan Kasikçki, Wilson Bell, Cynthia Ruder, Paul Werth, Andy Jenks, Susan Grunewald, and Lydia

Roberts. I am grateful to the anonymous reviewers at *Kritika* who read parts of chapter 3, which was published as an article in that journal; the participants in the second "Desert Workshop in Russian History"; and participants in the "Authoritarianism and Democratic Breakdown" workshop at the Hoover Institution, including Paul Gregory and Norman Naimark, who invited me to Palo Alto, California, for two productive weeks in July 2022 as I completed final revisions.

The long winter months in Komi were made much more enjoyable by the friendships of Liza Kalinina, Lauren Woodard, Nicholas Levy, Christiana Bonin, Anton Vakhotin, Maegan Boutot, Georgii Moiseenko, Tat'iana Goloven, and Natalia Chuprova, who I met in Syktyvkar, Moscow, and points in between.

This journey took me far from home, and I am forever grateful to my family, especially my parents Milt and Joan Kirk, who were a source of endless encouragement and love. My brother, Caleb, provided much needed respites fly-fishing on rivers throughout Maine. I would also like to express my immense gratitude to my extended family, the Carrs, who sent timely care packages to Syktyvkar, Russia; Tempe, Arizona; and Fairbanks, Alaska. I thank Miles Campos and Xiaohang Jiao for their friendship over many years. Finally, this book would not have been possible without the friendships and family I found in my new home in Fairbanks. Brandon Boylan, Nathan and Teal Belz, Phil and Steph Wight, Bill Schneider and Sidney Stephens, and Dan Darrow were invaluable sources of support when I needed it most. I am especially grateful for Willa Schneider, with her steadfast patience and unconditional love as I found my way. Thank you all for skiing with me through the taiga, fishing with me under the midnight sun, hunting with me for berries and caribou in the tundra, teaching me how to safely navigate rivers, and showing me how to live an Alaskan life. Finally, I'd like to thank Frøya, the Alaskan malamute, and Peace the Alaskan husky, who entered my life as I completed this book, for gently reminding me that it is time for a ski.

AFTER THE GULAG

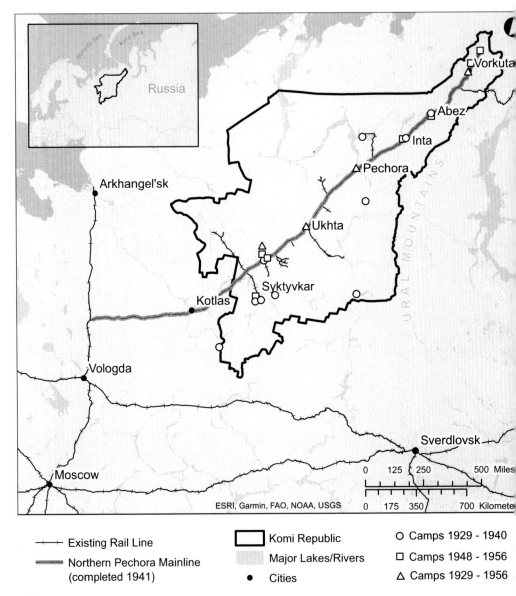

Map 0.1 Map of the Komi Republic depicting location of camps.
Source: Dr. Nathan P. Belz, University of Alaska Fairbanks.

Introduction

In 1991, following a brief exchange of letters, Gulag returnee Vitalii Ol'shevskii sent his memoir from Kiev to the Syktyvkar Memorial Society. The society was a branch of one of the Soviet Union's first civic organizations, founded in Moscow in 1987 to commemorate the victims of Stalinist repression. Although Ol'shevskii no longer lived in the Russian Far North, he felt that his memoir belonged in Syktyvkar Memorial's growing archive of survivor testimonies. Much had been written in the press in the few short years since President Mikhail Gorbachev relaxed censorship with his policy of *glasnost*. Like many other victims of political repression who sent their autobiographical narratives to local history museums and branches of the International Memorial Society (Memorial) throughout the Komi Autonomous Soviet Socialist Republic (ASSR), Ol'shevskii sought to contribute his insider's perspective to the reconstruction of a now permissible past. As he explained in the opening paragraphs of his memoir,

> I, like all of my countrymen, had to endure the terrible period in the history of our country, which the people have subsequently named the "Ezhovshchina"— and twenty years later, officially and publicly at the Twentieth Party Congress, [First Secretary Nikita] Khrushchev named it the "period of Stalin's cult of personality"—and to not only experience but to end up in the numbers of victims of that terror, which raged throughout the entirety of our vast motherland. There were very many of us, but neither the Twentieth Congress nor anyone else since has named the true number of victims.
>
> More often than not, [arrest] befell ordinary citizens who did not belong to the upper echelons of power, people who lived quietly, labored honestly, raised children . . .

> Since it fell to me to go through all levels of this human meat grinder, to endure all humiliations, all the physical and moral torture, and after fifteen years to exit to freedom and wait for recognition from the organs that I am not guilty of anything, I want to share the details about everything I experienced.[1]

Underscoring his authority to testify as one of the remaining survivors of Stalin's camps and the authenticity of his testimony as an ordinary political prisoner, Ol'shevskii presented his life as evidence of an unwritten and actively forgotten history of the Soviet Union: "The only thing that I wish is that this cruel, terrible epoch not pass away in memory. It should enter into history, so that it is never again repeated. I also want to underscore that there is not one grain of fiction, slander, or malevolence in these memoirs. I write only the truth, only about what I saw with my own eyes, what I experienced myself, or heard based on absolutely trusted sources. It is not my intention to take revenge on anyone. Those guilty of my tragedy left this life long ago. They got theirs without my intervention."[2] In the opening pages of his memoir, Ol'shevskii described what drove so many former prisoners to reveal themselves as victims of Stalinist repression in the final years of Soviet power. They sought to write themselves and their camp comrades into Soviet history at its end.

This book explores how ordinary political prisoners navigated life after release and how they translated their experiences in the Gulag and afterward into memoirs, letters, and art.[3] The construction of memory by former prisoners took place in the context of their relationships with each other and with nonprisoners—indeed, even the definition of "victim" was dependent on this interrelationship. Their autobiographical narratives informed the cultural memory of the Gulag in post-Soviet Russia during a period of tumultuous transition when Russians grappled with the painful chapters of their recent past in the hopes of building a democratic future. Using the Komi Republic as a case study shows how this memory crystallized in texts, ceremonies, monuments, and civil associations in the Russian Far North. Examining this memory project in a unique regional context breaks the idea of a centralized national culture of memory and reveals the influence of Russia's regions on Moscow. As people who bore the brunt of Stalinist violence and survived, Gulag returnees' life stories collected by Memorial serve as the basis of a powerful, alternate version of Soviet history. It is an alternate history because its evidence is to be found primarily in nonstate archives. This aspect is also what made the historical narrative that emerged from these new archives so powerful—the narrative was based on the details of the individual lives of thousands of ordinary Soviet citizens. Furthermore, these new testimonies expanded and went far beyond the memoirs and artistic representations of the camps published during the short-lived period of de-Stalinization under Khrushchev known as the "Thaw."[4] Eventually, the archive that survivors and their children built would be seen as a threat to President Vladimir Putin's regime. It is seen as a threat because it challenges the state's interpretation of the past by laying bare the crimes of the Soviet regime and juxtaposing them with the cult of victory of World War II— called the "Great Patriotic War," the Soviet-era moniker used in post-Soviet Russia as a symbol of Russian nationalism and military might.[5]

The mobilization of this new narrative was made possible by the formation of the Soviet Union's first civic organizations, which coalesced into a civil society in the late 1980s and early 1990s. The ranks of these civic organizations, typified by the International Memorial Society, were made up in part by Gulag returnees and their families. Once Gorbachev relaxed the controls on state censorship, thousands of victims and their families came forward, enabled by Memorial, to present new evidence of past crimes. This evidence quickly eroded the Communist Party's ability to limit its focus to Stalin and victimized party members.[6] Although discussion of the past was initiated from the top, the impetus for change was driven from below, much as it was in Western Europe following World War II.[7] The rise of memory at the end of the twentieth century, Nikolay Koposov writes, was affected by the democratization of history and the rise of the subaltern, the end of utopian projects and the Cold War, and the spread of human rights discourse.[8] Despite these universal trends, the production of cultural memory in Western and Eastern Europe, respectively, was shaped by two radically different events: the Holocaust in the West and the collapse of communist rule in the East.[9] Consequently, although the memory project of coming to terms with the Stalinist past was initiated by the Communist Party in Moscow, this book shows how memory lives in the provinces.

This book presents new evidence that sheds light not only on how Gulag returnees experienced life in Komi's towns but also on how they laid the foundations for the future commemoration of its past. While many prisoners left Komi after they were released, many more were not able to leave or chose not to when given the choice.[10] Originating in the camps as a means to survive, Gulag returnees' friendships grew into extended networks of informal associations after release. These informal mutual aid societies enabled the most vulnerable members of Soviet society to protect one another—or at least try to—from the state. They also provided Gulag returnees with a community of their own and a much-needed source of moral support and practical advice as they reintegrated into a society that remained largely suspicious and hostile toward them.[11] Gulag returnees who remained in Komi, and even those who left, continued to meet as friends, companions, and members of the "camp brotherhood." As many former prisoners wrote, these informal gatherings frequently turned into "evenings of memory" where they remembered the camps and the comrades they lost to "that world." Although it would be decades before many of them wrote memoirs, these informal gatherings formed the basis of a "community of memory" through which Gulag returnees defined themselves and their community.[12] This community was also shaped by the indelible stigma associated with former prisoners and the resistance they faced to their efforts to uncover and overcome dark chapters of the past, even in the post-Soviet period. As this book will show, Gulag returnees' friendships, social networks, and the greater mnemonic community they belonged to were integral to the success of the memory project of de-Stalinization in Komi and throughout the rest of the country.

Komi has a long history as a region of exile. As a hinterland of the Russian Empire, located in the northeastern corner of European Russia adjacent to the polar Ural Mountains, Komi became a place of exile in the late eighteenth and early nineteenth centuries.[13] At the start of the twentieth century, the region was sparsely populated by the native Finno-Ugric Komi people and a mix of free and unfree Russian settlers.[14] Before 1905, there were approximately 200 exiles living within the contemporary borders of the Komi Republic; by 1909, there were approximately 1,800 exiles in Komi.[15] Following the October Revolution and the Russian Civil War, the Bolsheviks continued to use the remote region as a dumping ground for undesirables.[16] It was not until 1929, when an expedition led by the Soviet secret police (the Joint State Political Directorate [OGPU] later known as the Peoples Commissariat of Internal Affairs [NKVD]) to survey the availability of natural resources in Komi disembarked at Chib'iu (now Ukhta), that the region embarked on a period of internal colonization with the growth of one of the first and largest networks of corrective labor camps in the Soviet Union.[17]

The demographics of Komi's prisoner population generally reflect camps throughout the rest of the Soviet Union. Based on the available statistics compiled by the Gulag administration, Alan Barenberg provides insight into the demographic profile of one of Komi's largest camp complexes in his history of Vorkuta. From 1942 to 1958, the majority of prisoners in Vorkutlag were ethnic Russians (between 38% and 63%). However, they were joined by other Soviet and foreign nationalities, including Ukrainians (the second largest contingent, between 10% and 31%), Belorussians, Georgians, Armenians, Tatars, Latvians, Lithuanians, Estonians, Jews, Germans, Poles, Chinese, Koreans, and miscellaneous others.[18] In terms of gender, universally, more men than women were imprisoned in the Gulag.[19] The same is true of the prisoner population of Vorkutlag. For example, from 1939 to 1958, men represented 85–99 percent of the prisoner population in Vorkutlag.[20] Despite their minority status in Komi's camps, the testimonies of female survivors provide important insights into the camps and life after release.[21] Statistics on prisoners' class origins are more difficult to obtain. Most prisoners in the Gulag were sentenced for nonpolitical crimes frequently associated with peasants, workers, thieves, and hardened criminals; however, the data on the convictions of Vorkutlag's prisoners complicate the general picture. From 1939 to 1955, between 68 and 75 percent of the prisoner population in Vorkutlag consisted of prisoners sentenced for "counter-revolutionary," or political, crimes.[22] This population largely differs from the Gulag system as a whole and suggests that the state saw Komi—with its harsh climate, barren landscape, and great natural wealth to exploit—as the perfect place to send those it deemed the least redeemable.

Although there were no camps in the city itself, Syktyvkar, Komi's capital city, came to be known in the late 1980s as "the capital of the camp republic."[23] Six of Komi's seven cities were built by people imprisoned in one of Komi's nine major camp complexes involved in the construction of vital infrastructure and the extraction of natural resources: timber, coal, oil, and uranium. In addition to these sprawling camps, of which there were twenty-two between 1929 and 1960, there were also villages for exiles scattered throughout the taiga and tundra known as "special settlements."[24] Syktyvkar was linked to all points of Komi's carceral archipelago by an infrastructure built on the bones of an unknown number of prisoners.[25] Estimates calculated from data in the archives of the Ministry of Internal Affairs (NKVD-MVD)—the institution responsible for the Gulag's operation—suggest that Komi's prisoner population grew from 10,000 in 1932 to 242,800 by 1950.[26] One of Komi's camp towns, Ukhta, for example, grew out of Komi's largest camp Ukhtpechlag, becoming a city of 16,000 (not including the prisoner population) in 1943.[27] Of these 16,000 civilians (vol'nonaemnye), 91.7 percent worked for Ukhtizhemstroi, a subsidiary of the corrective labor camp Ukhtizhemlag.[28] Considering that a total of 18 million people went through the hundreds of camps throughout the Soviet Union from their establishment in 1929 through 1960, the presence of so many prisoners concentrated in one region makes Komi unusual.[29] These demographics and the region's history also contributed to the formation of Komi's seven branches of the Memorial Society. Over time, Syktyvkar became the primary branch of the Memorial Society in Komi and formed the basis of a new organization known as the Repentance Foundation (hereafter Fond Pokaianie). Fond Pokaianie is the only organization of its kind in Russia. It was formed from a unique partnership between Syktyvkar Memorial and the provincial government in Komi, which funded the publication of books of memory (now in their fourteenth volume), erected monuments, sponsored museum exhibits, and contributed to Memorial's ongoing research and efforts to locate gravesites and "rehabilitate" victims of political repression. While many of these attributes make Komi unique, it is emblematic of other regions that underwent similar transformations into places of exile, imprisonment, industry, and death where branches of the Memorial Society emerged. In 1990, there were two hundred branches of the Memorial Society throughout the Soviet Union; however, by the mid-1990s, only thirty-five remained active.[30]

For those who survived the Gulag, rehabilitation was important because it not only restored their rights as Soviet citizens but also recognized their innocence by the state.[31] Rehabilitation first emerged as a political category after Stalin's death in 1953, when the Communist Party leadership initiated a limited de-Stalinization of Soviet society.[32] Between 1954 and 1961, approximately 800,000 Soviet citizens (both living and deceased) were rehabilitated by the state as victims of Stalinist repression.[33] This number represents less than one-third of the total of those who were sentenced for political crimes between the end of the Russian Civil War and Stalin's death.[34] The majority of former prisoners who were rehabilitated after Stalin's death were amnestied first and then applied for rehabilitation.[35] These petitions were handled on a case-by-case basis by committees at the Ministry of Justice and the Ministry of Internal Affairs in what was often a slow process.[36] Despite Khrushchev's denunciation of Stalin's "cult of personality" at the Twentieth Party Congress in 1956 and the removal of his body from Lenin's mausoleum following the Twenty-Second Party Congress in 1961, the party did little to streamline the process of rehabilitation to account for twenty-five years of mass repression and terror.

Because of the lack of institutional and legal support and the subsequent freeze on the discussion of Stalin's crimes under Leonid Brezhnev, most Gulag returnees remained unrehabilitated until Gorbachev returned to the issue in the late 1980s.[37] Gorbachev's efforts to update the former decree on rehabilitation led to the cancelation of all sentences handed down by extrajudicial organs (the infamous "troikas" and special boards of the Ministry of Internal Affairs) in 1989. This change resulted in the rehabilitation of 838,500 people and the reinstatement of 80,000 communists in the party in one year alone.[38] The discourse on rehabilitation also shifted during this period to focus on restoring the "good name" of the repressed.

Despite improvements to the process of rehabilitation and the expansion of the definition of "victim" under Gorbachev, the single most important piece of legislation on rehabilitation was passed under President Boris Yeltsin on the eve of the collapse of the Soviet Union. On October 18, 1991, the Supreme Soviet of the Russian Soviet Federative Socialist Republic passed the law "On the Rehabilitation of Victims of Political Repression," which formed the basis for the rehabilitation of an additional 650,000 people.[39] Although the new law extended rehabilitation to new categories of victims, such as dekulakized peasants, who were labeled class enemies and exiled to special settlements in remote regions of the Soviet Union during the height of Stalin's collectivization of agriculture, and those subjected to deportation and forced internment in psychiatric facilities, it did not include children who were born in the camps or in exile or who otherwise suffered as victims of political repression.[40] Over the course of the 1990s, an increasing number of people petitioned Memorial for help with obtaining rehabilitation, which contributed to the expansion of the definition of "victim" and the subsequent revision of the law on rehabilitation in 1993 that included the children of victims of political repression.[41] Although the data are incomplete, approximately 5,430 victims of political repression were living in Komi as of 1998.[42] More important, as of 2021, Syktyvkar Memorial and its successor, Fond Pokaianie, returned the names of 143,000 victims sent into exile and camps in Komi; these names are published in Fond Pokaianie's fourteen-volume book of memory, *Martirolog*.[43]

This book contributes to the growing historiography on the legacy of mass repression after Stalin. It highlights the prolonged struggle that Stalin's victims faced after release and attempts to make sense of the extraordinary mass violence of that era.[44] Works by Alan Barenberg, Miriam Dobson, and Nanci Alder illuminate the liminal position that Gulag returnees occupied in Soviet society and how they reintegrated into society after release.[45] *After the Gulag* presents new evidence of the essential role of social networks in the memory project coming to terms with the Stalinist past. It also builds on Barenberg's history of Vorkuta, which documents the porousness between the Gulag and the society that Gulag returnees reentered on release. It also engages Dobson's work, which describes how Gulag returnees were perceived in the eyes of Soviet citizens who had not been imprisoned and the ways in which former prisoners shaped the shifting political imaginary during the years of Khrushchev's Thaw. Dobson's work examines the petitions that former prisoners wrote to Soviet authorities, whereas the testimonies included in this work highlight how former prisoners felt about their experiences in the years after their release and show how they incorporated their imprisonment into their life narratives. The autobiographical narratives I examine defy Nancy Adler's contention that the "sentiments" of Gulag returnees who were not party members "require less complex explanation" because they did not need to justify their continuing faith in communism.[46] As shown by the evidence in this book, the things that ordinary Gulag returnees remembered, how they chose to represent them, and their motivations for doing so were quite complex.

The late 1980s was not the first time that the party and Soviet society attempted to come to terms with the Stalinist past. Polly Jones's and Alexander Etkind's studies of Soviet cultural memory after Stalin's death detail the diverse approaches that the state and society used in coming to terms with the legacy of mass repression during the Soviet and post-Soviet periods.[47] As Barbara Martin's recent work shows, dissidents also participated in this project with various intents and mixed results.[48] Although the individuals examined in this book drew from previously established genres, their autobiographical narratives went far beyond those written during the Thaw of the late 1950s and 1960s and established a new baseline for understanding the full scale and legacy of Stalinist repression. Furthermore, those who wrote in the late Soviet and post-Soviet periods were a more diverse group. Finally, when seen from the provinces rather than the center, the past looks somewhat different. The previously untapped personal archives that Gulag returnees donated to local history museums and branches of Memorial that form the basis of this book require reexamination—at a local level—of how "victims of political repression" continued to shape the production of cultural memory in the provinces long after the national obsession with the past began to fade following the collapse of the Soviet Union.[49]

Autobiographical narratives, such as memoirs, letters, memoir-letters, and—starting in the 1980s—questionnaires, were the predominant medium that Gulag returnees used to communicate their life stories. Examination of these texts requires consideration of the conventions of genre and the cultural contexts that informed their content. I define "autobiography" as a retrospective, first-person narrative of one's life.[50] While acknowledging the differences in form between "autobiography" and "memoir," following the work of Leona Toker and Irina Paperno, I use the terms interchangeably to describe Gulag returnees' autobiographical narratives, which combine elements of both to reconstruct the lives of individuals and the community they formed.[51] I also use the term "autobiographical narrative" to describe the primitive autobiographies that Gulag returnees composed in the questionnaires they completed for Memorial. Although these narratives were produced in response to set questions, Gulag returnees sometimes elaborated on their answers, going beyond what was asked. I likewise refer to the visual art and poetry that Gulag returnees created as a form of autobiographical "testimony." My broad application of these terms is intended to include more texts in my analysis, with the goal of illuminating the various autobiographical forms that Gulag returnees used to testify about the unwritten past.[52]

This book builds on and complicates the work of several literary scholars who have written on the Gulag. In her literary analysis of the corpus of memoirs produced by several generations of survivors, Leona Toker describes Gulag memoirs as a genre hybrid in which the camps occupy a central place with all other narrative details "leading down to that nadir."[53] Nevertheless, I have found that in many of these narratives—including those left unpublished—by ordinary political prisoners, the camps are but a chapter of the life story they tell. One reason for this major difference seems to have been that writing about the partial and unsatisfactory nature of reintegration before glasnost was to enter into conflict with the idea that rehabilitation solved the problem of false convictions. Another key feature of this genre is the tension between individual and collective concerns. In writing about their pasts, Gulag returnees felt it was imperative to combat the oblivion imposed by the regime, which attempted to erase its victims from history and only decades later began to "rehabilitate" them on a limited basis.[54] In addition to bringing individual lives into the public sphere and forming "textual communities," Irina Paperno argues that victims of repression who wrote memoirs in the late 1980s and 1990s claimed legitimacy as sources of historical testimony by placing "I" in a certain context (the Gulag) and tracing their origins to a formative moment in personal life and history.[55] Although the personal testimonies examined in this book include many of these motifs, they present something new: friendship, resistance, and the formation of the camp brotherhood.

Another important aspect of this book highlights the identities that former prisoners constructed for themselves. While most did not identify themselves as dissidents, they did construct identities that were outside of the predominant ideological discourses of Soviet society and the state. In my examination of Gulag returnees' autobiographical texts, I draw from John Paul Eakin's conceptions of autobiographical selves as "defined by and transacted in narrative process."[56] Such an approach highlights the agency of survivors and the intersection of memory and identity as it is reconstructed and enacted in the process of remembering. Although some returnees wrote about their lives before arrest, the majority examined in this book wrote only about their lives in the camps and after release. In attempting to bridge two chapters of their lives, life in the camps and life after release, these survivors often highlight the tension between the two parts of their lives—their two selves. The idiosyncrasies of individual lives make generalization difficult; however, it can be said that each of the former prisoners examined in this work connected their sense of self to the community of Gulag returnees they bonded with in the camps and after release. Exploring the tensions, silences, and overlaps in the stories they tell about themselves and how they chose to represent their experiences is part of the process of remembering that I illuminate in this research.

In a twist on Maurice Halbwachs's theory, I use the term "collected memories" in recognition of the diverse, often conflicting memories of the survivors about whom I wrote in this book.[57] Although they drew from socially constructed frameworks to articulate their experiences, their memories were their own. I use this term to highlight the plurality of memory, which informed the cultural memory of Stalinist repression at memorials throughout Komi. The term "cultural memory" emphasizes the artifacts that individuals, institutions, and societies use to reconstruct and represent the past in particular sociocultural contexts.[58] Cultural memory, as Aleida Assmann writes, unites memory (the contemporized past), culture, and the group (society), which enables the past to be reconstructed and transmitted to future generations who are far removed from the event.[59] In other words, cultural memory expands the focus of inquiry from specific groups to larger communities of memory, including those who were not repressed.[60] In the context of this book, the aim of this expanded concept of memory, as survivors and their allies saw it, was to communicate the memory of Stalinist repression to future generations and to commemorate its victims.

Building on and moving beyond Alexander Etkind's conception of the "hardware" (e.g., monuments) and "software" (e.g., texts, memoirs, histories, literature) at work in the production of cultural memory, I highlight the infrastructure of memory in Komi, which links cultural memory to the lived environment. While Etkind's metaphor aptly describes the interdependency of software and hardware in the production of cultural memory, his definition of "monument" is too narrow.[61] Memory, identity, and place, as Luissa Passerini and others have written, are fundamentally interconnected.[62] The infrastructure of memory, as Iwona Zarecka-Irwin writes, is not only built on texts, artifacts, and monuments but also encompasses the spaces that people use to remember the past.[63] Taking this concept a step further, I argue that Gulag survivors' testimonies transformed the buildings, railroads, and other infrastructure that prisoners built in Komi from monuments to socialist labor into monuments to political repression.

In his analysis of the instability of post-Soviet memory of Stalinist repression, Etkind points to the lack of hardware anchoring the content of soft memory to the landscape. Although this instability has created a space for attempts

INTRODUCTION   11

to co-opt commemoration by more state-friendly agents of memory—namely, the Russian Orthodox Church under Putin—such attempts have been less successful than scholars focusing on Moscow, St. Petersburg, and the Solovetsky Islands would make it seem.[64] On closer examination, a much more vibrant memory landscape exists in which the secular language of commemoration established by civic organizations, including Memorial, Fond Pokaianie, and the Sakharov Center, is the primary means through which the past is commemorated and understood thirty years after the collapse of the Soviet Union.[65]

The archives on which this history is based are dispersed. They can be found in local history museums, art galleries, libraries, and branches of the Memorial Society throughout Komi.[66] Some materials are kept in the National Archive of the Komi Republic. This distribution reflects the very real way in which the Soviet machinery of state repression scattered individual people throughout Komi's taiga and tundra. When we connect the dots representing these archives on the map, we draw the outline of Komi's camp infrastructure. Consequently, to work in these archives is, in a sense, to return to the sites of memory and to see the remnants of these physical and representational spaces that former prisoners documented in their autobiographical narratives.

I sought for these nonstate archives out of frustration with the restrictions I encountered at the National Archive of the Komi Republic. Although I found plenty of interesting documents, including the minutes of local party meetings, reports from the political departments of Komi's camps, camp newspapers, and even correspondence between remote camp officials and party bosses in Syktyvkar, these sources told me little about this history from the perspectives of former prisoners. When I discovered the richness of the archives of Komi's local history museums, I began to realize that perhaps this was what the former prisoners I was searching for had intended. After all, they did not send their precious documents, photographs, and manuscripts to state and party authorities who were the heirs to the system that they testified against; they sent them to branches of the Memorial Society and museums in Syktyvkar, Ukhta, Sosnogorsk, Pechora, Abez', Inta, and Vorkuta.

Not every Gulag returnee wrote a memoir. Some files include letters, memoirs, art, questionnaires, postcards, prisoner files, party cards, certificates of rehabilitation, and an array of other documents accrued over a lifetime, whereas others contain only a page-length autobiography, certificate of rehabilitation, and a photograph. Wherever possible, I included images of these documents and photographs of the former prisoners themselves to demonstrate the materiality of this archive and the connection between the people and the story they tell.

This book comprises five chapters and a conclusion. Chronologically, it takes us from the peak of glasnost in 1987 to the closure of the International Memorial Society on December 28, 2021. Despite the more recent nature of this history, the story it tells sheds new light on earlier periods of Soviet history through the eyes of those that the state repressed and then attempted to rehabilitate in its waning years. This book is not a history of the Gulag in Komi; rather, it aims to make the colossal nature of political repression accessible by grounding it in the complexities of individual people who survived it to better understand the legacy of this history in the places where it transpired. It is a history of the memory that Gulag returnees constructed when they entered into dialogue with those who had not been repressed. Although the research presented in this book focuses on the Komi Republic, the story it tells is emblematic of processes that unfolded and a past that came to light throughout the world's first socialist state as it came to an end.

Chapter 1 describes the emergence of the Memorial movement in Syktyvkar in 1987 and how its founding created an institution that former prisoners could write to without fear of persecution. The flood of correspondence that Memorial received during the late 1980s and throughout the 1990s formed the basis of an archive that represented the perspectives of the survivors of Stalinist repression. Working with these unexamined letters to Syktyvkar Memorial, I explore the institutionalization of Gulag returnees' collected memories. I show how their first attempts at telling what happened to them shaped the knowledge that this civic organization was able to collect and produce. This chapter also explores how the "repressed" shaped not only the developing cultural memory of the Gulag in Komi but also the definitions of "victim" and "rehabilitated."

Chapter 2 examines the shared themes, concerns, and conflicts of the corpus of Gulag memoirs written by Gulag returnees from Komi, most of which remain unpublished. I argue that Gulag returnees responded to the collapse of the Soviet Union by writing memoirs about their lives in captivity and after release, in which they sought to write themselves into Soviet history at its end. During this revolutionary period, former prisoners traced themselves back to a formative moment in their personal lives and constructed their identities in autobiographical memoirs. "We" and "I" are frequently interchanged and interspersed throughout Gulag returnees' memoirs. Highlighting the connection between the individual and the collective, their autobiographical narratives illuminate their belonging to a "brotherhood of *zeks* [prisoners]," a collective of "our own" (*svoi*), which was a core component of their identities.

Chapter 3 transitions from the camp brotherhood to focus on one survivor's testimony. It presents a case study of a Gulag returnee who never left Komi. On

INTRODUCTION   13

the basis of Konstantin Ivanov's personal archive, 154 letters he wrote to the Vorkuta Museum–Exhibition Center, and 53 artworks he created to represent his memories of the camp, I illustrate the process of remembering and address two major issues: how those who survived the brunt of Stalinist violence experienced life after release and how they defined themselves when finally given the chance in the last years of the Soviet Union. Before glasnost, Ivanov never wrote about the camps, choosing to put that most painful chapter of his life behind him. During glasnost and after the collapse of the Soviet Union, Ivanov—an artist by training—drew those parts of his life that he could not bear to write about in detail and wrote about his life after release in letters he sent to the Vorkuta Museum–Exhibition Center. Despite the relative openness of the post-Soviet period, Ivanov struggled to write about the camps. In this way, Ivanov is an outlier. He serves as a counterexample to those former prisoners who were empowered by the collapse of the Soviet Union to write memoirs. In many ways, Ivanov's story illustrates the same process of remembering that former prisoners engaged in when they wrote letters to Memorial about their lives in the camps and after. Ultimately, Ivanov was driven by his attachment to the region where he was once imprisoned and his desire to ensure that his fellow zeks and their contributions to the transformation of Vorkuta, from prison camp into a Soviet city, were commemorated in history.

Chapter 4 presents a different case study of a Gulag returnee who left Komi for Moscow after serving more than fifteen years behind barbed wire and in exile. Elena Markova represented her past in a completely different way in her memoir, her poetry, and the interviews I conducted with her in 2017. Markova explored what happens to one's sense of self in the camps and repeatedly asked, "How did I remain a human being?" In answering this question, Markova provides an example of a former prisoner who was, at the same time, part of and yet estranged from Soviet society. Unlike other Gulag returnees who at least attempted to identify themselves as Soviet people after they were released, Markova rejected this label and explored the ways in which her Gulag experience shaped her and the community of zeks to which she belonged. Although she did not identify as a Soviet person, Markova was not anti-Soviet and was proud of her country. This chapter, like the previous one, analyzes the unique features of Markova's testimony and explores themes raised in the corpus of Gulag returnees' memoirs examined in chapter 2.

Chapter 5 examines the expansive coverage of political repression in Komi newspapers from the late 1980s to 2021, when local publications emerged as the primary forum in which the past and its commemoration were debated and discussed. This chapter illustrates the ways in which Gulag returnees and those who had not been repressed came to terms with the past and traces the development of Komi's infrastructure of memory. It also examines the monuments and memory events that former prisoners and members of Memorial created as part of this infrastructure. What happened, who the victims and the perpetrators were, and how it all should be remembered posed intense dilemmas that played out in the local press. How were people supposed to view former "enemies of the people" who were now "victims of political repression"? Who was to blame for the mounting physical evidence of mass death that was literally being unearthed throughout Komi? Addressing these issues, the ways in which the public understood the past, remembered it, and commemorated it tell us much about the legacy of the Gulag and Stalinist repression and their place in cultural memory during a revolutionary moment in Soviet and post-Soviet history.

The epilogue discusses the state of cultural memory in Komi today in contrast with new memory projects in Moscow developed by the Russian state, Memorial, and the State Gulag History Museum. The process of remembering the Gulag is an ongoing one influenced by the infrastructure of memory developed in regions of the Soviet Union and the Russian Federation during the late 1980s and 1990s. However, the civic organizations that previously played the predominant role in commemorating the past have faced serious challenges from the state following Putin's election to a third term as president in 2012. The International Memorial Society has been ordered to close its doors by Russia's Supreme Court on the basis of spurious charges brought by the state prosecutor, who claimed that Memorial repeatedly violated the repressive law on foreign agents. The issue, which the state prosecutor made clear at Memorial's hearing in December 2021, is really about control over the past and Memorial's "false image of the Soviet Union as a terrorist state."[67] Despite these challenges, which have also affected Fond Pokaianie, the project of remembering the past continues in Komi with new museum exhibits, memorial markers, and research that sheds new light on the Gulag and its legacy.

The history you are about to read is a montage—a mixture of panoramic shots and close-ups. I tell this story through a series of biographies intermixed with regional and national events. At times, I let the survivors' autobiographies speak for themselves, as the survivors of this history intended—to tell their story in their own words. It is a story about the identities and agency of survivors of Stalinist repression who resisted being silenced and separated. The history of their memory is one that has much to tell about coming to terms with difficult pasts under conditions of authoritarian rule and the power of individual people and marginalized groups that engage in these memory projects.

Notes

1. Fond Pokaianie Archive (AFP) (V. B. Ol'shevskii, "Vyzhit! Ot Bamlaga do Pechlaga," Kiev, 1991, 1). The AFP is only partially organized. I give the full citation as listed in its finding aids if possible; however, in many cases, I list only the archive and the source.

2. Ibid., 2.

3. Although the majority of prisoners in the Gulag were criminals sentenced for a variety of crimes, this book is written on the basis of sources produced by "ordinary" political prisoners. These prisoners were not elites, members of the intelligentsia, or dissidents, nor were the majority of them members of the Communist Party. From the 1940s until Stalin's death in 1953, "counterrevolutionary" offenders, or those sentenced under article 58, represented approximately one-third of the camp population. I refer to these survivors as "Gulag returnees," not because they returned home (although some did if they had a home to go back to when given the choice) but because they returned to Soviet society. On the camp population, see Golfo Alexopoulos, *Illness and Inhumanity in Stalin's Gulag* (New Haven, CT: Yale University Press, 2017), 46.

4. Some non-elites wrote memoirs of their sojourn through the camps during the "Thaw," but the majority of these narratives were written by party members and those who sought reinstatement in the party. See Polly Jones, "Memories of Terror or Terrorizing Memories? Terror, Trauma, and Survival in Soviet Culture of the Thaw," *Slavonic and East European Review* 86, no. 2 (April 2008): 346–371; Nanci Adler, *Keeping Faith with the Party: Communist Believers Return from the Gulag* (Bloomington: Indiana University Press, 2012).

5. Jonathan Brunstedt, *The Soviet Myth of World War II: Patriotic Memory and the Russian Question in the USSR* (Cambridge: Cambridge University Press, 2021); David L. Hoffmann, ed., *The Memory of the Second World War in Soviet and Post-Soviet Russia* (New York: Routledge, 2022). Brunstedt notes how Russian state media deployed the memory of the war as a means to frame the Russia's invasion of Ukraine (6).

6. On this period of intense confrontation and (re)negotiation of the past, see Kathleen E. Smith, *Remembering Stalin's Victims: Popular Memory and the End of the USSR* (Ithaca, NY: Cornell University Press, 2009); R. W. Davies, *Soviet History in the Gorbachev Revolution* (London: Macmillan, 1989). For a broader consideration of restorative justice in Eastern Europe after 1989, see Tzvetan Todorov, *Memory as a Remedy for Evil*, trans. Gila Walker (London: Seagull, 2010).

7. Richard Lebow, Wulf Kansteiner, and Claudio Fogu, eds., *The Politics of Memory in Postwar Europe* (Durham: Duke University Press, 2006), 21.

8. Nikolay Koposov, *Memory Laws, Memory Wars: The Politics of the Past in Europe and Russia* (Cambridge: Cambridge University Press, 2018), 25.

9. See Lebow et al., *Politics of Memory*; Rubie S. Watson, ed., *Memory, History, and Opposition under Socialism* (Santa Fe, NM: School of American Research Press, 1994); Vladimir Tismaneanu and Bogdan C. Iacob, eds., *End and the Beginning: The Revolutions of 1989 and the Resurgence of History* (Budapest: Central European University Press, 2012); Jerzy W. Borejsza and Klaus Ziemer, eds., *Totalitarian and Authoritarian Regimes in Europe: Legacies and Lessons from the Twentieth Century* (New York: Berghahn, 2006). For a global perspective on the "memory boom" and transitional justice, see Béatrice Pouligny, Simon Chesterman, and Albrecht Schnabel, eds., *After Mass Crime: Rebuilding States and Communities* (Tokyo: United Nations University Press, 2007).

10. We will probably never know the true number of returnees due to lacunae in the archival record and lack of access to other archives, such as those of the Federal Security Service (FSB) and the Ministry of Internal Affairs (MVD); however, Nanci Adler estimates that around 5 million Gulag survivors returned to Soviet society in the 1950s. Nevertheless, it is important to note that she includes exiles and deportees in this figure; *Keeping Faith*, 4. To give an example of the social composition of a Komi city, Alan Barenberg estimates that that former prisoners and their families composed one-third of Vorkuta's population of approximately 175,000 by the end of the 1950s; Barenberg, *Gulag Town, Company Town: Forced Labor and Its Legacy in Vorkuta* (New Haven, CT: Yale University Press, 2014), 216–222.

11. In this way, Gulag returnees are similar to Soviet veterans of World War II. See Mark Edele, *Soviet Veterans of the Second World War: A Popular Movement in an Authoritarian Society, 1941–1991* (Oxford: Oxford University Press, 2008).

12. Iwona Irwin-Zarecka, *Frames of Remembrance: The Dynamics of Collective Memory* (New Brunswick, NJ: Transaction, 1993), 47. Irwin-Zarecka defines a "community of memory" as "a community created by that very memory." See Aleida Assmann, "Transformations between History and Memory," *Social Research* 75, no. 1 (Spring 2008): 52. Assmann writes of the construction of individual and group identities involved in the production of cultural memory: "Each 'we' is constructed through shared practices and discourses that mark certain boundaries and define the principles of inclusion and exclusion."

13. In 1897, Komi's population was approximately 170,600 people. See L. Prilutskaia, *Komi ASSR k 50-letiiu Sovetskoi vlasti: Statisticheskii sbornik* (Syktyvkar: Komi knizhnoe izd-vo, 1967), 8.

14. Local police kept files on exiles in Syktyvkar during the late eighteenth and nineteenth centuries. Although these files are not regularly accessible to researchers, they were shown as part of a public exhibition at the National Archive of the Komi Republic on the region's "history of repression" during the week of commemorative events leading up to the October 30 Day of Memory of Victims of Political Repression. These files included fingerprints, letters, reports from parole officers, and mugshots if available.

15. N. A. Morozov, "Istrebiteil'no-trudovye gody: Komi—krai politicheskoi ssylki," in *Pokaianie: Martirolog*, t. 1, ed. G. V. Nevskii (Syktyvkar: Fond Pokaianie, 1998), 15.

16. Skepticism notwithstanding, according to a 1967 collection of statistical surveys of the Komi ASSR, Komi's population grew from 224,900 in 1926 to 319,500 in 1939 and jumped again to 815,800 in 1959. In the year of publication, the collection estimated that 974,300 people lived in Komi. These numbers do not account for the prisoner population, but the growth in Komi's population of *vol'nonaemnye* largely follows that of the growth and spread of the Gulag throughout the region. See Prilutskaia, *Komi ASSR*, 8.

17. On internal colonization and the expansion of carceral networks in the Soviet Union, see Judith Pallot, "Forced Labour for Forestry: The Twentieth-Century History of Colonisation and Settlement in the North of Perm' Oblast,'" *Europe-Asia Studies* 54, no.7 (2002): 1055–1084; Lynne Viola, *The Unknown Gulag: The Lost World of Stalin's Special Settlements* (New York: Oxford University Press, 2007); Alan Barenberg, "'Discovering' Vorkuta: Science and Colonization in the Early Gulag," *Gulag Studies* 4 (2011): 1–20; L. A. Maksimova and L. V. Liamtseva, *GULAG kak factor modernizatsii na Evropeiskoi Severo-Vostoke* (Moscow: Izd-vo MGOU, 2011).

18. Barenberg, *Gulag Town*, 267. See also N. A. Morozov, "Mnogonatsional'nyi GULAG," in Nevskii, *Pokaianie*, vol. 1, 340–419.

19. Oleg V. Khlevniuk, *The History of the Gulag: From Collectivization to the Great Terror*, trans. Vadim A Staklo (New Haven, CT: Yale University Press, 2004), 315.

20. Barenberg, *Gulag Town*, 252–254.

21. See Wilson T. Bell, "Sex, Pregnancy, and Power in the Late Stalinist Gulag," *Journal of the History of Sexuality* 24, no. 2 (May 2015): 198–224; Elaine MacKinnon, "Motherhood and Survival in the Stalinist Gulag," *Aspasia* 13, no. 1 (2019): 65–94; Oksana Kis, *Survival as Victory: Ukrainian Women in the Gulag*, trans. Lidia Wolanskyi (Cambridge, MA: Harvard University Press, 2021).

22. Barenberg, *Gulag Town*, 254–259.

23. National Archive of the Komi Republic (GU RK NARK) 2 f. P-3800, op. 1, d. 38, l. 3 (M. B. Rogachev to Evgeniia Petrovna, April 8, 1993). Today, there are ten corrective colonies, four colony-settlements, three investigative isolators, and two medical clinics in Syktyvkar, Verkhnii Chov, Mikun', Kniazhpogost', Ukhta, Pechora, and Vorkuta. See Upravlenie Federal'noi sluzhby ispoleneniia nakazaniia (UFSIN) Rossii po Respublike Komi, "Istoriia UIS Komi," updated December 12, 2017, http://www.11.fsin.su/istoriya-uis-komi/. According to a 2011 article in a Syktyvkar newspaper run by human rights activists, *7x7*, this number is down from the twenty-eight places of confinement in Komi (thirteen colonies, twelve colony-settlements, three isolators) of various regimes of detention.

According to the same article, fifteen thousand people were imprisoned in these places of confinement. See Igor' Sazhin, "Kolonii Respubliki Komi," *7x7*, May 7, 2011, https://7x7-journal.ru/opinion/13939.

24. On special settlements, see N. M. Ignatova, *Spetspereselentsy v Respublike Komi v 1930–1950-e gg* (Syktyvkar: Institut iazyka, literatury i istorii Komi nauchnogo tsentra UrO RAN, 2009); Viola, *Unknown Gulag*; V. N. Zemskov, *Spetsposelentsy v SSSR, 1930–1960* (Moscow: "Nauka," 2003).

25. Despite the slight opening of the archives in the 1990s and work done on the numbers and categories of prisoners, to this day we still do not have exact numbers of Komi's prisoners. Given the increasing difficulty of access to MVD archives, we should not expect this to change any time soon.

26. E. P. Berezina, V. N. Kazarinova, and I. G. Zhukova, eds., *Politicheskie repressii v Komi krae (20–50-e gody): Bibliograficheskii ukazatel'* (Syktyvkar: Fond Pokaianie, 2006), 3. Barenberg notes that the number of prisoners in Komi's largest camp, Vorkutlag, grew from 16,096 in 1939 to 66,290 in 1949; *Gulag Town*, 252–253. The population of the Gulag peaked in 1950 at 2.5 million. According to Jeff Hardy, this puts the incarceration rate at 1,440 per 100,000; for comparison, the United States incarcerated 109 per 100,000 in 1950 (166,165 inmates); Hardy, *The Gulag after Stalin: Redefining Punishment in Khrushchev's Soviet Union, 1953–1964* (Ithaca, NY: Cornell University Press, 2016), 12.

27. E. A. Zelenskaia-Zysman, *Lagernoe proshloe Komi kraia (1929–1955 gg.) v sud'bakh i vospominaniiakh sovremennikov* (Ukhta: UPOO Memorial, 2016), 3.

28. Ibid.

29. N. A. Morozov estimates that a total of 3.5 million people went through Komi's camps during its thirty years of existence as part of the Gulag; Morozov, *Gulag v Komi krae, 1929–1956* (Syktyvkar: Syktyvkarskii Gosudarstvennyi Universitet, 1997), 181.

30. Susanna Pechuro, "Chto proiskhodit s oteleniiami Memorial?," *Memorial—Aspekt. Informatsionnyi biulleten' Moskovskogo Memoriala*, no. 1 (July 1993): 1, box 199; "Memorial za tri goda," *Svoboda i Kul'tura: Gazeta Moskovskogo Memoriala*, no. 2 (March 1991): 2, box 395, Soviet and Post-Soviet Independent Publications, Hoover Institution Library and Archives (hereafter Hoover Institution).

31. Rehabilitation removed the restrictions on former prisoners' passports and eliminated the requirement that they check in with local authorities twice monthly.

32. A. L. Kononov, "K istorii priniatiia rossiiskogo Zakona 'O reabilitatsii zhertv politicheskikh repressii,'" in *Reabilitatsiia i pamiat': Otnoshenie k zhertvam sovetskikh politicheskikh repressii v stranakh byvshego SSSR*, ed. Ian Rachinskii (Moscow: Memorial-Zven'ia, 2016), 5–28.

33. Matthew Stibbe and Kevin McDermott, "De-Stalinising Eastern Europe: The Dilemmas of Rehabilitation," in *De-Stalinising Eastern Europe: The*

Rehabilitation of Stalin's Victims after 1953, ed. Kevin McDermott and Matthew Stibbe (Baskingstoke: Palgrave Macmillan, 2015), 3. See also Miriam Dobson, "POWs and Purge Victims: Attitudes toward Party Rehabilitation, 1956–57," *Slavonic and East European Review* 86, no. 2 (April 2008): 328–345; Nanci Adler, *The Gulag Survivor: Beyond the Soviet System* (New Brunswick, NJ: Transaction, 2002), 30–31. Adler points out the lack of consensus among historians about the numbers of those who were rehabilitated and the percentage of repressed who remain unrehabilitated. The numbers she lists range from 258,322 to 737,182 rehabilitated between 1953 and 1961. In 1962, only 117 survivors were rehabilitated, and in 1963, this number dropped to 55.

34. Marc Elie, "Rehabilitation in the Soviet Union, 1953–1964: A Policy Unachieved," in McDermott and Stibbe, *De-Stalinising Eastern Europe*, 32.

35. Miriam Dobson, *Khrushchev's Cold Summer: Gulag Returnees, Crime, and the Fate of Reform after Stalin* (Ithaca, NY: Cornell University Press, 2009), 54, 59.

36. Elie, "Rehabilitation in the Soviet Union," 30–33.

37. Between 1962 and 1983, only 157,055 survivors were rehabilitated. See "Zapiska V. M. Chebrikova v TsK KPSS 'Ob ispol'zovanii arkhivov organov gosbezopasnosti,'" June 3, 1988, in A. Artizov, A. Kosakovskii, V. Naumov, I. Shevchuk, eds., *Reabilitatsiia: Kak eto bylo. Dokumenty Prezidiuma TsK KPSS i drugie materialy*, vol. 3, *Seredina 80-kh godov–1991* (Moscow: Mezhdunarodnyi Fond Demokratiia, 2004), 77.

38. Adler, *Keeping Faith*, 184.

39. Cathy A. Frierson, "Russia's Law 'On Rehabilitation of Victims of Political Repression': 1991–2011. An Enduring Artifact of Transitional Justice," working paper, National Council for Eurasian and East European Research, February 28, 2014, https://scholars.unh.edu/history_facpub/342/.

40. See Zakon Rossiiskoi Sovetskoi Federativnoi Sotsialisticheskoi Respubliki, "O reabilitatsii zhertv politicheskoi repressii ot 18 oktiabria 1991 g," in *Sbornik zakondatel'nykh i normativnykh aktov o repressiiakh i reabilitatsii zhertv politicheskikh repressii*, ed. V. Ia. Gribenko (Moscow: Izd-vo Respublika, 1993), 194–204.

41. Frierson, "Russia's Law," 3. Frierson notes that the law on rehabilitation has been amended sixteen times since its passage (1991–2011).

42. This number is based on lists that were compiled using pension records and published by Fond Pokaianie in vol. 2 of the Komi Republic book of memory, *Martirolog*. The lists are compiled by town and do not differentiate between categories of victims (prisoner, exile, special settler, child, or family member of victims of repression); however, the biographical data accompanying each name enable us to identify Gulag returnees. See G. V. Nevskii, ed., *Pokaianie: Martirolog*, t. 2, ch. 1 (Syktyvkar: Fond Pokaianie, 1999), 349–569.

43. N. M. Ignatova, ed., *Pokaianie: Martirolog*, t. 14 (Syktyvkar: Fond Pokaianie, 2021).

44. Adler, *Gulag Survivor*; Amir Weiner, "The Empire Pays a Visit: Gulag Returnees, East European Rebellions, and Soviet Frontier Politics," *Journal of Modern History* 78, no. 2 (June 2006): 333–376; Denis Kozlov and Eleonory Gilburd, eds., *The Thaw: Soviet Society and Culture in the 1950s and 1960s* (Toronto: University of Toronto Press, 2013); Kevin McDermott and Matthew Stibbe, *De-Stalinising Eastern Europe: The Rehabilitation of Stalin's Victims after 1953* (Baskingstoke: Palgrave Macmillan, 2015).

45. Barenberg, *Gulag Town*; Dobson, *Khrushchev's Cold Summer*; Adler, *Keeping Faith*.

46. Adler, *Keeping Faith*, 5.

47. Polly Jones, *Myth, Memory, Trauma: Rethinking the Stalinist Past in the Soviet Union, 1953–1970* (New Haven, CT: Yale University Press, 2013); Alexander Etkind, *Warped Mourning: Stories of the Undead in the Land of the Unburied* (Stanford, CA: Stanford University Press, 2013).

48. Barbara Martin, *Dissident Histories in the Soviet Union: From De-Stalinization to Perestroika* (London: Bloomsbury, 2021). The political prisoners of the 1950s–1980s recognized that they were different from the previous generation of prisoners who survived Stalin's camps. See *Vstrecha politzakliuchennykh 50–80-x godov*, St. Petersburg, August 11–12, 1990 (St. Petersburg: obshchestvo Memorial, 1991), Sankt-Peterburgskoe obshchestvo Memorial Collection, box 1, Hoover Institution.

49. Anatoly M. Khazanov, "Whom to Mourn and Whom to Forget? (Re)Constructing Collective Memory in Contemporary Russia," *Totalitarian Movements and Political Religions* 9, no. 2–3 (2008): 293–310. Khazanov links the decline in interest in coming to terms with the past to shifts in politics, but this view dramatically oversimplifies and overlooks much of the local production of cultural memory that influences and is influenced by central policies emanating from Moscow.

50. This definition is inspired by the works of John Paul Eakin and James S. Amelang. See John Paul Eakin, *How Our Lives Become Stories: Making Selves* (Ithaca, NY: Cornell University Press, 1999); James S. Amelang, *The Flight of Icarus: Artisan Autobiography in Early Modern Europe* (Stanford, CA: Stanford University Press, 1998).

51. Leona Toker, *Return from the Archipelago: Narratives of Gulag Survivors* (Bloomington: Indiana University Press, 2000); Irina Paperno, *Stories of the Soviet Experience* (Ithaca, NY: Cornell University Press, 2009), xiii. Regarding the hybridity of the Gulag memoir genre, Toker explains, "autobiography emphasizes authorial identity and memoir focuses on the public-interest data that the author has been in a position to store" (82). Paperno writes, "Memoirs, like other autobiographical texts, are retrospective narratives of individual life. What distinguishes memoirs from autobiographies (scholars maintain) is their emphasis

INTRODUCTION 21

on the negotiation between the self and community. Memoirs define themselves as accounts of lives embedded in a social matrix" (xiii).

52. I am supported in my approach by others who have adopted a broad definition of camp literature. See, e.g., Andrea Gullotta, *Intellectual Life and Literature at Solovki 1923–1930: The Paris of the Northern Concentration Camps* (Cambridge: Legenda, 2018).

53. Toker, *Return from the Archipelago*, 73.

54. Ibid., 77. On rehabilitation and the politics of memory in former Soviet countries, see Ian Rachinskii, ed., *Reabilitatsiia i pamiat': Otnoshenie k zhertvam sovetskikh politicheskikh repressii v stranakh byvshego SSSR* (Moscow: Memorial-Zven'ia, 2016).

55. Paperno, *Stories of the Soviet Experience*, 17, 25. On diaries, memoirs, autobiographical narratives, and the formation of textual communities, see Barbara Walker, "On Reading Soviet Memoirs: A History of the 'Contemporaries' Genre as an Institution of Russian Intelligentsia Culture from the 1790s to the 1970s," *Russian Review* 59 (July 2000): 327–352; Benjamin Nathans, "Talking Fish: On Soviet Dissident Memoirs," *Journal of Modern History* 87 (September 2015): 579–614.

56. Eakin, *How Our Lives Become Stories*. See also Jerome Bruner, *Acts of Meaning* (Cambridge, MA: Harvard University Press, 1990).

57. James Young, *The Texture of Memory: Holocaust Memorials and Meaning* (New Haven, CT: Yale University Press, 1993), xi–xii. As Young writes, "By maintaining a sense of collected memories, we remain aware of their disparate sources, of every individual's unique relation to a lived life, and of the ways our traditions and cultural forms continuously assign common meaning to disparate memories" (xii).

58. On cultural memory see Jan Assmann, "Moses the Egyptian: The Memory of Egypt in Western Monotheism," in *The Collective Memory Reader*, ed. Jeffrey K. Olick, Vered Vinitzky-Seroussi, and Daniel Levy (Oxford: Oxford University Press, 2011), 209–215. J. Assmann writes, "The concept of cultural memory comprises that body of reusable texts, images, and rituals specific to each society in each epoch, whose 'cultivation' serves to stabilize and convey that society's self-image." This is the stuff of which unity and identity are collectively constructed in a society's understanding of itself in the past. See also Assmann, "Transformations," 55–56.

59. Aleida Assmann and John Czaplicka, "Collective Memory and Cultural Identity," *New German Critique*, no. 65 (Spring/Summer 1995): 125–133.

60. Astrid Erll and Ansgar Nünning, eds., *A Companion to Cultural Memory Studies* (Berlin: De Gruyter, 2010), 5. Erll writes, "Just as socio-cultural contexts shape individual memories, a 'memory' which is represented by media and institutions must be actualized by individuals, by members of a community of

remembrance, who may be conceived of as *points de vue* (Maurice Halbwachs) on shared notions of the past. Without such actualizations, monuments, rituals, and books are nothing but dead material, failing to have any impact in societies." See also Adrian Forty and Susan Küchler, eds., *The Art of Forgetting* (Oxford: Berg, 1999).

61. On the interplay between the two ideas and their usage in studies of Soviet and post-Soviet memory, see Etkind, *Warped Mourning*, 40.

62. Luisa Passerini, ed., *International Yearbook of Oral History and Life Stories*, vol. 1, *Memory and Totalitarianism* (Oxford: Oxford University Press, 1992), 8; Pierre Nora, *Realms of Memory: The Construction of the French Past*, trans. Arthur Goldhammer (New York: Columbia University Press, 1992); Jay Winter, *Sites of Memory, Sites of Mourning: The Great War in European Cultural History* (Cambridge: Cambridge University Press, 1995).

63. Irwin-Zarecka, *Frames of Remembrance*, 13. Irwin-Zarecka describes the infrastructure of collective memory as "all the different spaces, objects, 'texts' that make an engagement with the past possible." Irwin-Zarecka was referencing Pierre Nora's "les lieux de mémoire," but as I show in the final chapter, this infrastructure includes the landscape of the lived environment, which was transformed by Gulag returnees' memoirs from monuments to Socialist labor to memorials to the Gulag.

64. For such works, see Zuzanna Bogumił, Dominique Moran, and Elly Harrowell, "Sacred or Secular? 'Memorial,' the Russian Orthodox Church, and the Contested Commemoration of Soviet Repressions," *Europe-Asia Studies* 67, no. 9 (November 2015): 1416–1444; Zuzanna Bogumił, *Gulag Memories: The Rediscovery and Commemoration of Russia's Repressive Past* (New York: Berghahn, 2018); Karin Hyldal Christensen, *The Making of the New Martyrs of Russia: Soviet Repression in Orthodox Memory* (New York: Routledge, 2018).

65. For works that examine memory in Russia's regions, see Bogumił, *Gulag Memories*; Wilson T. Bell, "Tomsk Regional Identity and the Legacy of the Gulag and Stalinist Repression," in *Russia's Regional Identities: The Power of the Provinces*, ed. Edith W. Clowes, Gisela Erbslöh, and Ani Kokobobo (London: Routledge, 2018), 206–225; Anne White, "The Memorial Society in the Russian Provinces," *Europe-Asia Studies* 47, no. 8 (1995): 1343–1366.

66. Pieces of the Memorial archive can be found in local history museums and in the private collections of its founding members.

67. "Memorial—O likvidatsii Mezhdunarodnogo Memoriala," Mezhdunarodnyi Memorial, December 28, 2021, https://www.memo.ru/ru-ru/memorial /departments/intermemorial/news/667. The prosecutor's words were reproduced on Memorial's website.

1

Letters to Syktyvkar Memorial

"Who Will Remember If I Forget?"

Peter Kotov wrote to the Syktyvkar Memorial Society in June 1990, a year after its establishment. In his first of several letters, Kotov identified himself as a former prisoner of Komi's camps and asked what he could do to help.[1] Kotov served nine years (1942–1951) in several camps in Komi, followed by seven more years in exile in Krasnoyarsk before being rehabilitated and returning to his native Poland in 1958.[2] Once home, Kotov kept regular correspondence with his former camp mates in the Soviet Union and wrote a memoir, which he sent to the Syktyvkar Memorial Society in 1991. A passage from his memoir perfectly encapsulates why Kotov, like so many other former prisoners, wrote autobiographical narratives about their experiences in the camps and shared them with Syktyvkar Memorial:

> It is remarkable that the caves and ruins of the first people remain, but there are not any traces of the former camps for prisoners. And the prisoners' cemetery was so [well] hidden that if you did not know, you would never guess that this was ALSO A BURIAL GROUND. . . . It is clear that after the liquidation of Stalin's prison camps, their creators and guards quite intentionally erased their traces, completely understanding that they committed crimes. Moreover, our duty, the responsibility of former prisoners of the Gulag who remain alive, consists in, to the degree possible, trying to raise from the dead the memory of what we lived through, to revive the memory of those people who remain forever in the hidden graves. As much memory is in a person, is as much humanity is in him.[3]

Many former prisoners who wrote to Syktyvkar Memorial echoed Kotov's sentiments: survivors had a duty to remember and record the evidence of the system of mass repression that once spanned the Soviet Union. In 1989, a former prisoner wrote from a small village in Komi to Syktyvkar Memorial, "My life is an entire book, and it's a shame that no one is interested while witnesses are still alive—after all, the dead don't speak."[4] As shown in the extensive correspondence between Syktyvkar Memorial and Gulag returnees, there was no shortage of interest in preserving their memories—evidence of Komi's unwritten history as one of the largest islands of the Gulag archipelago.

The flood of letters that Syktyvkar Memorial received from former prisoners raised many questions but also provided important insights into what motivated Gulag returnees to write after decades of silence. They showed what former prisoners revealed about themselves once they opened the floodgates of memory and how they defined themselves when finally given the chance. Nevertheless, this correspondence also sheds light on how the information they provided affected the memory project to commemorate the victims of political repression.

This chapter investigates the institutionalization of Gulag returnees' collected memories. The letters, questionnaires, and memoirs that Gulag returnees sent to Syktyvkar Memorial formed the basis of an archive, which made it possible to write an alternate history of the Soviet Union. It illustrates the development of the Syktyvkar Memorial Society and its search for Komi's camp past and reveals the importance of the friendships and social networks that Gulag returnees maintained after release. From the beginning, Syktyvkar Memorial relied on Gulag returnees' social networks to collect as much material as possible for its growing archive. Gulag returnees themselves were motivated to participate in this memory project by their desire to commemorate the victims of political repression. By participating, Gulag returnees fulfilled the roles of "ethnographer," eyewitness, and source.[5]

The launch of glasnost unintentionally created space for a diverse group of Soviet citizens to form the first Memorial Society in Moscow in January 1989. This group eventually became the International Memorial Society (Memorial)—the leader of a network of organizations and affiliated branches.[6] As the Soviet Union's first civic organization, called the Historical Enlightenment Society "Memorial," it petitioned for the construction of a memorial complex to commemorate the "victims of political repression." The movement it sparked coalesced in response to two decrees issued by the Presidium of the Central Committee, both aimed at completing the rehabilitation of "groundlessly repressed persons" as part of the "restoration of justice."[7] The decrees ordered the KGB, Procuracy, and regional party committees to review the cases of repressed persons who were subject to rehabilitation.[8] As the public response

LETTERS TO SYKTYVKAR MEMORIAL 25

to glasnost grew, Soviet citizens founded branches of Memorial in other parts of the country.[9]

By 1990, the Memorial Society had seven branches in Komi. With the exception of Syktyvkar, all were located in towns and cities that were founded by forced labor: Vorkuta, Inta, Abez', Pechora, Sosnogorsk, and Ukhta.[10] These regional branches were organized by coalitions of activists, former prisoners, and their relatives, who seized the moment to investigate Stalin's crimes and commemorate the victims of political repression. On April 20, 1989, the Syktyvkar Executive Committee (Gorispolkom) registered the "Syktyvkar volunteer historical-enlightenment Memorial Society." This step allowed the organization to meet and to begin collecting information, funds, and signatures for the construction of a memorial complex to honor the victims of political repression in Syktyvkar—completed in 2000.[11] Throughout the 1990s, the Syktyvkar Memorial Society's team of historians, anthropologists, archaeologists, and archivists worked with other branches of the organization in Komi to build a people's archive on the history of the Gulag and political repression.[12] When Fond Pokaianie was founded in 1998 as a partnership between Syktyvkar Memorial and the provincial government, the International Memorial Society wrote in a press bulletin, "Perhaps it is because of the density of tragic sites here in Komi, which remind us of Russia's not so distant past, that there are some of the most active branches of Memorial. Every one of my interlocutors spoke with great hope and pride about the regional governor's declaration of the program 'Pokaianie.'"[13]

The establishment of Syktyvkar Memorial created a place where former prisoners could write to about their pasts without fear. Gulag returnees trusted Memorial with their stories and requests for rehabilitation because the society was independent of the state. They also trusted Memorial because former prisoners and their children were among its most prominent members. Among them were Revol't Pimenov—the mathematician, dissident, former prisoner of the post-Stalin era, and friend of Andrei Sakharov—who was unanimously selected as the Syktyvkar Memorial Society's first chairman; Aleksandr Klein, a former political prisoner of Rechlag in Vorkuta; and Nikolai Morozov, who was born in Pechorlag in 1948 to two political prisoners.[14] Over the course of 1989–2002, Syktyvkar Memorial met with thousands of people at public receptions held twice weekly at the city's administration building. The society received hundreds of letters from a diverse array of former prisoners, special settlers, family members of purge victims, and children who were born in labor camps and on special settlements—all victims of political repression under the law.[15] Given the incomplete archival record, it is difficult to say exactly how many letters Syktyvkar Memorial received; however, the number is likely in the thousands.[16] The Moscow Memorial Society reported, for example, receiving thousands of letters each month from more than two hundred cities in the Soviet Union, post-Soviet Russia, and abroad starting in 1989.[17] The letters that Syktyvkar Memorial received range in length from a single paragraph to multiple letters of five to ten pages. The majority were written between 1989 and 1994 by former prisoners. Although many of these people left the region after they were rehabilitated in the 1950s, many Gulag returnees wrote to Syktyvkar Memorial from towns and villages in Komi where they were once prisoners. Interestingly, all the letters exhibit a keen sense of place that suggests attachment to the region that was once a place of imprisonment for them.

For many former prisoners, writing letters to Syktyvkar Memorial was the first time they wrote about their pasts and shared it with anyone.[18] As a result, some former prisoners wrote only a few lines in the genre of the "file autobiography," a document that Soviet people periodically wrote over the course of their lives for promotions, changes of employment, or entrance into the Communist Party.[19] When they finally revealed who they were, they addressed their prior silence as a matter of fact; the past was simply too dangerous to discuss before glasnost. Because this activity was relatively new for many people, some struggled to find the words to describe their experiences; others did not know what to write or how much to write about their lives in the Gulag and after release. Regardless of their ability or where they lived when the Soviet Union collapsed, Gulag returnees from Komi wrote to Syktyvkar Memorial to contribute their personal testimonies to the archive, to be rehabilitated, or simply to be heard.

Soon after it was founded, Syktyvkar Memorial became the organization that former prisoners trusted with their life stories. The information that these autobiographical narratives provided fundamentally shaped Syktyvkar Memorial's investigation into the past. These letters show the process of remembering that informed Gulag returnees' autobiographical narratives—a process shaped by the dialogue between former prisoners and Syktyvkar Memorial. An examination of these brief autobiographical narratives reveals what Gulag returnees felt was most important to know about their experiences and how they defined themselves. Following the collapse of the Soviet Union, a new law regarding the victims of political repression was passed that defined "victim" more broadly. Consequently, those who had been exiled to special settlements and the so-called children of the Gulag also began to write. While these letters consisted primarily of requests for assistance in obtaining rehabilitation and survivor benefits, they illustrate the challenges that victims faced as they found themselves under the jurisdiction of newly independent states.

The Founding of Syktyvkar Memorial

Just days before the Syktyvkar Executive Committee's decision, Syktyvkar Memorial held its founding conference on April 16, 1989. The conference was the subject of a long article in the central Komi newspaper, *Molodezh' Severa*, which reported that 100 of the 170 people in attendance voted to adopt the organization's charter. As *Molodezh' Severa* informed its readers, Syktyvkar Memorial planned to erect a monument to the victims of repression and to build an archive of survivors' testimonies.[20] In addition, the organization called on party officials to adopt a more comprehensive definition of "victim" that included non–party members and other categories of repressed people, such as former prisoners, *kulaks* (prosperous peasants who were branded class enemies for exploiting hired labor and sent remote special settlements), exiles, children born in camps, and "family members of enemies of the people." The article stated, "Having paid for [our] freedom, they should not fall out of history."[21] As one of the most important goals of Syktyvkar Memorial was the "education of the young generation," the program also called for the involvement of Komsomol activists, who were noticeably absent from the conference.[22] The article concluded by underscoring the necessity of Memorial's historic mission for the future health of Soviet society: "Comprehending that our country was fraught with spy-mania, we must never allow this again. Having united people of various ages and professions, those who suffered from Stalinist tyranny, and members of their family at its founding conference, Memorial's main tasks are the preservation of the memory of the victims of Stalinism and the restoration of historical justice."[23]

Despite its enthusiasm about the founding of Syktyvkar Memorial, the article did not describe the local origins of the organization. However, as noted in a letter written by Revol't Pimenov, Syktyvkar Memorial's origins were directly linked to the past the organization sought to uncover. In a letter to a colleague dated June 12, 1989, Pimenov described the origins of Syktyvkar Memorial as a unification of Komi's past and future: "When did the groups arise . . . ? One group, not open to the public, was virtually born from the date I was exiled here, reasonably considered sometime in the mid-1970s. The other, composed of youth, arose independently in the spring-summer of 1988."[24] Pimenov's comment is notable not only for its mention of the local community of exiles who stood at the origins of Syktyvkar Memorial but also for its statement about the merger of these exiles with youth activists inspired by *glasnost* to participate in its memory project.

Despite the fact that Syktyvkar Memorial's mission clearly contributed to glasnost's aim of overcoming the Stalinist past, not everyone was pleased with the movement's arrival in Syktyvkar. As Pimenov noted in his letter, the central Komi newspaper, *Krasnoe znamia*, received letters of protest that accused Memorial of "attempts to honor Banderites and Vlasovites" (anti-Soviet leaders Stepan Bandera and Andrei Vlasov, who collaborated with the Germans and actively fought against the Red Army during World War II) and demanded "that not one stone be laid in their honor."[25] Some threatened Memorial directly. The head of Syktyvkar Memorial's educational section, Igor' Bobrakov, shared a disturbing phone call he received at a meeting held on May 26, 1989: "'Your Pimenov is collecting information, yes?'—'Yes.'—'Don't you worry, we will build camps again just for you.' I don't want to scare anyone, I'm not scared, but I'm upset. Intolerance is alive and well. Despite shouting on every corner about Stalinism, a person can still be a virulent Stalinist on the inside."[26] Regardless of the conservative backlash, Pimenov noted that local authorities—namely, the KGB—exhibited cautious tolerance of the society: "The authorities' attitude [toward us] is determined, first, by their firm conviction that Bobrakov and Zil'berg [members of the board of Memorial] are actually secret members of the 'Democratic Union' [the first opposition party in the Soviet Union], and that Pimenov is an 'anti-Soviet twice over.'"[27] Authorities' tentative acceptance of the Syktyvkar Memorial Society also manifested in the form of partial access to state and party archives. Archivists at the Central State Archive of the Komi Autonomous Soviet Socialist Republic (ASSR) and the Regional Party Committee Archive (Komi Obkom) cooperated with Syktyvkar Memorial and gave them access to what documents they could. In contrast, the Ministry of Internal Affairs initially refused to recognize Memorial's right to collect data on behalf of the repressed persons who petitioned Memorial to do so.[28] Nevertheless, as Pimenov concluded in his letter, "Information coming from the central press has convinced me that the Memorial movement is legal, or at least looks legal."[29]

Former prisoners were initially uncertain about Memorial and hesitant about actively participating. As Pimenov wrote, "[We are] almost a nonentity. Very few people are interested, even fewer people actively participate. Former repressed persons are afraid, and the only thing that entices them is hope of material help from Memorial."[30] As a member of a different generation who was repressed because of his dissident political activities, it is perhaps unsurprising that Pimenov was willing to take greater risks. Initially, he was disappointed with the participation of the older generation of former prisoners. However, Pimenov's first impressions of their willingness to participate in Memorial were incorrect.

While Syktyvkar Memorial met, concerned citizens of Vorkuta and Ukhta were at work in April 1989 organizing independent branches. In Ukhta, approximately 150 people gathered at the founding conference of the Ukhta-Pechora Memorial Society (fig. 1.1). In addition to collecting materials on the history of the Ukhtpechlag and Ukhtizhemlag camps, the Ukhta-Pechora Memorial Society sought to "reveal the location and contents of the nameless graves, in which thousands of innocent people are buried."[31] Naming victims and marking sites of memory provided an impetus to write for former prisoners who were not interested in writing a memoir to finally break their silence. The opening of new branches was not the only sign that the Memorial movement had arrived in Komi. As *Molodezh' Severa* enthusiastically reported, Memorial's ideas spread to "the most remote corners of the republic," where "evenings of memory" dedicated to the "victims of Stalin's repressions" were held and included singing songs from the 1930s and 1940s, reciting poems, and sharing memories of those killed in the camps.[32]

As the movement gained traction, word spread outside the borders of the Soviet Union to the countries of the Warsaw Pact. Having read about Memorial and Pimenov's election to the Congress of People's Deputies, former prisoner Petr Kotov wrote to Syktyvkar Memorial from Gdansk, Poland. In his letter from June 1990, Kotov wrote to Pimenov, "The fact of your election as a deputy is very reassuring news, which is indicative of the change in the relationship to people of your fate on the part of the electorate of the Soviet Union."[33] On July 31, 1990, the deputy chairman of Syktyvkar Memorial, Mikhail Rogachev, replied to Kotov, "Revol't Ivanovich Pimenov was indeed elected as a People's Deputy of Russia. Moreover, he beat his opponent with a great majority. It is especially significant that the very people who voted for him were those who did not give him their vote in the [previous] election for People's Deputy of the USSR out of fear of voting for a former prisoner. Pimenov is not the only former political prisoner who has become a People's Deputy of the RSFSR [Russian Soviet Federative Socialist Republic]. Indeed, the times are changing."[34] The times were, indeed, changing. Not only was Pimenov elected as a people's deputy, but he was also elected despite his official biography, which listed his arrest and status as a former political prisoner.[35]

Those who had not been repressed played an important role in organizing Syktyvkar Memorial as it grew. If Gulag returnees were inspired by the changing times to write to Syktyvkar Memorial, their continued engagement with Memorial and the success of the organization was due to the small circle of volunteers who ran it. The first among them was Mikhail Rogachev, the deputy chairman and head of Syktyvkar Memorial's historical department. As the head of the historical department, Rogachev corresponded with all who wrote to Syktyvkar Memorial, in addition to meeting local survivors who visited the

Figure 1.1 A leaflet distributed by the Ukhta-Pechora Memorial Society in 1989 explains the society's mission and platform, lists its contact information, and, most importantly, states its status as a legally registered social organization. The leaflet reads in part, "The Ukhta-Pechora Memorial Society is for truth about the past and justice, a mixed economy, genuine democracy, a multiparty system, civil society, discipline, and order in the country. The Ukhta-Pechora Memorial Society is against any form of totalitarian regime, ethnic intolerance, chauvinism, monopolies in all spheres of life, a disdainful attitude toward the law, and permissiveness. Yes to Democracy! No to Totalitarianism!" Source: Ukhta State Technical University Local History Museum (AM UGTU f. Bulychev [listok Ukhto-Pechorskogo obshchestva "Memorial," 1989–1990]).

society's office hours.[36] When Pimenov died a year later from stomach cancer, Rogachev became the chairman of Syktyvkar Memorial. He continued to lead the organization after the founding of Fond Pokaianie in 1998 (discussed in chap. 5), which he led until his own death from COVID-19 in the first days of 2021. Born in Riga in 1952, Rogachev was the son of ordinary Soviet Russians who served in World War II. He never joined the Communist Party. On graduating from the history department of Leningrad State University in 1975, Rogachev was sent to Komi to work as a middle school teacher in the village of Tuiskerrossk. Although he did not receive his PhD (*kandidat*) until 2005,

Rogachev completed his graduate coursework in 1979 at the Komi Scientific Center—a branch of the Urals Academy of Sciences—where he continued to work as a researcher and taught courses in ethnography and history. Neither Rogachev nor any member of his family suffered repression.

So why did Rogachev join Syktyvkar Memorial in 1989? Rogachev was an ardent supporter of human rights, and he joined Syktyvkar Memorial out of his personal conviction to help others. Speaking directly into the camera at the close of a documentary film about his ongoing work at Syktyvkar Memorial, which aired on local television in 1995, Rogachev said, "We live in difficult times, just as we have before, and we survived and will survive these hard times. But if we do not help one another, if we cannot turn away from the concerns of everyday life at least for a moment and look around and try to help those in need, then I think that we will not survive, not only as Russians, as citizens, but we will likely not survive simply as people in the broadest sense of the word."[37]

Although he was not a young man when he joined, in many ways, Mikhail Rogachev was representative of the activist "youths" whom Pimenov described in his letter about the origins of Syktyvkar Memorial. As an outsider, so to speak, among Gulag returnees, Rogachev demonstrated to his interlocutors that he understood the difficulty of remembering the most traumatic chapters of one's life. As he wrote in response to a former prisoner's letter in 1990, "I understand that I ask too many difficult questions, but I hope that our correspondence will continue."[38] This candor is ultimately what made him trustworthy to the survivors, who remained wary of sharing their stories and exposing themselves to another round of repression, should Gorbachev's support for de-Stalinizing Soviet society come crashing down—as it had after Khrushchev's ouster in 1964. Luckily, however, this was not the case.

Syktyvkar Memorial began to receive letters from former prisoners from all over Komi and the Soviet Union over the course of 1989–1990. Its archive grew, and its mission came into focus. Many of these letters illustrate the uncertainty among former prisoners about what Memorial did. The letters that Syktyvkar Memorial sent in response to these inquiries enable us to see the development of the memory project. In a letter to a former prisoner in Kyiv, dated June 27, 1990, Rogachev explained Syktyvkar Memorial's work: "I consider our main task the collection of evidence of all the repressed from the Komi ASSR and to compile an all-encompassing martryology [martirolog], in order to preserve the memory of these people. We conduct research, collecting general facts regarding certain events and people."[39] In response to yet another inquiry about who Memorial's members were and what they did, Rogachev explained that the society was made up of a group of fifteen concerned citizens who, in addition

32 AFTER THE GULAG

to conducting research, helped relatives "looking for the graves of their loved ones who died in our camps."[40]

The expansion of the Syktyvkar Memorial archive was the result not only of cooperation with other branches but also of partnership with Gulag returnees in Komi and throughout the former Soviet Union.[41] This partnership was vital because Memorial still did not have state support or unrestricted direct access to state archives six years after the collapse of the Soviet Union. In a letter to a former prisoner in Kyiv, Rogachev asked for help collecting data for a Komi "Book of Memory":

> We finally intend to get down to work on the huge task of compiling the book of memory of information about all political prisoners and exiles, and those killed in the Komi ASSR from 1930 to 1950. But without state support, we will not manage this work because we don't have direct access to the camp archives. And we still haven't received any help from the state. We decided that we've waited long enough. Although it will be amateurish, we need to begin; otherwise, we will never finish. As you will understand, I write to you with a purpose, and I count on your help. Could you conduct surveys among the former prisoners and exiles you know in Kiev? Collect data on who remembers what about those who died in prison. The minimum data we need for the index—full name, year and place of birth, who they were before arrest, where they were arrested, when, by which organ, by which article they were sentenced, sentence, which camp they were in, where and when they died. The more detailed, the better. Even if the information is incomplete, we still need it—we can always specify later. I am writing to everyone I know to help. And we must do this, it is our duty. Do you agree?[42]

As Rogachev's letter indicates, Gulag returnees were not only sources of information but also partners in the project of recovering the past. Gulag returnees used their networks of camp comrades to gather testimonies for the Memorial archive, enabling Syktyvkar Memorial to offset its lack of access to state archives.

Syktyvkar Memorial's reliance on survivors' testimonies and memoirs was a product of the lack of archival access but also a fundamental part of its philosophy. Its efforts served to democratize Soviet history by bringing those who had been marginalized by the regime back into the picture. Despite the failings of memory and the amount of time that had passed for the survivors, Memorial saw their testimonies as an essential source in the reconstruction of the past. Rogachev himself admitted to searching the archives of the Komi Scientific Center when he was a graduate student in the late 1970s, looking for discussions about Stalinist repression that might have occurred in the early 1960s, but he found none.[43] As Memorial saw it, part of its mission was moving beyond the party's and the state's sources of information and transferring the authority on what happened in the past to those who experienced it. At a conference of the All-Union Memorial Society in Moscow on January 29, 1989, Pimenov observed, "In compiling new histories, apart from archival documents—which, by the way, are more likely to remain closed than open—the most important role belongs to the MEMORIES OF THE VICTIMS WHO ARE STILL ALIVE, as well as their CHILDREN AND RELATIVES. The historian must cite their memories in order to correct the documentary record."[44] More than a radical proposal from a known dissident and former prisoner, Pimenov's speech was a powerful statement about the agency of Stalin's victims as mnemonic actors to right injustices in historical memory. To understand the past, people had to listen to those who survived it.

The questionnaires that Gulag returnees completed were another important source of information. The questionnaire was designed to guide former prisoners who were uncertain about what they should write. In the Syktyvkar Memorial/ Fond Pokaianie archive, a total of 224 questionnaires were collected over the course of 1991–1992.[45] These questionnaires were used as both a self-interview, which former prisoners could complete on their own, and a template for interviews. The questionnaire asked for details about one's arrest, investigation, and sentencing; where the sentence was served and when; what the individual did in the camps; when they were released; whether they had been rehabilitated and when; and where they lived and worked after release.[46] This form became the standard for books of memory and databases that compile lists of former prisoners as evidence of actual lives touched by Soviet repression.[47]

This important tool for collecting information was also the product of collaboration between Syktyvkar and Moscow Memorial Societies. In June 1990, Syktyvkar Memorial received a letter from Moscow underscoring the difficulty reported by former prisoners completing the questionnaire. In a letter dated June 26, 1990, a historian at Moscow Memorial reported that it was "impossible" for former prisoners to complete the questionnaire on their own: "I've had to use the questionnaire [as the basis] of interview questions, asking the questions myself and filling in the answers with their words."[48] In his response, Rogachev stated that Memorial's researchers needed to adapt their methods to suit the "repressed": "I totally agree with you (my experience as an ethnographer speaks to this) that [survivors] filling out the questionnaire themselves will yield little. We should work using the interview method."[49] Despite their uncertainty about former prisoners' ability to complete the questionnaire, the Syktyvkar Memorial archive contains hundreds of these questionnaires (fig. 1.2). Clearly, they worked at a basic level.[50] The information Memorial

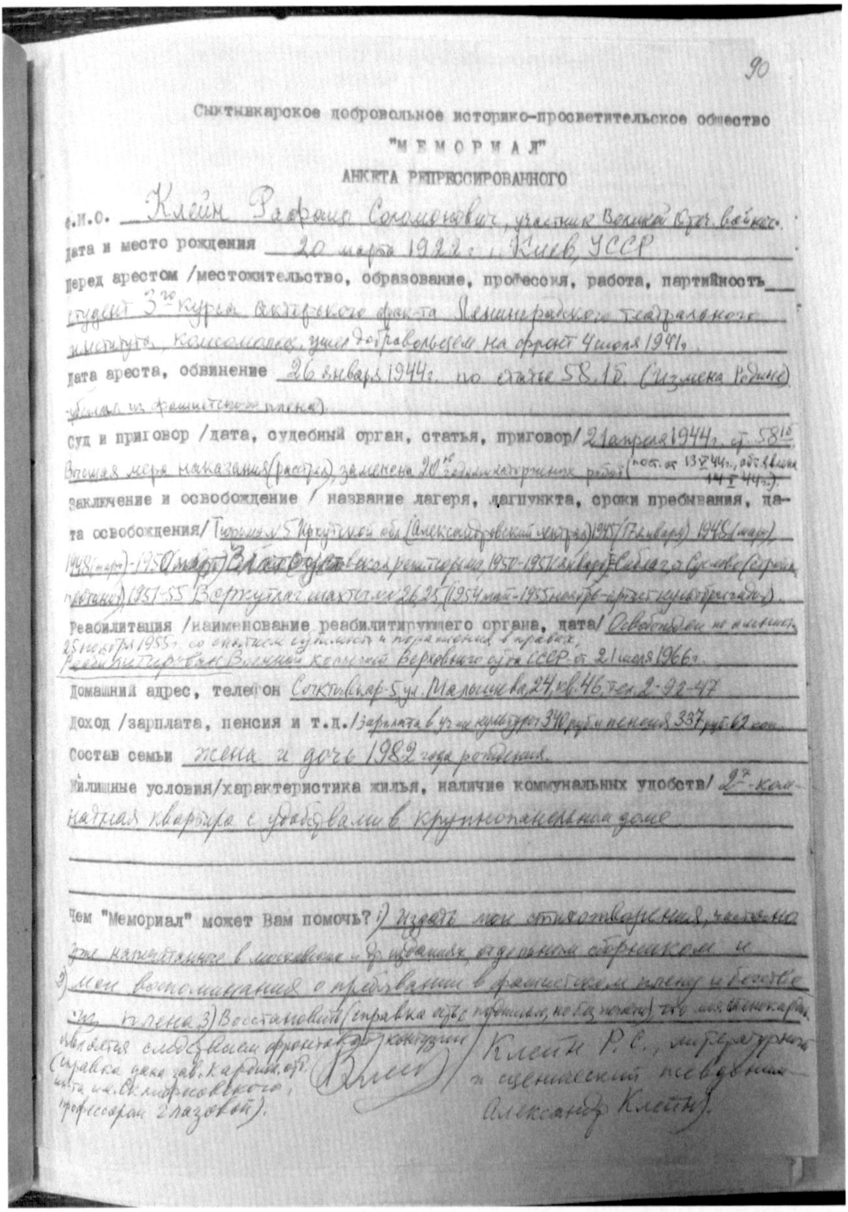

90

Сыктывкарское добровольное историко-просветительское общество
"М Е М О Р И А Л"
АНКЕТА РЕПРЕССИРОВАННОГО

Ф.И.О. Клейн Рафаил Соломонович, участник Великой Отеч. войны.
Дата и место рождения 20 марта 1922 г., Киев, УССР
Перед арестом /местожительство, образование, профессия, работа, партийность студент 3-го курса актерского фак-та Ленинградского театрального института, комсомолец, ушел добровольцем на фронт 4 июля 1941 г.
Дата ареста, обвинение 26 января 1944 г. по статье 58.1б. (измена Родине) (бежал из фашистского плена)
Суд и приговор /дата, судебный орган, статья, приговор/ 21 апреля 1944 г. ст. 58-1б. Высшая мера наказания (расстрел), заменена 20-ю годами каторжных работ
Заключение и освобождение / название лагеря, лагпункта, сроки пребывания, дата освобождения/ Тюрьма № 5 Иркутской обл. (Александровский централ) 1945 (7 января) – 1948 (март) 1948 (март) – 1950 (март) Владимирская ... 1950–1951 ... 1951–55 Воркутлаг шахты № 26, 25 (1954 май – 1955 ноябрь ...)
Реабилитация /наименование реабилитирующего органа, дата/ Освобожден ... 25 ноября 1955 г. со снятием судимости и поражения в правах. Реабилитирован Военной коллегией Верховного суда СССР от 21 июля 1966 г.
Домашний адрес, телефон Сыктывкар-5 ул. Малышева, 24, кв. 46. тел. 2-92-47
Доход /зарплата, пенсия и т.д./ зарплата в ... 340 руб. и пенсия 337 руб. 62 коп.
Состав семьи жена и дочь 1982 года рождения.
Жилищные условия/характеристика жилья, наличие коммунальных удобств/ 2-х комнатная квартира с удобствами в крупнопанельном доме

Чем "Мемориал" может Вам помочь? 1) издать мои стихотворения, частично уже напечатанные в ... изданиях, отдельным сборником и 2) мои воспоминания о пребывании в фашистском плену и бегстве из плена 3) Восстановить (справка ...) ... является следствием фронтовой контузии (справка ... профессора Глазовой).

Клейн Р. С., литературный и сценический псевдоним Александр Клейн.

Figure 1.2 Example of Syktyvkar Memorial's questionnaire filed by former prisoner Aleksandr Klein in 1991. The questionnaire became the basis for prisoner biographies in Fond Pokaianie's *Martirolog*. Source: Fond Pokaianie (AFP, Questionnaire of R. S. [Aleksandr] Klein, 1991, l. 90; Rogachev, ed., *Pokaianie: Martirolog*, t. 12, ch. 1, 294).

gathered from these simple forms enabled Syktyvkar Memorial to begin to grasp the immensity of the history that it was dealing with. As Rogachev concluded his letter, "Now the most complicated question is about the camps. In fact, we ourselves still have not completely figured out this eternally entangled system. On that score, we had more than seven camps."[51]

In completing these questionnaires, Gulag returnees transformed the dates and events of their lives into primitive autobiographies that made the system of mass repression comprehensible on a human scale. The pictured questionnaire filed by a former prisoner of Vorkutlag, Aleksandr Klein, offers an example of a Gulag returnee who used the form as a template for his autobiography. In the process of answering the questions, Klein constructed a narrative of his life that begins with his military service during World War II, goes through the camps, and ends with his life after release as a newspaper editor and educator. Although the questionnaire offers a limited view, it presents the life of a former prisoner who survived the camps and returned to Soviet society. It represents his effort to translate the details of his life into a publicly accessible document that could be written into a new history of the Soviet Union. It is also important to note that the form provided space for Gulag returnees to elaborate and emphasize chapters of their life that they felt were important. Not all Gulag returnees did so, but Klein's inclusion of the details of his life after release shows that the Gulag was an important chapter of his life, but it did not define him.

Following the collapse of the Soviet Union, Syktyvkar Memorial continued its mission to uncover the past and to assist "victims of political repression" with rehabilitation. This work expanded greatly in the years after 1991. In 1991, Syktyvkar Memorial began to hold public office hours in the city administration building.[52] This program started as a service to victims of political repression who otherwise might not have written to Syktyvkar Memorial; it also provided a means of gathering testimonies while assisting victims with the complicated process of rehabilitation. The process of obtaining the necessary documents created an inordinately difficult hurdle for those who spent most of their lives in Komi after their release and no longer knew anyone in their hometowns.[53] In a letter from 1993, Rogachev described the immensity of the problem, which only intensified after the collapse of the Soviet Union: "I thought that maybe we'd manage to finish up in a year—after all, our city is not very big, and already forty to fifty years have passed. Not likely! Every reception day, new people—they're elderly, naturally, but they don't forget. I've already registered more than six hundred people. Of course, it's indicative of the fact that Syktyvkar was the capital of the 'camp republic,' even though there were no camps in the city itself."[54]

The correspondence of Syktyvkar Memorial and the Syktyvkar Department of Social Security grew to such an extent that the May 15, 1992, issue of *Krasnoe znamia* published a long interview with the minister of social security, addressed to the former prisoners and special settlers in Komi, in which the minister answered questions about the process of rehabilitation and what such people were entitled to under the law.[55] Similar articles about rehabilitation and where one could go for help appeared in the local newspaper in Ukhta.[56] A year later, Rogachev wrote to a former prisoner about the slow pace of change and the inadequate government response to the needs of the repressed: "We finally started giving out identifications for the right to use privileges as victims of repression. . . . They sent four hundred to our city from Moscow. Can it be true that the bureaucrats can't surmise that Syktyvkar is a special city, the center of the land of camps? We have more than one thousand people who are eligible for this certification. I still don't know the exact number, because new people come every day."[57] By 1994, the number had doubled. As Rogachev wrote in a letter to a former prisoner who inquired about rehabilitation, "After all, the Komi Republic was a dreadful place. There were more camps here [than anywhere]. More than two thousand former political prisoners and exiles live in our small city (of 250,000 people)."[58] However, the number of rehabilitated victims continued to grow. By 1997, it had risen to more than three thousand.[59]

The idea that the Komi Republic was the center of the world of camps that engulfed the Soviet Union was reinforced not only by the large number of victims who came to office hours but also by the flood of correspondence that Syktyvkar Memorial received almost immediately after it was established. As will be shown, Gulag returnees' letters were one of the primary sources of Komi's camp past and contributed to the transformation of the entire region into a site of memory.

Letters to Syktyvkar Memorial: Reconstructing the Past, 1989–1992

The reconstruction of Komi's camp past during the late 1980s and early 1990s depended on Gulag returnees telling their life stories.[60] Former prisoners' autobiographical narratives were important not only because Syktyvkar Memorial did not have direct access to camp archives; they were also essential to the commemoration of the victims of political repression. Nevertheless, it is important to note that these narratives were shaped by dialogue. Taken as a whole, Gulag returnees' correspondence with Syktyvkar Memorial illustrates the process of remembering that informed their autobiographical narratives. As Elizabeth

Tonkin writes about the narration of our pasts, "memory makes us" and "we make memory."[61]

Many of the letters that flooded Syktyvkar Memorial's office read, "We are no strangers to Komi."[62] As this statement suggests, Gulag returnees' letters exhibited a strong sense of place. Former prisoners shared a connection to Komi, but their letters often highlighted a connection to a particular place, such as the camp where they served time or the town in Komi where they lived after release. This familiarity underscores the local aspect of their identities, which they often expressed in the sense of pride they felt about what they had built during the years of their forced labor. Gulag returnees' letters also reveal an important aspect of space, which is visible in their memoirs (in chap. 3). By setting their autobiographical narratives in Komi, Gulag returnees transformed the Far North into a site of memory. By underscoring their contributions to the development of the Far North, Gulag returnees' letters began the process of connecting the memory of the victims of political repression to the Komi landscape.

Memory as a source of the past is an important concept in Gulag returnees' letters. Echoing Pimenov's earlier statements, former prisoners often described their autobiographical narratives as sources of historical truth. This claim was based principally on their status as survivors and eyewitnesses, as they sometimes referred to themselves. As a repressed and marginalized population, authenticity was particularly important because Gulag returnees were countering the state narrative of the past without any documentation.[63] Vitalii Ol'shevskii's letter to Syktyvkar Memorial dated June 26, 1990, provides an example of how former prisoners framed their memories as a source of historical truth:

Dear Mikhail Borisovich!

During your stay in Moscow at the Memorial congress in May of this year, you spoke with comrade Siderskii, the chairman of Memorial Kiev. You told him about your interest in the history of the construction of the Northern-Pechora Railroad. It seems that he told you about me. In the memorable year of 1937, I fell into the clutches of the NKVD [People's Commissariat of Internal Affairs] and was sent to a far-off region. I served three years at BAM [Baikal-Amur Railway] at construction site no. 202, and then I was on the Northern-Pechora Railroad in Sevzheldorlag from 1940 to 1952. In Sevzheldorlag, I stayed alive because I worked as a surveyor. I worked on different parts of the railroad from Izhma to Vorkuta. I met many members of the [camp] leadership. I wrote a memoir about my life. My main goal was to depict the way of life of this kingdom. *I described only what I saw myself, without any fabrication* [emphasis added]. If my work interests you, I can send you a copy of the manuscript. I served a sentence under the KRD [counterrevolutionary activities] article. I've lived in Kiev, since [my] rehabilitation in 1955.[64]

Remembering was not an uncomplicated path that led directly to a lost past. Gulag returnees grappled with the problems of remembering in their letters to Syktyvkar Memorial. While all former prisoners thought that their stories ought to become part of a new narrative of Soviet history, they struggled with the silences or "blank spots" in their memories of the camps.[65] Some silences were a result of lingering fear about committing one's life to paper. In a letter from July 1990, former prisoner Vladimir Siderskii reflected on his memory and why it was difficult for other former prisoners to open up about their pasts: "Memory is not a very reliable custodian. After all, forty years have passed, plus age. Yes, for forty years I did not think about what I needed to remember, [or] that it would ever be of use. It was very dangerous to write, and even to think of this."[66] While Siderskii cast doubt on the reliability of memory due to the passage of time, his comment about the danger of writing about the past illuminates the lingering fear that prevented many Gulag returnees from writing about the past before glasnost. As another victim of political repression, L. Veselova, wrote to her local Memorial Society in Ukhta, "I was born in a camp, behind the barbed wire in 1941. A few years ago, I would not have told anyone about this. It was my terrifying secret. But now I speak about that which tortured me for years, without shame. After all, it's also a crime of Stalinism, when children were born in the camps and then suffered from a consciousness of inferiority. Deliverance from this feeling is a great blessing."[67]

Some Gulag returnees remained hesitant to write about their lives in the camps, whereas others were motivated to do so by what they read in the press. In these instances, the principal aim of their letters was setting the record straight while they still could. An additional motivating factor was the sense of duty that some people felt to honor the dead.[68] This feeling is what motivated two reluctant former prisoners from the Chuvash Republic on the Volga River, who read about Memorial's efforts throughout the country to uncover Stalin's crimes, to send a letter to Syktyvkar Memorial on January 31, 1989:

> Having read an article in the journal *Sobesednik* no. 46, 1988, I was compelled to write to you about what happened in [our] camp, where almost everyone was repressed in 1937. Our camp Lokchimlag was located on the territory of the Komi ASSR. Our camp section was located in Ust'kulomskii district close to the village Ust'nem across the river Vychegda.... Every night from the end of October to the beginning of November 1938, the third division of the NKVD took several people out of the zone after work. No one ever returned.... Five or

six of us were taken one night. They took them away to the forest in a covered truck and shot them. Everyone in the camp saw the lights. We did not know for sure where they took them, but we could hear the shots. This was carried out in about a month. They began to dig graves when the earth was no longer frozen, so that digging was easier.[69]

Although the primary aim of such letters was to correct the historical record with their own testimony, it is clear that the need for authenticity compelled former prisoners to construct a brief autobiographical narrative demonstrating their authority to testify. The second half of a letter collectively written by two prisoners provides a typical example of the ways in which former prisoners achieved this goal through their autobiographical narratives:

> Briefly about myself and my comrade: In August 1937, my comrade-neighbor, Spiridonov Sergei Nikoforovich (born 1918), and I, Arkhipov Ivan Andreevich (also born 1918), were repressed. We were held in preliminary detention at the NKVD headquarters in Krasnye Chetai, Chuvash ASSR. Without trial or investigation, I was sentenced to ten years by decree of a troika under the article "socially harmful element." My comrade was also sentenced to ten years under the article "socially dangerous element." Fourteen of us set out from prison together. Only the two of us returned. . . . We were considered enemies of the people, they treated us like animals. I can't find the words to describe what happened there. The prisoners who did not fulfill the norm received a punishment ration of 300 grams of bread and boiled water. Dysentery set in. Ten to fifteen people died in one day. We were released in 1947; since then, more than fifty years have passed, but we still know where the graves of those executed are. We can show you the place and help dig them up, there are about 1,500 people there.[70]

In addition to sharing their autobiographical narratives, Gulag returnees also wrote to Syktyvkar Memorial to contribute to the effort to comprehensively document life behind barbed wire. While these projects typically took the form of memoirs, others included artworks depicting landscapes and scenes from the camp, collections of poems composed in the camp and preserved in memory, and archives of correspondence with friends from the camps. In June 1990, former prisoner Leonid Gorodin wrote to Syktyvkar Memorial about his unique project to document the camps—an encyclopedic dictionary of the Gulag.[71] Over the course of several letters, Gorodin identified himself as "Vorkutinets" (a veteran of Vorkuta) and a "victim of Stalin's repressions" and described his project, which included more than seventeen thousand entries, as a "Museum for friends."[72] In a letter from August 3, 1990, Gorodin explained the significance of his encyclopedic dictionary: "For many years, I have collected and studied the language founded by the most fascinating and numerous group of people—prisoners. 'Thieves' songs are only a part of the prisoner language. Many words and expressions come from political *katorga*, or tsarist Russia. But inmates in prisons, [and] *zeks* [prisoners] from the camps and colonies [also] made significant contributions to the language during the postrevolutionary period."[73]

Such letters reveal that, for some, the process of remembering the Gulag began immediately after release. However, like others who wrote memoirs before glasnost, Gorodin did not take his dictionary out of his desk drawer until the late 1980s when he shared it with a few acquaintances in the hope that someone would publish his manuscript. It did not reach the public he so desperately tried to share his experiences with until 2021, when the State Gulag History Museum and Fond Pamiati published his dictionary and created a traveling museum exhibit about Gorodin's work.[74] The lifetime Gorodin spent documenting the language of the camps illuminates his prisoner experience as an essential part of his identity and shows his desire to contribute to the reconstruction of that world, which no longer existed, and to reveal its continued influence on Russian society through language. When Gorodin's project eventually made it out of the desk drawer and into the archive at Syktyvkar Memorial, Rogachev wrote to Gorodin, "Every testimony about the participants of the events in Ust'-Usa is very important and enables us to understand the essence of this drama."[75]

Gulag returnees frequently identified themselves as one of the group (*odno-etapniki*), a word from the camps that refers to prisoners on the same transport (*etap*).[76] In using this language, they identified themselves as one of the collective through descriptions of their collective suffering.[77] As a former prisoner from Kyiv, Lev Safronov, wrote in a two-page letter to Syktyvkar Memorial on July 16, 1990:

> It is possible that my memories about the days and years of my time in the Komi Republic will be interesting to you. I was one of the first to arrive at the construction of the railroad Kniazh-Pogost', Kozhva, Pechora, and onward to the North. I was a prisoner at the time, and what's more an "enemy of the people." From the beginning, we cut logging roads along the future railroad and laid the wooden bed [for the rails] along these tracts. We were divided into columns of three hundred to five hundred prisoners, or "zeks"; only civilians were the bosses of the colony and the upper echelon of the site. Although I was a zek and an "enemy of the people," fate made me a superintendent. . . .
>
> The living conditions, or more precisely living death, were severe. Half of my comrades were buried along the [railroad] tracks. . . . I don't think it would be an exaggeration if I said that one of my comrades lies under each tie of the Pechora

railroad. I survived because I was an exceptionally physically strong person, a Siberian hardened by the Siberian countryside, but southerners died like flies.[78]

Intrigued by Safronov's knowledge of where prisoners' bodies might lie, Rogachev encouraged Safronov to write as much as he could remember: "This is very important: more and more people come to us with requests, including people from Poland—people who are searching for the graves of their loved ones, and there is very little information saved in the archives. I think it's understandable how important it is to collect as much evidence of the participants of these tragic events as possible, and to restore the names and the graves of the victims of Stalinism."[79]

In his undated response to Rogachev's letter, Safronov included even more details in his narrative. Focusing on the relations between zeks and civilians, Safronov detailed the fine but distinct border between freedom and unfreedom:

> Years have passed, many memories have been blotted out, but I will try [to tell you] everything that I remember. . . . I often remember these first [months] now.
>
> Our crew boss in Kozhva was Boris Petrovich Podval'nyi—a very decent person, which was a rare quality among civilians in camp. . . .
>
> I especially remember one boss of the camp section. Although I remember his build and face, I'm sorry I don't remember his name. He was a son of the Komi people, the kindest person, he often used the word "Poshto" in conversation, and we called him citizen "POSHTO" behind his back, but this was without malicious intent or mockery; all of us zeks were grateful to him for his fairness and humaneness.
>
> There were many bosses, militarized guards, villains, scoundrels, and hangmen, but I'm sorry that I cannot name them. Overall, prisoners were approximately 90% political, including Poles after we annexed western Ukraine. The Poles' camp was on the northern bank of the Synia River close to the railroad tract.
>
> I wrote to you [last time] that the remains of a prisoner lie under every tie. This is figuratively speaking. The dead were kept close to the infirmary and camp sections. However, if you tallied the number of the dead, I'm certain that it would come to more than one person.[80]

Both of Safonov's letters describe Komi's northern railroad as a burial ground. This recurring metaphor highlights an important function of Gulag returnees' letters. By describing the railroad as a graveyard for prisoners, Safronov transformed the railroad from an infrastructural monument of Socialist achievement into a monument of Stalinist repression.[81] In claiming it as a product of prisoners' forced labor, he pushed back against the Soviet histories and newsreel films of polar industrialization that replaced prisoners with communist youth. In other words, Gulag returnees created sites of memory out of the products of their forced labor that anchored the memory of the Gulag to the landscape of the Komi Republic. As former prisoner Konstantin Flug wrote in his memoir in 1986, "Well, what is left of their labor? Vorkuta, Ukhta, Noril'sk, Magadan, Inta, Amdera, Kolymsk, Bratsk, Medvezhegorsk—the islands of Solzhenitsyn's archipelago—remain. The mining-metallurgical industry of the Soviet North remains, the Vorkuta-Pechora railroad remains, the Kolyma highway. Every one of the millions of toilers of the Gulag left their own mark, everyone has their own monument of labor."[82]

Although the infrastructure that prisoners built and some traces of the once vast network of camps could still be found throughout Komi, former prisoners were some of the last direct links to this vanishing world. The inclusion of this information in their letters and autobiographies initiated a search for the unmarked graves of prisoners (fig. 1.3); as will be shown in chapter 5, they became sites of memory where members of the public commemorated the victims of political repression.[83] Even when no graves were found, Gulag returnees' testimonies attached meaning to the small clearings in the taiga where the ruins of former camp buildings stood as sacred spaces (fig. 1.4). After an unsuccessful expedition to Lokchim, where Georgii Ustilovskii had not stepped foot since 1945, he proclaimed his memoir the only evidence of the mass death that he saw while imprisoned there:

> What did we see there? Signs that there had been zones there. Pine trees still hadn't managed to grow up in these places, but we saw the rotting barracks of the camp section. We could not find where the majority of people were buried. My testimony is the only evidence that many people were killed there. I know, I saw the destruction of people. Why didn't we find the gravesite? I contend for the following reason: they died primarily in the winter of 1937–1938, November, December, January, February, March. . . . The bodies were buried, if you can call it a burial, by weakened prisoners. They buried the bodies in the snow, not in the earth. In the spring, the snow melted, there was a very strong stench of [rotting] flesh. They closed camp sections 98, 100, 102. I think that large animals and birds dragged the bodies away. That is why there are no graves there and nothing dug into the ground. Personally, when we arrived at the place of the former camp section, I felt heartache. It was painful and bitter to look at the rotting barracks, to remember that bitter, hard life of dead camp mates, comrades, and friends.[84]

The creation of these sites of memory became increasingly important after the collapse of the Soviet Union, when the difficulty of the transition to capitalism

Figure 1.3 Unmarked prisoner graves, Pezmog, 1992. Source: Fond Pokaianie (AFP, collection of photographs, l. 1).

Figure 1.4 Remnants of Ust'vymlag after it was closed in 1962. Photographs taken 1964.
Source: Fond Pokaianie (AFP, collection of photographs, l. 2, 6).

stimulated nostalgia for the stability of days past.[85] As Safronov wrote in a two-page letter to Syktyvkar Memorial dated October 1996: "I'll try to expand on my memories about past tragedies, especially since many make it seem as if in Stalin's time everything was just GREAT. The truth is in our bones!!!"[86]

"I Want to Die Rehabilitated": Post-Soviet Letters, 1992–1997

In February 1992, the Komi newspapers *Molodezh' Severa* and *Krasnoe znamia* published two op-eds highlighting the difficulties experienced by local victims of political repression when they applied for rehabilitation.[87] Both articles served as publicity for the biweekly public office hours. The articles are noteworthy for the stories they include of those who came to Memorial seeking help and answers. One elderly woman, who served a sentence in the camps as a "family member of a traitor to the Motherland" and remained in Komi after release, told the reporter frankly, "I don't need any privileges. I want to die rehabilitated, nothing more."[88] However, as the second op-ed reported, despite the proclaimed importance of rehabilitation as "the restoration of justice," local authorities' management of the process was inept. "The daughter of A. K. Murav'eva, who was sentenced under the infamous article 58, said that her mother applied for rehabilitation to the Procurator of the Komi SSR more than six months ago, and to this day there has still been no answer."[89]

While Gulag returnees continued to write to Syktyvkar Memorial following the collapse of the Soviet Union to share their personal testimonies of repression, their letters increasingly focused on obtaining rehabilitation. During this period, Syktyvkar Memorial also received an increasing amount of correspondence from special settlers and children who were born in the camps. Although they focused on rehabilitation and the privileges that came with it, these letters offer insight into how a growing array of diverse people came to understand the definition of "victim" and how they altered it as they applied the term to themselves.

Gulag returnees appreciated the meager material aid they received. Perhaps more importantly, their letters indicate that they saw rehabilitation as a correction to the great moral, physical, and social injury they suffered at the hands of the Soviet regime. Even if they were rehabilitated in the 1950s or 1960s, privileges and a certificate of rehabilitation were especially meaningful as an acknowledgment of their innocence and a public symbol of their restored honor. As one Gulag returnee from Ukhta, who was imprisoned for having been taken prisoner of war during World War II, wrote to Syktyvkar Memorial in 1994, "Allow me to express my sincere gratitude for your help in the cause of the restoration of justice in my old case. Yes, thanks to your help, I, Soobtskov

Madinat Garunovich, am finally rehabilitated. I did just as you advised me and everything turned out well. Now, I receive privileges as a veteran of the war as I ought to according to the law."[90]

Not all the requests for rehabilitation turned out well. Although these letters shed light on the general difficulty of obtaining rehabilitation, they also illustrate the difficult financial situation many elderly former prisoners found themselves in after the collapse of the Soviet Union. On March 11, 1993, for example, ninety-five-year-old Evdokiia Meshcheriakova petitioned Syktyvkar Memorial to help her obtain privileges as a "victim of political repression." Explaining the difficulties that she encountered, which led to several failed petitions, Meshcheriakova pleaded:

> I write to you with a big request.... I have already written three times requesting them to send me a certificate [of release], but I have not yet received any reply. The first time I wrote to the head of special collections at the Komi MVD [Ministry of Internal Affairs] information center, A. A. Mikhail'chenkov, he wrote back on November 21, 1991, that my application was forwarded to Ukhta to the archive of the Administration of Internal Affairs of the Komi ASSR. I waited almost a year for an answer and was forced to write again on September 22, 1992, to the MVD archive of the Komi Republic, but there was no answer. I wrote once again on February 27, 1993, to the MVD archive in Ukhta. However, I am now uncertain that I will not receive the certificate I need. I am a very old person. I am ninety-five years old. I ought to be preparing for death. I need more money for a funeral. I urge you, Mikhail Borisovich, to help get this certificate of my release.[91]

While the ineptitude and understaffing of local agencies was a major problem that hindered the efficient processing of petitions for rehabilitation, letters from Gulag returnees and special settlers shed light on another significant obstacle created by the collapse of the Soviet Union. Some victims of political repression wrote to Syktyvkar Memorial about the rejection of their petitions for rehabilitation on the basis of their citizenship. Regardless of where they lived when the Soviet Union collapsed, if a victim had been arrested and sentenced by a court or extrajudicial organ in any of the former union republics, which were now independent states, their petitions were rejected, and they told to apply for rehabilitation in those states. Because many former prisoners who remained in Komi no longer had any ties in the places where they were arrested, this requirement created an inordinately large obstacle to achieving rehabilitation.[92] Nevertheless, the complications did not end there. As one former prisoner who remained in Inta after release wrote to Syktyvkar Memorial, "I've written to the Inta city council more than once requesting them to accept my certificate of rehabilitation to amend my length of service (*stazh*) to include the time that I spent in places of confinement. But they refuse me every time, citing the fact that I was rehabilitated by Ukrainian organs [of Soviet state security]. They will not accept certificates that were issued after 1985 by other republics. All together I earned thirty years toward my pension, and they do not pay out my pension in full."[93]

Children born in the camps and those who were children when their parents were repressed also identified themselves as victims of political repression. After the collapse of the Soviet Union, the so-called children of the Gulag consistently wrote to Syktyvkar Memorial. They primarily wanted to learn more about their parents who had shared very little about their lives in the camps.[94] However, those who remained in Komi with their parents after release also sought rehabilitation. They based their claim to the status of "victim of political repression" on their connection to the Gulag. In doing so, they cited their time in the camp system and in the homes for children of enemies of the people.[95] Although most of these children did not serve sentences alongside their parents, as Iwona Irwin-Zarecka writes, "the personal relevance of the traumatic memory, and not personal witness to the trauma" defines their status as part of the community.[96] For instance, Liubov' Shlezhkova, a child of a former prisoner living in Komi, wrote a letter to editor of the newspaper *Molodezh' Severa* in September 1993 that made its way to Syktyvkar Memorial. In addition to inquiring about the possibility of rehabilitation, her letter provides a detailed account of her family's repression:

> Since the publication of the article "Uprising of the Doomed" about Vorkutlag, I have [regularly] read your newspaper. I very much regret that, for unknown reasons, I did not save the precious article. You know, my father was also there; he was arrested in 1937 and sentenced to ten years plus another five years deprivation of rights under article 58-10. But I did not mean to talk about that now. Enough has already been written about these prisoners of Stalin's concentration camps and, moreover, I myself learn from Solzhenitsyn's books. This is the truth of life, that is the destruction of the country, of its dignity. I am the daughter of a repressed person, now posthumously rehabilitated, and my mother was also repressed and rehabilitated. I was the daughter of an "*enemy of the people*," but I didn't know it for many years. *I was born in the Vorkuta camps.* I know that privileges for the victims of political repression of the 1930s–1950s have been introduced. I know that the children of fascist concentration camps have privileges and compensation for the starvation, freezing, degrading work, and much more that they suffered. Now it has become known that Stalin's concentration camps surpassed the fascist camps. For some reason, the topic of Soviet children of the Gulag is

48   AFTER THE GULAG

not in the archives. Apparently, the documents were not preserved.... There were so many children born in the camps who were tortured, repressed, destroyed, dispersed, but you read almost nothing about them.

Underscoring the importance of the accounts of Gulag survivors, Shlezhkova thanked the newspaper and the Syktyvkar publishing house for publishing A. Voitalovskaia's memoir, *In the Steps of the Fate of My Generation*:

> Only from this book was I able to establish the life path of my father and mother in 1937–1938 (this was the beginning of the arrests). My mother did not tell me all of the terrible truth. Even though she told me some of her sorrowful confessions and stories with tears in her eyes, I could not believe all of it. It was unimaginable to me that this could be true. Dear editorial board of *Molodezh severa*, have there been any decrees about the restoration of privileges for us children of the Gulag? After all, we also suffered and bore the burden of the false guilt of our parents. The Stalinist saying that children do not bear responsibility for the guilt of their parents turned out to be an absurdity. I experienced this and was silent about it, but I remember all of it from an early age. I think that such people don't approach you that often. Once again, I wanted to ask if there is any kind of compensation for years spent in the camps for parents and their children? Parents have already died, but their children are still alive. Just ask us and we will respond, we are still alive and so is our memory of poverty, hunger, degradation, indifference, exile, and many years of silence. I received a birth certificate from the archives only a short while ago in 1992, and out of fear my mother didn't take my father's family name. I can't make sense of it. An entire book needs to be written on this topic. Please write to me. I await your response.[97]

Shlezhkova's letter is illuminating for several reasons. It reveals that newspapers and locally published Gulag memoirs were sources of information about the camps that made it possible for others to understand what their repressed family members could not. Like the others who wrote to Syktyvkar Memorial, Shlezhkova cited her personal testimony as an important piece of a developing but still incomplete narrative of the past. Shlezhkova's letter also illustrates how the children of Gulag returnees did not always know everything about their parents until much later in life. It also reveals that children also lived with a certain stigma attached to them as the "children of the Gulag." Similar to the criticisms voiced by living Gulag returnees who welcomed the commemoration of the past but felt that the state was not doing enough to help these people who were elderly and in need of material aid, Shlezhkova's letter also argued that if children who were born in the camps were not provided for under the law, then the law needed to be changed.[98] As one former prisoner wrote in an undated letter to Syktyvkar Memorial, "You write that your society Memorial helps in the search of graves and information about relatives—this is great, but there are no aid societies for the living. Nobody cares about them it seems."[99]

After the collapse of the Soviet Union, entire villages of former special settlers in Komi wrote to Syktyvkar Memorial seeking rehabilitation. The autobiographical narratives they composed, as part of their petitions, read like brief file autobiographies. In writing these file autobiographies, former special settlers offered little information about life in exile. A letter for rehabilitation dated October 16, 1993, from the Komi village Aikino reads, "In 1934, I was sent to a special settlement in the Komi ASSR, to the village Vet'iu in the Ustvymskii district. Since then, I have lived in the Komi Republic. I am eighty-six years old. I was born in 1907. With this application, I ask you to help with rehabilitation. I was sent from the BSSR [Belarus]."[100] It is unclear why they wrote so little about life in the special settlement; however, it seems possible that they did not disclose much because they simply did not know what to write about those years.

Despite the differences in their letters, both Gulag returnees and former special settlers expressed their sublime joy when they were finally rehabilitated. A special settler from the village Vet'iu wrote to Syktyvkar Memorial on August 18, 1993, to express her gratitude: "I thank you with all my heart for your care and goodness toward us. I received all the documents. . . . It seems that they came very quickly. And on my sixty-fifth birthday. No one has ever given me such a priceless gift."[101] Another former special settler residing in Komi described the feeling of rehabilitation as having a "stigma removed." She wrote,

> On October 18, 1991, the law on the rehabilitation of victims of repression came out. In order to get this certificate, I needed an archival certificate from the special collection of the MVD of the city of Syktyvkar. After receiving the archival certificate, I lost [my] composure and sleep. In the certificate, [my] entire family is listed; of eleven people, after each name is written the terrible word, "dead, dead," and so on nine times more—of them, two are not buried in Ichet-di. After prolonged correspondence, I received the long-awaited certificate of rehabilitation. Justice triumphed. The shameful brand of special settler, daughter of a kulak, was removed.[102]

Although the archival record from 1994 to 1996 is incomplete, Syktyvkar Memorial continued to receive letters from Gulag returnees, special settlers, their children, and relatives looking for their lost loved ones into the 2000s. The archival record picks back up in 1997. The majority of these letters were written by repressed persons seeking help with rehabilitation or obtaining information about a repressed parent. In a few instances, Gulag returnees who had not written to Syktyvkar Memorial wrote, but they did not do so with the same frequency as they had in the late 1980s and early 1990s. The slowing influx of letters from former prisoners can be explained by several factors. First, many of those who wrote memoirs and actively corresponded with Memorial in the late 1980s and early 1990s had passed away by the late 1990s. Second, although researching the history of the Gulag and commemorating the victims of political repression remained important in Komi, interest in the dark chapters of the Stalinist past declined nationally in the wake of the economic crisis of the 1990s, which made everyday survival a pressing issue.[103]

From the start, Syktyvkar Memorial was the main institution that former prisoners and other "victims of political repression" turned to. As one Gulag returnee said to a reporter during Syktyvkar Memorial's office hours, "It's easier to speak with a civilian than to go to the organs of power, who treated us harshly and unfairly in my time."[104] From 1989 to 1997, Gulag returnees actively corresponded with the Syktyvkar Memorial Society to tell their stories and to seek help obtaining rehabilitation. In the process, they formed a people's archive that preserved their autobiographical narratives as a part of an alternate history of the Komi Republic and the Soviet Union. As the product of the nascent civil society that emerged as the Soviet Union was collapsing, Syktyvkar Memorial played an essential role in the institutionalization of Gulag returnees' collected memories. Although Gulag returnees were initially motivated by anti-Stalinism, they continued to write to contribute to Syktyvkar Memorial's ongoing memory project commemorating the victims of political repression. After the collapse of the Soviet Union, former special settlers and children of Gulag returnees expanded this project when they wrote to Syktyvkar Memorial seeking rehabilitation as victims of political repression. Taken as a whole, this correspondence illustrates the ways in which victims of political repression identified themselves and were identified by the state.

The letters to Syktyvkar Memorial are as important for what they tell us about former prisoners as for their silences. For the most part, those who wrote to Syktyvkar Memorial mentioned their ethnicity only in passing. Although some former prisoners erected monuments to particular ethnic groups following the collapse of the Soviet Union, those who petitioned Syktyvkar Memorial did not divide their community along these lines. With few exceptions, former prisoners did not detail their lives after release in their letters. These large lacunae in their epistolary narratives show that these narratives were part of a dialogue with Syktyvkar Memorial, which was focused on documenting the system of political repression in the Komi Republic. Nevertheless, as the next chapter shows, Gulag returnees did write about their lives after release in the memoirs they sent to Syktyvkar Memorial and to local history museums throughout Komi.

Notes

1. National Archive of the Komi Republic (GU RK NARK) 2 f. P-3800, op. 1, d. 12, l. 13 (P. Kotov to R. I. Pimenov, June 25, 1990).

2. M. B. Rogachev, ed., *Pokaianie: Martirolog*, vol. 12, ch. 1 (Syktyvkar: Fond Pokaianie, 2016), 323.

3. GU RK NARK 2 f. P-3800, op. 1, d. 163 l. 33 (P. Kotov, "Vospominanie. Ch. 3: V Adake," Gdansk, Poland September 20, 1991–October 8, 1991).

4. GU RK NARK 2 f. P-3800, op. 1, d. 13, l. 25–26 (A. M. Stetsko to M. B. Rogachev, August 22, 1989).

5. Alexander Etkind, *Warped Mourning: Stories of the Undead in the Land of the Unburied* (Stanford, CA: Stanford University Press, 2013). Etkind refers to the camp intellectuals who wrote memoirs as "lay ethnographers" (82). See also Leona Toker, *Return from the Archipelago: Narratives of Gulag Survivors* (Bloomington: Indiana University Press, 2000), 77. Toker describes how the act of collecting data in the camps was an act of resistance to camp authorities' control of information. However, we can take this a step further. Gulag returnees' long-term collection of data is indicative of their plans for a larger memory project beyond the scope of their individual autobiography.

6. Although Memorial Moscow emerged in 1987, it was not registered as an "informal" organization until 1989; GU RK NARK 2 f. P-3797, op. 1, d. 57, ll. 3 ("K uchreditel'noi konferentsii," *Vedomosti Memoriala*, January 28, 1989); Natal'ia Baryshnikova, Sergei Bondarenko, Kiril Kozhanov, Nikita Lomakin, and Aleksei Makarov, "Pamiat' v proekte," International Memorial Society, accessed December 9, 2017, http://project.memo.ru; Stephen Kotkin, "Terror, Rehabilitation, and Historical Memory: An Interview with Dimitrii Iurasov," *Russian Review* 51, no. 2 (April 1992): 238–262.

7. The decrees were issued on July 11, 1988, and January 5, 1989. For the text of these decrees, see A. Artizov, A. Kosakovskii, V. Naumov, and I. Shevchuk, eds., *Reabilitatsiia: Kak eto bylo. Dokumenty Prezidiuma TsK KPSS i drugie materialy*, t. 3 Seredina 80-kh godov-1991 (Moscow: Mezhdunarodnyi Fond Demokratiia, 2004), http://www.alexanderyakovlev.org/fond/issues/62100. On the history of the development of the Soviet and Russian legal category of "Rehabilitation" see A. L. Konov, "K istorii priniatiia rossiiskogo Zakona 'O reabilitatsii zhertv politicheskikh repressii,'" in *Reabilitatsiia i pamiat': Otnoshenie k zhertvam sovetskikh politicheskikh repressii v stranakh byvshevgo SSSR*, ed. Ian Rachinskii (Moscow: Memorial-Zven'ia, 2016), 5–28. By 1989, the flood of those in need of rehabilitation grew to such proportions that the KGB and MVD recommended to the Procuracy and the Supreme Soviet that all sentences issued by extrajudicial organs be canceled, regardless of whether one submitted an application for rehabilitation (8–9).

8. Kathleen E. Smith, *Remembering Stalin's Victims: Popular Memory and the End of the USSR* (Ithaca, NY: Cornell University Press, 2009), 143. Smith writes,

"By the spring of 1991, a representative of the Moscow Procuracy claimed that it had resolved 90 percent of its cases that involved sentences by nonjudicial bodies—a large share of its 100,000 cases subject to review" (142). Ultimately, this number would turn out to be a fraction of those eligible for rehabilitation after the law was expanded in 1993.

9. On the spread of Memorial to Russia's regions, see Anne White, "The Memorial Society in the Russian Provinces," *Europe-Asia Studies* 47, no. 8 (1995): 1343–1366; Nanci Adler, *Victims of Soviet Terror: The Story of the Memorial Movement* (Westport, CT: Praeger, 1993); Margarita Masliukova, Ekaterina Mel'nikova, and Ekaterina Pavlenko, "Memorial: Epizod I," International Memorial Society, accessed February 12, 2019, http://prequel.memo.ru/about.

10. Unfortunately, not all of the archives for these local branches of Memorial have survived, and most are scattered throughout Komi. This makes a systematic study of the Memorial movement throughout all of Komi very difficult.

11. GU RK NARK 2 f. P-3797, op. 1, d. 24, l. 5–6 (R. I. Pimenov to O. A. Gorlanov, July 1, 1989). I analyze this monument in chap. 5.

12. Archival collections do not exist for the other branches of Memorial. Many of their documents were divided among various local history museums in Komi or lost.

13. V. A. Kucherenko, "Doroga pokaianiia," Memorial: Informatsionnyi biulleten' Pravleniia Mezhdunarodnogo istoriko-prosvetitel'skogo pravozashchitnogo i blagotvoritel'nogo obshchestva "Memorial," no. 14 (December 1999–January 2000): 36, box 510, Soviet and Post-Soviet Independent Publications, Hoover Institution Library and Archives (hereafter Hoover Institution).

14. Pimenov was arrested for organizing an illegal "anti-Soviet organization" that protested Stalinist repression and the Soviet Union's actions in Hungary in 1956. He was arrested in 1957 and sentenced to ten years imprisonment under art. 58–11. He spent five years in various camps before he was released from Vladimir Prison No. 2 in 1963. He returned to Leningrad, where he was rearrested for producing *samizdat* and sentenced to five years of exile in Komi in 1970. He was rehabilitated posthumously in 1991. For his biography, see Rogachev, *Pokaianie: Martirolog*, t. 12, ch. 2, 119.

15. M. B. Rogachev (chairman of Fond Pokaianie), interview with the author, December 7, 2017, Syktyvkar, Russia. The group kept no running total of rehabilitated persons, making the exact number difficult to estimate, with the exception of estimates documented in Komi newspapers. The number of letters is likely significantly higher. However, given the constraints and limited resources of the time, Syktyvkar Memorial's archive of these letters is incomplete. See Fond Pokaianie Archive (AFP) (K. Markizov, "Minui nas chasha sia," *Panorama stolitsy*, September 23, 1999). This article reports that the Syktyvkar Commission for the Restoration of the Rights of Victims of Political Repression

organized by the governor of Komi rehabilitated 1,594 people in 1996 and 1,884 people in 1999.

16. I have collected every file of correspondence available in the Syktyvkar Memorial/AFP. The files contain 790 pages of letters over ten files spanning 1989–1997. This does not include the memoirs of various lengths and archival documents, including certificates of rehabilitation, questionnaires, and other documents of a personal nature that were sent to Syktyvkar Memorial's archive, which is now in part in the holdings of GU RK NARK.

17. "Memorial za tri goda," *Svoboda i kul'tura: Gazeta Moskovskogo Memoriala*, no. 2 (March 1991): 2; and "Nasha pochta," *Svoboda: Gazeta press tsentra Moskovskogo Memoriala*, no. 11 (1990): 3, box 395, Soviet and Post-Soviet Independent Publications, Hoover Institution. The newspapers of Moscow Memorial *Svoboda i kul'tura* and *30 Oktiabria* are replete with similar articles spanning 1989–2021. See *30 Oktiabria*, box 2, Soviet and Post-Soviet Independent Publications, Hoover Institution.

18. While Gulag prisoners did write letters to family and to Soviet authorities for release, there are many silences in these letters. When they finally wrote full accounts of their lives in the camps and after release in the late 1980s and 1990s, many emphasized that they had not told anyone about the camps, except for fragments they shared with their families. For a discussion of letters from the camp as a potentially misleading source, see the memoir by former prisoner E. V. Markova, *Vorkutinskye zametki katorzhanki "E-105"* (Syktyvkar: Fond Pokaianie, 2005), 70–71. On reading between the lines of camp letters, see Arsenii Formakov, *Gulag Letters*, ed. and trans. Emily D. Johnson (New Haven, CT: Yale University Press, 2017).

19. For an example of this type of autobiographical document written by a Gulag returnee who remained in Ukhta after she was released, see Kaleria Anatol'evna Solov'eva, personal archive Syktyvkar, Russia, l. 33 (Moia avtobiografiia, 1953–1954); Kaleria Anatol'evna Solov'eva, l. 99–100 (Avtobiografiia, 1965). For instance, Solov'eva wrote in 1965, "As a fourth-year student, I was repressed in 1937 and sent to Ukhtizhemlag where I worked as a medic. I was released in 1945. From 1945 to 1946, I worked as a nurse at the clinic administered by the camp administration in Vetlosian. I left to finish my medical training. From 1946 to 1948, I studied at the Arkhangel'sk Medical Institute. From there, I was sent to Nar'ian-Mar in Arkhangel'sk province, where I was contracted to work as the head of the hospital until 1951. In 1951, I returned to Ukhta to work at the Ukhta Central Hospital, where I work at the present. I was rehabilitated on November 4, 1955, by the Military Tribunal of the Moscow Military District (no. N-3555/os). In 1936, my husband, Shmatov E. L., born 1905, was repressed and sent to Magadan where he died in 1938. He was rehabilitated posthumously on August 16, 1957, by decree of the Military Collegium of the Supreme Soviet of the USSR (no. 001504/37)." For

54 AFTER THE GULAG

an analysis of these documents from the 1950s through the 1970s, see Yury Zarets-kiy, "Confessing to Leviathan: The Mass Practice of Writing Autobiographies in the USSR," *Slavic Review* 76, no. 4 (Winter 2017): 1027–1047.

20. National Library of the Komi Republic (NBRK), A. Nikolaeva, "Memorial: Sleduiushchii shag," *Molodezh' Severa*, April 19, 1989. The newspaper underscored the popular support behind Syktyvkar Memorial: "On the popularity of Memorial, the numerous participants at the conference speaks for itself, those who consider it their duty to come up to the microphone and add their tasks. . . . There was no shortage of suggestions." For the charter adopted by the All-Union Memorial Society in Moscow (January 28, 1989), see Adler, *Victims of Soviet Terror*, 141–150. For the charter, see AFP op. 1, d. 1 ("Polozhenie o Syktyvkarskom dobrovol'nom istoriko-prosvetitel'nom obshchestve 'Memorial,'" April 16, 1989).

21. Nikolaeva, "Memorial: Sleduiushchii shag." I examine the evolution of this category in chap. 5, which provides an in-depth analysis of Komi newspapers.

22. AFP op. 1, d. 1 ("Polozhenie o Syktyvkarskom dobrovol'nom istoriko-prosvetitel'nom obshchestve 'Memorial,'" April 16, 1989).

23. Nikolaeva, "Memorial: Sleduiushchii shag." See also AFP op. 1, d. 1 (R. I. Pimenov, "Tsepochka neobkhodimykh deistvii obshchestva 'Memorial,'" January 29, 1989).

24. GU RK NARK 2 f. P-3797, op. 1, d. 24, ll. 4–5 (R. I. Pimenov to O. Gorlanov, June 12, 1989).

25. Ibid., 4. This was a shared concern among conservative members of Soviet society, who saw attempts to come to terms with the past as "blackening" the patriotic history of the country and saw mass rehabilitation of victims and the erection of monuments to all victims of political repression as seditious. For other examples of such letters to the editor, see GU RK NARK 2 f. P-3800, op. 1, d. 12, l. 1–2 ("Vse li zhertvy?," *Sovetskaia Chuvashiia*, June 18, 1989); GU RK NARK 2 f. P-3800, op. 1, d. 13, l. 6–12 (Mikhail Egorovich Khudoev, "I palach i zhertva," *Molodezh' Severa*, March 27, 1989). The terms "Banderites" and "Vlasovites" were the pejorative names given to followers of Stepan Bandera and Andrei Vlasov who led bands of local troops against the Red Army during World War II. In the postwar year, these names became shorthand for fascists and traitors.

26. AFP op. 1, d. 1 (Soderzhaniia protokola rabochego sobraniia Syktyvkarsk-ogo obshchestva "Memorial," May 26, 1989).

27. GU RK NARK 2 f. P-3797, op. 1, d. 24, l. 5 (R. I. Pimenov to O. Gorlanov, June 12, 1989).

28. AFP op. 1, d. 1 (Soderzhaniia protokola rabochego sobraniia Syktyvkarsk-ogo obshchestva "Memorial," May 26, 1989).

29. GU RK NARK 2 f. P-3797, op. 1, d. 24, l. 5 (R. I. Pimenov to O. Gorlanov, June 12, 1989).

30. Ibid.

31. Nikolaeva, "Memorial: Sleduiushchii shag." See also Archive of the Local History Museum at Ukhta State Technical University (hereafter AM UGTU) f. Bulychev (A. I. Terent'ev and V. Bulychev, "Khotelos' by vsekh poimenno nazvat,'" *Ukhta*, February 22, 1989); V. Bulychev, ed., *V nedrakh Ukhtpechlaga* (Ukhta: Ukhtinskaia tipografiia "Memorial," 1989).

32. Nikolaeva, "Memorial: Sleduiushchii shag." It is unclear whether they sang songs from the camps. Although it is doubtful that they did, as many political prisoners saw the coarse language of these songs as "uncultured."

33. GU RK NARK 2 f. P-3800, op. 1, d. 12, l. 13 (Petr Kotov to R. I. Pimenov, June 25, 1990).

34. GU RK NARK 2 f. P-3800, op. 1, d. 12, l. 15 (M. B. Rogachev to P. Kotov, July 31, 1990).

35. GU RK NARK 2 f. P-3800, op. 1, d. 7, l. 3 (Biography of Candidate for People's Deputy R. I. Pimenov, May 3, 1989).

36. AFP op. 1, d. 1 (Soderzhaniia protokola rabochego sobraniia Syktyvkarskogo obshchestva "Memorial," May 26, 1989).

37. Tat'iana Rozhina, dir., "Oni spasut Rossiu," Nezavisimaia studiia dokumental'nykh fil'mov "ASTI," 1995 (2019), YouTube video, 44:20, https://www.youtube.com/watch?v=XuUv5xixWxE&t=289s.

38. GU RK NARK 2 f. P-3800, op. 1, d. 12, l. 5 (M. B. Rogachev to V. B. Ol'shevskii, June 26, 1990).

39. GU RK NARK 2 f. P-3800, op. 1, d. 12, ll. 8–9 (M. B. Rogachev to L. M. Gorodin, June 27, 1990).

40. GU RK NARK 2 f. P-3800, op. 1, d. 12, l. 31 (M. B. Rogachev to V. G. Lipilin, July 31, 1990).

41. GU RK NARK 2 f. P-3800, op. 1, d. 12, l. 4 (V. B. Ol'shevskii to M. B. Rogachev, June 16, 1990), l. 5 (M. B. Rogachev to V. B. Ol'shevskii, June 29, 1990), ll. 22–22a (V. Z. Siderskii to M. B. Rogachev, July 5, 1990); and ll. 6–7 (L. M. Gorodin to M. B. Rogachev, June 19, 1990).

42. GU RK NARK 2 f. P-3800, op. 1, d. 78, ll. 7–7a (M. B. Rogachev to V. Z. Siderskii, February 24, 1997).

43. AFP op. 1, d. 1 (Soderzhaniia protokola rabochego sobraniia Syktyvkarskogo obshchestva "Memorial," May 26, 1989).

44. AFP op. 1, d. 1 (R. I. Pimenov, "Tsepochka neobkhodimykh deistvii obshchestva 'Memorial,'" January 29, 1989).

45. The breakdown of these questionnaires by category is sixty-nine prisoners, 133 special settlers, and twenty-four unknowns (i.e., people who did not completely fill out the questionnaire). The collection of questionnaires is incomplete. Despite the best efforts of Memorial activists to preserve every document, they failed to do so as a result of limited resources, manpower, and the overwhelming wave of people coming forward to tell their stories.

46. For an example of these forms, see AFP (Ankety repressirovannykh, vol. 1, A-K, ll. 109); AFP (Ankety repressirovannykh, vol. 2, K-Ia, ll.119).

47. See, e.g., International Memorial Society, "Zhertvy politicheskogo terrora v SSSR," updated July 12, 2017, https://www.memo.ru/ru-ru/collections /databases/modal_repression/.

48. GU RK NARK 2 f. P-3800, op. 1, d. 12, l. 16–18 (M. B. Smirnov to M. B. Rogachev, June 26, 1990).

49. Ibid., l. 19–21 (M. B. Rogachev to M. B. Smirnov, September 7, 1990).

50. M. B. Rogachev, interview with the author, March 3, 2017, Syktyvkar, Russia. This is also evident by the varied handwriting on these forms, which differs entirely from form to form.

51. Ibid.

52. GU RK NARK 2 f. P-3800, op. 1, d. 13, l. 3 (M. B. Rogachev to E. Petrovna, April 8, 1993).

53. GU RK NARK 2 f. P-3800, op.1, d. 38, l. 40–40a (E. D. Meshcheriakova to M. B. Rogachev, March 11, 1993) and l. 70 (I. P. Stasiuk to the Head of the MVD Archive of the Komi Republic, May 5, 1993). The burden of rehabilitation was on prisoners to obtain documents from the authorities of the regions where they were sentenced. This requirement often slowed down the process greatly, as documents were constantly lost and letters were misplaced or ignored. As Rogachev said in an interview with *Krasnoe znamia* in 1992, "More frequently than all, elderly people come here [to Syktyvkar Memorial's office hours], having fallen into despair of getting help and support from other organizations." See GU RK NARK 2 f. P-3800, op. 1, d. 102, l. 36 (M. Moiseeva, "Khotia rublem sud'bu ne ispravish', no . . ." *Krasnoe znamia*, May 15, 1992).

54. GU RK NARK 2 f. P-3800, op. 1, d. 13, l. 3.

55. GU RK NARK 2 f. P-3800, d. 102, l. 36. The minister noted, "In Syktyvkar, there are more former repressed who are supposed to be paid compensation than in other districts. The department of Social Security is overloaded with work, which is why its staff turned to the Memorial society for help, so that they collect the documents there and then send them to us."

56. AM UGTU f. Bulychev ("Gorispolkom i obshchestvo 'Memorial' provodiat registratsiiu lits bezvinno repressirovannykh," *Ukhta*, August 9, 1989).

57. These privileges included monetary compensation, free city transportation (excluding taxis), reduced taxes, and elimination of payments for communal utilities. GU RK NARK 2 f. P-3800, op. 1, d. 38, l. 59 (M. B. Rogachev to V. G. Lipilin, 1993).

58. GU RK NARK 2 f. P-3800, op. 1, d. 105, l. 9 (M. B. Rogachev to Aleksandr Konstantinovich, March 13, 1994).

59. GU RK NARK 2 f. P-3800, op. 1, d. 78, l. 9 (M. B. Rogachev to Iu. P. Grushin, March 25, 1997).

60. Andrew Lass, "From Memory to History: The Events of November 17 Dis/membered," in *Memory, History, and Opposition under Socialism*, ed. Rubie S. Watson (Santa Fe, NM: School of American Research Press, 1994), 91. Lass asks, "What happens to memories when they go on public display?" His answer underscores the role of eyewitnesses and memory as the sources for emerging identities and history in the Czech Republic after the Velvet Revolution of 1989.

61. Elizabeth Tonkin, *Narrating Our Pasts: The Social Construction of Oral History* (Cambridge: Cambridge University Press, 1992), 97. On the importance of memory and autobiography, see Luisa Passerini, ed., *International Yearbook of Oral History and Life Stories*, vol. 1, *Memory and Totalitarianism* (Oxford: Oxford University Press, 1992), 1–19.

62. I. L. Kuznetsov, ed., *Pechal'naia pristan'* (Syktyvkar: Komi knizhnoe izd-vo, 1991), 3. This volume was the first published collection of memoirs written by prisoners of Komi's camps. It was the direct product of the letters and manuscripts that Gulag returnees sent to Syktyvkar Memorial.

63. While Gulag returnees did face an uphill battle, the use of memory as a source of the past was not new. After the October Revolution, Bolshevik elites were obsessed with gathering oral histories and translating the experience of 1917 into cultural memory. Even the OGPU-NKVD held evenings of memory (vecher pamiati) to collect the accounts of those who participated in the 1929 expedition to Ukhta that founded the Gulag in Komi. For this collection of oral histories, see "Kollektsiia memuarov i literaturnykh proizvedenii," Arkhiv Memoriala (AM), f. 2, op. 3, d. 38, ll. 60 (V. Nadezhdin, ed., "Stenogramma vecherov vospominanii ob Ukhtinskoi ekspeditsii USEVLON-OGPU. Pos. Chib'iu," dekabr' 1932. Rukopis'). On mythmaking and the October Revolution, see Frederick C. Corney, *Telling October: Memory and the Making of the Bolshevik Revolution* (Ithaca, NY: Cornell University Press, 2004).

64. GU RK NARK 2 f. P-3800, op. 1, d. 12, l. 4 (V. B. Ol'shevskii to M. B. Rogachev, June 16, 1990). See also GU RK NARK 2 f. P3800, op. 1, d. 18, l. 1 (V. G. Lipilin to M. B. Rogachev, September 16, 1991); AM f. 2, op. 2, d. 112, l. 243 (V. E. Sollertinskii to Moscow Memorial, November 20, 1988). Sollertinskii wrote, "I send you the manuscript of my memoirs about the years of my life and the times, which fell to me. The memoirs are very personal, they are about only the events, which became my life and the lives of circle of people [who were] close to me. As a spontaneous positivist, I did not attempt to evaluate the quality of events, the manuscript is completely absent of exclamatory notes, although, of course, my relationship to the events examined is absolutely exact. There are several chapters pertaining to the times of Stalinist repressions, and sketches from nature from twenty years ago, clearly showing that the roots of repression essentially lay before Stalin."

65. GU RK NARK 2 f. P-3800, op. 1, d. 38, l. 101–103a (L. K. Shlezhkova-Vselova to M. B. Rogachev, September 2, 1993); f. P-3800, op. 1, d. 156, l. 2–17 (E. K. Makarova to M. B. Rogachev, April 2, 2000).

66. GU RK NARK 2 f. P-3800, op. 1, d. 12, l. 22–22a (V. Z. Siderskii to M. B. Rogachev, July 5, 1990); GU RK NARK 2 f. P-3800, op. 1, d. 78, l. 1–2 (Babushka Anastasiia to M. B. Rogachev, January 10, 1997). The same sentiment is also expressed in many letters. See, e.g., GU RK NARK 2 f. P-3800, op. 1, d. 13, l. 27–28a (Ivan Mikhailovich to the "Comrades of Memorial," June 23, 1989). This sentiment is also repeated in the oral history interviews collected by journalists from *Novaya Gazeta* in Komi and other former Gulag republics in the Russian Federation, see Anna Artem'eva and Elena Rachina, eds., *58-ia. Neiz"iatoe: Istorii liudei, kotorye perezhili to, chego my bol'she vsego boimsia* (Moscow: Izd-vo ACT, 2016).

67. Letter printed in Bulychev, *V nedrakh Ukhtpechlaga*, 17–18. Another letter from this booklet published by Memorial Ukhta read, "They rehabilitated me. I received a document from the Ministry of Internal Affairs in Vilnius that I am not guilty. Yeah, how could a girl be guilty at 16!?"

68. GU RK NARK 2 f. P-3800, op. 1, d. 12, l. 10 (L. M. Gorodin to M. B. Rogachev, July 2, 1990) and l. 29 (L. S. Safronov to M. B. Rogachev, not dated); GU RK NARK 2 f. P-3800, op. 1, d. 13, ll. 22–23a (A. M. Stetsko to M. B. Rogachev, June 22, 1989).

69. GU RK NARK 2 f. P-3800, op. 1, d. 12, l. 1–3 (I. A. Arkhipov and S. N. Spiridonov to Syktyvkar Memorial, January 31, 1989). These two also published a letter about what they witnessed in Lokchimlag in the newspaper *Sovetskaia Chuvashiia* entitled, "In the Forests of Komi." See GU RK NARK 2 f. P-3800, op. 1, d. 12, l. 3 ("V lesakh Komi," *Sovetskaia Chuvashiia*, June 14, 1989). This issue of *Sobesednik* did not feature an article on Komi; however, it did feature an article about Memorial's founding conference in Moscow, efforts to commemorate victims in Belarus, and a rebuttal from the editor in response to a letter to the editor about how Stalinist repression was fake.

70. GU RK NARK 2 f. P-3800, op. 1, d. 12, l. 1–3 (I. A. Arkhipov and S. N. Spiridonov to Syktyvkar Memorial, January 31, 1989).

71. The State Gulag History Museum in Moscow published Gorodin's dictionary in 2021. For the published version of Gorodin's dictionary, see Leonid Gorodin, *Slovar' Russkikh argotizmov: Leksikon katorgi i lagerei imperatorskoi i sovetskoi Rossii*, ot. red., Svetlana Pukhova (Moscow: Izdatel'skaia programma Muzei Istorii Gulaga i Fonda Pamiati, 2021), https://gmig.ru/upload/iblock/17f/17ff966718f1b4bca1d0e918f8e26e1d.pdf. Jacques' Rossi also compiled a Gulag dictionary, which was published in Russian (1991) and English (1989). Although Gorodin's was published later, it seems that he created his first. For Rossi's dictionary, see Jacques Rossi, *The Gulag Handbook: An Encyclopedia Dictionary of Soviet Penitentiary Institutions and Terms Related to the Forced Labor Camps*, trans. William A. Burhans (New York: Paragon House, 1989).

72. GU RK NARK 2 f. P-3800, op. 1, d. 12, ll. 6–7 (L. M. Gorodin to M. B. Rogachev, June 19, 1990); GU RK NARK 2 f. P-3800, op. 1, d. 12, l. 10 (L. M. Gorodin to M. B. Rogachev, July 2, 1990); GU RK NARK 2 f. P-3800, op. 1, d. 12, l. 37–40 (L. M. Gorodin to M. B. Rogachev, August 3, 1990). Gorodin included a letter from one of his friends in the dictionary: "Any dictionary, especially one of a particular epoch, reflects real life and over the years it becomes more and more valuable. . . . A dictionary is an entire world of its own type a sort of spiritual cosmos. And a dictionary of 'Russian slang' is also a cosmos, a unique world of the language of outcasts, which is also a part of the society that gave birth to it." See GU RK NARK 2 f. P-3800, op. 1, d. 17, l. 133 (Letter to L. M. Gorodin, May 27, 1985).

73. Ibid., 40. Gorodin saw his dictionary not only as a source of history and illuminative of the meaning behind Gulag returnees' writings but also as a source to be used by criminologists, writers, historians, students, researchers, and translators. He truly wanted to share his work with the world. In this way, Gorodin joins the likes of repressed scholars and intelligentsia who used their camp experiences as the basis of some of their academic work. On writing history after the Gulag and the repressed intelligentsia, see Etkind, *Warped Mourning*, 60–82. Etkind highlights Bakhtin, Likhachev, and others whose academic work was shaped by their camp experience.

74. "Vystavka: Iazyk [ne]svobody," Muzei istorii GULAGa, June 10–July 25, 2021, Yeltsin Center, https://gmig.ru/museum/exhibitions/yazyk-ne-svobody/; Kseniia Filimonova, "Leksikograf rukotvornogo ada," Gor'kii, May 20, 2021, https://gorky.media/reviews/leksikograf-rukotvornogo-ada/; Liliia Pal'veleva, "Slovar' [ne]svobody. Lagernoe naslediie russkogo iazyka," Radio Svoboda, February 10, 2021, https://www.svoboda.org/a/31092341.html.

75. GU RK NARK 2 f. P-3800, op. 1, d. 12, l. 12 (M. B. Rogachev to L. M. Gorodin, July 30, 1990). See also GU RK NARK 2 f. P-3800, op. 1, d. 12, l. 36 (M. B. Rogachev to L. M. Gorodin, September 12, 1990).

76. Rossi, *Gulag Handbook*, 262. This word is commonly found in Gulag memoirs. An *odnoetapnik* is a "fellow prisoner from the same transport, each of the individuals travelling or who travelled in the same transport" (*etap*).

77. GU RK NARK 2 f. P-3800, op. 1, d. 12, l. 30 (V. G. Lipilin to M. B. Rogachev, letter not dated [presumably 1990, judging by Rogachev's response]) and l. 43–44 (B. S. Siniavskii to M. B. Rogachev, not dated); GU RK NARK 2 f. P-3800, op. 1, d. 105, l. 10–1-a (A. Stroikovskii to M. B. Rogachev, February 7, 1994).

78. GU RK NARK 2 f. P-3800, op. 1, d. 12, l. 25–25a (L. S. Safronov to M. B. Rogachev, July 16, 1990). In addition to his long letter, Safronov sent a handwritten copy of his certificate of rehabilitation he wished to be added to the collections of the nascent Syktyvkar Memorial archive. See GU RK NARK 2 f. P-3800, op. 1, d. 12, l. 26 (Certificate of Rehabilitation given to L. S. Safronov May 5, 1981, by the Ministry of Justice Kazakh SSR).

79. GU RK NARK 2 f. P-3800, op. 1, d. 12, l. 27 (M. B. Rogachev to L. S. Safronov, July 29, 1990).

80. GU RK NARK 2 f. P-3800, op. 1, d. 12, l. 29 (L. S. Safronov to M. B. Rogachev, not dated).

81. On the "infrastructural monuments" of Stalinism, see Anna Neimark, "The Infrastructural Monument: Stalin's Water Works under Construction and in Representation," *Future Anterior* 9, no. 2 (Winter 2012): 1–14. Neimark argues that Stalinist infrastructure was meant to be monumental and thus served as the task of "representing memory, sovereignty, and history." See also Cynthia Ruder, *Building Stalinism: The Moscow Canal and the Creation of Soviet Space* (New York: I. B. Taurus, 2018).

82. Archive of the Vokuta Museum of Geology (AVMG) (K. Flug, "Chernyi ostrov GULAGa," 1986), 8. See GU RK NARK 2 f. P3800, op. 1, d. 18, ll. 50 (V. G. Lipilin, "Vospominaniia," 1991); AFP (G. I. Ustilovskii, "Gor'kaia zhizn,'" Sosnogorsk, 2000). Lipilin also used the imagery of a graveyard to describe Komi as a monument to the victims of political repression: "O, ancient, fragile Komi land, the most disfigured, you laid to rest under your soil hundreds of thousands, millions of innocently murdered! Almost 1,500 versts [994 miles], you bear the most extensive monument to the buried—the railroad from Kotlas to Vorkuta. A prisoner is buried under each tie. This is a figure of speech, there are actually two prisoners under each tie" (2). This idea frequently appears in the oral histories of former prisoners and guards who remained in Komi. See also Anna Artem'eva, Elena Racheva, *58-Ia. Neiz"iatoe: Istorii liudei, kotorye perezhili to, chego my bol'she vsego boimsia* (Moscow: Izd-vo ACT, 2016).

83. GU RK NARK 2 f. P-3800, op. 1, d. 159, l. 9 (E. A. Griaznova, "Vospominanie," Syktyvkar, undated); GU RK NARK 2 f. P3800, op. 1, d. 18, l. 2 (V. G. Lipilin, "Vospominaniia," 1991); Kuznetsov, *Pechal'naia pristan.'*

84. AFP (G. I. Ustilovskii, "Gor'kaia zhizn,'" Sosnogorsk, 2000), 6. See also AM UGTU (Kotvitskii, "O chem molchit istoriia"), 77. Kotvitskii is one of many other prisoners who wrote about camp authorities' uncouth burial practices and disrespect for dead prisoners: "They dumped them with a tag on their foot in a grave somewhere under a fir or a pine tree and carelessly sprinkled it with some earth. And who can say how they died and where their nameless grave is? The taiga devoured many of them, but she—fierce and silent—can keep her secret" (77).

85. On this topic see Svetlana Boym, *The Future of Nostalgia* (New York: Basic, 2001); Serguei Oushakine, "'We're Nostalgic, but We're Not Crazy': Retrofitting the Past in Russia," *Russian Review* 66 (July 2007): 451–482.

86. GU RK NARK 2 f. P-3800, op. 1, d. 78, l. 78, p. 28–28a (L. S. Safronov to M. B. Rogachev, October 8, 1996).

87. GU RK NARK 2 f. P-3800, op. 1, d. 102, l. 28 (E. Oteva, "Chotb ne propast' poodinochke," *Krasnoe znamia*, February 4, 1992) and l. 29 (K. Markizov, "Khochu umeret' reabilitirovannoi," *Vechernii Syktyvkar*, February 22, 1992).

88. Ibid., 29.

LETTERS TO SYKTYVKAR MEMORIAL

89. Ibid., 28.

90. GU RK NARK 2 f. P-3800, op. 1, d. 105, l. 4–4a (M. G. Soobtskov to M. B. Rogachev, February 10, 1994). See GU RK NARK 2 f. P-3800, op. 1, d. 105, l. 5 (M. B. Rogachev to M. G. Soobtskov, February 28, 1994). Gulag returnees underscore the importance of rehabilitation to them but also its effect on their loved ones. Former prisoner Boris Serov described how he initially was denied rehabilitation because his sentence had been rescinded sometime after his release, presumably in the 1950s. As Serov wrote in the introduction to his 1989 memoir, "I applied for rehabilitation and they answered that my conviction was rescinded, which made it impossible to rehabilitate me. And to this day, I live with the weight of being an unrehabilitated former prisoner. My daughters write in questionnaires: 'My father was sentenced, article 58 . . .' Well, let this weigh on the conscience of those who created such a life, who were indifferent to human lives. For them people are a gray faceless mass. They will be swept away and we will endure. There, I cast off this old injustice. What are you going to do about it!" See GU RK NARK 2 f. P-3800, op. 1, d. 156, ll. 25–26 (B. D. Serov, "Piat' let i vsia zhizn,'" Pechora, 1989).

91. GU RK NARK 2 f. P-3800, op. 1, d. 38, l. 40–40a (E. D. Meshcheriakova to M. B. Rogachev, March 11, 1993). In June 1993, Meshcheriakova wrote again to thank Rogachev for his help: "Thank you for your care and attention, which you showed having sent an archival certificate about my stay in places of confinement. I can imagine how much time you spent on the search for the necessary information." See GU RK NARK 2 f. P-3800, op. 1, d. 38, l. 42 (E. D. Meshcheriakova to M. B. Rogachev, June 6, 1993).

92. GU RK NARK 2 f. P-3800, op. 1, d. 102, l. 28. The article cites the cases of repressed Ukrainians, Belorussians, Lithuanians, and Latvians who settled in Komi after release.

93. GU RK NARK 2 f. P-3800, op. 1, d. 38, l. 85–85 (A. K. Sysak to M. B. Rogachev, 1993).

94. GU RK NARK 2 f. P-3800, op. 1, d. 102, l. 41 (K. Markizov "Deti GULAGa," *Vechernii Syktyvkar*, October 30, 1992); N. A. Morozov, interview with the author, May 19, 2017, Moscow, Russia. The majority of Gulag children were eventually taken from their parents, especially when they were political prisoners, and taken either to the children's camp section attached to the camp or a regional orphanage for children of "enemies of the people." On children born in the camps and children's homes for enemies of the people, see Cathy A. Frierson and Semyon S. Vilensky, eds., *Children of the Gulag* (New Haven, CT: Yale University Press, 2010).

95. Syktyvkar Memorial received many of letters from children of Gulag returnees. See, e.g., GU RK NARK 2 f. P-3800, op. 1, d. 105, l. 23–23a (A. V. Vladimirovich to M. B. Rogachev, February 20, 1994), l. 20–20a (E. V. Mikhaileva to M. B. Rogachev, February 18, 1994), and l. 15–15a (N. A. Babkina to M. Rogachev, February 18, 1994).

96. Iwona Irwin-Zarecka, *Frames of Remembrance: The Dynamics of Collective Memory* (New Brunswick, NJ: Transaction, 1993), 49. In her analysis communities of memory, Irwin-Zarecka points out that the boundaries of these communities shift over time, expanding beyond the group of original eyewitnesses, as events of the past enter into public discourse and other memory actors participate in the commemoration of the past in question (48).

97. GU RK NARK 2 f. P-3800, op. 1, d. 38, l. 101–103a (L. K. Shlezhkova-Vselova to the editor of *Molodezh' Severa*, September 2, 1993). The article Shlezhkova cited was about a prisoner uprising that occurred in 1942.

98. It is unclear whether children of victims of former prisoners were provided for under the October 1991 version of the law; however, they were included in later redefinitions of *victim* and *repression*.

99. GU RK NARK 2 f. P-3800, op. 1, d. 12, l. 43–44 (B. S. Siniavskii to M. B. Rogachev, not dated). See also GU RK NARK 2 f. P-3800, op. 1, d. 156, l. 57 (P. I. Siamtomov, "Ispoved," memoir based on letters received from P. I. Siamtomov, October 1990–January 1991).

100. GU RK NARK 2 f. P-3800, op. 1, d. 38, l. 98 (L. M. Kovelenko to M. B. Rogachev, October 16, 1993), l. 21–22 (K. A. Krauze-Gladchenko "citizen of the Komi ASSR" to M. B. Rogachev, February 11, 1993), 27–28 (S. A. Gubert-Konovalovaia to M. B. Rogachev, March 1, 1993), and l. 43 (L. Fedorovna Shrainer to M. B. Rogachev, March 1, 1991). See also GU RK NARK 2 f. P-3800, op. 1, d. 38, l. 29–31a (A. A. Krail' to M. B. Rogachev, March 1, 1993). This former special settler wrote from the village Vet'iu. It seems from the amount of correspondence received that the entire village wrote to Syktyvkar Memorial for rehabilitation once the word got out. GU RK NARK 2 f. P-3800, op. 1, d. 38, l. 38 (Erna B. Arnold-Miuller, application for rehabilitation, March 10, 1993). This former special settler returned to Komi when she married and found work as a guard at a nearby corrective labor colony in Komi.

101. GU RK NARK 2 f. P-3800, op. 1, d. 38, l. 94 (L. K. to M. B. Rogachev, August 18, 1993).

102. GU RK NARK 2 f. P-3800, op. 1, d. 156, l. 97 (Klavdiia Petrovna Chudinova "Vospominaniia o perezhitom proizvole podvergshimsia repressiiam po politicheskim motivam pri raskulachivaniimore," not dated).

103. On the national decline of anti-Stalinism, see Smith, *Remembering Stalin's Victims*, 174–193. On the collapse of the Soviet Union and everyday survival during the financial crisis that ensued, see Olga Shevchenko, *Crisis and Everyday Life in Postsocialist Moscow* (Bloomington: Indiana University Press, 2009).

104. GU RK NARK 2 f. P-3800, op. 1, d. 38, l. 29 (K. Markizov, "Khochu umeret' reabilitirovannoi," *Vechernii Syktyvkar*, February 22, 1992).

2

The "Brotherhood of *Zeks*"

Constructing Community and Identity through Memoirs

In 1989, Gulag returnee Boris Serov wrote a memoir and sent it to the newly formed Syktyvkar Memorial Society from the northern city of Pechora, where he once served a five-year sentence.[1] He described the first years after his release in 1946, when he continued to gather with his friends from the camps to remember those they lost to its darkest depths. Then his thoughts turned toward recent efforts to come to terms with the Stalinist past:

> We remembered our comrades in misfortune and laughed and cried. Memory did not always give us joy. Remembering those times, we cried more often than we laughed! . . . This is a small piece of my life. At times life spoiled me, but often repressed and scoffed at me. Although that's life, isn't it? People oppressed me, jeered at me out of envy, career goals, or just out of spite. And then they repeated over and again: forget! Everything was good, there was no fear, no degradation. You were always happy! But how is it possible to forget the way it was with us, with the whole country? If we forget everything that happened to us, we will not know our history. And after all, the history of the Motherland is the history of our mother. Since you can't remember your mother, you don't think of her? If a child loses his mother, is he really alone? No. Kind people will take him in, or the children's home will shelter the unfortunate one, and he will be full and warmly dressed. But he will nonetheless long for and dream about meeting his mother. One would think that he has everything, what doesn't he have? He doesn't have a mother! Not knowing what a mother is, can you live for her? That is what the motherland is. Our collective mother. Not knowing her, is it possible to love her unconditionally? And love helps us forgive her mistakes and correct them, rebuilding her life and the life of all society.[2]

Like many Gulag returnees who wrote memoirs in the late 1980s, Serov understood the necessity of Gorbachev's glasnost. If Soviet society was to be rebuilt, the crimes of Stalinism had to be confronted. However, without the perspectives of ordinary citizens whom Stalin repressed, was such a reckoning even possible?

This chapter suggests that Gulag returnees responded to glasnost and the collapse of the Soviet Union by writing autobiographical narratives in which they wrote themselves as a community into Soviet history at its end. As those who bore the brunt of Stalinist repression and survived, it was important to them to contribute their life stories as evidence of Stalin's crimes. Consequently, Gulag returnees joined the national conversation about the past as key witnesses. However, because more than forty years had passed since many of them were released, Gulag returnees had to trace their lives back from the present to this formative moment. In doing so, they formulated identities in which the individual and the collective were intertwined. Interchanging and interspersing "we" and "I" throughout their autobiographies, Gulag returnees referred to themselves as a "brotherhood of zeks [prisoners]."[3] To identify themselves as a community, they used words such as svoi (us, ours), nashi (ours), and my (we), as well as camp slang such as byvshie ("formers"; i.e., former prisoners), lagerniki (camp inmates), kontriki (counterrevolutionaries, political prisoners), bratia 58 ("brother 58-ers," fellow political prisoners sentenced under article 58), and "zek" (short for Z/K, "prisoner").

Jochen Hellbeck and others have argued that one of the primary aims of the Soviet experiment was the unification of the individual and the collective embodied by the state.[4] These scholars have used diaries, autobiographies, and correspondence from the 1930s and 1940s to illustrate how ideology shaped the efforts of Soviet people to construct selves that joined them with the collective; they argue that people achieved this without a loss of individuality but rather an integration of the two selves. Others, such as Alexander Etkind and Sarah J. Young, point to the shattering of the "New Soviet Man" in the camps as evidence of the failure of this project.[5] Autobiographical narratives written by Gulag returnees during the twilight of Soviet power illustrate this same process of attempting to merge the individual and the collective, albeit in a different context and with a radically different intent. Unlike diarists from the 1930s who attempted to join the collective embodied by the state, Gulag returnees wrote autobiographies in the late 1980s and 1990s to join a collective of former enemies of the state. Although Gulag returnees also identified themselves by the subgroups they belonged to in the camps—divided by ethnicity, criminal caste, and class—they underscored the brotherhood of zeks as an important part of their identity when they reconstructed their lives.[6] Membership in this community formed the basis of a collective identity, which was a function of identifying themselves as survivors of political repression to bring the past to light.[7] In some ways, the brotherhood of zeks resembles the alternative public that dissidents formed, which Barbara Martin describes in her work.[8] However, dissidents were a much less cohesive group than the former prisoners examined in this book.

This chapter also engages the work of historians and literary scholars who examine the cultural history of autobiographical writing in Russia and the Soviet Union. In particular, I refer to works by Irina Paperno, Barbara Walker, and Benjamin Nathans, who examine the autobiographical writings of intellectuals and dissidents and the use of this form in constructing a virtual community. Although the memoirs examined in this chapter were shaped by the same culture of autobiographical writing that informed the memoirs of intellectuals and dissidents, Gulag returnees' texts describe a totally different set of concerns, conflicts, and qualities that they used to represent and define their community.[9] In other words, while the form may look the same, the communities they constructed were anything but.

Following the collapse of the Soviet Union, hundreds of Gulag returnees sent autobiographies to local history museums and branches of the Memorial Society in towns throughout Komi where they had once been prisoners. This chapter examines approximately one hundred of these texts, which were written mainly between 1988 and the late 1990s. Although a few of these texts were written before glasnost, as Paperno writes, they "belong to the present moment, when they are assembled, framed, and put into the public domain for everybody to see."[10] The authors of these texts were not intellectuals from Moscow and Leningrad; they were peasants, workers, engineers, builders, doctors, party members, artists, and teachers from all over the Soviet Union who served time for (mostly) imagined political crimes in Stalin's Gulag.[11] While some left the region after their rights as Soviet citizens were restored, many remained in Komi for the rest of their lives. Regardless of where they lived when they wrote their memoirs, survivors of Komi's camps underscored their connection to the region decades after release. As former prisoner Leonid Safronov wrote in his 1993 memoir, "Years pass and fewer and fewer of us former prisoners of Ukhtpechlag remain. There are a handful of us in Kiev. Sometimes we meet, we remember the camps [and] the guards with hate, but the Pechora is our second motherland and the Komi people—our brothers."[12]

This chapter is composed of three sections. In each section, I draw from texts that belong to the corpus of memoirs written by the survivors of Komi's camps.

66   AFTER THE GULAG

The first section explores the camp origins of the brotherhood of zeks. While some survivors briefly touched on their lives before arrest, the majority of the autobiographical narratives begin with life in the camp, which often included the period of predeparture imprisonment and interrogation. However, many survivors featured in this chapter omitted this stage of their camp journey either because it had been described elsewhere or was too difficult to revisit. These narratives overwhelmingly emphasize the importance of friendship to their survival and the preservation of their humanity. The second section examines life after release. Gulag returnees underscored the continued importance of the camp brotherhood, which enabled them to reintegrate back into Soviet society. Their inclusion of this part of their lives, and their emphasis on life after release, illustrates that the Gulag alone did not define them. The third section examines the various statements survivors made about why they wrote memoirs when they did. Given that many of them wrote after the publication of Aleskandr Solzhenitsyn's *One Day in the Life of Ivan Denisovich* and the samizdat publication of *The Gulag Archipelago*, Solzhenitsyn was an important figure who factored into their reasons for writing. This section also explores some of their responses to Solzhenitsyn's writings about the Gulag, which they tended to highly praise or sharply criticize.

Writing after the Return: The Origins of the Brotherhood of Zeks

By offering their life stories as evidence of Stalinist repression, Gulag returnees sought to fill the silences of history books, which did not capture their experiences. While the details of individual accounts vary, their descriptions of life in the camps reveal the origins of the brotherhood of zeks. Gulag returnees described the topography of the camps set among the taiga (forests) and arctic tundra of Komi as part of the natural landscape and as the setting where they formed the camp brotherhood. They illustrated this environment with details about the violence they suffered at the hands of camp authorities and hardened criminals, the deplorable conditions of camp barracks, the dangerous working conditions, and the physical toll that insufficient rations and hard labor exacted on their bodies. The details of their lives in the camps assigned meaning to the carceral spaces they described throughout the Komi landscape. Furthermore, as Leona Toker writes, gathering this information was a form of prisoner resistance against Gulag officials who attempted to keep uncensored information about the camps from reaching the Soviet public before glasnost.[13]

Many well-known Gulag returnees, such as Aleksandr Solzhenitsyn, Varlam Shalamov, and Evgeniia Ginzburg, described the distrust between inmates and the camps as a place of the destruction of self; however, the former prisoners in this chapter frequently referred to the camps as their "university." Although it would be easy to simply read this as a sarcastic comment about the environment that prisoners were prescribed for "reeducation"—and, indeed, some used this metaphor to mock Maxim Gorky, who proclaimed the redemptive features of forced labor in his book about the construction of the Belomor Canal—many Gulag returnees used this metaphor as an earnest description of their experience. They wanted to extract something useful from their suffering.[14] When former prisoner Vladimir Sollertinskii decided, for instance, to write an autobiography for his grandchildren in 1984, the search for the source of who he became led him back to the camps: "The true impulse to write this narrative was vague and indefinite at first, and then it spontaneously revealed itself; it was the desire to understand where I came from. In the process of working on the manuscript and summarizing my thoughts, it became clear that it [the Gulag] shaped every aspect of my development as a human being. The conclusion is trivial enough, but my example shows its universality."[15] Despite the horrors Sollertinskii witnessed in the Gulag, he remembered the camps as a site of personal development: "The atmosphere of the 1930s, when the necessity of service to the common cause was accepted without discussion. The camp, which seemed to be a misfortune in every way, turned out to be a stroke of good luck. Here the grandiose intellectual and spiritual potential of my surroundings completed the work of my human development, here my spirit was freed and learned to be free."[16]

Although Sollertinskii described the impact of his imprisonment in a positive light, he was not blind to its destructiveness. The effects of years behind barbed wire cut both ways. For some, including Sollertinskii's brother and father, the camps destroyed them. Contrasting his memory of the camps with the memory of his father and brother when they came to live with him after their release, Sollertinskii testified to the Gulag's destruction of the man his father had been before arrest: "I didn't recognize him. . . . He was indifferent to everything, and if I insisted on something, he would submit, but only then. They lost the hunger for life, the will to live in the adversities they endured."[17] Although they were transformed in different ways, the Sollertinskiis survived thanks to their "comrades in misfortune."

The severe conditions in Komi's camps limited the chances of surviving on one's own. Although mortality rates were worse in the agricultural camps and corrective labor colonies located in regions with more moderate climates, the climate of the Far North compounded the harmful effects of the unsanitary barracks, squalid rations, violence, and backbreaking manual labor, which quickly reduced able-bodied workers into walking skeletons.[18] Learning to survive from other prisoners was one of the most important lessons at the camp university. Furthermore, caring for their comrades in misfortune despite their own critical condition was a defining characteristic of the camp brotherhood. In his undated autobiography, former prisoner Aleksandr Gurevich wrote that he owed his own survival to the camp brotherhood's sense of collective responsibility for the well-being of its own:

> It is no exaggeration to say that I owe these people. They taught me everything I learned. Most of them received a basic education before the Revolution, and in the years after the Revolution, they were among the most educated and cultured scientists and specialists who preserved institutions of higher education on the ruins of Russian universities. These people were distinguished by their keenness when they worked, energy, drive, and sense of responsibility. They commanded authority and were able to influence their subordinates and camp bosses. They generously shared their knowledge and experience in a way that was quite humble in comparison with today's leaders. As the most "conscientious" workers, they were of course masters of padding the numbers [*tufta*], though not for the sake of personal gain, but for the sake of additional portions of bread, scoops of porridge, [and] seven grams of sugar for the workers.[19]

To be sure, however, Gulag returnees also learned to survive from seasoned criminals (*ugolovniki*). Because many political prisoners were new to the camps and did not have the slightest understanding of the world they had entered, attending the camp university also meant learning to adapt. Former prisoner Vitalii Ol'shevskii recalled in his undated memoir that the first lessons of this education began from the moment of arrival at the camp:

> By the time we joined the column, there were already thirty camp old timers [*lagernikov*] who were mainly criminals [*ugolovnikov*] shipped here from the Far East. Apparently, their role was to test our mettle, to make us into a productive camp collective out of a formless mass of normal citizens. They taught us all the complex laws of the camp order and interrelations in a graphic, easy-to-understand way. This unwritten law was so barbaric that many of us could not grasp it and, as a result, they died. The first to die was Aleksei Putriu. Many more died later. They all died in different situations, but as a matter of fact, they died because they could not adapt to this life.[20]

Gulag returnees forged powerful bonds in the camps that formed the basis of lifelong friendships. These friendships not only enabled inmates to survive but also helped them adapt to life after release. Such friendships were one of the ways in which prisoners resisted the degradation of the camp environment and "remained human beings." Arrested as an eighteen-year-old high school student and sent to the strict-regime camp in Inta, Susana Pechuro described the importance of friends who saved her life by getting her reassigned from general labor to the camp cultural-educational department (fig. 2.1). These people became her family after she was torn from her own:

> Friendship in prison—it is a topic of a separate conversation, yes, there has already been much written about this. A friend in prison is more than a friend. A person with whom you become close, having lost everything that people live by in the normal world, replaces those close ones you lost. You give your camp friend all of your warmth, all of your soul. That is why in the camp, more than anything, [prisoners] fear being transferred. People cannot imagine how they can bear another loss, the loss of a camp friend. God, how many of such losses I came to bear during the years of my imprisonment! It turns out that it's possible to survive all of it and not lose the ability to love, to be happy.[21]

For Pechuro, her camp comrades were more than friends. They were her family. These bonds were the foundation of the brotherhood of zeks. For them, surviving without friendship would have been impossible. As Pechuro continued in her six-page description of the camp brotherhood,

> The friendship that connected us there has remained for all our lives. We realized a lot there, which we might not have been able to understand without having gone through the experience of imprisonment. There, evil and good were expressed clearly and simply. A person in prison cannot mask themselves. There is nowhere to hide. There are no decorations that could hide his essence. It is impossible to hide even from oneself there. People are divided by the principle, "You die today—I die tomorrow," or, on the contrary, "I agree to die today, so you can live until tomorrow." Bad people became even worse, but good people ascended to the heights of human nobility.[22]

Although friendship was the foundation of the brotherhood of zeks, Gulag returnees defined this community in opposition to the "criminal other." They frequently characterized camp criminals (*ugolovniki, vory*) in their memoirs as violent, immoral, and, most importantly, the guilty ones. Criminals were the opposite of brothers and sisters, and thus they did not belong to the camp brotherhood. By defining themselves in opposition to the criminal other, Gulag returnees used this prisoner subcategory to consolidate their collective identity as innocent victims of Stalinist repression.[23] When former prisoner Andrei

Figure 2.1 (*left*) Undated photograph of Susana Pechuro included with the memoir she sent to Syktyvkar Memorial in 1995. (*center*) Vladimir Sollertinskii, Sosnogorsk, not dated. (*right*) Grigorii Rivkin, Vorkuta, 1946. The photographs Gulag returnees included in their memoirs were reminders that real people were behind these narratives of repression, survival, and life. Source: Fond Pokaianie and the International Memorial Society (GU RK NARK 2 f. P-3800, op. 1, d. 163, l. 159; AM f. 2, op. 2, d. 112, l. 239; AFP op. 1, d. 31, l. 1).

Evstiunichev wrote his autobiography in 1991, for example, he described Gulag returnees as a community defined by their resistance to the moral abyss of the camp world personified by the criminals:

> Identifying oneself with the others [*mezhdu soboiu*], we morally supported one another, raising hope for survival by morally strengthening the spirit and one's physical condition. The majority of political prisoners [*politicheskie zakliuchennye*] set themselves the goal to survive, to not lose one's human essence, to not stain oneself with criminal filth, despite everything to not lower one's morals, to not lower oneself to the level of criminality. Not allowing our minds to become stale, we read books to renew them, which came to us in various ways; we studied different fields; played chess; participated in theater; held debates (except politics); shared our knowledge of art, ethics, and much more, striving to remain a HUMAN BEING. Leaving the camp to freedom, every person carried a fear of return.[24]

By identifying himself as a member of a community that enabled him to survive, Evstiunichev underscored the correlational nature of Gulag returnees' collective identity. As shown in Evstiunichev's autobiography, this community was also defined by the division between political prisoners and criminals.[25]

By revealing who the real criminals were in their autobiographies, Gulag returnees asserted their own innocence as victims of political repression. In concert with a growing number of voices, Gulag returnees attempted to alter the perception that those sentenced under article 58 of the Soviet penal code were counterrevolutionaries, traitors, and enemies—still a widespread belief among conservative members of Soviet society in the late 1980s.[26] As former prisoner Anton Kotvitskii wrote in the memoir he sent to the Ukhta-Pechora Memorial Society in the late 1980s, "In earlier times, murderers, thieves, swindlers, and bandits sat in prison. . . . The isolated endured impoverishment and deprivation. Tortured by remorse, badly dressed, unshaven, and mean, they served time for crimes. As it should have been in our time . . . But who is sitting in this stinking cell? Who . . . ?"[27]

For Gulag returnees writing in the 1980s and 1990s, ethnicity was not a determining factor in their definition of who belonged to the brotherhood of zeks.[28] Although there was a preponderance of Russians, the omission of ethnicity in Gulag returnees' memoirs is striking given the diversity of Komi's camps.[29] Nevertheless, to be a member of the brotherhood of zeks, one had to live by the principle of "I'll die today so you can live to tomorrow." As one Gulag returnee and native of Poland, Petr Kotov, wrote about the camp brotherhood in 1992, "There were people of different nationalities, but there was no division of people by ethnic category. People unselfishly helped one another—a phenomenon that you see rarely in the camps, especially in such a collective form."[30] Although Kotov saw this help as rare, many Gulag returnees who sent their autobiographies to the Memorial archive and local history museums throughout Komi suggest that it was more common than Kotov realized. Former prisoners, such as Susana Pechuro, underscored that political prisoners had much more in common with each other than the subgroups they belonged to in the camps suggested:

> It must be said that the relations of prisoners of different nationalities were far from simple. I experienced this for the first time in my life. Listening to their stories, I felt tortuous shame for my country, which brought so much sorrow and suffering "to the liberated peoples." In conversations with them, I never tried to justify these actions. I said, since we are here together on the bunks, I am not your enemy. Just like you, I am an enemy of [Soviet] power. Indeed, they stopped looking askew at me; on the contrary, we related to one another with empathy and sympathy. We started to talk about our pasts, to share our thoughts and our meager packages, if they came.[31]

Although Pechuro's background made her more of an "intellectual" than the other prisoners featured in this book, her example highlights the intersectionality of the community that Gulag returnees formed through friendship, solidarity born out of survival, and the process of remembering.

Some Gulag returnees dedicated a significant amount of space in their autobiographies to describing their attitudes toward work. Although such descriptions seem remotely related to how they remembered their lives in the Gulag, the differences in their attitudes toward work illustrate one of the important nuances of their collective identity. Some Gulag returnees, like Konstantin Marushchiak, maintained their belief that justice would prevail. Although they were certain of their innocence, this group of prisoners highlighted their exceptional work performance as the only thing that made life in the camps easier. As Marushchiak wrote in his 1989 autobiography, "My camp life continued in difficult and severe conditions . . . but it was necessary to endure and to work. Only conscientious labor and fulfilling the assignments smoothed over the difficulties and made life better. I understood this and tried to fulfill the production quota."[32]

Despite his early release for "good work performance," Marushchiak remembered the stigma attached to him as a former prisoner. To overcome this invisible brand, like other Gulag returnees, Marushchiak described how he worked harder than everyone else after release to prove that he belonged as a member of Soviet society:

> I understood excellently that I was innocent, but nonetheless the shortening
> of my sentence was a holiday to me. This was very rare at the time; it lifted
> my morale. However, it did not matter. I constantly thought about what
> sins they had torn my life apart for. A thought haunted me: "Well, OK, they
> captured you, put you down, pinned the label of an enemy of the people on
> you, moreover they persecuted your family." Despite this, it was necessary to
> honestly work, to fulfill the production assignments. I worked and believed
> in impending justice. But still I had to endure nine years of a hard existence. I
> always had a conscientious attitude toward labor.[33]

Like many Gulag returnees, Marushchiak continued to work in the camp after release.[34] Besides the fact that he was no longer a prisoner, little changed during that first year except for his residence; Marushchiak moved from barracks in the zone to barracks in town.[35] Despite his good standing as an employee of the Ministry of Internal Affairs (MVD), the need to outperform his colleagues never left Marushchiak until he was finally promoted to chief engineer of the Department of Major Construction at Ust'vymlag in 1955: "This position was confirmed in Moscow. Such an assignment and confirmation [conferred] a lot of trust [in me]. By granting me such a position, the leadership, political department, officer corps, party and union organizations acknowledged me as an honest devotee to the cause of the Communist Party of Lenin, a Soviet person. Everything I knew, everything I could [give], I gave to the cause of fulfilling the plan without considering how long it would take or my own strength. This was my answer to the trust that was shown to me."[36]

On the surface, Marushchiak seems to be one of the former prisoners who "kept faith in the party" and attempted to reconcile who he was before arrest with who he became after release.[37] However, he was not rehabilitated until 1957 and did not join the Communist Party until 1960.[38] Although his career path seems unique—he eventually rose to the rank of lieutenant colonel—his story reveals that release did not end the need to perform one's rehabilitation.[39] It was a lifelong process.[40] Perhaps most important, his autobiography illuminates the complexity of Gulag returnees' identities, which overlapped in some areas with those of other Soviet people who expressed both idealism and alienation.[41] Nikolai Volkov wrote in his memoir about the complex feelings that the state's recognition of one's hard work inspired in former prisoners: "A state award is a major event in anyone's life, but for us it was like the beginning of our exit from the vicious circle created by a difficult fate. Then there was ceremony where they congratulated us with warm words and gave us our awards. The 'formers' [former prisoners] hugged each other and even shed a few tears. It was unbelievable like in a dream."[42]

Although some prisoners accepted the idea that it was possible to return to Soviet society through hard work, others saw the camps as intentionally designed to destroy their work ethic. Despite their return and ongoing attempts to reintegrate, many Gulag returnees feared that their imprisonment had irrevocably damaged their attitude toward work, which prevented them from rising above the bottom rung of the social ladder. After serving a total of eighteen years in the camps and in exile, Leonid Gorodin was released in 1954.[43] Despite having gone on to a career as the editor of a newspaper in Sverdlovsk, he feared that the camps permanently destroyed his work ethic. As he wrote in his 1989 autobiography,

> You know what thought has relentlessly haunted me for some time now? Maybe the camps were devised by enemies who were given the task of arousing an aversion for labor in people. Take me, for example. I experienced satisfaction from labor all my life. It relaxed me. I burst forward from prison into the camp, I wrote a petition, I even declared a hunger strike so that they would quickly send me away [to the camps] because there is no worse punishment for me than idleness. I knew that difficult, forced labor awaited me—which is why it was a thousand times more difficult. But it didn't

74 AFTER THE GULAG

scare me. But now I notice how a hatred toward labor grows in me, not only because it is forced but because it is senseless.[44]

Unlike Marushchiak, Gorodin did not feel that his labor in the camps transformed him into an "honest" Soviet citizen. Instead, Gorodin felt alienated from labor and thus unable to completely rejoin Soviet society. With that door closed to him, Gorodin sought a new collective to join after release, which he found in the camp brotherhood (fig. 2.2).

In addition to telling their own stories, Gulag returnees' autobiographical narratives serve as textual monuments to their fallen comrades. Gulag returnees memorialized their friends by returning their names from the abyss with the hope that someday someone will learn the fate of a loved one.[45] In addition to listing their names, Gulag returnees also incorporated their stories into their own testimonies.[46] By telling their comrades' stories as part of their own, Gulag returnees preserved their memories and expanded the scope of their own testimony. Furthermore, and perhaps most important, the inclusion of their comrades' stories illustrates the entangled nature of the history they were trying to write. In 1996, Irina Skakovskaia wrote an autobiography with the explicit aim of preserving the memory of the Gulag returnees she lived among as she waited for her mother's release in Vorkuta: "In these pages, I wanted to speak about the people whom I knew and loved in my youth. It's possible that there are some inaccuracies in the details since much time has passed already. But I have not sinned against the spirit of Vorkuta, which formed me as a person. . . . And I am grateful to my *Vorkutiane* [native/veteran of Vorkuta] for their steadfastness, bravery, and the lofty moral ideals that they followed despite those difficult times."[47] These themes also made their way into the poems that former prisoners wrote. As Anna Bokal wrote in a poem about the camp brotherhood,

> Oblivion is worse than sacrilege,
> Friends I cannot forget.
> Love and the camp brotherhood,
> I've kept in my heart ever since.[48]

While memoirists from the late 1980s and 1990s readily name names, those written before glasnost do not often attach stories to any particular person other than the author.[49] Such omissions were made to protect their friends in the event that the manuscript fell into the hands of the state security services. This happened to Vladimir Sollertinskii in 1983 when the KGB confiscated his autobiography after he tried to send it to a friend in the mail.[50] However, as Sollertinskii wrote, the omission of names also underscored the shared nature of

  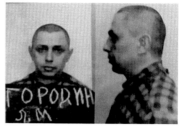

Figure 2.2 (*left*) Leonid Gorodin's mugshot, 1936. (*center*) Portrait after release, Vorkuta, 1947. (*right*) Mugshot after second arrest, Vorkuta 1950. Source: State Gulag History Museum (GBUK MIG [personal file of L. M. Gorodin]).

the experiences he documented: "I don't name names and I won't name them: any in the mass of those who were with me and those whom I singled out in these pages could have been Ivanov, Petrov, Sidorov, or myself."[51] Other Gulag returnees chose not to name names simply because they did not want to incur doubt regarding the veracity of their memoir by assigning the wrong biography or event to someone.[52]

Life after Release

In the longest chapter of his 1991 memoir, entitled, "Freedom, What an Immense, Fine-Sounding Word," Andrei Evstiunichev described the joyous day of release and the disappointment that followed when the reality of life as a Gulag returnee set in:

> Before every prisoner, after release, stands the question: "How to live on?" According to our Soviet laws, a convicted person is deprived of all the rights of citizenship and human rights. [One's] apartment is confiscated for the use of the state, all [one's] belongings are requisitioned, redistributed—more accurately, stolen. Prisoners sentenced for political crimes often have relatives who were also subjected to repression—[they are often sent] to the camp or into exile as family members of an enemy of the people. . . . Having been released from the camp, a person, having no means of existence, no place to lay one's head at night, receiving a refusal to be hired at work, frequently became easy prey for vigilant police officers and would be brought to court as a person without a definite place of residence or work and was once again returned to the familiar environment of camp "citizens."[53]

After his release, like other Gulag survivors, Evstiunichev faced an uncertain road ahead. Not only was he limited in where he could live and work, but like most Gulag returnees, he also faced continued persecution from authorities and suspicion from his neighbors.[54]

Gulag returnees universally highlighted the first days of release in their autobiographies. Although some dedicated only a few pages to their lives after release, many wrote at great length about this new chapter of their lives. Their memories of release ranged from vivid descriptions of their first impressions to detailed accounts of the process of leaving "the zone to freedom."[55] Regardless of how they described release in their autobiographies, Gulag returnees tended to underscore the continued weight of their past.[56] Despite this burden, they emphasized that there was indeed life after release.[57] Taken as a whole, this aspect of Gulag returnees' autobiographical narratives describes the continued importance of the camp brotherhood, which enabled survivors to rebuild their lives and join a collective of their peers who understood, better than anyone, what they had gone through. In light of their changed status and the new concerns they had on the outside, their narratives illustrate the continuities and evolution of the community they formed in the brotherhood of zeks.

Gulag returnees faced many questions on release. They returned from the camps bearing the scars of years of hard labor, which distinguished them from other citizens. If it were not apparent by looking at them, then a quick check of their documents would confirm their status. If one was not sentenced to eternal exile, passport restrictions severely limited one's options. Nevertheless, despite the obstacles and the difficulty of this transition, Gulag returnees reintegrated into Soviet society (to varying extents). They adapted to life after release just as they had survived the camps, by forming informal mutual aid associations under the auspices of the camp brotherhood. These factors all affected Vladimir Novokhatskii's decision not to return to his native Ukraine, which he explained in his 1992 memoir (fig. 2.3):

> Questions arose in my mind every day and every night: I'm free!! But where should I go? Who will take me in? Who needs me? Where will I work and what will be my profession? How should I build my future life so what I endured doesn't happen again? Every person dreams of returning to their native land, to the country of their childhood, to their family and loved ones. But what awaits me in my motherland? My mother and stepfather are there, but they are very old and live in the countryside . . . and I thought, I'll return to the motherland disgraced for all my life so long as the USSR and the Stalinist regime exist. I decided that I would not return home—I will stay in the North, I will go to Ezhid-Krytu and get fixed up in a job. I'll earn enough, if only for some civilian clothes—I won't go back to the padded camp jacket

and camp boots. And then, when I assume the look of a human being, maybe I will go to the motherland. At that time, many prisoners ended up living where they served their time. They knew each other well. In the first days after release, they helped one another get fixed up in a job and helped one another. And so, I firmly decided that I would stay in the North. Maybe not for a long time. But you see, I live in the North to this day. I tried to return to [my] mother Ukraine. I went there, but at that time, I was still an "enemy of the people." And if I had not come back to the North, they would have definitely found a reason to imprison me again.[58]

Without the support of their community, which enabled them to find housing and work, it was unclear to former prisoners how long it would be before they might be arrested and sent back to the camps.[59]

After many long years behind barbed wire, Komi became home for many Gulag returnees. Even if one could leave, it would mean abandoning the community that meant so much to them.[60] As Vladimir Sollertinskii wrote in 1984, "Not a single thread connected me to normal life: my family was scattered throughout the world, friends stopped being friends—in any setting outside the camp, I was an undesirable outsider."[61] In many instances, after many years of imprisonment, friends from the camps were the only family that Gulag returnees had left. Camp friends provided an important source of comfort and support during the tumultuous transition to freedom. As Lev Safronov wrote about a member of his adopted family in 1993, "This was my older brother, not by blood but in spirit. F. G. is an optimist, and he helped me a lot in the development of my spiritual state; he helped me strengthen my optimism to not give in and to endure, and I endured."[62]

Some former prisoners from the Baltic countries, which were annexed by the Soviet Union in 1940, also remained in Komi after release. Having lived in Vorkuta for many years after release, for example, Kraulis Visvaldis moved to Syktyvkar in 1961, where he worked as a studio artist. Not even an offer from his brother to live with him in Canada enticed Visvaldis to change his mind. He had married a local woman, and his life was now in Komi. Gulag returnee Konstantin Ivanov wrote about his Latvian friend in 1997: "When I asked him why he didn't move to Canada (after all, his brother offered him a house there), he logically explained to me that without a knowledge of English, there is nothing for him and Galia to do. I will die, and Galia won't find work anywhere, and it will be bad for her. 'Why don't you go to Riga?' I asked him. In Riga, now, there are just the same barracks as there are here. And again Galia . . . She will always be foreign there."[63]

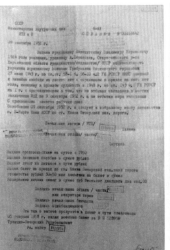

Figure 2.3 After escaping from a German prisoner-of-war camp near Stalingrad, Vladimir Novokhatskii was sentenced to ten years in 1943. He included photographs of (*left*) his release papers (1952), (*center*) his many medals, and (*right*) his certificate of rehabilitation in his memoir (1957). Source: Ukhta State Technical University Local History Museum (AM UGTU [Novokhatskii, "Rokovaia chernaia shinel,'" l. 22, 1, 22]). Novokhatskii wrote, "Not everyone knows that captivity is hell! And even worse, if you survive and break out of this hell, the brand of traitor to the motherland will hang over you for the rest of your life. And I went through this hell [twice!]," 12).

Gulag returnees frequently mention their ability to identify *svoi* at a glance. As Aleksandr Gurevich wrote in an undated memoir, "Seasoned prisoners had a specific facial expression and deadened eyes. By these traits—many years later, in the happiest environment—they recognized each other, strangers with a mutual fate."[64] Gurevich's description of those who returned vividly depicts the transformation that prisoners underwent in the camps. Some writers included these details as part of what Alexander Etkind refers to as the "parable of misrecognition"—a trope used in Gulag literature and memoirs that symbolizes the loss of identity as the cost of survival—whereas others used them to illustrate their ability to recognize others like them.[65] The ability to recognize and identify with other former prisoners, who they did not know, contributed to the expansion of the collective. In his 1986 memoir, Konstantin Flug described how he bonded with another Gulag returnee who recognized him on a trolleybus in Stalingrad: "Not long ago, on Border Guard Day, an old-timer in a blue beret came and sat next to me on the trolley and quietly asked, 'Were you in the Arctic?' 'Yes.' 'Where?' 'In Vorkuta.' 'And I am from Kolyma.' And then he revealed his toothless mouth, just like mine, as if we were relatives. It's possible that we were brothers-in-arms. Brothers of the 70th parallel!"[66] While this seems like a minor detail, it shows how small interactions between former prisoners created an extended network that reached far beyond the small towns and villages of the Far North.

Gulag returnees not only recognized other political prisoners as their peers but also saw themselves as superior to those who had not been repressed. Gulag returnees expressed their superiority in their descriptions of the interactions they had with other civilians who treated them as second-class citizens.[67] Petr Kotov's memoir about this part of his life reveals the tension between the two groups: the "formers" (*byvshie*) and the "civilians" (*vol'nonaemnye*).[68] Drawing from the experiences he shared in exile with his closest friend and "comrade in unhappiness," Nina Sobinova, Kotov described how the treatment of former prisoners in the 1950s contributed to their sense of superiority:

> The leadership and the workers who were not exiles at the meat factory tried to show her that they were superior at every step. Because she was an exile, she didn't exist. It's true that the law was on the side of nonexiles. However, in my experience, exiled people were significantly superior to nonexiles. I don't say this without providing any proof, which comes from my life experience and observations. Having met many exiled people and interacted with bosses who were not exiles while I was in exile in the village Maklakova in Krasnoiarskii krai, I came to the conclusion that the absolute majority of people in power at that time, the so-called rulers, were much more stupid than their subordinates, especially than the exiles.[69]

Not all civilians treated former prisoners with suspicion, as the relationships and marriages between these two groups attest.[70] Although the party frowned on these unions, it did not stop civilians and Gulag returnees from marrying.[71] Vladimir Sollertinskii, for example, married a local woman in Sosnogorsk in 1945 (two years after his release). Shortly after they registered the marriage, Galina Ivanovna was summoned to the political department of the local party headquarters, where she was told to break off the marriage or return her party card. She laid her card on the table and left without a word; however, she did not remain unaffiliated for long. A few days later, Galina Ivanovna's boss at the telegraph office returned her party card with no fuss or further trouble.[72]

Kotov's memoir stands out for his focus on life after release. This part of Kotov's autobiography draws from his extensive correspondence with Sobinova, which lasted from the end of their exile in 1956 until 1989.[73] He reproduced many of these letters in his memoir as evidence of his continued friendship with the prisoners he met in the Adak camp for invalids and in exile. These letters tell stories about their imprisonment and exile, inquire about the health and status of other "former *Adakovtsy*," and offer critiques of the writings of other Gulag returnees.[74] They demonstrate the permanence of these relationships, which Kotov and his friends maintained via correspondence long after he returned to Poland and they moved to cities throughout the Soviet Union:

> In the very beginning, I had the intention of cutting Nina Mikhailovna's letter to the minimum, but I chose not to after reading it [again]. It seems to me that everything Nina Mikhailovna writes about is very important to get a sense of the life and fate of people who were imprisoned in Adak and exiled in Eniseisk. From her letter, it's clear that these people did not lose touch with one another and helped each other after release, that they concerned themselves with our physical and moral victory over ourselves, to which they ceaselessly strived. They absolutely did not manage to smash and destroy us (former prisoners and exiles). They weren't able to do this because, although these people were going through the most dreadful stage of their lives in inhuman conditions, they nonetheless preserved their qualities as human beings and tried to realize them in life.[75]

While the bonds that Gulag returnees shared were sources of strength, they were concerning to camp officials and police. Despite the porousness of the boundaries between the camp zone and the town, the authorities seemed to especially disapprove of relationships between Gulag returnees and their comrades who remained in the zone, which the authorities saw as potentially subversive.[76] Nikolai Volkov recalled in his 1970 memoir being warned to part ways with his friends after he exited the camps: "But remember! You are now citizens (*vol'nonaemnye*). We expect that you will once and forever be done with your past [ways]. Everything that led you to be prisoners yesterday must end today. Any connections between prisoners discredit a free person.... Although we understand that you just returned from the camps and that this [cutting ties] will not be easy for you to do, but do this, you must. Your new position obliges you to do so."[77] Nevertheless, camp authorities were not able to permanently, or even temporarily, disrupt the relationships that began in the zone and continued after release.[78] They simply pushed them into private spaces, and the camp brotherhood lived on.[79]

Writing at the End: Why Gulag Returnees Wrote Memoirs

A workplace reading of Khrushchev's speech, "On the Cult of Personality and Its Consequences," in Ukhta is one of the most powerful moments of Anton

Kotvitskii's 1970 memoir, written "for the drawer." Kotvitskii remembered how the large crowd of former prisoners, exiles, and their children became emotional and even angry as the text was read aloud in 1956:

> An unusual rumor spread throughout the city in October: they read a secret letter at the oil refinery—Khrushchev unmasked Stalin. People were disturbed, slept badly.... The next day they read the letter out loud at the Geological Trust, where I worked at the time. The building was completely full of people. There was nowhere to sit or stand.... It was as if a strong clap of thunder on a clear day stunned the people. People listened intensely, totally silent and with bated breath. They were afraid to cough, to make a sound.... Except for a few party members, the overwhelming majority of people there were former "enemies of the people," the repressed, special settlers, exiles, and so on. All those who populated the Komi ASSR... People from the world of the unfortunate, innocent victims, survivors of prison dungeons and concentration camps who lived to this unusual and happy day. ... When the massive stone crushing them and blocking out the sun crashed to the ground ... Old Bolsheviks who I sat with in prison spoke poorly of Stalin, but what Khrushchev said was awe inspiring and terrifying.... When they read about Kossior [Stalin's First Secretary of the Ukrainian Communist Party], I couldn't take it and cried out: "But they turned me, and those like me, into ground meat." ... Several women fell into hysterics. Their husbands had been shot, and they had suffered for a long time themselves in the concentration camps.[80]

However, Kotvitskii continued, "Khrushchev did not speak about everything."[81]

Like many of his peers, Kotvitskii saw Khrushchev's attempt to come to terms with the Stalinist past as a failure because it did not present a full account of what they, the survivors of Stalinist repression, knew about the camps. When the topic resurfaced during glasnost, Kotvitskii took his memoir out of the drawer and immediately sent it to the Ukhta-Pechora Memorial Society: "One should not casually tell a lie that demands high-flown words and many decorations. It's possible to be silent about a book [or] events. But one shouldn't keep silent about an entire epoch when tragedy is presented as prosperity and baseness as greatness."[82]

The desire to overcome the silences of the state's narrative of the past explains why so many sent their autobiographies to branches of Memorial and local history museums, but Gulag returnees were motivated by other reasons as well. Some, such as Konstantin Marushchiak, were motivated by anti-Stalinism: "For all time, there is no and will be no forgiveness for him [Stalin] and his henchmen. Stalin cannot be counted in the lists of Communists; his remains should not be preserved in the Kremlin wall. Stalin's remains should be scattered into the dust and filth as he scattered the remains of millions of innocent people into camp dust."[83] Others, such as Nikolai Volkov, wrote because they wanted others to know about their contributions to Soviet society, including who really built the cities of the Far North:

> Cities do not rise out of nothing; they are built over years. Everything has its beginning. They come into existence only once, from the first tent, earthen dugout, or house. And having said this, do not cast even the smallest shadow on the greatness of the service of all the subsequent builders, including some civilians among the few first builders, several of whom came here following the dictates of their heart. But one question for any honest historian must be clear: THE CITY OF A DIFFICULT FATE was founded and built in the harsh conditions of the Arctic under the leadership of the Communist Party and sincere Soviet people. But you have a right to say that not only you, recently rehabilitated, participated in the construction of the city, and even in the very beginning, a significant number of real criminals, who had the title thieves, bandits, counterfeiters, and so on, participated.[84]

New memoirs continued to arrive in the mail at local branches of Memorial even after the collapse of the Soviet Union. Despite the ongoing rehabilitation of "victims of political repression," many Gulag returnees were alarmed by the decline of public interest in the past during the mid-1990s.[85] Gulag returnees, such as Lev Safronov, submitted their autobiographies to combat the "gathering strength of the Stalinists," who they feared were gaining power again after they traded their party cards for the "robes of democrats." As Safronov wrote in 1993, former prisoners feared for their families and for the future of the country:

> The reason why I, an old man of eighty-two years, sat down to write my memoirs is fear—not fear for myself, [but] fear for my children's future, my grandchildren's, and my countrymen. This fear arose long ago, but it has deepened after I saw on the television waves of raging crowds on the streets of Moscow, red calico flags—the symbol of blood; portraits of Stalin—a symbol of blood; Communist slogans—another symbol of blood. . . .
>   Today, in all echelons of power, there are still hidden Stalinists, descendants, and followers of those who tortured us, who show our relatives, who drove our country into the darkness and into poverty. This is borne out by the difficulty it took me to get a certificate [of rehabilitation]. . . . I write about myself and my comrades in misfortune [ondnobedtsy], but this was a road traveled by millions of victims of terror. Some of them made it to today, but

most of them remain in the frozen ground of our northern regions, which they conquered in the name of constructing a "bright future."

The relatives and close ones of those who were shot, killed, remain. The authorities have only one phrase in their answers to their inquiries about them: "Place of burial unknown." The living cannot pray at the graves of their fathers, mothers, brothers; they cannot lay flowers [because] the gravesite is unknown.[86]

Although the memory project of coming to terms with the Stalinist past in Komi developed exponentially over the course of the 1990s, Gulag returnees continued to emphasize the necessity of remembering the past. In 2000, former prisoner Georgii Ustilovskii wrote that the only way to prevent the return of the past was to remember it:

> Our main task, the task of all tasks, is to remember, to tell, to record, [and] to confirm with our testimonies the facts of these grave crimes of the bloody Stalinist-Brezhnevite regime against the people of our Great country. To name as many of the hangmen and oppressors as possible, those who mocked honest people who were not guilty of anything, so that the future generation knew the truth and only the truth so that our testimonies prevented anyone from ever making a fool of our ancestors, so that such savage barbarism, abasement, offense, inhumane tortures, and suffering were never again repeated.[87]

While all of the above factored into why Gulag returnees contributed their life stories to the Memorial archive, survivors also wrote to respond to Aleksandr Solzhenitsyn. As Toker argues, the presence of founding texts written before glasnost and the collapse of the Soviet Union relieved those who came forward in the 1980s and 1990s of the need to capture it all in their memoirs.[88] However, they were also a source for comparison, which inspired Gulag returnees to contribute their own stories to inform a more complete understanding of the past.[89] Just as it was in the debates over history and reform during the "Thaw," Solzhenitsyn's work was an important focal point in Gulag returnees' autobiographies of the late 1980s and 1990s.[90] These latter-day memoirists challenged, praised, criticized, and debated the merits of Solzhenitsyn's representation of the camps. The resulting overlaps and conflicts between Solzhenitsyn's work and the memoirs written by Gulag returnees from Komi illuminate the development of the collective story they tell.[91]

By referencing other Gulag literature and memoirs, in addition to the stories of those they knew in the camps, Gulag returnees connected their individual experiences to a community based in a shared past. In 1996, Gulag returnee

84   AFTER THE GULAG

Konstantin Ivanov sent a four-page letter to the Vorkuta Museum–Exhibition Center in which he compared Ivan Denisovich from Solzhenitsyn's novel to one of his camp mates. Reflecting on his own difficulty adapting, Ivanov contrasted his experience with his memory of his friend's "total adaptation" to camp life: "You could say that in the camp, Savos'ko felt like a fish in water. And later when I read Solzhenitsyn's *One Day in the Life of Ivan Denisovich*, I immediately thought that Solzhenitsyn copied several of Denisovich's characteristics from Savos'ko."[92] Contrasting his experience with such a widely recognizable character as Solzhenitsyn's Ivan Denisovich, Ivanov presented his testimony as a contribution to a fuller picture of what it was like in the camps: "I tried to describe everything from my 'belfry'—how I saw, understood, and experienced everything. Someone, maybe, saw it all differently and experienced it all in their own way."[93]

Petr Kotov dedicated sixteen pages of his memoir to discussing *One Day in the Life of Ivan Denisovich*, combining excerpts of his correspondence with Nina Sobinova from 1962 and his own memories of the camps in 1993. Both Sobinova and Kotov saw *One Day in the Life* as a founding text on the "camp theme," but they disagreed about Solzhenitsyn's portrayal of the camp "stooges" (*pridurki*).[94] In December 1962, Sobinova wrote to Kotov: "Of course, I read *One Day in the Life of Ivan Denisovich*. It's a wonderful story! I only disliked his disdainful attitude toward the 'stooges.' After all, 'stooges' like Nikolai Vladimirovich Podobedov, and others who worked as rate-fixers, secretaries, and doctors, saved people if they were kind and good hearted."[95] However, Kotov did not think that Solzhenitsyn was unfair in his depiction of those who obtained easy jobs in the camps. Kotov criticized his friend's position in 1992: "I knew a 'stooge' who was a genuinely good person and tried to help his fellow brother-prisoners. But this does not mean that in every place of confinement they were such people."[96] He continued, "It seems to me that Nina Mikhailovna is exaggerating the author's 'disdainful' attitude toward the 'stooges.' Not all of the 'stooges' in the novel are the bad sort. For example, Tiurin, the brigadier of the 104th Brigade, and his assistant Pavel are not at all the bad type. And the author's attitude toward them is not 'disdainful,' but totally serious and benevolent."[97]

Their debate over Solzhenitsyn's portrayal of camp "stooges" is noteworthy for two important reasons. First, their attitudes toward the camp stooges illuminate the moral code of the camp brotherhood, which informed their reading of Solzhenitsyn. According to Sobinova, Solzhenitsyn's mistake was that he did not consider the actions of stooges who helped their "brother-prisoners" in the camps, which made them members of the camp brotherhood and not, as she felt Solzhenitsyn portrayed them, villainous servants of the regime. Second, their dialogue illustrates that Gulag returnees were empowered by their status "as the ones who know camp life" to judge the truth of Solzhenitsyn's representation.[98] Both Sobinova and Kotov drew from their own memories of life in the camps to critique Solzhenitsyn's portrayal of one of the most painful and formative chapters of their lives.

While many accepted the general "truth" (*pravda*) of Solzhenitsyn's writing, some were motivated to "set the record straight." As former prisoner Konstantin Flug wrote in his 1986 memoir: "Solzhenitsyn is a great writer, but I don't accept his truth."[99] Flug submitted his memoir for publication to *Novy Mir* in 1987 under the title *One Day in the Life of Konstantin Valerianovich*, which was rejected because the journal simply could not publish all of the memoirs it received after Gorbachev initiated glasnost.[100] Throughout his fifty-page memoir, Flug continuously highlights the contradictions between his depiction of the camps and Solzhenitsyn's. Although he wanted to write about the "darkness" of the past, as Solzhenitsyn did, Flug remembered only "life": "Many condemn me because I only saw the good in the camps. But it was just this way. Solzhenitsyn saw the bad. . . . The truth of the good is more valuable to me. It is impossible to forget the good."[101] At another point in his memoir, Flug interrupts his narrative to underscore another difference between his and Solzhenitsyn's accounts: "It's curious that we had several people in common, but in his 'Archipelago,' they were victims, and in my chronicle, they were happy people."[102]

It seems that the underlying issue is victimhood. Although he accepted the label "victim of political repression" as the state's recognition of his innocence, Flug did not see himself as a victim; he was a survivor.[103] Perhaps the greatest evidence of this overarching theme in Flug's autobiographical narrative is the letter that he wrote to the Vorkuta Party Committee (Gorkom) in 1983, which he reproduced in the opening pages of his memoir, chastising the party for not acknowledging his achievements as a zek and one of the founders of Vorkuta:

> On Vorkuta's fortieth anniversary, I ask you to accept the congratulations of a pioneer of the Polar Stokehold, one of the first explorers of the virgin lands of the Vorkuta-Pechora coal basin! I participated in the construction of the city long before the official date of its founding, as far back as 1933! . . . Having raised me from a prisoner student to a genuine specialist, Vorkuta has always been for me a geological virgin land, a school, for which I am grateful to this day to the political and operations organs of Vorkutpechlag NKVD-MVD. I gave almost twenty years of my life and labor to Vorkuta. And I am sincerely grateful to you personally, Gorkom CPSU [Communist Party of the Soviet Union], that you named me a veteran of the Arctic in 1979!

86 AFTER THE GULAG

Indeed, I participated in the birth of Vorkuta, which, alas, I cannot visit the forty-year-old city due to my seventy-two years. And that's why I have the right to honestly confess to you that I am a little offended that my labor is never remembered, that the heroic pioneers and founders of the Arctic have been totally forgotten! This is a bit unjust against the general background of the party's and the government's constant concern for veterans of the war and veterans of labor. After all, only a few of the first cadres of the GULAG, like me, remain.[104]

Despite Flug's insistence that his testimony was so radically different from Solzhenitsyn's, he too saw the Gulag as an important chapter of the country's history, which had not yet been written in full. As he wrote in 1986,

Vorkuta is not only an arctic coal basin, it is an entire epoch, from dekulakiza-tion to victory during World War II—it is people's fate! Vorkuta is one of the industrial giants of the development of the Soviet Arctic during the years of the first five-year plan. It is the history of our country! Even now, in Soviet literature, they attempt to evade the topic of human fates during the years of this unique—as it is unrepeatable—epoch of two state systems in one country: Soviet power and the People's Commissariat of Internal Affairs [NKVD], when the people's labor was divided between trade unions and the assignments of the GULAG NKVD.[105]

Although they sometimes debated the accuracy of Solzhenitsyn's representation of the camps, Gulag returnees contributed their testimonies to paint a more complete picture of what it was like in "that world" (*tot svet*). Their mentions of Solzhenitsyn's writings emphasize that writing about the Gulag was not just for the intellectuals. Furthermore, in these collected memories, there were elements of dialogue and debate that shaped their views of camp history. Recording this unwritten chapter of Soviet history before they were gone was what united such diverse figures as Flug, Sollertinskii, Skakovskaia, Pechuro, Sobinova, Kotov, and other members of the camp brotherhood.

The era of glasnost and the collapse of the Soviet Union produced a flood of new testimonies from Gulag returnees who had previously remained silent. Once they understood what Memorial was and the moment they were living in, Gulag returnees submitted their autobiographies to the Memorial archive at local history museums and branches of Memorial in Komi, Moscow, and other cities. In doing so, they participated in the memory project of coming to terms with the Stalinist past. What began as testimony about their lives in the camps transformed into a process of autobiographical writing that extended to their lives after release. Through this process, Gulag returnees remembered their pasts and defined themselves as members of a community that they referred to as the "brotherhood of zeks."

Although they came from all walks of life and belonged to various groups in the camps and after release, this community of *svoi* was the primary source of the identities they constructed in their autobiographical narratives. In these texts, Gulag returnees often explained how they survived the camps and reintegrated into Soviet society after release. In doing so, they described the most important features of their community: selflessness, devotion to one's comrades in misfortune, and humaneness. The qualities they described to personify this diverse group and the methods they used to rejoin Soviet society after release can be seen as contributing to the formation of their community, which shaped the cultural memory of the Gulag in the Komi Republic and the rest of the country. Although motivated by a variety of reasons, these ordinary political prisoners wrote autobiographies to combat the legacy of Stalinism, to memorialize their friends, and to write themselves as a community into Soviet history at its end. As the next two chapters show through two very different autobiographies, the process of remembering the past was complicated.

Notes

1. Serov was sentenced on November 19, 1937, by a People's Commissariat of Internal Affairs (NKVD) troika under article 58.11 (organization of anti-Soviet groups or activities) and sentenced to five years of imprisonment followed by three years of deprivation of rights. For his biographical information, see International Memorial Society, "Victims of Political Terror in the USSR," accessed April 1, 2018, http://lists.memo.ru/index18.htm.

2. National Archive of the Komi Republic (GU RK NARK) 2 f. P-3800, op. 1, d. 156, ll. 27–28 (B. D. Serov, "Piat' let i vsia zhizn,'" Pechora, 1989).

3. Alexei Yurchak, *Everything Was Forever, until It Was No More: The Last Soviet Generation* (Princeton, NJ: Princeton University Press, 2006), 131–132. Yurchak identifies "publics of *svoi*" among members of the last Soviet generation who had not been in the camps. Although he describes this as a feature of late Socialism, it seems that the experience of being "within" but invisible to the system also applies to Gulag returnees.

4. Jochen Hellbeck, *Revolution on My Mind: Writing a Diary under Stalin* (Cambridge, MA: Harvard University Press, 2006). See also Igal Halfin, *Terror in My Soul: Communist Autobiographies on Trial* (Cambridge, MA: Harvard University Press, 2003); Thomas Lahusen, *How Life Writes the Book: Real Socialism and Socialist Realism in Stalin's Russia* (Ithaca, NY: Cornell University Press, 1997); Oleg Kharkhordin, *The Collective and the Individual in Russia: A Study of Practices* (Berkeley: University of California Press, 1999).

5. Alexander Etkind, "Soviet Subjectivity: Torture for the Sake of Salvation?," *Kritika: Explorations in Russian and Eurasian History* 6, no. 1 (Winter 2005): 171–186; Sarah J. Young, "Recalling the Dead: Repetition, Identity, and the Witness in Varlam Shalamov's *Kolymskie rassazy*," *Slavic Review* 70, no. 2 (Summer 2011): 353–372.

6. On these prisoner subcategories in the Gulag, see Alan Barenberg, *Gulag Town, Company Town: Forced Labor and Its Legacy in Vorkuta* (New Haven, CT: Yale University Press, 2014), 206; Steven Barnes, *Death and Redemption: The Gulag and the Shaping of Soviet Society* (Princeton, NJ: Princeton University Press, 2011), 185–197; Federico Varese, "The Society of the *vory-v*-zakone, 1930–1950s," *Cahiers du Monde russe* 39, no. 4 (1998): 515–538; Leona Toker, *Return from the Archipelago: Narratives of Gulag Survivors* (Bloomington: Indiana University Press, 2000), 15–24.

7. Iwona Irwin-Zarecka, *Frames of Remembrance: The Dynamics of Collective Memory* (New Brunswick, NJ: Transaction, 1993), 47–52. Irwin-Zarecka writes about the dynamics of collective memory and the formation of "communities of memory," which are formed when groups engage in the work of remembrance. I see the community that Gulag returnees formed in their memoirs and autobiographies as such a community. Irwin-Zarecka writes, "A community of memory is created by that very memory" (47–48).

8. Barbara Martin, *Dissident Histories in the Soviet Union: From De-Stalinization to Perestroika* (London: Bloomsbury, 2021), 4, 7.

9. For these studies of autobiographies written by the Soviet intelligentsia and dissidents, see Barbara Walker, "On Reading Soviet Memoirs: A History of the 'Contemporaries' Genre as an Institution of Russian Intelligentsia Culture from the 1790s to the 1970s," *Russian Review* 59 (July 2000): 327–352; Irina Paperno, "What Can Be Done with Diaries?," *Russian Review* 63 (October 2004): 561–573; Benjamin Nathans, "Talking Fish: On Soviet Dissident Memoirs," *Journal of Modern History* 87 (September 2015): 579–614.

10. Irina Paperno, *Stories of the Soviet Experience* (Ithaca, NY: Cornell University Press, 2009), xii.

11. Although some did transgress the law, it is difficult to consider their actions a crime. I focus on ordinary political prisoners because those sentenced for "everyday life crimes" (*bytoviki*) and criminals (*blatnye/urki*) typically did not write memoirs.

12. GU RK NARK 2 f. P-3800, op. 1, d. 40, l. 31–32 (L. S. Safronov, "Doroga vo mrake bez nadezhdy na prosvet," 1993).

13. Toker, *Return from the Archipelago*, 77. Toker writes, "On arrival at each penal facility, most prisoners investigated the lay of the land: collecting facts was necessary for practical adaptation. Yet collecting *maximum* data, in excess of what was needed for daily survival, was also a form of resistance to the authorities'

control of information. One ceased being a victim and turned into a subversive intern, a witness-in-training. Curiosity was also a psychological aid to endurance."

14. Fond Pokaianie Archive (AFP) (M. D. Baital'skii, "Znai istoriiu goroda v kotorom zhivesh': Na kirpichnom zavode," *Zapoliar'e*, September 19, 2000). In one part of his memoir, which was published as part of a six-part series of articles in the Vorkuta newspaper *Zapoliar'e* in 2000, Baital'skii wrote on why he wrote about the camps: "I speak about camp customs not for the sake of exotics, but to show the environment which we recent communists, and hundreds of thousands of ordinary workers, were prescribed for correction." For Baitail'skii's memoir manuscript, see AFP op. 1, d. 23, ll. 1–394 (M. D. Baital'skii, *Tetradi dlia vnukov*, Moscow, 1976). Gorky's book on the Belomor Canal was published in the West as propaganda in 1935. See Maxim Gorky, ed., *Belomor: An Account of the Construction of the New Canal between the White Sea and the Baltic Sea*, trans. S. G. Firin (New York: H. Smith and R. Haas, 1935). On the correlation between the destruction and creation of the self in the camps and the reeducation of prisoners, see Barnes, *Death and Redemption*, 38, 58; Julie Draskoczy, *Belomor: Criminality and Creativity in Stalin's Gulag* (Boston: Academic Studies, 2014), 23, 26.

15. Archive of the International Memorial Society (AM) f. 2, op. 2, d. 112, l. 176 (V. E. Sollertinskii, "Kuda bog smotrit, vospominaniia," Sosnogorsk, 1984). See also AFP op. 1, d. 31, l. 38 (G. I. Rivkin, "Po dorogam proizvola," 2005).

16. Ibid.

17. Ibid., 225. Contextualizing his father's and his brother's broken spirit after release, Sollertinskii wrote about the difficulties they had describing what they had seen: "I already spoke about the aversion that our brother 58 [*brat-58*] felt toward discussing the details of the camp underworld, which is why father did not speak about them, and I did not ask. It's unlikely that the details differ much from what is written in *One Day in the Life of Ivan Denisovich*, and I won't talk about them either."

18. Mikhail Nakonechnyi, "'They Won't Survive for Long': Soviet Officials on Medical Release Procedure," in *Rethinking the Gulag: Identities, Sources, Legacies,* ed. Alan Barenberg and Emily D. Johnson (Bloomington: Indiana University Press, 2022), 103–128; Golfo Alexopoulos, *Illness and Inhumanity in Stalin's Gulag* (New Haven, CT: Yale University Press, 2017), 85–109; Wilson T. Bell, *Stalin's Gulag at War: Forced Labor, Mass Death, and Victory in the Second World War* (Toronto: University of Toronto Press, 2018).

19. AM f. 2, op. 2, d. 22, l. 43 (A. S. Gurevich, "Vospominaniia," not dated). Judging by the references he made to the *Gulag Archipelago* and other texts, including newspapers, it seems likely that Gurevich wrote his autobiography between 1988 and 1992.

20. AFP op. 1, d. 29, l. 57 (V. B. Ol'shevskii, "Vyzhit! Ot Bamlaga do Pechlaga," not dated). Ol'shevskii's memoir is not dated; however, part of the 308-page

text was published in 1991 in the first edited volume of memoirs written by former prisoners from Komi. For the condensed, published version, see Vitallii Ol'shevskii, "Vyzhit!" in *Pechal'naia pristan'*, ed. I. L. Kuznetsov (Syktyvkar: Komi Knizhnoe izd-vo, 1991), 257–268.

21. GU RK NARK 2 f. P-3800, op. 1, d. 163, ll. 163–164 (S. S. Pechuro, "Vospominanie," not dated). Pechuro wrote, "The camp taught me, a young uneducated girl, and everyone else, about human kindness, self-confidence, and brotherhood" (165). On friendship and the bonds that tie, see also A. L. Voitolovskaia, *Po sledam sud'by moego pokoleniia* (Syktyvkar: Komi knizhnoe izd-vo, 1991), https://www.sakharov-center.ru/asfcd/auth/?t=author&i=616; GU RK NARK 2 f. P-3800, op. 1, d. 163 ll. 27–145 (Petr Kotov, "Vospominanie," Gdansk, Poland, 1991). Kotov wrote, "Indeed the 'camp brotherhood' shared the difficult experiences that bring people together. This is clear in Nina Mikhailovna's interactions and relationships with former prisoners who were in prison and exile with her. The principle: 'Political prisoners of all countries unite!' was close to us and we tried to apply it in practice of our lives" (131).

22. Ibid., 168–169. See also Pavel Rachkov, "Kak my tam zhili (zapiski ssylnogo)" in *Pechal'naia* pristan', ed. I. L. Kuznetsov (Syktyvkar: Komi Knizhnoe izd-vo, 1991), 20–21; AFP op. 1, d. 33 (Vladimir Shervinskii, "Vospominanie," Riga, 1963–1965); AFP op.1, d. 25, ll. 1–219 (L. M. Gorodin, "Avtobiografiia, pis'ma, vospominaniia," 1982). Gorodin writes about members of the camp brotherhood who taught him "about the simple things, without which it would have been difficult for me to survive; a person who gave me a drink of water, when I thirsted, who lifted me up when I lost heart and became a friend to me and a brother" (119).

23. Barnes, *Death and Redemption*, 81. Barnes writes, "Categorization in the Gulag served as a source of power, both in the relationship between authorities and prisoners, and among the prisoners themselves."

24. A. P. Evstiunichev, *Nakazanie bez prestupleniia* (Syktyvkar: Memorial, 1991), 258. See also AFP op. 1, d. 29, l. 224 (Ol'shevskii, "Vyzhit'!"). Vitalii Ol'shevskii expressed this sentiment in a slightly different way: "I am proud that despite everything I experienced, I preserved my name as an honest person, I did not become a scoundrel, traitor, or an informant." I will explore this theme in greater detail in chap. 4.

25. The group solidarity that Gulag returnees documented in their memoirs seems also to have been a response to the well-documented fact that criminals ran the camps. It was not uncommon for criminals to serve as guards and crew bosses and in other positions of power over political prisoners. On the documentation of these divisions in the camps by NKVD and Ministry of Internal Affairs (MVD) officials, see Vladimir Kozlov, ed., *Istoriia Stalinskogo GULAGa*, t. 6 (Moscow: ROSSPEN, 2004), 67. See also Kate Brown, "Out of Solitary

Confinement: The History of the Gulag," *Kritika: Explorations in Russian and Eurasian History* 8, no. 1 (Winter 2007): 93–94; Janusz Bardach, *Man Is Wolf to Man: Surviving the Gulag*, trans. Kathleen Gleeson (Berkeley: University of California Press, 1998).

26. AM f. 2, op. 2, d. 112, l. 143 (Sollertinskii, "Kuda bog smotrit"). Sollertinskii wrote that criminals saw themselves as "genuine citizens of the USSR. They were obliged to persecute any and all enemies of the people they encountered, that is our brother 58-ers."

27. Archive of the Local History Museum at Ukhta State Technical University (AM UGTU) (A. A. Kotvitskii, "O chem molchit istoriia," Kiev, 1970), 17. See also AFP op. 1, d. 29, l. 64 (Ol'shevskii, "Vyzhit!"); GU RK NARK 2 f. P-3800, op. 1, d. 40, l. 13 (Safronov, "Doroga vo mrake bez nadezhdy na prosvet"); AFP op. 1, d. 23, l. 69 (Baital'skii, "Tetradi dlia vnukov," 1976).

28. These groups are well documented in the memoir literature; see Aleksandr I. Solzhenitsyn, *The Gulag Archipelago: An Experiment in Literary Investigation*, vol. 2 (New York: Harper & Row, 1975), 265, 350–351; Joseph Scholmer, *Vorkuta*, trans. Robert Kee (New York: Henry Holt and Co., 1955), 121–155; Tamara Petkevich, *Memoir of a Gulag Actress*, trans. Yasha Klots and Ross Ufberg (Delkab: Northern Illinois University Press, 2010).

29. Alexopoulos, *Illness and Inhumanity*, 44–45. According to Alexopoulos, from 1930 to the 1950s, the majority of prisoners were ethnic Russians. Barenberg's work confirms this and provides a breakdown of the ethnic composition of Vorkutlag and Rechlag in the years for which data is available, 1942–1954; Barenberg, *Gulag Town*, 264–265.

30. GU RK NARK 2 f. P-3800, op. 1, d. 163, l. 91 (Kotov, "Vospominanie," 1992). See also AM f. 2, op. 3, d. 59, l. 25 (K. P. Marushchiak, "Biograficheskaia rukopis' vospominanii," Syktyvkar, 1989); AFP op. 1, d. 25, l. 65–67 (Gorodin, "Avtobiografiia, pis'ma, vospominaniia"); AM f. 2, op. 2, d. 81, ll. 25 (I. V. Skakovskaia, "Vospominaniia o Vorkute i vorkutianakh, 1946–59," 1996).

31. GU RK NARK 2 f. P-3800, op. 1, d. 163, l. 165 (Pechuro, "Vospominanie," not dated). See also E. V. Markova, *Vorkutinskye zametki katorzhanki "E-105"* (Syktyvkar: Fond Pokaianie, 2005), 65, http://www.sakharov-center.ru/asfcd /auth/?t=book&num=821. Markova wrote of the new arrivals from the Baltic countries in her camp: "Two years after their arrival in the zone, they looked like typical *katorzhane* in filthy, torn quilted jackets, pants, and *ushanki*. Everyone looked the same, only their numbers distinguished them."

32. AM f. 2, op. 3, d. 59, l. 24 (Marushchiak, "Biograficheskaia rukopis' vospominanii"). Marushchiak repeats himself for emphasis on the next page: "Faith in justice gave me the strength to work conscientiously and overcome all the difficulties. We worked for twelve to fourteen hours straight. Everyone, of course, was half-starving, but the will to live gave us strength. Among the camp

administration there were fair, kind people who helped us overcome all of life's burdens." See AM f. 2, op. 3, d. 59, l. 25.

33. Ibid., 26. See also AFP op. 1, d. 34, l. 33 (N. P. Volkov, "Gorod trudnoi sud'by," 1965–1970).

34. Barenberg, *Gulag Town*, 161–197. Barenberg underscores the necessity of hiring former prisoners to maintain the production of coal in Vorkuta, which was undoubtedly an issue faced by authorities everywhere where prisoners composed a significant segment of the local labor force. Barenberg writes, "Many ex-prisoners had already secured jobs and housing in the city before they were released, as was the case with the thousands of dezoned prisoners who were given permission to live outside the camp zone after Stalin's death. . . . The release of tens of thousands of prisoners in such a short period of time, combined with the transition of Vorkuta's mines to nonprisoner labor, created an enormous demand for workers, particularly those with skills and experience" (199). See also Nanci Adler, *The Gulag Survivor* (New Brunswick, NJ: Transaction, 2002), 71–72.

35. This movement from the camps to the town just outside the barbed wire is well documented in state archives and Gulag returnees' memoirs. See, e.g., Leonid P. Markizov, *Do i posle 1945: Glazami ochevidtsa* (Syktyvkar: Fond Pokaianie, 2003), 156; AFP op. 1, d. 34, l. 54 (Volkov, "Gorod trudnoi sud'by").

36. AM f. 2, op. 3, d. 59, l. 28 (Marushchiak, "Biograficheskaia rukopis' vospominanii"). See also AFP (A. I. Sapozhnikova, "Vospominanie," Syktyvkar, 2012), 18. Sapozhnikova wrote about her reinstatement in the party: "In 1958 they accepted me into the party. Why did I need this? It was important to me to prove to those around me that although I was repressed, I was not guilty of anything."

37. Nanci Adler, *Keeping Faith with the Party: Communist Believers Return from the Gulag* (Bloomington: Indiana University Press), 28–92.

38. AM f. 1, op. 3, d. 3123, l. 1–2 (K. P. Marushchiak, Moscow Memorial Society questionnaire, 1989); AFP (K. P. Marushchiak, Syktyvkar Memorial Society questionnaire, not dated).

39. It is unclear how common this was; however, given the fact that most people who worked in the camps had very little education, it is perhaps unsurprising that camp officials tried to keep as many of the educated, skilled workers as they could. On education levels of camp officials in 1945, see N. V. Petrov, ed., *Istoriia Stalinskogo GULAGa*, t. 2 (Moscow: ROSSPEN, 2004), 256. For other examples of former prisoners who joined the MVD after release, see AM f. 2, op. 1, d. 77, ll. 54 (Iakov Kuperman, "Piat'desiat let, 1927–1977: Vospominaniia," not dated). Kuperman worked as an engineer for the MVD after release and recounts meetings with Naftalii Frenkel', who rose from prisoner to chief of the Directorate of Railroad Construction (GULZhDS). Andrei Krems is another example of a former prisoner who became a prominent member of the local MVD. Although he never wrote a memoir, the apartment where he spent the rest of his life after his

release in 1940 has become a museum in Ukhta. For Krems's biography, see M. B. Rogachev, ed., *Pokaianie: Martirolog*, t. 12, ch. 1 (Syktyvkar: Fond Pokaianie, 2016), 329.

40. On the lifetime of performing to fit in after release, see also Markova, *Vorkutinskye zametki*; GU RK NARK 2 f. P-3800, op. 1, d. 156, ll. 22–45 (Serov, "Piat' let i vsia zhizn'"); GU RK NARK 2 f. P-3800, op. 1, d. 163, ll. 5–6 (K. M. Aleksandrovna, "Vospominanie," undated).

41. Yurchak, *Everything Was Forever*, 288–290.

42. AFP op. 1, d. 34, l. 33 (N. P. Volkov, "Gorod trudnoi sud'by," 1965–1970).

43. Rogachev, *Pokaianie: Martirolog*, 184. Gorodin was arrested in 1936 and sentenced to five years of imprisonment in Ukhtpechlag. His release was delayed until the end of World War II. As a result, he was transferred to Vorkutlag in 1942. For "good work performance," he was released "early" in 1944. In 1950, he was arrested again and sentenced to eternal exile in Vorkuta. He was released from exile in 1954 and continued to work in Vorkuta. He moved to Sverdlovsk after he was rehabilitated in 1956.

44. AFP op. 1, d. 25, l. 98 (Gorodin, "Avtobiografiia, pis'ma, vospominaniia"). See also Evstiunichev, *Nakazanie bez prestupleniia*, 261; Veniamin Vasil'ev, "V'iugi Vorkutlaga," in *Pechal'naia Pristan'*, ed. I. L. Kuznetsov (Syktyvkar: Komi knizhnoe izd-vo, 1991), 175; AFP op. 1, d. 23, l. 155 (Baital'skii, Tetradi dlia vnukov). Baital'skii wrote, "The re-education of criminals, from what I observed, as it was to be expected, turned into the most extreme form of *tufta*, into total deception. Criminality, even the so-called 'everyday' [*bytovaia*] crime didn't decrease in the slightest" (155).

45. AFP (Viktor Lozhkin "Material on the repressed Jewish intelligentsia in the camps of Abez'," May 19, 2001). See also AM f. 2, op. 1, d. 74, ll. 834 (I. K. Koval'chuk-Koval', "Svidanie s pamiat'iu: Vospominaniia," not dated); AM UGTU (V. K. Novokhatskii, "Rokovaia chernaia shinel'," 1992, ll. 64); V. A. Samsonov, *Zhizn' prodolzhitsia: Zapiski lagernogo lekpoma* (Petrozavodsk: Kareliia, 1990). GU RK NARK 2 f. P-3800, op. 1, d. 163, l. 80 (P. Kotov, "Vospominanie," 1991). Petr Kotov provides an example of this aim of Gulag returnees' memoirs: "It turns out that the word *Adak* [in Komi] means *whirlpool*—a word that very precisely relates the character of that place and those relationships, where I came to spend quite a long time. My fate turned out so that I managed to sail out of that whirlpool. Many remain there forever, and I remember them."

46. Toker, *Return from the Archipelago*, 80. Toker writes, "Each memoir produces a specific new tension between a number of highlighted portraits and the undifferentiated mass of people who both remain at the background and press in upon one in overcrowded cells, trains, or barracks." For examples of this, see GU RK NARK 2 f. P-3800, op. 1, d. 163, l. 53 (Kotov, "Vospominanie"); AM f. 2, op. 1, d. 139, ll. 308 (S. P. Shur, "Pod kolesom istorii, ch. 2," 1960).

94 AFTER THE GULAG

47. AM f. 2, op. 2, d. 81, l. 25 (Skakovskaia, "Vospominaniia o Vorkute i vorku-tianakh, 1946–59," 1996). Skakovskaia's parents met in exile in Syktyvkar before they were re-arrested and sentenced to camps. See also GU RK NARK 2 f. P-3800, op. 1, d. 163, l. 80 (P. Kotov, "V Adake barrak no.2," Gdansk, 1991); AM f. 1, op. 3, d. 3123, l. 7–11: (K. P. Marushchiak to I. R. Liubavina, September 19, 1989); AM f. 2, op. 1, d. 101, ll. 226 (D. M. Rakhlin, "Griaznia istoriia," 1989–1990).

48. Quoted in GU RK NARK 2 f. P-3800, op. 1, d. 163, l. 131 (Petr Kotov, "Vo-spominanie," Gdansk, Poland, 1991). Bokal was a prisoner of Vorkutlag 1936–1945. For her biographical information see Memorial's database of "Victims of Political Terror in the USSR," accessed January 22, 2018, http://base.memo.ru/person/show/372910.

49. See Martin's discussion of the need for secrecy, *Dissident Histories*, 180.

50. AM f. 2, op. 2, d. 112, ll. l 95–100 (Sollertinskii, "Kuda bog smotrit"). Soller-tinskii described the "polite talk" he had with local KGB officers in his rewritten manuscript: "To conclude the conversation, they had me sign a paper, which enu-merated everything 'bad' with a checkmark next to each. . . . The word 'allegedly' was put next to each adversity that I mentioned in the manuscript. I was warned about never allowing this to happen again and that the district procurator had been notified. I asked: 'For what? Is writing forbidden?' 'No,' they said, 'you can, it is your right.' 'But I can't write about this?' 'You know, it depends who will read it.' I signed on the line and sighed, 'How slowly the times change!' 'What, what?' I explained that we already went through this, truly, in several other forms" (96–97). See also AM UGTU (Kotvitskii, "O chem molchit istoriia"); AFP op. 1, d. 34, l. 74 (Volkov, "Gorod trudnoi sud'by").

51. AM f. 2, op. 2, d. 112, l. 164 (Sollertinskii, "Kuda bog smotrit, vospominaniia").

52. See, e.g., GU RK NARK 2 f. P-3800, op.1, d. 16, l. 26 (Gorodin, "Rasskazy, vospominaniia," 1962–1977); GU RK NARK 2 f. P-3800, op. 1, d. 159, ll. 24–48 (Z. A. Dunchenkin, "Vospominanie perezhitogo detstva v ssylke," Verkhnyi Chov, 1992–1994); GU RK NARK 2 f. P-3800, op. 1, d. 159, ll. 54–79 (I. Iz"iurov, "Vozvrashchaias v tridtsat' sed'moi," undated).

53. Evstiunichev, *Nakazanie bez prestupleniia*, 231–232. See also AM f. 2, op. 2, d. 81, l. 25 (Skakovskaia); Aleksandr Klein, *Ulybki nevoli: Nevydummanaia zhizn'. Sobytiia. Sud'by. Sluchai* (izd-vo 'PROLOG', 1997), 277–287; AM f. 2, op. 2, d. 90, ll. 134 (T. V. Tigonen, "Souchastie v prave: Vospominaniia," Leningrad, 1982–1989).

54. On passport restrictions placed on Gulag returnees under articles 38 and 39 "of the Instructions on Internal Passports" with the notation "OMZ" (released from places of confinement), see Jacques Rossi, *The Gulag Handbook: An Encyclo-pedia Dictionary of Soviet Penitentiary Institutions and Terms Related to the Forced Labor Camps*, trans. William A. Burhans (New York: Paragon House, 1989), 263,

THE "BROTHERHOOD OF ZEKS"   95

294. Gulag returnee Elena Markova referred to the 101-km radius around major cities and border areas where former prisoners could not live as "another zone." See Markova, *Vorkutinskye zametki*, 153. This status was so common among former prisoners that it earned its own term in camp slang: "passport with a temperature." See GU RK NARK 2 f. P-3800, op. 1, d. 17, l. 22 (Gorodin, "Slovar' Russkikh argotizmov").

55. See, e.g., GU RK NARK 2 f. P-3800, op. 1, d. 156, ll. 48–89 (P. I. Siamtomov, "Ispoved,'" Syktyvkar, October 1990–January 1991); GU RK NARK 2 f. P-3800, op. 1, d. 156, ll. 22–45 (Serov, "Piat' let i vsia zhizn'"); GU RK NARK 2 f. P-3800, op. 1, d. 163, ll. 5–6a (M. A. Kalimova, "Vospominanie," undated); L. M. Gurvich, "Zareshechennye gody," in . . . *Imet' silu pomnit': Rasskazy tekh, kto proshel ad repressii*, ed. L. M. Gurvich (Moskva, Moskovskii rabochii, 1991), 151–180.

56. On the effect of "having a past" on Latvians who wrote narratives of their exile and imprisonment after Latvia was annexed by the Soviet Union in 1940, see Veida Skultans, *The Testimony of Lives: Narrative and Memory in Post-Soviet Latvia* (London: Routledge, 1998), 67–82.

57. AM f. 2, op. 2, d. 112, l. 149 (Sollertinskii, "Kuda bog smotrit"). As Sollertinskii wrote about his release: "Life continued, LIFE CONTINUED."

58. AM UGTU (Novokhatskii, "Rokovaia chernaia shinel,'" 1992), 55.

59. On former prisoners' social networks, see Alan Barenberg, "From Prisoners to Citizens? Ex-Prisoners in Vorkuta during the Thaw," in *The Thaw: Soviet Society and Culture in the 1950s and 1960s*, ed. Denis Kozlov and Eleonory Gilburd (Toronto: University of Toronto Press, 2013), 118–144; Adler, *Gulag Survivor*, 57–58. For descriptions of these mutual-aid associations in Gulag returnees' memoirs, see Klein, *Ulybki nevoli*, 278; Markizov, *Do i posle 1945 goda*, 156; AM f. 2, op. 2, d. 81, l. 25 (Skakovskaia, "Vospominaniia o Vorkute i vorkutianakh, 1946–59").

60. AM f. 2, op. 1, d. 139, l. 187 (S. P. Shur, "Pod kolesom istorii, ch. 2," 1960). Shur described life after release in Inta as a new spring: "Every morning, arising from sleep, we head off to work, we all thought about: what will today bring? We lived fully, feeling that another time had come, that the air was saturated with electricity, that things are shifting, that things are disappearing which were firmly rooted in our way of life, that something new was coming, the best, that smelled of the renewal of our tired, joyless lives."

61. AM f. 2, op. 2, d. 112, l. 163 (Sollertinskii, "Kuda bog smotrit").

62. GU RK NARK 2 f. P-3800, op. 1, d. 40, l. 26 (Safronov, "Doroga vo mrake bez nadezhdy na prosvet"). Safronov and his friend were reunited in Syktyvkar after the collapse of the Soviet Union.

63. Archive of the Vorkuta Museum–Exhibition Center (VMVTs) f. OF 4327, op. 1, d. 26, l. 10 (K. P. Ivanov to Z. N. Fesenko, January 3, 1997). I examine Ivanov's extensive archive of memoir-letters in the next chapter.

64. AM f. 2, op. 2, d. 22, l. 10 (A. S. Gurevich, "Vospominaniia," not dated); AM f. 2, op. 2, d. 112, l. 152 (Sollertinskii, "Kuda bog smotrit"); AFP op. 1, d. 29, l. 278 (Ol'shevskii, "Vyzhit!"); Evstiunichev, *Nakazanie bez prestupleniia*, 260; AFP op. 1, d. 25, l. 67 (L. M. Gorodin, "Avtobiografiia, pis'ma, vospominaniia," 1956–1992); AM f. 2, op. 2, d. 81, l. 21 (Skakovskaia, "Vospominaniia o Vorkute i vorkutianakh, 1946–59").

65. Alexander Etkind, "A Parable of Misrecognition: *Anagnorisis* and the Return of the Repressed from the Gulag," *Russian Review* 68 (October 2009): 623–640.

66. Archive of the Vorkuta Museum of Geology (AVMG) (K. Flug, "Chernyi ostrov GULAGa"), 31.

67. On attitudes toward returning prisoners in the 1950s and after, see Miriam Dobson, *Khrushchev's Cold Summer: Gulag Returnees, Crime, and the Fate of Reform after Stalin* (Ithaca, NY: Cornell University Press, 2009), pt. 2; Marc Elie and Jeff Hardy, "'Letting the Beasts Out of the Cage': Parole in the Post-Stalin Gulag, 1953–1973," *Europe-Asia Studies* 67, no. 4 (June 2015): 579–605; Amir Weiner, "The Empires Pay a Visit: Gulag Returnees, East European Rebellions, and Soviet Frontier Politics," *Journal of Modern History* 78, no. 2 (June 2006): 333–376; Barenberg, *Gulag Town*, 208–209.

68. GU RK NARK 2 f. P-3800, op. 1, d. 163, ll. 89–113 (Kotov, "Nina Mikhailovna Sobinova," in "Vospominanie" Gdansk, Poland, 1992). Although *"vol'nonaemnye"* can refer to former prisoners who continued to work in town as free people, in this case, it refers to Soviet citizens who had not been repressed.

69. Ibid., 102. For other examples, see AFP op. 1, d. 25, ll. 115–117 (L. M. Gorodin, "Vospominaniia byvshego politzakliuchenñogo," Vorkuta, 1990); GU RK NARK 2 f. P-3800, op. 1, d. 156, ll. 48–89 (Siamtomov, "Ispoved").

70. See, e.g., AM f. 2, op. 2, d. 112, l. 187 (Sollertinskii, "Kuda bog smotrit"); AM f. 2, op. 1, d. 74, l. 674 (I. K. Koval'chuk-Koval', "Svidanie s pamiat'iu: Vospominaniia," not dated); AM UGTU (Novokhatskii, "Rokovaia chernaia shinel'"), 58; GU RK NARK 2 f. P-3800, op. 1, d. 40, ll. 33 (Safronov, "Doroga vo mrake bez nadezhdy na prosvet"); Evstiunichev, *Nakazanie bez prestupleniia*, 255.

71. GU RK NARK 2 f. P-2576, op. 1, d. 4, ll. 55–70 (Intinskii raikom KPSS gorsoveta, January 4, 1955–December 27, 1955). A report from the Inta city soviet reports the case of a party member who allowed her daughter—a Komsomol teacher—to marry a "citizen who was only just released from prison, not reinstated in his civil rights. This citizen, T. Likhtenshtein, lives in a family of party members. Sokolova rushed to marry a former convict, who has still not proven himself to others. How can this be seen as anything but political negligence?" See also GU RK NARK 2 f. P-2576, op. 1, d. 2, ll. 10, 16 (Intinskii raikom KPSS "Protokola zasedanii biura i Partiinykh sobranii," January 8, 1953–January 19, 1954).

72. AM f. 2, op. 2, d. 112, l. 187 (Sollertinskii, "Kuda bog smotrit").

THE "BROTHERHOOD OF ZEKS" 97

73. GU RK NARK 2 f. P-3800, op. 1, d. 163, ll. 89–113 (P. Kotov, "Nina Mikhailovna Sobinova," in "Vospominanie," Gdansk, 1992). Despite the danger of doing so and the ban on his passport, Kotov and his wife traveled to Leningrad to visit Nina Mikhailovna and her husband. The couples became close in the camps and remained so after release. Kotov writes about an episode in which they were caught during their trip and summoned to the local police precinct, but no problems followed: "It was a totally different time" but "we did worry that we would be arrested again [because of our records]." For this episode see, GU RK NARK 2 f. P-3800, op. 1, d. 163, l. 86 (P. Kotov, "Byvshie Adakovtsy v inykh obstoiatel'stvakh" in "Vospominanie," Gdansk, undated).

74. Kotov repeatedly refers to himself and his fellow former prisoners as "Adakovtsy." See, e.g., GU RK NARK 2 f. P-3800, op. 1, d. 163, l. 133. Others grouped themselves by camp or region in Komi as well; see GU RK NARK 2 f. P-3800, op. 1, d. 159, l. 9 (E. A. Griaznova, Vospominanie, undated, Syktyvkar); AVMG (K. Flug, "Chernyi ostrov GULAGa"), 50; GU RK NARK 2 f. P-3800, op. 1, d. 40, ll. 33 (Safronov, "Doroga vo mrake bez nadezhdy na prosvet").

75. GU RK NARK 2 f. P-3800, op. 1, d. 163, l. 94 (P. Kotov, "Nina Mikhailovna Sobinova," in "Vospominanie," Gdansk, 1992). See also AFP op. 1, d. 34, l. 72 (Volkov, "Gorod trudnoi sud'by"); A. Klein, *Kleimenye, ili Odin sredi odinokikh: Zapiski katorzhnika* (Syktyvkar, Komi Respublikanskaia tipografiia, 1995), 197, https://www.sakharov-center.ru/asfcd/auth/?t=book&num=1942.

76. Barenberg, *Gulag Town*, 198–230. Barenberg details the numerous ways in which former prisoners were systematically discriminated against and surveilled.

77. AFP op. 1, d. 34, l. 49 (Volkov, "Gorod trudnoi sud'by").

78. GU RK NARK 2 f. P-3800, op. 1, d. 163, l. 88 (Kotov, "Vospominanie"). Kotov writes, "Of course, it gladdens me, and I am happy that there is such a strong connection between former prisoners and former exiles. After all, the authorities always tried to divide us, they tried to poison us against one another. Sometimes they managed to do this, but the majority did not follow. Solidarity between former prisoners prevailed, which in soviet reality directed a person to think about reconsidering the cynicism of life."

79. This contrasts with the experience of Soviet veterans of World War II, who were able to form an entitlement group and, eventually, a popular movement under the regime. See Mark Edele, *Soviet Veterans of the Second World War: A Popular Movement in an Authoritarian Society, 1941–1991* (Oxford: Oxford University Press, 2008).

80. AM UGTU (Kotvitskii, "O chem molchit istoriia"), 100–101. Stanislav Kossiov was one of Stalin's deputies who was directly involved in both collectivization of agriculture, which directly contributed to the famine that killed millions in Ukraine known as the "Holodomor," and the initial stages of the Great Purges.

98   AFTER THE GULAG

He was removed from his post as first secretary of the Communist Party of the Ukrainian SSR, sentenced as an enemy of the people, and shot in 1939. He was rehabilitated by Khrushchev (who replaced him as first secretary in Ukraine) following the Twentieth Party Congress in 1956.

81. Ibid.

82. Ibid., 78–79.

83. AM f. 2, op. 3, d. 59, l. 24 (K. P. Marushchiak, "Biograficheskaia rukopis' vospominanii," Syktyvkar, 1989). See also GU RK NARK f. P3800, op. 1, d. 18, l. 8 (V. G. Lipilin, *Vospominaniia*, 1991); AM UGTU (A. A. Kotvitskii, *O chem molchit istoriia*, l. 87, Kiev, 1970); AM f. 2, op. 1, d. 21, ll. 23 (V. I. Belkin, "Protiv Stalina pri Staline: Zametki uchastnika i ochevidtsa," 1988); GU RK NARK f. P-3800, op. 1, d. 163, l. 165 (S. S. Pechuro, "Vospominanie"); AVMG (K. Flug to Vorkuta Gorkom KPSS, November 26, 1983 reproduced in K. Flug, "Chernyi ostrov GULAGa"), 4–5; AFP op. 1, d. 25, l. 97 (L. M. Gorodin, "Avtobiografiia, pis'ma, vospominaniia," 1956–1992).

84. AFP op. 1, d. 34, l. 28 (Volkov, "Gorod trudnoi sud'by"). See also AM UGTU (Kotvitskii, "O chem molchit istoriia"), 69. Although it was published after Volkov's memoir was written, Vasily Grossman depicts a similar scene in his novel about Gulag returnees after Stalin's death, *Everything Flows*: "'I've got prisoners working on my construction site,' he said on one occasion. 'Their name for people like you is 'layabouts.' But when the time comes to decide who built communism, no doubt it'll turn out to be you lot who did all the plowing'"; Grossman, *Everything Flows*, trans. Robert Chandler, Elizabeth Chandler, and Anna Aslanyan (New York: New York Review Books, 2009), 5.

85. AM f. 2, op. 3, d. 59, l. 34 (Marushchiak, "Biograficheskaia rukopis'"); AM f. 2, op. 2, d. 112, l. 243 (V. E. Sollertinskii to Memorial Moscow, November 20, 1988); AFP (A. I. Dering, "Letopis' moei zhizni," Novocherkassk, 1990), 33.

86. GU RK NARK 2 f. P-3800, op. 1, d. 40, ll. 3–4 (Safronov, "Doroga vo mrake bez nadezhdy na prosvet"). Safronov describes in detail how he traveled to the KGB archives in Pavlodar and gained access to his father's, brother's, and his own case files. During his interaction with the officer/archivist on duty, they discuss why there will be no Soviet Nuremberg, which, for Safronov, justifies his fears of the continued vulnerability of Gulag returnees in post-Soviet society. For this story, see GU RK NARK 2 f. P-3800, op. 1, d. 40, ll. 20–23.

87. AFP (G. I. Ustilovskii, "Gor'kaia zhizn'," Sosnogorsk, 2000), 7.

88. Toker, *Return from the Archipelago*, 100.

89. Ibid., 103. Toker writes, "*The Gulag Archipelago* expressly invites emendations. Its use of unverified testimony and its insufficiency of archival documentation are undisguised. . . . Later sources are *expected* to complement Solzhenitsyn's data and correct his factual misprisions." For instance, from 1989 to 1998, the newspaper *Ukhta* published dozens of the hundreds of memoirs and

THE "BROTHERHOOD OF ZEKS" 99

autobiographical letters sent to the editors and the Ukhta-Pechora Memorial Society. See, e.g., AM UGTU f. Bulychev.

90. Miriam Dobson, "Contesting the Paradigms of De-Stalinization: Readers' Responses to 'One Day in the Life of Ivan Denisovich,'" *Slavic Review* 64, no. 3 (Autumn 2005): 581. See also Denis Kozlov, *The Readers of Novy Mir: Coming to Terms with the Stalinist Past* (Cambridge, MA: Harvard University Press, 2013); Polly Jones, *Myth, Memory, Trauma: Rethinking the Stalinist Past in the Soviet Union, 1953–1970* (New Haven, CT: Yale University Press, 2013), 147.

91. Toker, *Return from the Archipelago*, 90; Paperno, *Stories of the Soviet Experience*, 41. See also AM f. 2, op. 1, d. 77, ll. 54 (Kuperman, "Piat'desiat let, 1927–1977: Vospominaniia"). For example, Kuperman interrupts his narrative with brackets and inserts a comment about how his interrogation experience was "detailed by Solzhenitsyn in [his novel] *In the First Circle*" (8). Referencing Solzhenitsyn as the master description of the interrogation experience, Kuperman spares himself the burden of reliving the gory details and continues his autobiographical narrative.

92. VMVTs f. OF 4327, op. 1, d. 5, ll. 4 (Ivanov to Fesenko, February 19, 1996).

93. VMVTs f. OF 4270, op. 1, d. 18, l. 4a (Ivanov to Trukhina, August 18, 1992).

94. A *Pridurok* worked office or light-duty jobs in the camps. For instance, office workers, specialists, and doctors were considered "fools" or "stooges" because of the comfortable positions of the work they did for the camp regime. See Rossi, *Gulag Handbook*, 334.

95. GU RK NARK 2 f. P-3800, op. 1, d. 163 ll. 109–111 (Kotov, "Nina Mikhailovna Sobinova," in "Vospominanie," Gdansk, Poland, 1992).

96. Ibid., 112.

97. Ibid.

98. Ibid., 119, 122. Kotov also reviewed Boris D'iakov's memoir about the Gulag published under the title "*Perezhitoe*" in the journal in *Zvezda* in 1963. Kotov's criticism of D'iakov sheds some light on his own political beliefs: "To praise the power that sent him to *katorga* as an innocent person. Is this not an unnatural phenomenon?" (118).

99. AVMG (Flug, "Chernyi ostrov GULAGa"), 49.

100. AVMG ("Editorial Board of *Novyi mir* to K. Flug, September 14, 1987" reproduced in "Chernyi ostrov GULAGa"), 2.

101. AVMG (Flug, "Chernyi ostrov GULAGa"), 13, 49.

102. Ibid., 7.

103. Ibid. On Gulag returnees' acceptance of the label of "victim of political repression" and the denial that they were victims, see AFP op. 1, d. 29, l. 1 (V. B. Ol'shevskii, "Vyzhit! Ot Bamlaga do Pechlaga," Kiev, 1991); AM f. 2, op. 3, d. 59, ll. 33–34 (Marushchiak, "Biograficheskaia rukupis' vospominanii"). See also GU RK NARK 2 f. P-3800, op. 1, d. 16, l. 9, 49 (L. M. Gorodin, "Rasskazy, vospominaniia"

1962–1977); GU RK NARK 2 f. P-3800, op. 1, d. 156, ll. 22–45 (Serov, "Piat' let i vsia zhizn'"); GU RK NARK 2 f. P-3800, op. 1, d. 156, l. 46–47 (L. A. Skriabina-Puzakova, "Ichet-Di," Ichet-Di, 1997); GU RK NARK 2 f. P-3800, op. 1, d. 156, l. 96–97 (K. P. Chudinova, "Vospominaniia o perezhitom proizvole podvergshimsia repressiiam po politicheskim motivam pri raskulachivanii," not dated).

104. AVMG (K. Flug to Vorkuta Gorkom KPSS, November 26, 1983 reproduced in "Chernyi ostrov GULAGa"), 4–5.

105. Ibid., 6.

3

Alternative Forms of Autobiography

Konstantin Ivanov's Letters and Art

After years of corresponding with the Vorkuta Museum–Exhibition Center following the collapse of the Soviet Union, Gulag returnee and artist Konstantin Petrovich Ivanov explained why he never wrote a memoir. In a letter to the museum from December 1996, Ivanov described himself as "derailed" from a life worthy of documenting:

> I don't need to write memoirs, but a confession. When I wrote you about my friends—comrades and, as you say, "in connection to them I mentioned my own affairs"—I could manage.... But to write about myself... that is already a pretension... a claim to be someone. But I am a nobody. I am the most ordinary mediocrity. And generally, I think that only a worthy person can write memoirs. A person who, despite everything in his life, achieved his sacred goal and benefited society with his labor, creativity, and craft, and thus thanked the society for having raised, taught, [and] fed him.[1]

Despite the painfulness of remembering and his hesitancy, Ivanov continued to write his "memoir-letters." He was driven by his attachment to the region where he was once imprisoned and his desire to ensure that his fellow *zeks* and their contributions to the transformation of Vorkuta from prison camp into a Soviet city were commemorated in history: "I never like my scribble, and I send it out only because I feel a debt to the small piece of the history of culture of the great city of Vorkuta.... I am very satisfied by the fact that, in some way, I have managed to be useful to you in your painstaking work in search of the truth (*istina*)."[2] On the basis of Ivanov's archive, this chapter provides a case study of a Gulag returnee that addresses two major issues: how those who survived the

AFTER THE GULAG

brunt of Stalinist violence experienced life after release and how they defined themselves when finally given the chance in the last years of the Soviet Union.

Like the other former prisoners described so far, Ivanov's contribution to the search for the "truth" about the past came toward the end of a period of intense fixation on political repression sparked by glasnost and the collapse of the Soviet Union. Ivanov was one of the hundreds of ordinary political prisoners of Komi's camps who wrote memoirs during this period of renewed interest in the past. Although Ivanov's memoir-letters include many of the central themes of the Gulag memoir genre explored in the previous chapter, such as the tension between individual and collective concerns, they present us with something new.

In contrast to most Gulag memoirs, which are more finished works, Ivanov's memoir-letters illustrate the process of remembering that former prisoners engaged in when they corresponded with Memorial. Despite the time that had passed since his release and the relative openness of the period in which he wrote, Ivanov struggled to write about the camps. Over the course of eight years, Ivanov reconstructed the two parts of his life, two corresponding selves, in an autobiographical narrative of his life in the camps and after release.[3] His narrative is rife with unresolved tension between the two parts of his life and is evident in the frequent chronological shifts he made in his attempt to bridge them.[4] Nevertheless, his letters reveal a deep connection to the city of Vorkuta—the place of his imprisonment and his home for ten years after release among a group of former prisoners that he befriended in the camps; he referred to this group as the "union of outcasts." Like many of his peers, Ivanov described the camps as his "university," despite the horrors he witnessed there. Ivanov focused on the relationships that enabled him to survive the camps and that sustained him after release as he reintegrated into Soviet society. However, Ivanov's letters are unique for their focus on his life after release and shed new light on the bonds among prisoners, friendship, and identity.

The short autobiography that Ivanov recorded in the questionnaires he submitted to Memorial and the Vorkuta Museum–Exhibition Center in 1991 marked the beginning of a process of autobiographical writing. He sent 154 letters to the museum over the course of the last eight years of his life, 1991–1999. The letters that Ivanov regularly wrote to the museum vary in length from one to eighteen pages (with an average length of three to four pages). Although his letters are primarily descriptive, they are punctuated at times with powerful emotion. In addition to this correspondence, Ivanov donated his personal archive to the museum; the archive contained artifacts from his life as a Gulag returnee and a series of artworks themed "Hope Dies Last" (*Nadezhda umiraet poslednei*).[5] From 1983 until his death, Ivanov created fifty-three pieces, which he described as his "memories" of his camp life.[6] These drawings captured the experiences that he could not bring himself to write about.

From 1945 to 1955, Ivanov was a prisoner of Vorkutlag and then Special Camp No. 6 (Rechlag).[7] Located in the Far North, just west of the Ural Mountains, Vorkuta was the capital of one of the first and most populous epicenters of the Gulag.[8] Before his arrest, Ivanov attended art school in Odessa until his studies were interrupted by the outbreak of World War II. Like many Soviet citizens who found themselves in occupied territory during the war, Ivanov was arrested by the People's Commissariat of Internal Affairs (NKVD) following the Red Army's recapture of Sevastopol'. On May 25, 1944, he was sentenced to fifteen years of hard labor (*katorga*) and five years of deprivation of rights under article 58-1a (treason) of the criminal code of the Russian Soviet Federative Socialist Republic.[9] In 1955, a Ministry of Internal Affairs parole board reviewed Ivanov's file, reduced his sentence to ten years, and released Ivanov without the right to leave Vorkuta. Over the next ten years as a citizen of Vorkuta, Ivanov worked as an applied artist at the Vorkuta State Drama Theater and the Vorkuta Television Studio. In 1965, Ivanov was invited to work in the capital of the Komi Autonomous Soviet Socialist Republic (ASSR) at the Syktyvkar Television Studio. After twenty years of living in the Arctic, he left Vorkuta for good. Ivanov chose to live the rest of his life in Syktyvkar with his wife, who had also been repressed and who he met in 1957 while on tour with the Vorkuta Theater.[10] The region that was once his place of imprisonment and exile had become home over the course of many years.[11]

I have organized Ivanov's letters thematically following the chronology of his life as he constructed it. In this way, I am able to illustrate the process of remembering through his letters and art. The first section examines Ivanov's memoir-letters about life in the Gulag, focusing on how he portrayed those years and the link he drew between survival and the development of his sense of self. The second section explores Ivanov's narrative of adaptation to life after release in Vorkuta. In a town one step removed from the Gulag, friends and work as an applied artist were key to Ivanov's reintegration into Soviet society. Ivanov's focus on this period of his life underscores that the Gulag alone did not define him. The third section analyzes Ivanov's Gulag art as a component of his autobiographical narrative. Ivanov's representations of his memories of the Gulag shed light on his attempt to overcome the silences in his memoir-letters by taking us into the darkness of the camps.

Behind Barbed Wire: Narrating Life in the Gulag

Ivanov's writing about life in the camps is sparse.[12] He never takes us down to its darkest depths in his memoir-letters.[13] Instead, when Ivanov did write about life in the camps, he described them as his "university."[14] Like his comrades from the "camp brotherhood" examined in the previous chapter, Ivanov remembered the Gulag as the site of his development. However, because survival depended on certain knowledge that was unavailable to those uninitiated, Ivanov also used this metaphor as a reference to learning to survive the camps. In a two-page letter from 1996, he explained that the strict-regime camp was where he befriended many intellectuals and cultural figures who aided his development as an artist, person, and survivor:

> Rechlag—it was a separate, large chapter of my life. . . . It was a strict-regime camp for only political prisoners sentenced for article 58 with a sentence of at least fifteen years (with the brand KTR—that is, a *katorzhanin*—with a number [on his clothes]). . . . In a way, the strict regime camp turned out to be, especially for the strata of intellectuals, a blessing for us. . . . I met a lot of famous people there. In general, for me, it was one of the most significant courses of my 'university.' I could write a whole book of memoirs about this one camp, which is why I will stop knowing that I will get carried away.[15]

Ivanov's first encounter with the intellectuals in the barracks was one of his most prominent memories of Rechlag. Developing his university metaphor, Ivanov described this moment of self-awareness in an eighteen-page letter from 1996: "They were all strong men who managed to survive and acquired new professions, having become good, law-abiding specialists and leaders of labor. But among them there were also intellectuals: doctors, teachers, scientists, and simply intellectuals."[16] Uncertain about his place among this group of elites, Ivanov continued: "And how did I wind up here in their company? I couldn't make sense of it. You see, I was neither one nor the other. . . . And then I learned that I wasn't the only one who thought about all this. From [our] collective reflections, the following conclusions emerged. . . . [Our zone] was the 'brain trust' of the 'society of zeks' [*mozgovaia chast' obshchestva zekov*]."[17] Although Ivanov eventually befriended many of these men and lived among them after release, he did not define himself as an intellectual.[18]

Ivanov presented his memories of the camps in a mosaic of contrasting images. He found friendship and learned about the art of survival in the special camp, whereas the general-regime camp, Vorkutlag—where he was sent on temporary reassignment to work as a laborer—was an education of an entirely different kind. There Ivanov struggled to put the destructiveness of the camps into words, which he alluded to in a six-page letter from March 1996: "Everyone looked at me, with my numbers on my hat, jacket, and pants, like I was a scarecrow. No one greeted me. No one wanted to complicate their life. They brought a *katorzhanin*, well, let him be and let us live on our own."[19] There is no further mention of his physical state or the toll of hard labor on his body in the rest of Ivanov's letter. This aspect makes Ivanov's simile, "like I was a scarecrow," all the more powerful. It is a glimpse into what Ivanov endured, which we do not fully see until he reveals it to us in his illustrations of prisoners' emaciated bodies breaking under the weight of the daily production quota.[20] It is also a statement about the added difficulty of surviving with the brand of *katorzhanin*, whom Solzhenitsyn referred to as "the doomed."[21]

Katorzhane were supposed to be isolated from the rest of the prisoner population and put to extreme hard labor with sentences of up to twenty-five years. Known by its tsarist-era name, *katorga* was a punishment reserved for those accused of especially egregious crimes against the Soviet people or Red Army prisoners of war, such as collaboration with the enemy; the term was introduced by decree in 1943.[22] Rather than being physically branded, as they had been during the tsarist era, *katorzhane* in Stalin's camps wore numbers on their clothing, unlike other prisoners. Furthermore, mortality rates among this contingent were some of the highest in the Gulag system.[23] As Steve Barnes, Alan Barenberg, Golfo Alexopoulous, and Mikhail Nakonechnyi have shown, *katorzhane* such as Ivanov existed within a "hierarchy of detention" intended not only to isolate, punish, and reeducate but also to exploit prisoner labor for economic ends, which created conflicts between Soviet legal theory and how it was practiced in the camps.[24]

One of the keys to Ivanov's survival and development was his circle of camp comrades. While Ivanov "learned as much as he could" about art and self-preservation from his circle of close friends, these prisoners also provided an important source of mutual aid. Ivanov received a temporary stay of this "dry execution" thanks to the efforts of his friends, who intervened on his behalf to get him released from lockdown in the strict-regime barracks and temporarily transferred to the camp-planning division, where he illustrated blueprints for architects.[25] As Ivanov explained in one of his longest letters in 1996, "Their intrigue turned out in my favor. Under pressure from the intellectuals, the boss of the architecture department of the planning division took me under his protection, and I was taken on as a copier, and then I took Konstantin's place [as a drafter]. I began to draw and color architectural plans. Of course, the main 'foundations' were done by the architects themselves, but I gradually mastered this field."[26]

Another key to Ivanov's survival was, to use Golfo Alexopoulos's phrase, "avoiding physical exploitation."[27] In the same letter from 1996, Ivanov underscored the importance of his life-saving, permanent reassignment to work as an artist in the cultural-educational department: "It was what I needed. It was as if I received a mandate from the very head [of the camp section] to work illegally at the cultural-educational department. What a stroke of luck. By that time in my journey through hell, I'd gone through 'fire, water, and bronze pipes,' and therefore I learned well 'to strike while the iron was hot.'"[28] With this reference to his "journey through hell," Ivanov once again alludes to the painful memories he was only able to convey through his art. For Ivanov and other prisoners, such as Thomas Sgovio, who survived the camps of Kolyma, obtaining a "soft job" was deliverance from the slow death of becoming a lifeless "goner" on the path to "early release"—death.[29] In addition to explaining his survival, Ivanov included these details to contextualize the continuity between his life in the camps and after release.

Ivanov did not write in a vacuum. Comparing his memoir-letters with the more finished works of his comrades led Ivanov to reflect on the incompleteness of his remembering.[30] In a brief note to a camp mate in 1992, Ivanov thanked his friend for sending him the first published collection of memoirs written by survivors of Komi's camps, *Sorrowful Pier.*[31] Despite feeling that he was not up to the task of writing a memoir, Ivanov expressed regret that he did not contribute to the collection: "The memory of that experience (such a long gone past) is so close to the heart. It is a very interesting collection of memoir authors. *Sorrowful Pier*—it is my refuge. My comrades-in-education [*odnokashniki*] write so well. It grieves me that, in my own time, I did not manage to do the same, but for that, one needs facts, and I don't have any."[32] It seems Ivanov doubted that his memories were enough to serve as historical testimony. Like so many of his peers, accuracy was important to Ivanov as he realized that his letters had become a part of the larger effort to rewrite the past. Despite the incompleteness of his memory, he continued to write to the museum to ensure that his comrades and their contributions to the city of Vorkuta were remembered: "I am endlessly happy that, thanks to your initiative, I managed to briefly tell about my friend, about that time—that, although only to a small extent, I helped you draw back the curtain of time concealing the years past."[33]

ALTERNATIVE FORMS OF AUTOBIOGRAPHY

107

Life after Release in Vorkuta, 1955–1964

If the Gulag was his university, then Vorkuta during the "Thaw" was where Ivanov found himself. In a letter from 1992, he described this part of his life as "a time of a great change . . . The golden age of the 'Thaw' . . . the time of mass releases of political prisoners . . . a time, for a while, of select complete rehabilitations. For us [it was] a bright ray of hope! We emerged from the darkness! Faith in tomorrow appeared. [It was] a time of spiritual emancipation."[34] Although the process of adapting to his new life was not easy, Ivanov managed to reintegrate into Soviet society. Ivanov's intense focus on his life after release marks a departure from the Gulag memoir genre, which typically ends with release.[35] "In Gulag memoirs the issue of homecoming," Leona Toker writes, "is treated more or less extensively only when it involves problems of re-adaptation. Release from the camps is not tantamount to homecoming."[36] This is not the case with Ivanov. While he documented the struggles he faced as he readapted to civilian life, Ivanov's focus on "homecoming" reveals his strong connection to Vorkuta, which he referred to as "the city of my unhappiness and small joys."[37] Ivanov, who lived in Vorkuta for ten years after release before he moved to Syktyvkar, strongly identified with the city where he began his "new life" after release.[38]

The story of his release and first days of freedom are an important moment in Ivanov's memoir-letters that mark the beginning of the next part of his life. In the second half of an eighteen-page letter from July 1996, Ivanov vividly described the day of his release after ten years of confinement and the hostility he faced as a former prisoner:

> And then came the day of my own release . . . On the first day of my free life, I visited the Polish artist Cheslava Upatuv [Tsidzik; "Chesia"]. We became acquainted while we were still in 'the raspberry patch' at mine no. 2. We kept secret correspondence through a Muscovite, Raisa Pervina, her former camp comrade in the women's camp at the brick factory. At that time, Chesia had already been released and lived as if in a free town, in an apartment-style barracks outside the zone at the brick factory OLP. We had not even said a word, when women—camp guards who protect the innocence of civilian women—burst into her room. They arrested me, having accused me of an attempt to have intercourse with the former prisoner Upatuv. Chesia cried, trying to show the purity of my intentions with regard to her. But they were implacable. For three hours, they held me in an isolation cell. And when they let me out, they drove me to the bus stop and said, 'Forget the road to our

neighborhood, find yourself a woman there, where you were imprisoned. Or else a certificate won't help you—we will throw you in prison again and you'll cry for your freedom.' At first, during the period of general releases, we encountered such paradoxical incidents. Zealous servants of the regime could not come to peace with real events—the mystery of the prisoners' period of transition.[39]

Figure 3.1 K. P. Ivanov, Vorkuta, December 1955 (eight months after release). Source: Personal collection of A. A. Popov, Syktyvkar, Russia.

Although many of Vorkuta's residents at that time were former prisoners, others did not know what to think of their new neighbors and had difficulty shaking the image of them as "enemies of the people." This image had been reinforced by decades of propaganda and the chaos that ensued after the 1953 amnesty that released many of Vorkutlag's criminals.[40] In addition to prolonged suspicion, Gulag returnees also faced legal discrimination in housing and at work, even in places like Vorkuta, where approximately one-third of local residents in the 1950s were former prisoners.[41] Ivanov remembered release not as an end to his persecution, leading to the restoration of his status as an upstanding Soviet citizen, but rather as the beginning of a new time in which he navigated a gray zone between freedom and unfreedom (fig. 3.1).[42]

Work at the Vorkuta State Drama Theater played an important role in Ivanov's transition back into Soviet society. It was at the theater where Ivanov felt he redeemed the time he lost and contributed something to Soviet society. Ivanov obtained employment at the Vorkuta theater in 1955 through his friend and fellow former prisoner Konstantin Gusev, who had been released only a few months earlier.[43] As the city's cultural center, the Vorkuta State Drama Theater was originally an institution of Vorkutlag's political department, which was responsible for the reeducation of prisoners, and a source of entertainment for local residents. In a twelve-page letter from 1994, Ivanov described working at the theater as "the more important time of my life."[44] In another ten-page letter dated 1996, Ivanov described the theater as a place of personal redemption, where he recovered the youth he lost to the camps: "You served eleven years in a camp—this is the time when you're supposed to be developing yourself an artist. Time passed, you won't catch up." However, Ivanov continued, "I found myself in the niche at the theater. Self-reliance, independence, and spiritual satisfaction."[45] The theater served as a sort of halfway house where repressed artists practiced their craft and participated in the development of culture in Vorkuta—a microcosm of the Soviet society they built in the Far North.[46]

In his role at the theater, Ivanov produced ideologically infused art that kept within the bounds of Soviet cultural norms.[47] Although Ivanov adhered to the standards of the time in his artwork, he was given free rein to create. His work at the theater did not go unnoticed by party officials from Syktyvkar, who made the trip north to attend the theater incognito. In a twelve-page letter written in 1994, Ivanov remembered being summoned to the director's office after the performance, where he was met by the deputy minister of culture and the deputy director of the cultural department of the Komi Obkom. Much to his relief, the two officials praised Ivanov's set design and costumes and invited him to drink with them.[48] As an episode in Ivanov's narrative, the details of his work in the theater and his emphasis on the praise it received from party officials demonstrate the importance of work as a means of surviving exile. Perhaps most important, Ivanov's story shows how he performed his rehabilitation by successfully presenting himself as a Soviet person through his mastery of Soviet culture.[49]

In another four-page letter written in 1993, Ivanov expanded on the theme of his work and the gradual softening of local authorities' attitudes toward former prisoners. In 1957, the "union of outcasts" was hired by the city soviet and the executive committee to decorate "our gray city" in preparation for the youth festival.[50] Ivanov painted a mural depicting "smiling boys and girls on a background of a bright blue sky with white clouds. They were dressed in various, colorful national costumes surrounded by flowers with the slogan, 'Peace to the earth,' and to so on—stereotypes of those quite cheerful, heady days of freedom."[51] Although the mural was well received and the artists were paid on time, things did not end there. When they divvied up their collective pay, the former prisoners registered some of the earnings to others who contributed to the project, which also enabled them to avoid paying their full share of taxes. This drew the attention of the police, who initiated a criminal investigation into corruption:

Two weeks later, I received a summons to report to the investigator. But we were lucky that this happened in those years! It was our golden time, as they say, "our hour of triumph." The investigator that we ended up with was an intelligent and reasonable man. . . . I wrote my testimony in about two hours. I honestly described everything (there was nothing for me to hide). [I wrote] only what I concealed from the woman who uncovered our trickiness when she signed the ledger, but she didn't react in any way. The investigator carefully read my testimony, smiled and said, "You described it well." He saw our decorations [around the city], which he liked. It turned out by the time we met that he had almost finished the investigation of the case against us. He had questioned many witnesses, certified the description of [our] work and the expenses, but he didn't find anything criminal anywhere. "Of course," he said, "it would be possible to accuse you of tax evasion, but what you did in this case is not a violation of the law as it is written." . . . Generally, it all blew over. This was also a sign of those times. For lack of evidence of a crime, the case was dismissed.[52]

The documents that Ivanov selected for donation to the archive of the Vorkuta Museum–Exhibition Center, which included playbills, art, identification cards, photographs, and letters of recognition from the Union of Soviet Artists of the Komi ASSR, also demonstrate Ivanov's pride as a former prisoner and artist who participated in the reformation of Vorkuta into a Soviet city (fig. 3.2).[53] Ivanov included these artifacts from his archive with his letters to the museum to historicize his membership in the community and to verify his narrative of forced migration and a life in the arts: "I don't know whether you need them? It seemed to me that these [things] are also history."[54] As Ivanov commented on the theater programs and photos he sent to the museum in 1993, "I look at them and then a warm breeze of years long past warms my soul a little."[55] The fact that the things he donated came from his postcamp life underscores the importance of this period. The Gulag alone did not define him.

The letter that accompanied these artifacts also tells us something about how Ivanov related to his postcamp self from the present. Among the documents he donated to the museum was the transcript of a televised speech he delivered in 1961 on the meaning of art under communism and the creation of an authentic Soviet self. It read in part, "The theory of communism originates from the idea that every pursuit of any person is, in a communist society, an authentic creation (work)—it is an active and indisputable development of man himself, a manifestation of the highest possibilities of his reason, his feelings, his arms and body."[56] Reading these lines thirty-two years later in 1993, Ivanov reflected on this former version of himself: "It seems that at that

Figure 3.2   Ivanov's theater identification card issued in 1957. Source: Vorkuta Museum–Exhibition Center (VMVTs f. OF 4262, op. 1, d. 2, l. 1).

time I still worked as a propagandist-artist for the enlightenment-educational division of Vorkuta . . . I thought that I had matured since then, but reading these old records, I now realize the crudity and primitiveness of [my] thought. Maybe more is understood [now], but this is not education—it's amateur."[57] Throughout Ivanov's correspondence, there is tension between the two periods of his life—in and after the Gulag—in his memoir-letters. As Ivanov read his old manuscripts in the wake of the Soviet collapse, there is tension between the present in which Ivanov wrote and the past he reconstructed through the process of remembering. This tension between Ivanov's past and present was a product not only of the genres he drew from his memoir-letters but also of the need he felt to explain himself and how he fit into Soviet society.[58] It is worth noting that when he reflected on his past words, Ivanov did not say that he did not believe these words when he wrote them, despite having been imprisoned and exiled by the communist state for decades.

A core component of Ivanov's memoir-letters is his memorialization of those who helped him readapt to civilian life after release.[59] In a ten-page letter written in 1992, Ivanov wrote at length about the friendships that sustained him and the community of Gulag returnees that became an essential part of his new life. He described this community as the "Vorkuta Union of Artists," an informal "club of survivors and those released from the camps, of unaccomplished dropouts. We weren't a union, more so we thought of ourselves as a band of bohemians, an assembly of like-minded lovers of chatting about art, and we were all united in conscience."[60] The group, formed before Ivanov's release by fellow artist and camp comrade Iakov Vunder, worked on official projects. Members shared the profits "as it should have been under 'failed communism.'"[61]

AFTER THE GULAG

Although the Vorkuta Union of Artists was initially an informal group comprised of former prisoners, it eventually became a branch of the Komi ASSR Union of Soviet Artists—the main organization that employed and helped artists, especially those who had been imprisoned, find work in their respective fields.[62]

In this same letter, Ivanov described how former prisoners banded together and helped each other adapt to civilian life:

> Everyone needed to exchange their camp overalls for a normal civilian suit. Everyone needed to find a shelter, a roof over one's head, to get fixed up in a job, especially in one's field. After all, we still did not have the right to go home or to move to another place. They freed us from the camps with the right to live only in Vorkuta. Collective actions helped us to adapt more quickly to [our] new life. And thus, our so-called "Union" was "a voluntary club of artists and outcasts." [It was] a club without a meeting place or manual. The organizer of this union, of all of us half-starving artists after release, was the artist Iakov Iakovlevich Vunder—the soul of the club. His home was our first shelter. His poor wife—the [vol'nonaemnaia] ballerina Maria Grigor'evna Vunder—had to put in a lot of thought and physical energy to feed this crowd of outcasts during our meetings . . . although, at that time in the city, already more than half of the population consisted of "formers." In almost every Vorkuta family, you met guests who were not of one's station [ne po odezhke], who themselves in the past bore the many burdens of deprivation [of freedom]—all of whom were welcoming and hospitable. Back then there were none of today's publicized charitable organizations. We did everything by ourselves, without profit or publicity.[63]

Ivanov's "comrades-in-education" clearly played an essential role in his readaptation to Soviet society. However, his letter also emphasized the self-reliance of the group, which it seems Ivanov saw as almost superior to those who did not experience the Gulag. As Alan Barenberg shows, such social networks were widespread in Vorkuta, even among those who did not know one another.[64] The shared experience of imprisonment and the continued discrimination they faced after release formed a powerful social bond, especially among prisoners of the same camp contingent.

In subsequent letters, Ivanov underscored the importance of the union of outcasts as a source of emotional support: "We were all in need of spiritual warmth of one's neighbor. We had this in our 'club' and in every social outcast in the city."[65] Ivanov's letters reflect Gulag returnees' usage of the language of svoi and nash (one of our own), which, as noted in the previous chapter, they used to identify themselves as members of the camp brotherhood.[66] Emphasizing the importance of this community in a letter from 1994, Ivanov described the letters and postcards he received from his camp "classmates" as a "symbol of the warmth and tenderness of people who survived a tragedy together."[67] The names on the postcard shown in figure 3.3 suggest that Ivanov befriended a circle of Polish girls in the camps who were likely repatriated in 1956; they would have been among the very last. Tens of thousands of Polish citizens had been sent to special settlements and camps in the Soviet Union in 1939, following the sweeping wartime deportations that decimated the western borderlands and Poland, and not amnestied in 1941.[68]

In a ten-page letter about the "union" from 1992, Ivanov remembered one of the most important events at the start of his "new life" after release. In autumn 1955, just months after Ivanov was released from Rechlag, the Vorkuta Union of Artists held its first exhibition in the foyer of the Vorkuta State Drama Theater. The exhibition, organized by Iakov Vunder, featured the art of former prisoners Konstantin Gusev, Kraulis Visvaldis, Iurii Shepletto, and Cheslava Tsidzik.[69] As his first exhibition after his release, the show was important to Ivanov not only as a cultural event but also as a means of demonstrating that he belonged in Soviet society. As he wrote in another letter from 1995, "After all, the exhibition is the life of the artist."[70] Despite his newfound freedom, Ivanov remembered the self-censorship required of former prisoners if they wished to remain free.[71] "At the first city exhibition," he recalled, "I showed small portraits of miners and different Rechlag prisoners. Of course, I removed the numbers from the overalls otherwise they would not have made it to the exhibit. I also did not indicate the family names. They went out under the general subtitle, 'Toilers of the Arctic Stokehold.'"[72] Furthermore, when prisoners' artwork was shown at all-union exhibitions in Moscow, it went out under the general title, "Exhibition of Komi Artists." As Ivanov explained in a six-page letter from 1995, "When our artists [nashi] from Vorkuta, Syktyvkar, Ukhta, Inta presented at all-union exhibitions in Moscow, they were called artists from Komi, or an exhibition of artists of Komi (that is the Komi branch of the union)."[73]

The subjects of Ivanov's artwork during this period suggest his desire to document the remnants of the camps, the origins of the city, and Ivanov's "university" before they disappeared as Vorkuta rapidly grew. This work was influenced by the education he received from his camp comrade, which continued outside the barbed wire. Ivanov accompanied his friend Vunder on trips into the tundra as field artist to document the natural environment of the Arctic for the Vorkuta Geological Expedition.[74] In 1960, Ivanov participated in the "Second Exhibition of Vorkuta Artists" to mark the opening of the Vorkuta Regional History Museum. Once again, Ivanov's artistic eye was fixed on Vorkuta's flora and fauna, which we see in his landscape of the remnants of the "infamous" camp section no. 59, entitled "Usinsk Street" (fig. 3.4).[75] The painting depicts a gray,

Figure 3.3 Postcard sent to Ivanov from his friends on the Vorkuta-Moscow train home after release, 1956. (*above*) The postcard reads, "Dear Kostia! We send you a heartfelt hello from the road. We're getting along wonderfully. We are not worried for Chesia, she will leave soon too. You probably have heard the news as well. Don't forget us. Barbara, Broni, Taniia, and Frank." (*facing*) Front: Ostankino Palace-Museum of Serf Art. Source: Vorkuta Museum–Exhibition Center (VMVTs f. OF 4262, op. 1, d. 2, l. 3).

derelict camp section. The prisoner barracks are surrounded by guard towers and a barbed-wire fence, which separates the camp zone from the city just outside its gates. The painting is emblematic of Ivanov's position in Vorkuta—a former prisoner shaped by the camps and bound to the city as an exile. This theme is featured in another one of Ivanov's landscapes from the same period. We see two parts of Ivanov's life rendered in a landscape of the coal mine, "Kapital'naia," as seen from the attic of the original drama theater that burned in 1958 (fig. 3.5).[76] In another landscape from the same period, Ivanov shows us the space where he transitioned into his life as a free man, with a landscape of the street on the outskirts of town cast in a golden hue by the midnight sun of the Arctic (fig. 3.6).[77] The colors of this landscape are noticeably brighter, and despite the ramshackle appearance of the buildings on the outskirts of town, the midsummer light that Ivanov captured reflects the warmness he described in his letters about life after release and the community to which he belonged.

Ivanov also sent a landscape of the Iun'-Iaga mine to the museum, which he sketched as it was undergoing construction in 1958 (fig. 3.7), although there is no indication that he presented it at the 1960 exhibition. The sketch is a part of the visual record that Ivanov created to document the city "of his unhappiness and small joys." By juxtaposing the four perspectives, we see the camp origins of the city and its rebirth as an Arctic mining town at the start of Ivanov's "new life."

Figure 3.4 K. P. Ivanov, "Usinsk Street," April 1959, oil on canvas. Source: Vorkuta Museum–Exhibition Center.

Figure 3.5 K. P. Ivanov, "View of the Mine 'Kaptial'naia' from the Attic of the Burned Theater," 1957, watercolor. Source: Vorkuta Museum–Exhibition Center.

Figure 3.6 K. P. Ivanov, "Summer. Midnight. On My Roof," 1959–1969, oil on canvas. Source: Vorkuta Museum–Exhibition Center.

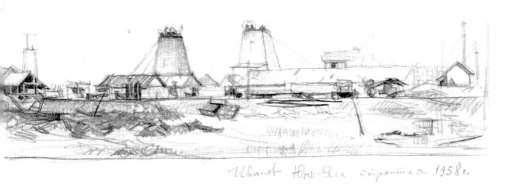

Figure 3.7 K. P. Ivanov, "Iun'-Iaga Under Construction," 1958, pencil. Source: Vorkuta Museum–Exhibition Center (VMVTs f. NVF, op. 1, d. 4, l. 1).

A recurring theme in Ivanov's memoir-letters is the pride he felt and the painful lack of recognition of Gulag returnees' contribution to Vorkuta's growth.[78] Citing their suffering as prisoners and their work as artists after release, Ivanov emphasized the significance of "union members" who, "despite everything, made their massive contribution to the development of culture in Vorkuta."[79] In another three-page letter from 1993, Ivanov elaborated on the role that former prisoners played in the city's transformation:

> The fact is that in those old times, every factory, office, enterprise needed a person capable of performing font graphic works or other artistic design works for the implementation of the so-called visual agitation, starting from the wall press, slogans, the design of signs and diagrams, to scenery for amateur artistic performances. Previously, all these works were performed free of charge by artists from the camps. But new times had come. The talented workforce was no more. But the demand for visual agitation remained. There were no studios that could have fulfilled this demand in the city. Furthermore, even if they existed, they would not have been able to staff daily. And thus, bosses began to offer artists permanent employment as staff, but they were not registered as artists. Instead, artists started [to work] as engineer-technicians or some sort of high-paying job as a technical worker.[80]

The lack of acknowledgment fueled Ivanov's efforts to ensure that his comrades and their contributions would be remembered. However, the emotions raised by these memories led Ivanov to question the distorting effect they may have had on his process of remembering: "So, without pretending to the truth (*istina*), I described our heroes, my colleagues, comrades, and friends. I tried to be objective. But my memory lets me down."[81]

Ivanov moved to Syktyvkar with his family in 1964. Although he briefly mentioned this period of his life in several letters, he did not say much. It seems that Ivanov was not happy about the move to Syktyvkar, nor were his friends in Vorkuta, but he moved anyway because his wife was in poor health. As Ivanov wrote in 1994, "I did not really want to leave Vorkuta. I lost a lot in pay, but my wife's health was more important. Iasha was very upset about my departure. Iasha and Amman accompanied us [to the landing strip]."[82] Despite his sadness about leaving the Arctic city that had become his home, Ivanov was happy to see another old friend and fellow artist from the camp, Kraulis Visvaldis, who was waiting for him at the airport.[83]

Ivanov's memoir-letters frequently digress from the topic at hand to illustrate an episode from the camp or describe a comrade to properly contextualize his life after release. As Ivanov wrote after a series of detours in 1993, "Forgive me for another long digression. When remembering the past, images arise, which are difficult to ignore. And the more positive occurrences are remembered, and the negative are left in the remote of the past. The good is more easily remembered. The bad you always want to forget."[84] These digressions throughout his correspondence reveal the porousness between the two periods of his life and the pain of remembering, which he attempted to overcome in his art.

"Hope Dies Last": Art as Memory and Narrative

Six years after his release from Rechlag, on November 24, 1961, Ivanov delivered a televised speech announcing the grand opening of the Vorkuta Art School and Studio, which he directed. It was a place where former prisoners and young artists came together to develop their craft and to study life in the tundra.[85] Ivanov's speech celebrated the achievements of Vorkuta's cultural scene and the role of art in building Soviet society. For Ivanov, art was more than entertainment. It was the means of elevating and transforming man and society: "For artists, paintings are a specific means of studying the world. This method makes it possible not only to recognize forms of nature but also to creatively capture them—that is, to turn them into forms of art."[86] Ivanov expounded on the purpose of art and the manifestation of one's true self: "Art is needed because it is in art that man is higher, a more complete manifestation

ALTERNATIVE FORMS OF AUTOBIOGRAPHY

of his versatile capabilities. Knowledge of art offers that which science cannot: it reflects man and all the world in its integrity, its correspondence and value from an aesthetic point of view of the ideal representation of harmony."[87] As a former prisoner addressing his neighbors by radio, Ivanov posited a vision of art as a tool for the spiritual mastery of the world, a means of overcoming the limitations of man. How, then, did Ivanov use those tools to represent his memories of the Gulag?

In a one-page letter to the Vorkuta Museum written in 1995, Ivanov described his Gulag art series as "the history of my life, my memory,"[88] which was valuable to him "not as works of art, but as memory."[89] Much like other repressed artists, Ivanov produced artwork as documentation of those formative years and representation of his memories.[90] The artwork he produced is a component of the same process of remembering that produced his memoir-letters; however, Ivanov felt much more comfortable reliving the past through this medium.

Time and again, Ivanov refused to write a memoir, citing the unpleasantness of remembering and writing about those difficult times. In a letter to the Vorkuta Museum dated June 26, 1996, Ivanov wrote that he wanted to refuse Syktyvkar Memorial's request to interview him for a documentary film about the society and its ongoing work to commemorate the victims of political repression. Nevertheless, he did not refuse because Syktyvkar Memorial helped him obtain rehabilitation in 1992, when he had thought it was a lost cause after decades of rejected petitions. Furthermore, he thought of Mikhail Rogachev, Syktyvkar Memorial's deputy chairman and head of the historical department, as his "guardian angel" for the care and respect he showed Ivanov as a survivor of Stalinist repression.[91] However, despite his willingness to testify, Ivanov explained that when they asked to speak about life in the camps, it was difficult for him to remember and to decide what to say—the camera made him nervous. Ivanov preferred to sit and write letters and to draw his memories in calm and quiet.[92] Ivanov's choice to use visual art as the media of his Gulag memoir should be read in the way it was intended, as a part of his autobiographical narrative. His artwork is a manifestation of his self looking back as a survivor.

In a letter to the Vorkuta Museum and Exhibition Center written in 1995, Ivanov explained that he began the project while he was imprisoned in Rechlag but did not resume it until his retirement in 1983.[93] When he was asked again about his Gulag art by Rogachev in the 1995 documentary film *Oni spasut Rossiiu*, Ivanov replied, "When I retired, I decided to remember all of that life. And

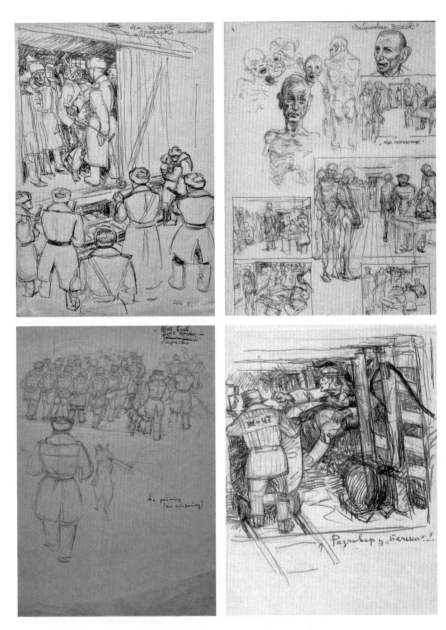

Figure 3.8 K. P. Ivanov, (*top left*) "En Route, 1944"; (*top right*) "Prisoner Selection"; (*bottom left*) "Step to the Left, Step to the Right, I Shoot"; (*bottom right*) "Conversation by the Stove." Ivanov made several sketches of prisoner convoys that included his prisoner number A-837. Source: Vorkuta Museum–Exhibition Center and A. A. Popov (for "Prisoner Selection" and "Conversation by the Stove," see VMVTs f. OF 3673, op. 1, d. 16, ll. 4, 18; "En Route, 1944" and "Step to the Left, Step to the Right, I Shoot" are from the personal collection of A. A. Popov, Syktyvkar, Russia).

Figure 3.9　K. P. Ivanov, "Plank Beds." Source: Vorkuta Museum–Exhibition Center (VMVTs f. OF 3673, op. 1, d. 16, l. 17).

Figure 3.10　K. P. Ivanov, "Prayer-Roll Call." Source: Vorkuta Museum–Exhibition Center (VMVTs f. OF 3673, op. 1, d. 16, l. 16).

Figure 3.11 K. P. Ivanov, "Without a Last One!" Source: Vorkuta Museum–Exhibition Center (VMVTs f. OF 3673, op. 1, d. 16, l. 3).

I began to do the sketches for future compositions."[94] He began the project with several portraits of prisoners done "from nature" in pencil "behind the barbed wire," which he smuggled out of the camp zone and subsequently gave away.[95] Although Ivanov lost the originals, he wrote that the experiences were ingrained in his memory and described his Gulag art as his "memoirs about the distant past."[96] The pieces he completed were part of a planned larger work that ultimately went unfinished.[97] The fact that Ivanov started this work in the camps and returned to it thirty-two years later shows not only that his memories of the Gulag remained with him but also that he felt the importance of documenting his experiences in the camps through art; he sketched "for the drawer" before the return of the topic of political repression to public discourse during glasnost. Although he did not expect his art would ever see the light of day, it is important to note that Ivanov returned to this project with the intent of transmitting the memory of Stalinist repression to future generations. As he wrote in the margins of one untitled storyboard sketch: "For the eternal memory of future generations. The terrible chapters of my country in illustrations."[98] Ivanov's art explores themes developed in his memoir-letters,

Figure 3.12 K. P. Ivanov, "Godfathers Play Cards/Criminal Group." The caption next to Stalin's face associates Stalin with common criminals. It reads, "Boss, teacher, father (godfather)." Source: Personal collection of A. A. Popov, Syktyvkar, Russia.

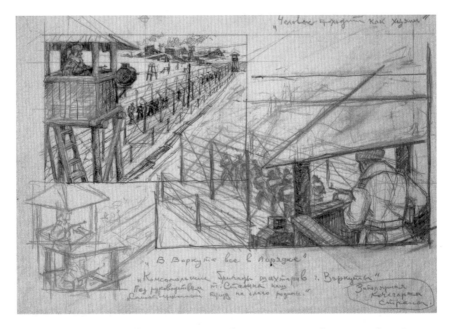

Figure 3.13 K. P. Ivanov, "A Man Passes By Like a Master, in Vorkuta Everything Is Alright." Source: Vorkuta Museum–Exhibition Center (VMVTs f. OF 3673, op. 1, d. 16, l. 8).

especially his description of the Gulag as a place of his derailment but also his development. His works capture the fierceness and beauty of the camp environment and the bonds prisoners forged by surviving it (figs. 3.8–3.24).[99]

"Hope Dies Last" recreates scenes from his life in Vorkutlag and Rechlag, illustrating the entire cycle of the prisoner experience from transport to selection and assignment on arrival to "early release" through death.[100] By including his own prisoner number (A-837) in some of his illustrations, such as "Miners KTR '45–'46" (fig. 3.20) and "The Path to Early Release" (fig. 3.17), Ivanov reveals the link between his individual experiences and the collected memory of the camps, which he shared with his "comrades in misfortune" and documented in his art. Unlike other Gulag returnees' art done in a more fantastic and surrealistic fashion, Ivanov's works represent a genre that Katya Pereyaslavska calls "authentic realism."[101] Ivanov's artworks document the landscape, camp architecture, prisoner clothing, and scenes from everyday life to illustrate prisoners' humanity and the inhumanity of the camps. They represent the environment that shaped Ivanov and his fellow union members.

Figure 3.14 K. P. Ivanov, "Untitled." Source: Vorkuta Museum—Exhibition Center (VMVTs f. OF 3673, op. 1, d. 16, l. 19).

Such works, Pereyaslavska writes, offer their "own version of 'reality in its revolutionary development.'"[102]

In Ivanov's contributions to this genre, such as his drawings of miners, we see the *katorzhane* who provided coal to the country. However, in this version, the numbers Ivanov once removed to pass the censor are restored to reveal the true identities of the lauded heroes of socialist labor. In his sketch, "A Man Passes By Like a Master" (fig. 3.13), Ivanov mocks the official narrative that

Figure 3.15 K. P. Ivanov, "Polar Stokehold of the Country." Source: Vorkuta Museum–Exhibition Center (VMVTs f. OF 3673, op. 1, d. 16, l. 15). Ivanov wrote about "Polar Stokehold of the Country": "The wire passage from the mine zone to the residential zone. I passed through this passage from OLP-2 to mine no. 2"; see VMVTs f. OF 4327, op. 1, d. 22, l. 3 [Ivanov to Fesenko, December 16, 1995]).

Komsomol brigades built Vorkuta by juxtaposing prisoners passing through a corridor of barbed wire on their way to work under the deadly eyes of automatic rifles, with the slogan, "Komsomol brigades of miners of the city of Vorkuta. Under the leadership of comrade Stalin, we dedicate our selfless labor to the benefit of the motherland."[103] In "Plank Beds" (fig. 3.9), "Prayer-Roll Call" (fig. 3.10), and "Goner" (fig. 3.16), Ivanov shows the emaciated bodies of prisoners on their "last legs," which he could not bring himself to describe in his letters. In "Without a Last One!" (fig. 3.11), Ivanov visually represents the violence that he and other political prisoners suffered at the hands of the criminals and camp staff. And in "The Path to Early Release" (fig. 3.17), Ivanov reveals the most frequently traveled road out of the camps: death—the path that Ivanov was spared by his friends' intervention. This artwork disrupts the socialist realist image of prisoners reforged by their labor and reveals the reality of the camps through the eyes of a survivor. Many of these images show the numbers

Figure 3.16 K. P. Ivanov, "Goner." Source: National Museum of the Komi Republic.

Figure 3.17 K. P. Ivanov, "The Path to Early Release." Source: Vorkuta Museum–Exhibition Center (VMVTs f. OF 3673, op. 1, d. 16, l. 6).

that *katorzhane* were forced to wear, which Ivanov frequently described in his letters as a "brand."[104]

The obvious exceptions are Ivanov's only finished pieces in the series, entitled "Love in the Mine," "Despair," and "Memory of Vorkuta" (fig. 3.24). In "Love in the Mine" (fig. 3.24a), Ivanov provides a glimpse of a relationship between a man and a woman, which was forbidden in the camps, and suggests that there was romance, as well as friendship. The darkness surrounding the couple in the center of this piece suggests the light and comfort that such a relationship brought two suffering people. This is also the theme of an unfinished sketch with the same title (fig. 3.24c) that features prisoners underground in a coal mine cradling a child born into "that world." While sex in the Gulag was frequently documented in acts of violence, it

Figure 3.18   K. P. Ivanov, "Untitled" *or* "Miners of the Polar Stokehold"? Source: Vorkuta Museum–Exhibition Center (VMVTs f. OF 3673, op. 1, d. 16, l. 14).

Figure 3.19   K. P. Ivanov, "Architectural Forms of Stalinist Prosperity." Source: Vorkuta Museum–Exhibition Center (VMVTs f. OF 3673, op. 1, d. 16, l. 20).

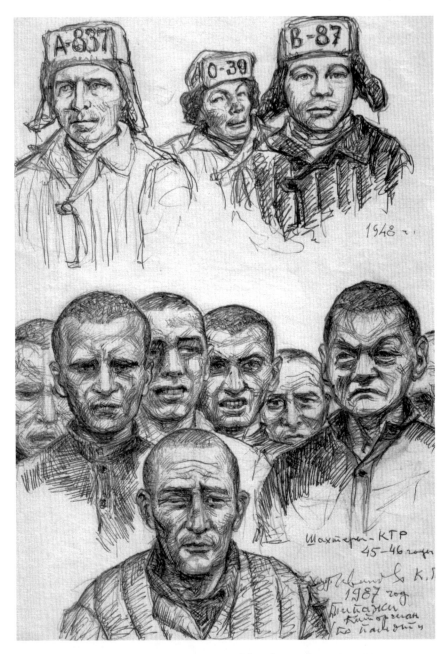

Figure 3.20 K. P. Ivanov, "Miners KTR '45–'46" (1987). Source: Vorkuta Museum–Exhibition Center (VMVTs f. OF 3673, op. 1, d. 16, l. 11).

Figure 3.21 K. P. Ivanov, "Miners-*katorzhanki* '45–'46." Source: Vorkuta Museum–Exhibition Center (VMVTs f. OF 3673, op. 1, d. 16, l. 10).

Figure 3.22 K. P. Ivanov, "A Check of the Correctness of the Number on My Padded Jacket." Source: Vorkuta Museum–Exhibition Center (VMVTs f. OF 3673, op. 1, d. 16, l. 7).

was also, as Wilson Bell writes, a form of prisoner resistance and a source of pleasure.[105] In contrast, "Despair" represents the darkness of the mine, and the dread it filled Ivanov with, in a woodcut and ink print (fig. 3.24d). And finally, Ivanov's most polished work, "Memory of Vorkuta" (fig. 3.24b), surreally depicts the living skeletons that built Vorkuta and the rivers of blood that carried prisoners to its coal mines and bonded them in barbed wire. In this image, the ghosts of the past man the watchtower as Stalin's gaze looks through the viewer out into the tundra. In such images of the camps, as Alexander Etkind writes, the distortions of surrealism combine representation of the past and "frightening" images to express the artist's subjectivity.[106] In Ivanov's only finished pieces, we see both the love and friendship he described in his letters about life after release and the darkness he wanted to forget, which he feared distorted the testimony he produced in his memoir-letters.

Figure 3.23 K. P. Ivanov, "Women Miners Hauling Coal at Mine no. 2." Source: Vorkuta Museum–Exhibition Center (VMVTs f. OF 3673, op. 1, d. 16, l. 12).

Ivanov's work is intended not only as visual evidence of an experience for which there is little photographic evidence but also as a representation of the memories of his camp life he could not convey in words. He felt it was important to include these memories to overcome the silences in his memoir-letters and to explain the person he became. In a three-page letter written in 1995, Ivanov described his art as a return to Vorkuta, "the cradle of my formation from prisoner (Z/Ka-exile) into a person."[107] In using art to tell his story about life in the Gulag, Ivanov employed skills he learned in Rechlag and continued to develop after release as he trained with the artists of the union of outcasts and the Vorkuta Union of Artists, which enabled him to create a bridge between the present and his "distant past."

Although Ivanov never exhibited this artwork, he contributed several pieces to Fond Pokaianie's *Martirolog*, a book of memory containing the names,

Figure 3.24 K. P. Ivanov, (*a, top left*) "Love in the Mine"; (*b, top right*) "Memory of Vorkuta"; (*c, bottom left*) "Love in the Mine [sketch]"; (*d, bottom right*) "Despair." Source: A. A. Popov and Vorkuta Museum–Exhibition Center ("Love in the Mine," "Love in the Mine [sketch]," and "Despair" are from the personal collection of A. A. Popov, Syktyvkar, Russia; for "Memory of Vorkuta," see VMVTs f. OF 3673, op. 1, d. 16, l. 22).

memoirs, and archival sources that document the history of the Gulag and political repression in the Komi Republic.[108] Nevertheless, he still had to be convinced that the testimony of his memoir art was of value to Syktyvkar Memorial and others who wanted to understand the truth about those times. As Rogachev told Ivanov about the importance of his work to the growing Memorial archive, "They are trying to save everything. It isn't a museum or art gallery in the usual sense of the word. Rather, it is an archive of art in which every testimony is extremely valuable and not only the originals done in the camps."[109] Perhaps, as he once wrote about Rechlag, Ivanov was painting the book he could not bring himself to write.

In one of his final letters almost a year before his death, Ivanov wrote to the museum about what their correspondence had meant to him. His words were mixed with satisfaction, doubt, and the hope that he remembered as best he could. As Ivanov wrote on August 24, 1998,

> Despite what it cost to remember, I wrote these memories down as they arose. Now, when I begin to write about myself . . . breaking through the thick fog of the long, distant past . . . A place . . . which wasn't!? And a small, bright, happy childhood, and adolescence. And such sicknesses, disorders in our little family . . . and the storm of war . . . occupation, prison, the camps . . . The struggle for life, for a place under the sun with honorable and dishonorable methods. Scribbling with a quill about open wounds, I tried to write about everything. But I could not withstand the pain and dropped the quill. In fact, I turned out to be a weak person [I was not up to the task].[110]

Ivanov's life was shaped by his experiences as a prisoner and an exile in Vorkuta. For him, the Gulag was many things. It was the source of his "derailment" and the "university" that shaped his development as a human being and an artist. His emphasis on the Gulag's influence on the development of his sense self raises questions about the impact of the camps on Gulag returnees as they adapted to life after release. As Ivanov's memoir-letters show, he remembered this period of his life as a prolongation of his alienation as a "former" (i.e., former prisoner), which raises a central question to be explored in the remaining chapters: How did Gulag returnees experience the collapse of the Soviet Union?

Although Ivanov never intended to write a memoir, the letters and art he produced in the process of remembering transformed into a memoir of his life, which started in the camps and evolved into a story about his life after release. While the collapse of the Soviet Union made it possible for Gulag returnees to share their pasts without fear of reprisal, Ivanov provides us with an example of a former prisoner who struggled to write—a struggle other ordinary Gulag returnees also faced. Although Ivanov tried to remember as much as he could, he could not and did not want to put it all down on paper. Writing about the Gulag was too painful, too difficult, and perhaps Ivanov felt that he could not add anything new to the history of political repression at a time when so many of his comrades came forth with their own testimonies.

Ivanov's memoir-letters and art should not be read as a book with a beginning, middle, and end. They should be read and analyzed not only for their content but also for what they so vividly illustrate—the process of remembering. While Ivanov's autobiographical narrative is unique for its focus on life after release, his letters contain themes of the Gulag memoir genre and provide testimony about how Gulag returnees were simultaneously part of and estranged from Soviet society. Ivanov's letters likewise illustrate how the continued discrimination faced by Gulag returnees shaped the formation of their community—the camp brotherhood. The contents of Ivanov's archive underscore what he felt was important for those who had not been imprisoned to know about the Gulag and its former prisoners. By returning to the Gulag to contextualize his life after release, Ivanov traced his origins to a formative moment (in his personal life and history) and claimed an identity that was informed by the union of outcasts, of which he was a member.

Notes

1. Archive of the Vorkuta Museum–Exhibition Center (VMVTs) f. OF 4327, op. 1, d. 16, l. 2 (K. P. Ivanov to G. V. Trukhina, December 10, 1996).

2. VMVTs f. OF 4270, op. 1, d. 6, l. 1 (Ivanov to Trukhina, April 20, 1993). Ivanov's letters served as memoirs. Throughout this article, I refer to his letters as *memoir-letters*.

3. John Paul Eakin, *How Our Lives Become Stories: Making Selves* (Ithaca, NY: Cornell University Press, 1999). On the construction of identity in narrative and autobiographical memory, Eakin writes, "The self in question is a self defined by and transacted in narrative process." See Jerome Bruner, *Acts of Meaning* (Cambridge, MA: Harvard University Press, 1990), 105–106.

4. Alessandro Portelli, *The Death of Luigi Trastulli And Other Stories: Form and Meaning in Oral History* (Albany, NY: SUNY Press, 1991), 20–21, 59–60. Portelli argues that chronological shifts in the narrative are a function of memory captured in oral history testimony. Overlaps in chronology occur when the subject seeks to break down a continuous life narrative into sequential events.

ALTERNATIVE FORMS OF AUTOBIOGRAPHY

5. VMVTs f. OF 4327, op. 1, d. 22, ll. 3 (Ivanov to Z. N. Fesenko, December 16, 1995).

6. VMVTs f. OF 4270, op. 1, d. 22, ll. 9 (Ivanov to Fesenko, September 11, 1995).

7. M. B. Rogachev, ed., *Pokaianie: Martirolog*, t. 12, ch. 1 (Syktyvkar: Fond Pokaianie, 2016), 251; VMVTs f. NVF 3698, op. 1, d. 1, ll. 4 (Collection of materials on the repressed Ivanov).

8. Alan Barenberg, *Gulag Town, Company Town: Forced Labor and Its Legacy in Vorkuta* (New Haven, CT: Yale University Press, 2014), 252–254. Barenberg writes that the prisoner population of Vorkutlag grew from 16,096 in 1939 to 66,290 in 1949. In 1949, the combined prisoner population of Vorkutlag and Rechlag, which was formed as a special camp in 1948 to house especially dangerous prisoners, was 73,064. The prisoner population between the two camps peaked at 77,700 in 1950. After Stalin's death and the mass releases that followed, the prisoner population declined significantly until the camps were shuttered at the end of the 1950s. On the basis of Gulag records, Barenberg estimates that twenty thousand prisoners died in Vorkuta between 1942 and 1954.

9. VMVTs f. NVF 3698, op. 1, d. 1, l. 2 (Ivanov's questionnaire to Moscow Memorial, March 23, 1991). *Katorga* was reintroduced in 1943 as a replacement for the death penalty and was reserved for the worst enemies of the Stalinist regime. It was originally a form of punishment in tsarist Russia and was initially banned by the Bolsheviks. It was reinstated by decree of the Presidium of the Union of Soviet Socialist Republics (USSR) Supreme Soviet "on measures for punishing German fascist villains, spies, and traitors to the Motherland and their accomplices" on April 19, 1943. See Golfo Alexopoulos, *Illness and Inhumanity in Stalin's Gulag* (New Haven, CT: Yale University Press, 2017), 197.

10. VMVTs f. OF 4279, op. 1, d. 15, ll. 4 (Ivanov to Trukhina, April 28, 1993). This is one of the only references Ivanov makes to his wife in all of his correspondence, which focused on his camp family. According to the questionnaires he filed, they had two children.

11. Ivanov was rehabilitated in 1992. He described the bittersweet feeling of rehabilitation in a letter to a camp comrade: "When I received this unexpected news . . . Tears, bitter tears, splashed from my eyes. I waited for this day for almost fifty years." See VMVTs f. NVF 3698, op. 1, d. 3, ll. 2 (Ivanov to Volodia, February 8, 1992).

12. His letters about the camps detail his arrival at Vorkutlag, transfer to the special camp Rechlag, the camp environment and the division between political prisoners and criminals, hard labor, the dehumanization of having to wear a number, and work as an artist for the camp architectural department and cultural-educational department.

13. As a *katorzhanin* (a prisoner sentenced to hard labor, *katorga*), Ivanov clearly saw some of the worst of the camps.

14. VMVTs f. OF 4327, op. 1, d. 16, ll. 2 (Ivanov to Trukhina, December 10, 1996); VMVTs f. OF 4270, op. 1, d. 9, l. 2 (Ivanov to Trukhina, June 15, 1993).

15. VMVTs f. OF 4327, op. 1, d. 16, l. 1.

16. VMVTs f. OF 4327, op. 1, d. 11, 1. 8 (Ivanov to Trukhina, July 30, 1996). In another letter, Ivanov references his friend and artistic mentor, Iakov Vunder, whom he met in Rechlag. Ivanov describes how they learned much (about themselves and their craft) in the camps from "masters" of Soviet painting Petr Bendel' and Boris Deineka, as well as cinematographer Aleksei Kapler. See VMVTs f. OF 4270, op.1, d. 9, l. 2 (Ivanov to Trukhina, June 15, 1993). Kapler also became a huge mentor to former prisoners Iulii Dunskii and Valerii Frid in Rechlag. See Kathleen E. Smith, *Moscow 1956: The Silenced Spring* (Cambridge, MA: Harvard University Press, 2017), 131–132.

17. VMVTs f. OF 4327, op. 1, d. 11, 1. 8 (Ivanov to Trukhina, July 30, 1996).

18. Aleksandr I. Solzhenitsyn, *The Gulag Archipelago: An Experiment in Literary Investigation*, vols. 1–3 (New York: Harper & Row, 1975), 2:280–281. This scene resonates with Solzhenitsyn's rejection of the idea that all political prisoners (and the "trusties" among them) were intellectuals: "Over the years I have had much occasion to ponder this word, the *intelligentsia*. We are all very fond of including ourselves in it—but you see not all of us belong. . . . An intellectual is a person whose interests in and preoccupation with the spiritual side of life are insistent and constant and not forced by external circumstances, even flying in the face of them."

19. VMVTs f. OF 4220, op.1, d. 1, l. 3 (Ivanov to Trukhina, March 12, 1996).

20. Ibid., 8. On katorga, Solzhenitsyn wrote, "Little attempt was made to conceal their purpose: the *katorzhane* were to be done to death. These were, undisguisedly, murder camps: but in the Gulag tradition murder was protracted, so that the doomed would suffer longer and put a little work in before they died"; *Gulag Archipelago*, 2:8. See also Alexopoulos, *Illness and Inhumanity*, 198, 227–231.

21. Solzhenitsyn, *Gulag Archipelago*, 3:7.

22. On the tsarist system of katorga, see Sarah Badcock, *A Prison without Walls? Eastern Siberian Exile in the Last Years of Tsarism* (Oxford: Oxford University Press, 2016); Daniel Beer, *House of the Dead: Siberian Exile under the Tsars* (New York: Knopf, 2017). As Jeff Hardy notes, the Bolsheviks avoided using terms linked to the ancient regime when designing their own penal system; Hardy, *The Gulag after Stalin: Redefining Punishment in Khrushchev's Soviet Union, 1953–1964* (Ithaca, NY: Cornell University Press, 2016), 10–11.

23. Alan Barenberg, "Soviet Katorga Reconsidered: Retribution, Punishment, and Social Control in Wartime and the Postwar," in *Social Control under Stalin*

ALTERNATIVE FORMS OF AUTOBIOGRAPHY 139

and Khrushchev: The Phantom of a Well-Ordered State, ed. Immo Rebitschek and Aaron Retish, 135–160 (Toronto: University of Toronto Press, 2023).

24. Steven Barnes, *Death and Redemption: The Gulag and the Shaping of Soviet Society* (Princeton, NJ: Princeton University Press, 2011), 16–17; Alexopoulos, *Illness and Inhumanity*, 184; Mikhail Nakonechnyi, "'Factory of Invalids': Mortality, Disability, and Early Release on Medical Grounds in GULAG, 1930–1955" (Phd diss., University of Oxford, 2020).

25. Solzhenitsyn described the impossibly high production quotas and low rations in the "destructive labor camps" as "dry execution"; *Gulag Archipelago*, 2:199.

26. VMVTs f. OF 4327, op. 1, d. 11, l. 18 (Ivanov to Trukhina, July 30, 1996).

27. Alexopoulos, *Illness and Inhumanity*, 227–228. See also Leona Toker, *Return from the Archipelago: Narratives of Gulag Survivors* (Bloomington: Indiana University Press, 2000), 17. Toker highlights the concept of "dragging someone out [*vytashchit'*]" of general labor as a central motif of the Gulag memoir genre.

28. VMVTs f. OF 4327, op. 1, d. 11, l. 7 (Ivanov to Trukhina, July 30, 1996).

29. Thomas Sgovio, *Dear America! Why I Turned against Communism* (New York: Partners, 1979), 170–171. Solzhenitsyn described death as "early release" as "the most basic, the steadiest form of Archipelago output there is—with no norms"; *Gulag Archipelago*, 2:221.

30. Ivanov also refers to memoirs written by his friends from Vorkuta, as well as newspapers and books about the Gulag. VMVTs f. NVF 3298, op.1, d. 4, l. 1 (Ivanov to Volodia, April 10, 1992); VMVTs f. NVF 3298, op. 1, d. 5, l. 1 (Volodia to Ivanov, November 3, 1992); VMVTs f. NVF 3298, op. 1, d. 6, ll. 2 (Ivanov to Volodia, October 28, 1992).

31. I. L. Kuznetsov, ed., *Pechal'naia pristan'* (Syktyvkar: Komi Knizhnoe izd-vo, 1991).

32. VMVTs f. NVF 3298, op. 1, d. 4, ll. 1 (Ivanov to Volodia, April 10, 1992).

33. VMVTs f. OF 4270, op. 1, d. 11, l. 1 (Ivanov to Trukhina, October 20, 1992).

34. VMVTs f. OF 4270, op. 1, d. 18, l. 2 (Ivanov to Trukhina, August 18, 1992).

35. Toker, *Return from the Archipelago*, 93.

36. Ibid., 270.

37. VMVTs f. OF 4270, op. 1, d. 1, l. 1 (Ivanov to Trukhina, January 25, 1995).

38. Other Gulag returnees who described release in these terms include, the Archive of the Local History Museum at Ukhta State Technical University (AM UGTU) (A. A. Kotvitskii, "O chem molchit istoriia," Kiev, 1970); Fond Pokaianie Archive (AFP) op. 1, d. 34, ll. 74 (N. P. Volkov, "Gorod trudnoi sud'by," 1965–1970); Archive of the International Memorial Society (AM) f. 2, op. 3, d. 59, ll. 34 (K. P. Marushchiak, "Biograficheskaia rukopis' vospominanii," Syktyvkar, 1989). It seems Ivanov only ever left Komi once after he was sent there. He visited

140   AFTER THE GULAG

Crimea on a honeymoon with his newlywed wife in 1957. See VMVTs f. OF 4279, op. 1, d. 15, ll. 4 (Ivanov to Trukhina, April 28, 1993).

39. VMVTs f. OF 4327, op. 1, d. 11, l. 14 (Ivanov to Trukhina, July 30, 1996).

40. Barenberg, *Gulag Town*, 125; Miriam Dobson, *Khrushchev's Cold Summer: Gulag Returnees, Crime, and the Fate of Reform after Stalin* (Ithaca, NY: Cornell University Press, 2009), 31.

41. Barenberg, *Gulag Town*, 216–222. Barenberg estimates that former prisoners and their families composed one-third of Vorkuta's population of approximately 175,000 by the end of the 1950s.

42. Other Gulag returnees remembered similar experiences, AM f. 2, op.1, d. 88, ll. 22 (P. I. Siamtomov, "Ispoved': Vospominanie," Syktyvkar, Oct. 1990–1991); A. P. Evstiunichev, *Nakazanie bez prestupleniia* (Syktyvkar: Memorial, 1991); AM UGTU (Novokhatskii, "Rokovaia chernaia shinel,'" 1992).

43. VMVTs f. OF 4262, op. 1, d. 9, ll. 12 (Ivanov to Trukhina, January 22, 1994).

44. Ibid., 1.

45. VMVTs f. 4327, op. 1, d. 44, l. 9 (Ivanov to Trukhina, July 30, 1996).

46. Ibid.

47. VMVTs f. OF 4262, op. 1, d. 9, ll. 12 (Ivanov to Trukhina, January 22, 1994). Ivanov describes a patriotic play he worked on about Bukovina under German occupation during World War II. He also lists non-Soviet plays, such as Mikhail Lermontov's *Masquerade Ball*, Molière's *Scapin the Schemer*, Hugo's *Maria Tudor*, Anton Chekhov's *Uncle Vanya*, and *Grushenka* based on Nikolai Leskov's "The Enchanted Wanderer." Ivanov notes how "the charm of this play overwhelmed the public."

48. VMVTs f. OF 4262, op. 1, d. 9, l. 9.

49. Like many others, Ivanov recounted working harder than his coworkers who had not been imprisoned to overcome the stigma of their past. VMVTs f. OF 4270, op. 1, d. 6, ll. 6 (Ivanov to Trukhina, April 20, 1993); VMVTs f. OF 4327, op. 1, d. 26, ll. 11 (Ivanov to Trukhina, February 3, 1997). See also Leonid P. Markizov, *Do i posle 1945 goda: Glazami ochevidtsa*, ed. M. B. Rogachev (Syktyvkar: Pokaianie, 2003), 196; National Archive of the Komi Republic (GU RK NARK) 2 f. P-3800, op. 1, d. 156, ll. 22–45 (Serov, "Piat' let i vsia zhizn,'" Pechora, 1989).

50. VMVTs f. OF 4279, op. 1, d. 15, l. 1 (K. P. Ivanov to G. V. Trukhina, April 28, 1993). Ivanov mistakenly wrote 1956; the World Festival of Youth and Students was held in the USSR in 1957.

51. Ibid., 2.

52. Ibid., 3–4.

53. Former prisoner Konstantin Flug also described the pride and attachment he felt to the city of Vorkuta and his role in its transformation: "Vorkuta is my

life's achievement and my youth!" See also Archive of the Vorkuta Museum of Geology (AVMG) (Flug, "Chernyi ostrov GULAGa," 50). Eugenia Ginzburg similarly commented on the "ridiculous pride" she felt on returning to Magadan after a seven-year absence and seeing the city she and countless other zeks built: "We treasure each fragment of our life, even the bitterest"; Ginzburg, *Within the Whirlwind*, trans., Ian Boland (New York: Harcourt Brace Jovanovich, 1981), 201. For the letter of recognition Ivanov received from the Komi ASSR Union of Artists for his entries in the 1955 exhibition, see VMVTs f. NVF 4362, op. 1, d. 6 (V. Poliakov to Ivanov, letter of appreciation for participation in 1955 exhibition).

54. VMVTs f. OF 4262, op. 1, d. 9, l. 1 (Ivanov to Trukhina, January 22, 1994).

55. VMVTs f. OF 4270, op. 1, d. 9, l. 1 (Ivanov to Trukhina, June 15, 1993).

56. VMVTs f. NVF 4363, op. 1, d. 7, ll. 10–11 (Ivanov text of televised speech in Vorkuta, November 24, 1961).

57. VMVTs f. OF 4270, op. 1, d. 9, l. 1 (Ivanov to Trukhina, June 15, 1993).

58. Irina Paperno, *Stories of the Soviet Experience* (Ithaca, NY: Cornell University Press, 2009), xiii. Paperno explains this tension as inherent to the memoir genre, in which the author attempts to connect their past self to their present self.

59. Toker, *Return from the Archipelago*, 80. Toker identifies the memorialization of one's camp comrades as a key feature of the Gulag memoir genre.

60. VMVTs f. OF 4270, op. 1, d. 18, l. 1 (Ivanov to Trukhina, August 18, 1992). See also AM f. 2, op. 2, d. 112, l. 164 (Sollertinskii, "Kuda bog smotrit"). Gulag returnee Vladimir Sollertinskii described the group of friends he kept after release in a similar way: "We talked about literature, music, the land-surveyor read his poems, under [their] influence, I also started to compose some, [which] were of no quality in comparison with those that the land surveyor wrote. Sometimes the regular military officer of a high rank joined us, a tankman, and we discussed the details of the war."

61. Ibid.

62. The Union of Soviet Artists Komi ASSR was founded in 1943 by Valentin Poliakov who organized political-educational groups, Komsomol brigades, and exhibitions of Komi's artists. He was the first civilian artist to visit Vorkuta in the early 1950s and an advocate of Gulag returnees. Ivanov includes a letter of recognition from Poliakov in the materials he sent to the Vorkuta Museum. See N. Zh. Beliaeva, "V. V. Poliakov i ego vospominnanki" and "Uchastie repressirovannykh khudozhnikov v Komi respublikanskikh vystavkakh 1940-x godov," *Materialy i issledovaniia* vypusk 2 (Syktyvkar: Natsional'naia galereia Respubliki Komi, 2008), 60–69, 73–99.

63. VMVTs f. OF 4270, op. 1, d. 18, l. 1 (Ivanov to Trukhina, August 18, 1992).

64. Barenberg, *Gulag Town*, 222–227.

65. VMVTs f. OF 4270, op. 1, d. 18, l. 1 (Ivanov to Trukhina, August 18, 1992). See also VMVTs f. OF 4270, op. 1, d. 6, ll. 6 (Ivanov to Trukhina, April 20, 1993).

66. Ibid., 3; VMVTs f. OF 4270, op. 1, d. 17, l. 1 (Ivanov to Trukhina, September 15, 1992); VMVTs f. OF 4270, op. 1, d. 14, ll. 8 (Ivanov to Trukhina, May 17, 1994).

67. VMVTs f. OF 4262, op. 1, d. 9, l. 2 (Ivanov to Trukhina, January 22, 1994).

68. On the deportees to Komi, see M. B. Rogachev, *Pokaianie: Martirolog*, t. 5 (Syktyvkar: Fond Pokaianie, 2002). Between 1987 and 1997, Syktyvkar Memorial received six hundred letters from Poles who had spent time in camps and in exile in Komi. Rogachev notes that 64 percent, or 20,806 special settlers and former prisoners, were amnestied in 1941 and left Komi in 1944. Approximately fifteen thousand immediately joined the front with the Polish Army in 1942. However, some opted to remain in Komi and left in 1946 at the behest of a resettlement commission organized by Sovnarkom in 1945 to relocate "free citizens," or those who were no longer under the administration of the NKVD (367–416).

69. VMVTs f. OF 4270, op. 1, d. 18, l. 2 (Ivanov to Trukhina, August 18, 1992). Ivanov and Vunder also presented at the Eleventh Exhibition of Works of Artists of the Komi ASSR in Syktyvkar in October 1955. See Archive of the National Gallery of the Komi Republic (NGRK) (V. V. Poliakov, red., *Ministerstvo Kul'tury Komi ASSR XI-ia Vystavka rabot khudozhnikov Komi ASSR: Katalog*, Syktyvkar, 1955). Although Ivanov never comments on divisions in the camps along ethnic lines, his descriptions of friends from the camps who were not Russian illustrate how these divisions did not matter so long as they were *svoi*.

70. VMVTs f. OF 4327, op. 1, d. 19, l. 6 (Ivanov to Trukhina, November 9, 1995).

71. On release, prisoners were obliged to sign nondisclosure agreements. These legal documents prohibited writing about, representing, or discussing what they witnessed or heard in the camps. The penalty for disclosing these "state secrets" was eight to ten years. For an example of this document, see VMVTs f. NVF 2917, op.1, d. 3, ll. 2–3 (Personal file of Ia. Vunder).

72. VMVTs f. OF 4270, op. 1, d. 18, l. 2 (Ivanov to Trukhina, August 18, 1992). In subsequent letters to the Vorkuta museum, Ivanov notes that many of the pieces he displayed at the 1955 exhibition were painted "from nature" in the camps and smuggled out during release.

73. VMVTs f. OF 4327, op. 1, d. 19, l. 2 (K. P. Ivanov to G. V. Trukhina, September 11, 1995).

74. VMVTs f. OF 4327, op. 1, d. 12, ll. 4 (Ivanov to Trukhina, September 13, 1996); VMVTs f. OF 4270, op. 1, d. 9, l. 2 (Ivanov to Trukhina, June 15, 1993).

75. VMVTs f. OF 4270, op. 1, d. 21, ll. 4 (Ivanov to Trukhina, January 27, 1994). This letter contains a list of all works presented at the exhibition; VMVTs f. OF 4327, op. 1, d. 19, ll. 6 (Ivanov to Trukhina, November 9, 1995). For K. P. Ivanov, "Usinsk Street," April 1959, oil on canvas (fig. 3.4) see "Ulitsa Usinskaia,"

displayed online as part of the multimedia project "Kraevidenie: Respublika Komi glazami khudozhnikov," accessed July 27, 2021, http://www.kraevidenie .ru/hudozhniki/32.

76. For K. P. Ivanov, "View of the Mine 'Kaptial'naia' from the Attic of the Burned Theater," 1957, watercolor (figure 3.5) see "Vid na shaktu 'Kapital'naia' iz okna cherdachnogo pomeshcheniia sgorevshego teatra," displayed online as part of the multimedia project "Kraevidenie: Respublika Komi glazami khudozh-nikov," accessed July 27, 2021, http://www.kraevidenie.ru/hudozhniki/32.

77. For K. P. Ivanov, "Summer. Midnight. On My Roof," 1959–1969, oil on can-vas (fig. 3.6) see "Leto. Polnoch'. U moego krylechka," displayed online as part of the multimedia project "Kraevidenie: Respublika Komi glazami khudozhnikov," accessed July 27, 2021, http://www.kraevidenie.ru/hudozhniki/32.

78. VMVTs f. OF 4270, op. 1, d. 6, l. 1; VMVTs f. OF 4270, op. 1, d. 7, ll. 6 (Iva-nov to Trukhina, February 2, 1993); VMVTs f. OF 4270, op. 1, d. 8, ll. 4 (Ivanov to Trukhina, January 30, 1993).

79. VMVTs f. OF 4327, op. 1, d. 26, l. 3 (Ivanov to Trukhina, February 3, 1997). "Union members" is both a reference to Ivanov's "union of outcasts" and camp slang meaning former zeks. On the meaning of this slang term and others, see GU RK NARK 2 f. P-3800, op. 1, d. 17, l. 22 (L. M. Gorodin, "Slovar' Russkikh argotizmov," 1984–1985).

80. VMVTs f. OF 4270, op. 1, d. 6, l. 2 (Ivanov to Trukhina, April 20, 1993).

81. VMVTs f. OF 4327, op. 1, d. 26, l. 3 (Ivanov to Trukhina, February 3, 1997).

82. VMVTs f. OF 4270, op. 1, d. 14, l. 7 (Ivanov to Trukhina, May 17, 1994).

83. Visvaldis moved to Syktyvkar in 1961. Although he was not rehabilitated at the time, the Union of Soviet Artists of the Komi ASSR facilitated his move. See VMVTs f. OF 4327, op. 1, d. 26, l. 3 (Ivanov to Fesenkov, January 3, 1997).

84. VMVTs f. OF 4270, op. 1, d. 7 (Ivanov to Trukhina, February 2, 1993). Iva-nov echoes Varlam Shalamov, who wrote: "A human being survives by his ability to forget. Memory is always ready to blot out the bad and retain only the good. . . . We had all been permanently poisoned by the north, and we knew it"; Shalamov, *Kolyma Tales*, trans. John Glad (New York: Norton, 1980), 66.

85. VMVTs f. OF 4270, op. 1, d. 14, ll. 8 (K. P. Ivanov to G. V. Trukhina, May 17, 1994).

86. VMVTs f. NVF 4363, op. 1, d. 7, ll. 11 (K. P. Ivanov text of televised speech in Vorkuta November 24, 1961).

87. Ibid., 9.

88. VMVTs f. NVF 4363, op. 1, d. 15, l. 1 (Ivanov to Trukhina, August 5, 1991).

89. VMVTs, f. OF 4270, op.1, d. 16, l. 2 (Ivanov to Fesenko, September 7, 1995).

90. A. B. Roginskii, ed., *Tvorchestvo i byt GULAGa: Katalog muzeinogo sobra-niia Obshchestvo "Memorial"* (Moscow: Izd-vo Zven'ia, 1998). Thomas Sgovio and Evfrosiniia Kersnovskaia also included drawings of their memories in their

144   AFTER THE GULAG

memoirs. See Sgovio, *Dear America!*; Thomas Sgovio papers, box 1, "Paintings and drawings depicting living and working conditions in Soviet forced labor camps," Hoover Institution Library and Archives; Evfrosiniia Kersnovskaia, *Naskal'naia zhivopis'* (Moscow: SP Kvadrat, 1991). Former prisoner Nikolai Miller did not write a memoir, but he showed the artworks he made in Ukht-pechlag in an exhibition in Ukhta in 1989. See V. Sergeev, "Nepokornost' sud'be," *Ukhta*, October 11, 1989. The Memorial Society and the State Gulag History Museum hold two major collections of Gulag art, part of which can be seen here (accessed September 21, 2017): https://yandex.ru/collections/user/yndx-collections/kollektsiia-zhivopisi-muzeia-istorii-Gulaga/. Other works of art done by prisoners while they were in the camps and after release are still coming to light. See, e.g., O. M. Ranitskaia, *Meteo-chertik. Trudy i dni*, ed. Alena Skhanova (Moscow: Avgust Borg, 2017); Ksenia El'iashevich, "'My v plenu u svoikh': Repressirovannyi khudozhnik iz Minska v kartinkakh opisal tiur'mu, sud, i lageria," *Novosti Tut.By*, September 22, 2017, https://news.tut.by/society/560412.html.

91. VMVTs f. OF 4327, op. 1, d. 10, ll. 2 (Ivanov to Fesenko, June 26, 1996). Ivanov's interview is featured in the documentary film, *Oni spasut Rossiiu*, dir. Tat'iana Rozhina (Syktyvkar: Nezavisimaia studiia dokumental'nykh fil'mov "ASTI," 1995) posted 2019, YouTube video, 22:04, https://www.youtube.com/watch?v=XuUv5xixWxE&t=289s.

92. Ibid., 2.

93. VMVTs f. OF 4270, op. 1, d. 22, l. 9 (Ivanov to Fesenko, September 11, 1995). Ivanov was not the only one to make sketches of "nature" in the camps. In a letter from October 1992, Ivanov writes about how Evgenii Ukhnalev used to secretly sketch in the zone. See VMVTs f. OF 4270, op. 1, d. 11, l. 1 (Ivanov to Trukhina, October 20, 1992).

94. Rozhina, *Oni spasut Rossiiu*, 17:32.

95. VMVTs f. NVF 4363, op. 1, d. 15, l. 1 (Ivanov to Trukhina, August 5, 1991). This letter indicates that he gave some of these works to Cheslava Tsidzik, his friend from Rechlag and fellow member of the union, with whom he kept in touch with after she returned to L'viv. In a letter from 1992, Ivanov laments that he lost these works from the camps: "And now, when it turned out that I have no present and there will be no future, I live only by the past—these works have suddenly become dear to me." See VMVTs f. OF 4270, op. 1, d. 11, l. 1 (Ivanov to Trukhina, October 20, 1992).

96. VMVTs f. OF 4270, op. 1, d. 22, l. 9 (Ivanov to Fesenko, September 11, 1995).

97. VMVTs f. OF 4327, op. 1, d. 22, l. 3 (Ivanov to Fesenko, December 16, 1995).

98. K. P. Ivanov, "Untitled," from the personal collection of A. A. Popov, Syktyvkar, Russia. This sketch features a rough storyboard, which includes images of specters floating in the heavens above the coalfields of Vorkuta.

ALTERNATIVE FORMS OF AUTOBIOGRAPHY 145

99. VMVTs f. OF 4327, op. 1, d. 12, l. 3 (Ivanov to Trukhina, September 13, 1996).

100. Ivanov's art can be compared to Shalamov's *Kolyma Tales* and Solzhenitsyn's *One Day in the Life of Ivan Denisovich*. Although their approaches to writing about the Gulag differed, they thought the only way to represent their lived experiences was through literary art based on real life that depicted the entire cycle of the Gulag experience. Aleksandr I. Solzhenitsyn, *One Day in the Life of Ivan Denisovich*, trans. Ralph Parker (New York: Signet Classic, 1998).

101. Katya Pereyaslavska, "Gulag Art: Elusive Evidence from the Forbidden Territories," *Art Documentation* 30, no. 1 (2011): 33–42. Pereyaslavska writes, "With no access to photography, these images remain the only form of visual documentation providing a glimpse into the Soviet concentration camps. What Gulag art seems to offer is exactly what Socialist Realism sought to obscure—the *actual* post-revolutionary Soviet reality or, what one could call *Nastoiaschii realism*, the true, authentic Realism" (34). See also Svetlana Boym, *Territories of Terror: Mythologies and Memories of the Gulag in Contemporary Russian-American Art* (Seattle: University of Washington Press, 2006), 17.

102. Pereyaslavska, "Gulag Art," 35.

103. VMVTs f. OF 3673, op. 1, d. 16, l. 8 (Ivanov, "Hope Dies Last").

104. Gulag returnees frequently described feeling as if they had been branded by the numbers on their clothing. Ivanov describes this repeatedly in his memoir-letters. See, e.g., VMVTs f. OF 4220, op. 1, d. 1, ll. 6 (Ivanov to Fesenko, March 12, 1996); VMVTs f. OF 4327, op. 1, d. 11, ll. 7 (Ivanov to Trukhina, July 30, 1996).

105. Wilson T. Bell, "Sex, Pregnancy, and Power in the Late Stalinist Gulag," *Journal of the History of Sexuality* 24, no. 2 (May 2015): 199. See also Elaine MacKinnon, "Motherhood and Survival in the Stalinist Gulag," *Aspasia* 13, no. 1 (2019): 66.

106. Alexander Etkind, *Warped Mourning: Stories of the Undead in the Land of the Unburied* (Stanford, CA: Stanford University Press, 2013), 93. Etkind focuses on surrealist examples of Gulag art that enabled artist-survivors to represent the unimaginable and inhumane in the camps.

107. VMVTs f. OF 4327, op. 1, d. 22, l. 1 (Ivanov to Fesenko, December 16, 1995).

108. VMVTs f. OF 4327, op. 1, d. 33, ll. 4 (Ivanov to Trukhina, August 24, 1998). For these images, see G. V. Nevskii, ed., *Pokaianie: Martirolog*, t. 1 (Syktyvkar: Komi knizhnoe izd-vo, 1998) and *Pokaianie: Martirolog*, t. 2 (Syktyvkar: Komi knizhnoe izd-vo, 1999). I discuss the *Martirolog* and Fond Pokaianie in chap. 5. Ivanov's Gulag art was presented alongside the artworks of his friends-in-misfortune in October 2021 at the Vorkuta Museum-Exhibition Center. See Artur Arteev, "Nasledie repressirovannykh khudozhnikov," *Respublika*,

October 6, 2021, http://respublika11.ru/2021/10/06/nasledie-repressirovannyih
-hudozhnikov/; Vorkuta Museum–Exhibition Center, "Vystavka grafiki i zhivopisi iz fondov Vorkutinskogo muzeino-vystavochnogo tsentra otkrylas' v Gorodskom vystavochnom zale Vorkuty," October 5, 2021, http://museumworkuta.ru
/novosti_809/vystavka-grafiki-i-zhivopisi-iz-fondov-vorkutinskogo-muzejno
-vystavochnogo-centra-otkrylas-v-gorodsk/.

109. Rozhina, *Oni spasut Rossiiu*, 28:09.

110. VMVTs f. OF 4327, op. 1, d. 33, l. 3 (Ivanov to Trukhina, April 24, 1998).
Ivanov died on May 9, 1999.

4

"How I Remained a Human Being"

*Elena Markova's Spiritual Resistance
Inside and Outside the Gulag*

In Moscow in 2017, Gulag returnee Elena Vladimirovna Markova concluded a
two-hour lecture about her time in the Gulag with the following words:

> Vorkuta was always with us. Do you understand? Vorkuta remained in our
> hearts. . . . Spiritual resistance is connected to the spiritual life of prisoners.
> This is what saved prisoners. Yes, the theater was an escape [*ostrov spaseniia*],
> but it was also our independent action, camp poetry, and the environment
> [we created] where you were surrounded by smart, cultured people. This
> is spiritual salvation [*dukhovnoe spasenie*]. And when I moved to Moscow
> after seventeen years in Vorkuta, I had such a [negative] reaction to the
> Muscovites—forgive me, Muscovites. I thought, oh my God, what unin-
> teresting, petty, small-minded people. In Vorkuta, we really had a different
> public, a totally different milieu. Vorkuta has always remained with me in my
> soul. I am at the end of my life now, but the paradox of *katorga* [which led
> to the creation of this public] is the most astonishing phenomenon to me.
> There were such good people there whom I associated with, whom I drew
> strength from, and who spiritually saved me. In Moscow, I did not have such
> an environment.[1]

Gulag returnees frequently asked themselves in their memoirs, "How did
I remain a human being in such conditions?"[2] For Markova, the answer was
"spiritual resistance." As she wrote in her 1993 memoir, "Those who survived
physically understood that long-term incarceration in a concentration camp
meant moral and spiritual degradation. Those who survived also resisted spiritual death. For their spiritual self-preservation, they sought several compensatory mechanisms."[3] These compensatory mechanisms included composing and

memorizing poems, which they recited to one another; creating art; writing illegal letters to one another; and friendship. All of these practices can be seen as what Alexei Yurchak defines as *obshchenie* or "both a process and a sociality that emerges in that process, and both an exchange of ideas and information as well as a space of affect and togetherness."[4] While these practices enabled Markova to endure the camps during some of the deadliest years of its existence, they were also an important part of her life after release.[5]

Historians have focused previously on how prisoners physically survived the camps; however, this chapter puts an in-depth focus on the strategies they adopted to survive psychologically.[6] Based on Markova's memoir, correspondence with her camp comrades from the 1950s and 1990s, and interviews that I conducted with her in 2016 and 2017, this chapter explores the ways in which Markova's spiritual resistance in and after the Gulag strengthened her sense of self and the "public" of zeks she belonged to in Vorkuta and Moscow.

Like many Gulag returnees, Markova was both a part of and estranged from Soviet society. As she wrote in a 1995 essay about her past, "Everything that I achieved after release cannot erase what I experienced in prisons and the camps."[7] However, unlike other former prisoners who at least attempted to identify as Soviet people after they were released, Markova rejected this label. Although she was neither anti-Soviet nor a dissident, Markova felt more kinship with those who survived the Gulag than with her countrymen who had not been "there." This bond was not just the product of having survived a traumatic experience together and experiencing the ongoing discrimination that Gulag returnees faced after release; it was also based on the common set of values espoused by the act of spiritual resistance.

Markova and Konstantin Ivanov traveled in some of the same circles in Vorkuta, and their solidarity with other members of the camp brotherhood (*svoi*), their status as *katorzhane* (prisoners sentenced to extreme heavy labor—*katorga*), and the pride they felt as *Vorkutiane* (veterans of Vorkuta) illuminate important connections between them. Nevertheless, they could not be more different. Unlike Ivanov, Markova emphasized her status as a survivor. Although her time in the camps was no less difficult, Markova felt empowered to write an autobiography after the collapse of the Soviet Union, whereas Ivanov was reluctant to write at all. As Markova told me in an interview in 2017, "The collapse of the Soviet Union presented a chance to write, and when the opportunity arose, I took it."[8] Furthermore, Markova did not refer to the camp as her "university." Although she saw her imprisonment as a formative chapter of her life, she assigned a different meaning to it. Markova represented both her years in the Gulag and her life after release as a time of prolonged development, when her identity was shaped by her simultaneous habitation of two temporal spaces. As she wrote in 1993, "Many years have passed after my release, but the past is not forgotten.... Such is the way you live, in two temporal spaces. One—Moscow, the present; the other—the past, Vorkuta."[9] In addition, by her own words, Markova is an exceptional Gulag returnee for another reason.[10] Unlike many of her friends from the camps, Markova and her husband were completely rehabilitated during the 1950s and even given an apartment in Moscow.[11]

The intertextual shifts in her memoir, much like oral history, reveal the collected memories of the Gulag that shape and are shaped by individual identity.[12] To impart scope to her memoir and to show that the story she had to tell was not just her own, Markova frequently drew from the lives of others she knew in the camps and after release. In addition to her memories of the past, Markova included material from the archive of testimony that she built over the years. This archive includes official documents, letters, poems, notes, photographs, and stories that Markova collected over the years. She sent some of this material to her mother while she was imprisoned, "through all means, both legal and illegal."[13] These sources, which are reproduced throughout Markova's memoir, tell about the experiences of the punishingly heavy labor of *katorga*, survival, release, and the struggle to adapt to civilian life in real time. As part of a remembered past, however, the narrative Markova constructed in her memoir also conveys the meaning she assigned to these experiences as she looked back on her life from her present. Markova's emphasis on friendship, the "camp brotherhood," and spiritual survival suggest that the post-Soviet context in which she wrote reinforced her feelings of alienation from society and the importance of the camp brotherhood that she belonged to. Although the collapse of the Soviet Union made it possible for her to tell her story, the process of remembering—including the construction of her own personal Gulag archive—unfolded over the rest of her life.

This chapter contains three sections. Taken as a whole, the subsections of this chapter illustrate the various aspects of Markova's life that defined her. The first section provides a brief overview of Markova's biography, which creates a timeline of her life from the 1920s to her life in Moscow in the 1960s. The second section examines Markova's life in the Gulag through the lens of spiritual resistance. This section explores how spiritual resistance and spiritual life laid the foundation for the "public" of zeks that Markova joined after release. The third section illustrates the continued importance of spiritual resistance after release. Although Markova did not write at length about this part of her life, this part of her memoir provides new insights into the extended network of former prisoners, which Markova referred to as the "Vorkuta diaspora."

Markova's Life History

Elena Vladimirovna Markova (Ivanova) was born in Kiev to schoolteachers in 1923. Before her own arrest in March 1943, political repression had already devastated her family. Her paternal grandfather, an Orthodox priest, died trying to save his church's library after a band of militant atheists set fire to it in 1922. In 1937, Markova's father was arrested and shot as the "Great Terror" raged throughout the Soviet Union, sweeping away hundreds of thousands of innocent people.[14] Markova's mother was imprisoned for a year and a half following her husband's arrest, as the "wife of an enemy of the people."[15] Temporarily orphaned by the People's Commissariat of Internal Affairs (NKVD), Markova was saved from an orphanage by her maternal grandmother. They fled to a remote village where they lived an impoverished life as family members of "enemies of the people," which, as Markova wrote in 1993, "in those times was scarier than the plague."[16] After the repressions that tore apart the Ivanov family in the 1920s and 1930s, Markova lived a quiet life with her mother and maternal grandmother, who was an ethnic German. Markova was an excellent student who loved learning and dreamed of attending university in Leningrad. On June 21, 1941, Markova graduated from tenth grade filled with excitement about her plans for higher education; however, the next morning, Nazi Germany invaded the Soviet Union, postponing Markova's education and sending her on a course that would change her life forever.

Soon after the German invasion of the Soviet Union during World War II, Markova and her mother were deported to the small village Krasnoarmeiskii in the Donbas region of Ukraine, along with other ethnic German families.[17] Eventually, their village was captured by advancing Wehrmacht and SS units and occupied until 1943.[18] In February of that year, the Red Army liberated Krasnoarmeiskii, but not for long. During the ensuing battles to retake the village, Markova heroically gathered the wounded Red Army soldiers and treated them in a makeshift field hospital. When the village was overrun and recaptured by the Wehrmacht, Markova hid the wounded who could not escape among families in town as the Red Army hastily retreated. Knowing that the Wehrmacht would search for and execute the wounded Red Army soldiers on sight when they returned, Elena Vladimirovna collected their weapons and documents and stashed them at her family home.[19] To prove that the unfamiliar faces in the village were indeed local residents Markova forged residency documents, which listed the wounded soldiers as citizens of Krasnoarmeiskii. However, this was only a temporary measure to forestall inquiry into the increase in the village's population. On the orders of Major A. N. Ul'ianov, the commander of the Red Army medical battalion who remained in hiding in Donbas, Markova enrolled in the German labor exchange in town with the aim of obtaining work permits for the walking wounded.[20] Ul'ianov entrusted this dangerous assignment to the nineteen-year-old Markova because of her fluency in German. Markova's successful deception saved the lives of seventy-six men and earned her a military commendation signed by Major Ul'ianov.[21]

Despite the commendation for her heroism at great personal risk, Markova was arrested by the NKVD when the Red Army drove the Wehrmacht out of Donbas and recaptured the village. On December 1, 1943, Markova was convicted of treason by an NKVD military tribunal. As an alleged collaborator and German spy, she was sentenced to fifteen years of hard labor (*katorzhnykh rabot*) and an additional five years of deprivation of civil rights: "My guilt lay in the fact that for two and a half months, I worked on the German labor exchange. Why I wound up working there did not interest my interrogators, although the letter of reference [from Ul'ianov] was in my file."[22] Following Markova's interrogation, she was sent to prison no. 1 in Stalino, where her father was executed and her mother served time after her husband's arrest.[23] After months of interrogation, Markova was sent by cattle car to the Far North in May 1944. In June 1944, she passed through the barbed wire gates at Vorkutlag and was sent to work in the coal mines of Vorkuta.

In 1950, Markova was transferred to the adjacent strict-regime camp, Rechlag, where she continued to work in the harshest conditions on the construction of the railroad to the village Mul'de. Markova's fortune changed dramatically when she was reassigned to the camp clinic, where she treated the sick and dying inmates and infants that were born in the camps.[24] Another lucky break came in 1951. Thanks to the persistence of her mother, who tracked down the soldiers that Markova saved in Krasnoarmeiskii and got them to petition on Markova's behalf for leniency, the Military Collegium of the Supreme Court of the Union of Soviet Socialist Republics (USSR) reviewed Markova's file and reduced her sentence to ten years.[25] In November 1953, Markova was released without the right to leave Vorkuta.

In 1954, after release, Markova married former prisoner Aleksei Alekseevich Markov, whom she met through the camp theater. Markov was arrested in 1943 in Moscow for uttering an anti-Soviet anecdote, sentenced to *katorga*, and sent to Vorkuta.[26] The amnesty of September 17, 1955, released Markova from exile; however, she remained in Vorkuta as an unrehabilitated former prisoner.[27] In 1957, she gave birth to her daughter Inna. In 1959, Markov was rehabilitated. A year later, Markova was rehabilitated by the Supreme Court of the USSR, which dismissed her case "for lack of evidence of a crime." After she was rehabilitated

152   AFTER THE GULAG

in 1960, the Markovs moved to Moscow.[28] Although she missed Vorkuta and her friends there, living in the capital afforded her the opportunity to pursue the education that she had always dreamed of. Even though she was rehabilitated, Markova still found it difficult to find work or gain entrance to the university because of the stigma attached to her status as a former prisoner. In 1962, she enrolled in correspondence courses at the Moscow State University of Economics, Statistics, and Informatics. In 1965, she defended her candidate degree, followed by her doctorate in engineering six years later.[29] After her husband passed away in 1973, Markova continued to live with her daughter in Moscow, where she still lives as of this writing.

Spiritual Resistance in the Gulag

For Markova, spiritual resistance was not connected to any institutional religion. Instead, spiritual resistance was a form of self-preservation—a means to maintain her humanity amid the inhumanity of the camps. In other words, spiritual resistance was a practice, a feeling, a faith in one's self and one's friends.[30] That is not to say that religion was absent from the Gulag, for it was not.[31] Markova did not mention her encounters with Russian believers in the camps, but when she interacted with foreign believers in the camps, she remembered feeling a belief in something greater. However, as Markova wrote in 1993, it was not religion: "Not once was the discourse about God. As children of the atheistic times, we did not delve into religious questions, we didn't know the prayers.... We felt the need to something higher, but how, with what words?"[32]

To withstand the destructiveness of her environment, Markova retreated inward and remembered pieces of the life that she left behind.[33] Markova found "something higher" and the words to express it through "internal migration."[34] However, she did not do so alone. By interacting and associating with other political prisoners, Markova forged solidarities with her camp comrades who retreated inward with her. As she wrote in her memoir:

> The reality [of the camps] was so terrible, that it seemed I would not last one day. And I faced a sentence of fifteen years. In order to somehow save myself, I constantly lived by memories of my former life. Working in the mine, I recited poems, committed to memory favorite songs or old romances that my mother sang. The total starvation of information was tortuous, an excommunication from books, journals, newspapers, and radio. We lived as if we had been transported back to the prehistoric epoch when writing hadn't been invented yet. The only thing that we had left was conversation with our close friends in spirit. I highly valued such conversations and tried my hardest to

find interesting people to converse with. This is how I attempted to resist the sinister process, which was supposed to turn us *katorzhanki* into dull, soulless creatures.[35]

In the harsh conditions of the Arctic, bread was symbolically and literally life. However, as Markova wrote, "We didn't live by bread alone."[36] For Markova and her friends, poetry and intellectual comradeship were the metaphorical bread that sustained them. Although there were libraries at the cultural-educational department of the camp, Markova and the other *katorzhane* were not allowed access to the books. To fill the void, they remembered the poems of Marina Tsvetaeva, Nikolai Gumilev, Anna Akhmatova, Osip Mandelshtam, and others, as Markova wrote, "whom we only began to talk about openly only after the 'Thaw.'"[37] Poetry was a form of resistance that enabled Markova to "remain human."

In addition to reciting the poems of other well-known poets, Markova composed and collected camp poems, which she memorized.[38] The creative and mnemonic processes involved in composing poems served as a way for prisoners to document their environment for future generations:

> But most importantly, we wrote poems ourselves. Often, they were unskillful, childish poems, which specialists and lovers of high poetry disdainfully relate to. But I think that one must apply a special measure to amateur camp art. It is original documentary evidence of our spiritual life, our emotions, interactions, and relations to camp events. After all, there is simply no other documentary evidence [that captures these aspects of camp life]. Some letters have been saved, but they were composed with the censor in mind, and in order to not worry our loved ones, we expressed ourselves very carefully. In camp poems, [authors wrote about] resistance to the slave, *katorzhnoi* life, overcoming spiritual death, the search for paths of intellectual development. *Poems were a unique chronicle of our unfree life* [emphasis added]. Alas, more than anything, they recorded the chronicle of terrible, bloody events. . . . Camp poems are poetic resistance in the Gulag, a violation of the regime, which was punished harshly.[39]

Markova saw the poems that she and her friends composed as evidence of the "spiritual world of the camps."[40] These unique works of art represented their experiences in the camps more than the letters they wrote home. Because letters home had to pass the censor, as Markova wrote, "no one ever risked completely unburdening one's heart."[41] In contrast, camp poems "were not intended for print—composing poems, we didn't think about the camp censor. Camp poems are a mirror of our spirituality, a unique camp diary."[42]

These poems also enabled survivors to describe the indescribable and relay it to their families and future generations. As Alexander Etkind notes, "lyric poems written by the survivors—ordered, understandable, shared pieces of speech that communicated bygone worlds—worked as effective, popular acts of resistance."[43] By composing poems in their heads, prisoners assigned meaning to their experiences as they lived them. However, because these poems changed over time as they were remembered, recited, and recorded, they reflect the same process by which Gulag returnees constructed their autobiographies.[44]

One of the unifying motifs of Markova's and other Gulag returnees' camp poetry is the tundra.[45] These poems capture the beauty and harshness of the Arctic and describe their relationship to it. As Markova wrote, the tundra represented "the personification of our troubles and the single source of beauty [in the camps]."[46] In Markova's poetry, the tundra represented a "parallel world" that she was simultaneously a part of and separated from.[47] As Josephine von Zitzewitz notes in her analysis of Varlam Shalamov's and Nikolai Zabolotsky's camp poetry, the "lyricism of nature images"—such as that found in Markova's camp poems—can be read as a continuation of the Russian classical tradition in which the celebration of the "austere natural environment" was a source of hope for "renewal" and a space uncorrupted and untouched by the destructive world of the camps.[48] However, the tundra was not just a theme in camp poetry; it was a continuous source of inspiration and spiritual resistance for other Gulag returnees. For instance, Iakov Vunder, Konstantin Ivanov, and a host of other Gulag returnee-artists frequently traveled into the tundra at different times of the year to capture the movement of light and darkness across the pristine landscape as the seasons changed above the Arctic Circle.[49]

Over the course of her nine years behind barbed wire, Markova corresponded with her mother and other prisoners in the camp through legal and illegal channels.[50] As Markova wrote in 1993, these letters "were a kind of symbol of spiritual salvation. . . . They were ineradicable like the camp poems. It was the prisoners' moral resistance against the hated GULAG."[51] Markova's "illegal" letters were passed to other sections of the camp through a network of inmates, friendly civilians, and corrupt guards. At times when Markova was separated from her "circle of friends in katorga" (*kruzhok druzei po katorge*), camp correspondence enabled the group to continue their "spiritual life" (*dukhovnaia zhizn'*) together. Furthermore, these letters illustrate the great risk that Markova and others were willing to take to maintain these meaningful relationships in the camp.[52] Underscoring this point, Markova continued in her memoir, "These letters served as a window to another world—a world of human

Figure 4.1 Self-portrait that G. M. Rontal' sent to E. V. Markova in 1952. Source: State Gulag History Museum (GBUK MIG f. 5, d. 3, l. 30).

emotions, lofty impulses, and thoughts. These gray pieces of paper, covered in writing in pencil, were of inestimable significance to long-term prisoners."[53]

Many of the letters from Markova's archive are from her close friend and fellow *katorzhanin* Georgii Rontal' (fig. 4.1), who was released in 1955.[54] The letters Markova received from Rontal' mention the poems that Markova composed, which shows that she shared her poems with prisoners in other camp sections. Although we only have one side of this dialogue, these letters reveal the variety of topics that Markova and Rontal' discussed in their illicit correspondence, which included literature, art, and music (fig. 4.2).[55] Most important, these letters illustrate that Gulag returnees risked harsh punishment—solitary confinement, reduced rations, added time on their sentence, or worse—simply to comfort and remind each other that they were valued members of a community.

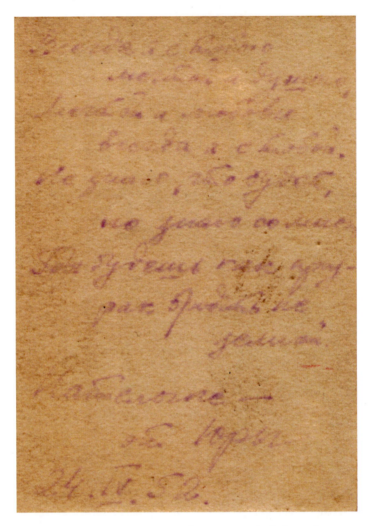

Figure 4.2 Poem that G. M. Rontal' wrote to E. V. Markova, September 24, 1952. The poem reads, "I am always with you, in your dreams and in your soul, I am always with you. I do not know what will come, but I know that you will, like a specter, roam the heavens." Source: State Gulag History Museum (GBUK MIG f. 5, d. 3, l. 300b).

Furthermore, it illustrates the porousness of the camp regime, which even *katorzhane*, who were supposed to be totally isolated, were able to evade like other prisoners. Rontal' wrote to Markova in a letter dated December 21, 1950, about how her turn outward to her friends coincided with an improvement in her emotional well-being:

> With all my heart, I send you congratulations and wishes for the utmost happiness in everything in the New Year. I hope the New Year brings you much happiness and joy and relief from the weight of the separation from your mother and me. I am very glad to hear that you have cheered up now, thanks to your friends and acquaintances who have a good influence on your mood and thoughts. It is so good that in the end, you renounced your reticence, which you found yourself in for the last few years, and embarked on the path of the community. Remember the words of Shosta Rustaveli: 'He who does not look for friends, is an enemy to himself'? . . . Lenok, I am very glad *that you're well* and cheerful. For the first time, (in your letter from 19.XII) you write that your days are interesting and that you are even writing poetry. And I am unable to read them . . . how annoying! Perhaps they reflect your change in mood? Thank you, my dear, for the [other] poems. I like both editions, the old and the new.[56]

Rontal's letters illustrate how members of the community, who were scattered throughout different camp sections, interacted and how turning outward to one another buoyed their ability to spiritually resist. His letters also shed new light on how members of the camp brotherhood identified themselves while they were imprisoned. Although he used a false name to conceal his true identity, lest his letters fall into the wrong hands, Rontal' identified himself and Markova as members of the camp brotherhood by referring to himself as her brother.[57] In a letter to Markova dated December 1951, for example, Rontal' encouraged her not to lose heart with such little time left on her sentence (fig. 4.3): "My beloved Lenusia! Happy New Year 1952! I wish you, dear, very much happiness, joy, and health. I hope the new year brings you long awaited freedom, and with it the happiness of meeting with all your close ones and friends and with science, art, and music. You can be certain that despite the distance separating us, I will always be with you with all my being. Be well and cheerful, my dear sister. Sending you my love. Heartily embracing and kissing you. Always your brother, Vsevolod."[58]

Spiritual resistance was not confined to conversations, inner thoughts, and illicit letters; it had a space—the camp theater—that was organized by the state. Although she did not work in the theater herself, it represented a refuge for Markova, who worked grueling shifts underground and then, later, with sick children born in the camp. It was also the place where Markova met her future husband and many of the friends with whom she would spend the rest of her life (fig. 4.4).[59] Most important, Markova remembered performances at the camp theater

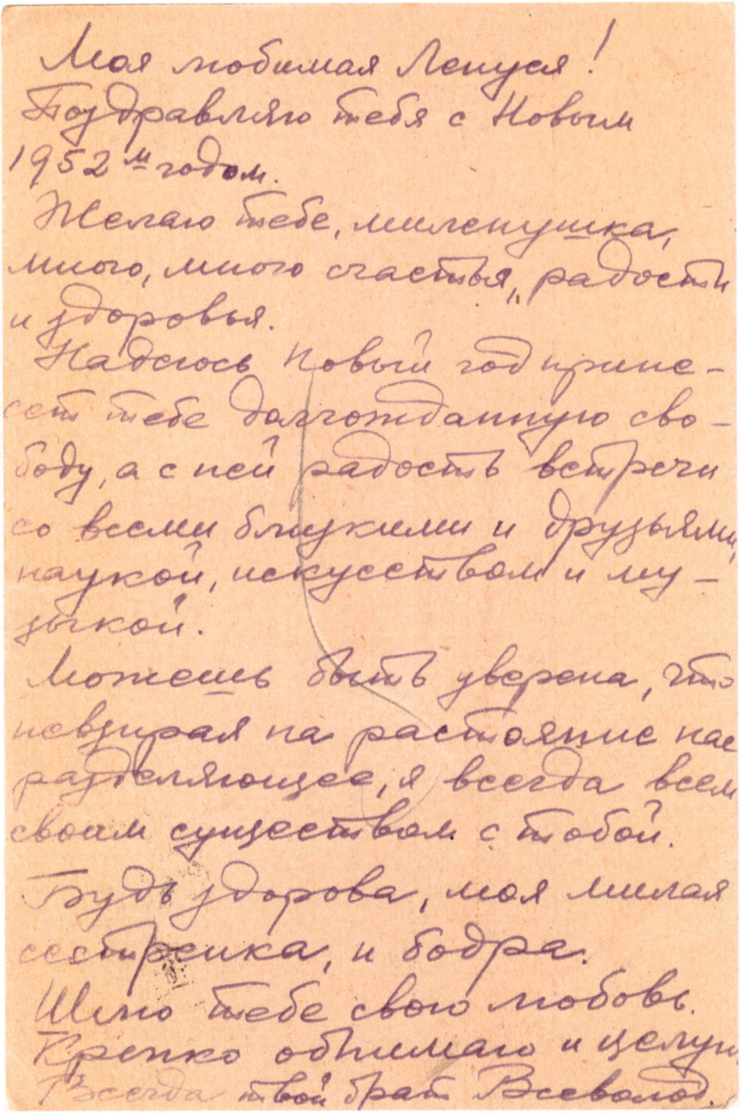

Моя любимая Ленуся!
Поздравляю тебя с Новым
1952м годом.
Желаю тебе, миленушка,
много, много счастья, радости
и здоровья.
Надеюсь Новый год прине-
сет тебе долгожданную сво-
боду, а с ней радость встречи
со всеми близкими и друзьями,
наукой, искусством и му-
зыкой.
Можешь быть уверена, что
невзирая на растояние нас
разделяющее, я всегда всем
своим существом с тобой.
Будь здорова, моя милая
сестренка, и бодра.
Шлю тебе свою любовь.
Крепко обнимаю и целую.
Всегда твой брат Всеволод.

Figure 4.3 *(above and facing)* Letter from G. M. Rontal' to E. V. Markova, December 1951. Source: State Gulag History Museum (GBUK MIG f. 5, d. 3, l. 27).

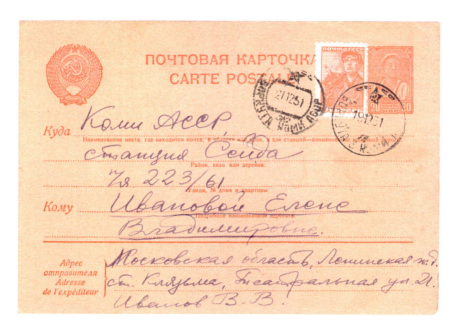

as a temporary inoculation against the horror of her environment. As evidence of how much the theater meant to her and other prisoners, Markova reproduced a letter from one of her friends who wrote and performed music for the camp theater. Larisa Guliachenko's letter to Markova from 1990 illuminates how Gulag returnees also bonded over their memories of the theater and not just the things they endured: "Now I warmly remember those long-past times, our stage (our pitiful stage), our performances and concerts (poor, miserable!). And once again, with sadness, I am firmly convinced that after Usa [river camp], I never experienced such creative energy, such an incomparable joy, and enthusiasm as then!"[60]

The Vorkuta Diaspora: 1953–1993

As the time left on her sentence expired in September 1953, Markova penned a farewell note to her friends. She reproduced this note in her memoir as an illustration of just how much their friendship meant to her:

> Midnight. The hazy-pale, starless, arctic night is the personification of our existence, so far from real life. The concert is tomorrow. I'm writing to you, my friends.... But why such pain? We will soon part and will no longer march together.... It's difficult to imagine that the day is coming when it will no longer be our shared day, they will be different days for us, separated by uncertainty....

Figure 4.4 (*top*) E. V. Markova (middle) visiting Larisa Guliachenko (right) and her daughter Ira (left), who was born in Rechlag, in Kiev. (*bottom*) The caption on the back reads, "Kiev, 1956 or 1958." It seems more likely that this photo was taken at a later date, as Markova was not rehabilitated until 1959 and, according to her memoir, did not leave Vorkuta until 1960. Source: State Gulag History Museum (GBUK MIG f. 5, d. 11, l. 11).

"HOW I REMAINED A HUMAN BEING"   161

In our life together, deprived of everything that could have filled the soul with happiness and light, we had only one thing—our friendship! Thanks to it, we were happy in misfortune. We thought and felt, when we should have turned into mindless creatures! We asked ourselves about good and evil as lawlessness and tyranny ruled around us. Our camp stage—our small world of beauty and light among pitch darkness—gave me new life. I will hold the sacred memory of our poor camp stage, on which you, my dear friends, were the greatest, most talented artists to me. OLP "Zapoliarnyi" on the Usa River. September 1953.[61]

Despite thinking at the time that her release meant saying goodbye, Markova continued to maintain these friendships on the other side of the barbed wire. The "epistolary fever," as Markova aptly described it, that gripped prisoners in the camp continued after release. Faced with new concerns and the challenge of blending into a society that remained suspicious of them, Markova and other Gulag returnees who exited the camps in the 1950s found these relationships to be even more important. As Markova wrote in her memoir, "They [the prisoners] found a spiritual outlet in the letters, which they valued above all else. But here approaches the long-awaited release [with] new impressions, worries, and concerns.... One would think that they no longer need the letters. But no! The epistolary fever continued more than ever, my personal archive attests to this."[62] As Gulag returnees adapted to civilian life after years in the camps, letters between prisoners—however infrequent—offered a connection to something familiar during the difficult period of adjustment.

As evidence of the effect and meaning of these letters, however infrequently they came after release, Markova and others saved this correspondence as their memories of the past. Nevertheless, these letters were also a link to the "community of zeks," which grew and shrank as friends left the camps and then left Vorkuta after they were rehabilitated.[63] While Markova and her husband remained in exile in Vorkuta, she conducted correspondence with close friends who managed to leave. She reproduced selected letters in her memoir narrative as evidence of the ties between herself and other Gulag returnees but also as proof that these relationships did not end at release: "Our friendship continued through regular correspondence, including many photos that [he] took, which we cherished very much."[64] One letter, which Markova reproduced in full, described the incredible feeling of leaving the camp zone and reuniting with friends. As Edgar Shtyrtskober wrote to Markova from Leningrad on January 28, 1956—one of the most important days of his new life, "My mind is in a tangle from happiness.... Up until the last moment when I got on the train, I had the feeling that I was there to say goodbye and not to leave.... Imagine my state as I sat in my compartment across from my neighbor and wondered what to do. I was thinking of you, and then suddenly a wave of memories about

162 AFTER THE GULAG

Leningrad, my loved ones, and my sister washed over me, and I sat there on pins and needles totally intoxicated [with delight]."[65]

When Markova moved to Moscow with her family in 1960, she did not experience the same rapturous delight. Markova remembered the transition to Moscow as jarring. The capital was like a foreign country to her.[66] Finding work in Moscow was difficult for Markova, who, despite her total rehabilitation, continued to suffer from the stigma associated with her status as a *byvshii* (former prisoner). It did not help, as Markova wrote in her memoir, that she freely disclosed her status to would-be employers: "In my scrupulousness, I did not hide my Vorkutlag past, even though I was rehabilitated. At the end of interviews, I would usually say, 'I should tell you that I was sentenced under the political article of the law and served a sentence.'" She continued, "No further explanations were necessary. I especially remember the reaction of the head of the personnel department at one academic institute: 'How dare you show your face in our institute with such a biography!'"[67] Despite the fear that her past evoked in many people, Markova eventually found work at the Central Automatization Complex (TsNIIKA) in Moscow.

Her work as an engineer took her to many different factories throughout the Soviet Union. On trips to Stalinogorsk (now Novomoskovsk), she would stay with her friends from Vorkuta, the Korovins, who left the Far North in 1960 after twenty-four years of prison and exile.[68] The decision to leave Vorkuta was difficult for the Korovins, who, Markova wrote, "participated in the transformation of Vorkuta from nothing into the capital of the vast tundra, into the center of Pechora coal mining. In Vorkuta, they had a 'mighty bunch' of friends in freedom who supported them and made life interesting. They perceived Stalinogorsk as a foreign city, unattractive and uninteresting."[69]

When the Korovins eventually moved to Moscow, they became part of the "Vorkuta diaspora," which included other Gulag returnees such as Pavel Shapiro, Iurii Volkov, Vadim Iasnyi, Aleksei Eisner, and Leonid Raikin.[70] Many of their gatherings took place at the homes of Shapiro and Nikolai Korovin.[71] Although the circle of former prisoners did not meet often, Markova remembered these gatherings as "the most interesting, dear visits of my life. Contrary to Soviet tradition, the main thing was not the feast, but thoughts of high aspiration."[72] Although these gatherings enabled Markova to reconnect with the community that she thought she had left behind when she moved to Moscow, they were important for another reason.[73] Because writing about the past remained dangerous until *glasnost*, these meetings were also a means to keep the memory of those times alive by reminiscing about their "Vorkuta past."[74] As the collective remembered its shared origins, it became clear to Markova that the spiritual resistance, which saved her, had also formed the group. As Markova wrote amid the chaos of the ongoing transformation of post-Soviet Russia in 1993, "It turned out that the Vorkuta brotherhood was stronger than those times of annihilation."[75]

The second generation of *Vorkutianie* continued their parents' traditions. Although many of them lived in Vorkuta for only a few years, they shared the same attachment to the city as their parents and identified themselves as members of the Vorkuta brotherhood. These children of former prisoners spent the summers of their youth and adulthood together at the Korovins' dacha outside Moscow. As Markova wrote about the "second generation of the Vorkuta brotherhood" in her memoir, "The second generation of *Vorkutiane*—the children of the Korovins and their friends who spent their childhood in Vorkuta—continue these traditions to this day. . . . Although she left Vorkuta at the age of one year [and] four months, my daughter Inna also considers herself a *Vorkutianka*, and she also gravitates toward the second generation of the Vorkuta brotherhood."[76] Although it is unclear how many other Gulag returnees agreed with Markova's sentiment, the letters that children of Gulag returnees sent to the Syktyvkar Memorial Society starting in the late 1980s reinforce the idea that they also considered themselves members of the extended community.[77]

The Vorkuta diaspora was not limited to Moscow. As Markova told me during our second interview in October 2017, "They were everywhere—Kharkov, Kyiv, Moscow, Leningrad, Vorkuta."[78] Although it remains unclear how much contact Markova had with the Vorkuta brotherhood outside of Moscow, this network of former prisoners enabled Markova to connect with those she had not heard from since they left Vorkuta in 1960. Following the collapse of the Soviet Union, Markova obtained the address of one of her long-lost friends—Iosif Virzhonis, who returned to Lithuania sometime after Markova left Vorkuta—and began corresponding with him. Over the course of 1992–1993, Markova and Virzhonis sent each other a total of eleven letters. Although some of the letters allude to current events—the collapse of the Soviet Union and the independence of the Baltic states—Markova and Virzhonis primarily discussed Vorkuta, their friends, and their camp past.[79] The most striking aspect of this correspondence is its depiction of how Markova and Virzhonis, who had not spoken for forty years, connected with one another and their community by remembering their shared past. The first letter that Markova sent to Virzhonis on July 1, 1992, reads, in part,

> I began to write you and involuntarily paused to imagine your surprise—who sent this from Moscow? Markova who? Yes, we met a long time ago in Usa in OLP "Zapoliarnyi" in 1952, forty-years ago! ~~Maybe you don't remember.~~ I was not Markova then, but Ivanova, not Elena Vladimirovna, but Lenochka. You came under guard to the men's section of the OLP to work in the medical

Figure 4.5 (*top*) E. V. Markova with camp friends V. V. Oliger (left) and Iosif Virzhonis (right), Vorkuta, 1955. (*bottom*) The caption on the back reads, "Birthday April 24, 1955. My two comrades from the state farm '*Zapoliar'e*' Usa (1951–52). Vasilii Viktorovich Oliger, Iosif Virzhonis." Source: State Gulag History Museum (GBUK MIG f. 5, d. 3, l. 32, 32ob).

unit. I was glad to chat with you and our good comrades Valentin Viktorovich Oliger, Tikhon Subokov, and Volodia. Do you remember that time? Alas, I don't know anything about the fates of our friends who remained in Usa. When I learned that Volodia had your address and asked him to give it to me. I hope it's OK that he shared it with me without your knowing! I am so happy to have the opportunity to speak with you after so many years! To hear your voice is like another life! Iosif, I have not had any information about you and Olia since 1955, when [I] last saw you in my apartment. I've kept our "tortured path to starvation" in my memory. And with gratitude, I fondly remember the comrades and friends, who, by the kindness of their heart, warm words, and care, helped me survive and remain a human being. Now, in the twilight of life, I am increasingly detached from the reality of the present. . . . I have begun to collect memoirs and poems about our camp life for the Vorkuta local history museum. After I hear back from you, I will write more. I will answer all of your questions. I eagerly await your letter and hope to receive news from you about Oliger. I am sending you a photograph [of us] from 1955 [fig. 4.5]. Wishing you all the best. A big hello to your family.[80]

Unable to contain his excitement, Virzhonis responded in a rambling four-page letter on July 14, 1992. Despite the time that had passed, Virzhonis reassured Markova that he had not forgotten anything and expressed his happiness about reconnecting with his old friend and camp comrade:

Forty years is a huge length of time—it is an entire lifetime, which has flown by in a flash. But its light constantly illuminates those unforgettable days when fate brought such people together—Valentin Viktorovich, Aleksandr Vasil'evich Khokhlov, and even you and me—when we were still young and stupid despite our humbling camp experience. . . . I remember you very well, especially since I still have the photo you gave me. Even then it was possible to find such good conversation with your family, such discourse was welcome to those who thirsted [for contact] like people thirst for water in the desert.[81]

Despite the decades that had passed since their imprisonment, the memory of their spiritual resistance to the camps united Markova, Virzhonis, and other members of the Vorkuta diaspora. The same networks of mutual aid that united prisoners in the camps also enabled them to find one another after release.

On October 30, 1993, Markova stepped foot in Vorkuta for the first time since 1960. She returned to the city as a member of a delegation from Moscow to participate in the observance of the Day of Victims of Political Repression. After the ceremony, she visited the Ministry of Internal Affairs archive in town, where she hoped to find some information about the fates of several of her

166   AFTER THE GULAG

"friends in *katorga*," of whom she had lost track many years before. Despite her status as a rehabilitated victim of political repression and a *Vorkutianka*, Markova remembered how the archivist treated her with suspicion and disrespect: "The head of the archive greeted me like in the old, bad days. I immediately felt like a *katorzhanka* again."[82] The officer did not give Markova the files; instead, she read Markova's personal file aloud and said goodbye.[83] This experience confirmed the necessity of her trip to the Far North and her decision to write her own testimony about Stalinist repression and its afterlife.

Although Markova's memoir contains motifs that can be found in the memoirs of other Gulag returnees, she stands apart for several reasons. While other former prisoners spoke of the importance of friendship and community to surviving the Gulag and adapting to life after release, Markova's memoir is unique for its detailed illustration of exactly how prisoners resisted the destructiveness of their environment. And yet, the story she tells is much bigger than that. Markova's story of spiritual resistance is also the story of how those who were discarded by the state formed a public of zeks that existed within Soviet society, despite the regime's attempts to curb the formation of independent groups. Drawing from her personal archive of letters, photographs, poems, and stories, Markova provides time-stamped evidence of the development of this community and its collected memories from its origins in the camps to the present in which she wrote. Indeed, the ongoing resistance she faced undoubtedly reinforced the community she identified with, as it did for other Gulag returnees who picked up their pens following the collapse of the Soviet Union. Despite the fact that Markova and her fellow prisoners had been repressed, traumatized, and stigmatized for a lifetime, they documented their struggles and their triumphs, not only for themselves or each other but also for the country as it grappled with the dark chapters of its past.

Notes

1. E. V. Markova, "Lektsiia: Dukhovnoe soprotivlenie v GULAGe," Sakharov Center, April 20, 2017, YouTube video, 2:31:54, https://www.youtube.com /watch?v=rHk-j2t3Cyg.

2. See chaps 2 and 3. See also National Archive of the Komi Republic (GU RK NARK) f. P-3800, op. 1, d. 17, l. 13 (Gorodin, "Slovar' Russkikh argotizmov"). In the introduction to his Gulag encyclopedia dictionary, Gorodin illustrates how prisoners celebrated humanity. Calling someone a *Chelovek* (person) was the highest honor prisoners could bestow on one another.

3. E. V. Markova, *Vorkutinskie zametki katorzhanki "E-105"* (Syktyvkar: Fond Pokaianie, 2005), 144. Markova's memoir was written over the course of 1992–1993. Markova discussed writing her memoir in an interview with the author by phone, October 10, 2017.

"HOW I REMAINED A HUMAN BEING"

4. Alexei Yurchak, *Everything Was Forever, Until It Was No More: The Last Soviet Generation* (Princeton, NJ: Princeton University Press, 2006), 149–150. In other words, Gulag returnees formed a community of *svoi*, which they referred to as the Vorkuta "brotherhood," through the practices they used to spiritually resist the camps.

5. The mortality rate in Vorkutlag for those sentenced to katorga (KTR) in 1944 (the year Markova arrived) was 377.96 deaths per thousand. The next year it dropped to 197.62 and continued to decline in the years afterward. For mortality rates in Vorkutlag and Rechlag, see Alan Barenberg, *Gulag Town, Company Town: Forced Labor and Its Legacy in Vorkuta* (New Haven, CT: Yale University Press, 2014), 270.

6. Golfo Alexopoulos is the most recent author to write on the question of physical survival; Alexopoulos, *Illness and Inhumanity in Stalin's Gulag* (New Haven, CT: Yale University Press, 2017). For other works that explore this topic, see Steven Barnes, *Death and Redemption: The Gulag and the Shaping of Soviet Society* (Princeton, NJ: Princeton University Press, 2011); Aleksandr I. Solzhenitsyn, *The Gulag Archipelago: An Experiment in Literary Investigation*, vols. 1–3 (New York: Harper & Row, 1975); Michael David-Fox, ed., *The Soviet Gulag: Evidence Interpretation, and Comparison* (Pittsburgh, PA: University of Pittsburgh Press, 2016); Mikhail Nakonechnyi, "'They Won't Survive for Long': Soviet Officials on Medical Release Procedure," in *Rethinking the Gulag: Identities, Sources, Legacies*, ed. Alan Barenberg and Emily D. Johnson (Bloomington, IN: Indiana University Press, 2022), 103–128. An exception is a gender analysis of Romanian women sent to Soviet camps; see Jill Massino, "Gender as Survival: Women's Experiences of Deportation from Romania to the Soviet Union, 1945–1950," *Nationalities Papers* 36, no. 1 (March 2008): 55–83.

7. E. V. Markova, "Doroga, kotoruiu ia ne vybirala," *Radost'*, no. 3–4 (1995): 126–133, http://www.sakharov-center.ru/asfcd/auth/?t=page&num=2793.

8. E. V. Markova, interview with the author by phone, October 10, 2017. She qualified her answer by explaining why she waited so long to write about the past: "None of us wrote about our lives in the camps in those times because it was so strictly forbidden. You would receive another sentence if you were caught writing about the camps. We all had to sign an agreement of nondisclosure when we left the camps that was kept in the organs. And besides, I didn't think anyone would care [about my story]."

9. Markova, *Vorkutinskie zametki*, 130. See also E. V. Markova, interview with the author, May 17, 2017, Moscow, Russia.

10. Markova, interview, May 17, 2017. This was one of the first things that Elena Vladimirovna said to me as we sat down to discuss her life and experiences in the Gulag. It is a reference to the fact that many former prisoners did not survive long after release or were not as successful as she and her husband were in rebuilding their lives after release.

11. This seems to have been somewhat rare. Rehabilitation usually entailed a dismissal of all charges and the lifting of passport restrictions.

12. Alessandro Portelli, *The Death of Luigi Trastulli and Other Stories: Form and Meaning in Oral History* (Albany, NY: SUNY Press, 1991), ix, 1. Portelli informs my interpretation of Markova's memoir. He argues that historical fact confirms something existed or happened, but memory of something tells us about the meaning of that event as it pertains to identity and culture. As a cultural form produced through the process of remembering, memoir illuminates the connection between the individual's identity and their community.

13. Markova, interview, October 10, 2017. Markova gave parts of her archive to the Sakharov Center and the State Gulag History Museum in Moscow.

14. On the basis of extensive work in declassified Soviet archives, the consensus among historians is that more than 1 million people were victims of political repression during the Great Terror (1936–1938); of that number, approximately 700,000 were executed in 1937–1938. See J. Arch Getty and Oleg V. Naumov, *The Road to Terror: Stalin and the Self-Destruction of the Bolsheviks, 1932–39* (New Haven, CT: Yale University Press, 1999), 591; Hiroaki Kuromiya, *The Voices of the Dead: Stalin's Great Terror in the 1930s* (New Haven, CT: Yale University Press, 2007), 1.

15. Markova, *Vorkutinskie zametki*, 31.

16. Ibid., 11. See also Markova, interview, May 17, 2019.

17. Pavel Polian, *Against Their Will: The History and Geography of Forced Migrations in the USSR* (Budapest: Central European University Press, 2004), 123–139. Polian writes that during the war, 1.2 million of 1.5 million Soviet ethnic Germans were subject to internal forced migration and resettlement. As of 1942, there were 1,031,300 ethnic Germans registered as special settlements throughout the central and eastern regions of the USSR. Markova's family was part of a cohort that was more or less left in place due to the rapidity of the German advance into Ukraine.

18. Markova, *Vorkutinskie zametki*, 7.

19. Ibid., 15–16.

20. Ibid., 13–14.

21. Ibid., 23. Markova's commendation dated March 20, 1943, is reproduced on this page.

22. Ibid., 31.

23. Ibid.

24. Alexopoulos, *Illness and Inhumanity*, 85–109. Gulag labor camps, colonies, and construction sites were always in need of medical personnel and often recruited prisoners with either experience or training to staff these positions, as civilians would often not last very long at camp sites.

25. Markova, *Vorkutinskie zametki*, 9.

26. Markova, interview, May 17, 2017. Markov worked alongside Iakov Vunder and Konstantin Ivanov at the Vorkuta State Drama Theater.

27. There were major differences between these legal categories, which greatly affected a Gulag returnee's prospects after release. Release as a result of a term expiring, amnesty, pardon, or conditional early release did not expunge former prisoners' criminal records. If a prisoner's sentence was not overturned with rehabilitation or other administrative action, the release did not restore their civil rights. See A. Artizov, A. Kosakovskii, V. Naumov, and I. Shevchuk, eds., *Reabilitatsiia: Kak eto bylo. Dokumenty Prezidiuma TsK KPSS i drugie materialy* Mart 1953-fevral' 1956, t. 1 (Moscow: Mezhdunarodnyi fond "Demokratiia," 2004), 45–48, 257–259. See also Nanci Adler, *The Gulag Survivor* (New Brunswick, NJ: Transaction, 2002), 26–34.

28. Markova, *Vorkutinskie zametki*, 9, 215. See also Markova, interview, May 17, 2017.

29. M. B. Rogachev, ed., *Pokaianie: Martirolog*, t. 12, ch. 2 (Syktyvkar: Fond Pokaianie, 2017), 27–28. See also Sakharov Center, "Markova Elena Vladimirovna (urozhd. Ivanova)," accessed March 27, 2019, https://www.sakharov-center.ru/asfcd/auth/?t=author&i=593.

30. Markova, *Vorkutinskie zametki*, 115.

31. See, e.g., Solzhenitsyn, *Gulag Archipelago*, 2:309–310; Janusz Bardach, *Man Is Wolf to Man: Surviving the Gulag*, trans. Kathleen Gleeson (Berkeley: University of California Press, 1998), 209–210, 235.

32. Markova, *Vorkutinskie zametki*, 115.

33. Arrest and imprisonment split Markova's life in two. This is reflected in the recurring metaphors and imagery she uses to describe the splitting of her autobiographical self. Markova wrote, for instance, "Two banks [of a river]— two worlds. One dark, hair-raising, the other—light, free, serene. The gates of the dark world open, and the convoy drives us in, like a flock of livestock to the slaughter"; *Vorkutinskie zametki*, 34.

34. Yurchak, *Everything Was Forever*, 132–133. Yurchak uses the metaphor of internal migration to describe the formation of publics of *svoi* during late Socialism that were simultaneously invisible within and a part of Soviet society. I use it here to describe how Markova retreated inward with other prisoners to "spiritually resist" the environment that actively destroyed their bodies and their sense of self. This retreat ultimately contributed to the formation of the public of zeks that she constructs in her memoir.

35. Markova, *Vorkutinskie zametki*, 51. For other examples, see 65, 67–68.

36. Ibid., 114–115. Markova also repeated this statement in our interview and her lecture at the Sakharov Center.

37. Ibid., 70–71.

38. Ibid., 52. On memorizing poems in the camps as a form of self-preservation, see M. D. Baital'skii, "Znai istoriiu goroda v kotorom zhivesh': Na kirpichnom zavode," *Zapoliar'e*, September 19, 2000; Archive of the International Memorial Society (AM) f. 2, op. 2, d. 81, l. 21 (I. V. Skakovskaia, "Vospominaniia o Vorkute i vorkutianakh (1946–59)," 1996); AM f. 2, op. 2, d. 112, l. 164 (V. E. Sollertinskii, "Kuda bog smotrit, vospominaniia," Sosnogorsk, 1984); A. Ia. Istoginoi, ed., *Intaliia: Stikhi i vospominaniia byvshikh zakliuchennykh Minlaga* (Moscow: Vest', 1995).

39. Markova, *Vorkutinskie zametki*, 76. On writing letters that would pass camp censors, Markova made sure to write in her usual romantic, spirited language "of her old self" as a proof of life for her mother and an indicator of her unbroken spirit. In this sense, Markova's poems are like Gulag letters, which Emily Johnson describes as "a time-stamped window on a past that was still unfolding"; Arsenii Formakov, *Gulag Letters*, ed. and trans. Emily D. Johnson (New Haven, CT: Yale University Press, 2017), 16.

40. Markova, *Vorkutinskie zametki*, 114–115. See also L. K'eralli, "Poeziia GULAGa kak literaturnoe svidetel'stvo: teoreticheskie i epistemologicheskie obosnovaniia," *Studia Litterarum* 3, no. 3 (June 2018): 144–163.

41. Ibid.

42. Ibid.

43. Alexander Etkind, "Sites and Sounds of the Camps: Commentary on the 'Legacies' Section," in *Rethinking the Gulag: Identities, Sources, Legacies*, ed. Alan Barenberg and Emily D. Johnson (Bloomington: Indiana University Press, 2022), 278.

44. For an example of a Gulag returnee who wrote autobiographical poems, see Aleksandr S. Klein, *Moi nomer "2P-904": Avtobiograficheskie stikhi i poema* (Syktyvkar: Komi respublikanskaia tipografiia, 1992).

45. Markova, *Vorkutinskie Zametki*, 72–82. Other themes include love, friendship, and memorializing the dead. Markova dedicates an entire chapter of her autobiography to the tundra.

46. Ibid., 71.

47. Ibid.

48. Josephine von Zitzewitz, "The Role of Nature in Gulag Poetry: Shalamov and Zabolotsky," in Barenberg and Johnson, *Rethinking the Gulag: Identities, Sources, Legacies*, 213.

49. For descriptions of this work, see chap. 3.

50. For Markova's correspondence with her mother while she was in Vorkuta, see Archive of the State Gulag History Museum (GBUK MIG) f. 5, d. 2 (1944–1958). Markova managed to keep many of the illegal letters that she received over the years. After release, she also managed to collect some of the letters she sent to others. These letters are also included in this archive.

51. Markova, *Vorkutinskie zametki*, 151.

52. Ibid.

53. Ibid.

54. From 1950 to 1952, Rontal' wrote seventy-four illegal letters to Markova who, it seems, was imprisoned in a separate camp section. For Rontal's brief biography, see E. V. Markova, V. A. Volkov, A. N. Rodnyi, and V. K. Iasnyi, *Gulagovskie tainy osvoeniia severa* (Moscow: Stroiizdat, 2001), 315. The biographical data Markova gives is incomplete. For more complete data, see Fond Ioffe, "Elektronnyi arkhiv Fonda Ioffe," 2010, https://arch2.iofe.center/person/33276.

55. See, e.g., GBUK MIG f. 5, d. 3, l. 29 (Note from G. M. Rontal' to E. V. Markova, not dated); GBUK MIG f. 5, d. 3, l. 24 (G. M. Rontal' to E. V. Markova, December 28, 1950); GBUK MIG f. 5, d. 3, l. 23 (G. M. Rontal' to E. V. Markova, December 24, 1950). In our phone interview on October 10, 2017, Markova said the following to me about the topics of her illegal camp correspondence: "We didn't whine about deprivations in our letters. We wrote about music, culture, spiritual life. And this saved us."

56. GBUK MIG f. 5, d. 3, l. 22 (G. M. Rontal' to E. V. Markova December 21, 1950).

57. In his letters, Rontal referred to Markova as his "dear sister" and signed them as "your brother."

58. GBUK MIG f. 5., d. 3, l. 27 (G. M. Rontal' to E. V. Markova, December 1951).

59. For other images from the personal archive of E. V. Markova that she donated to the Sakharov Center, see "Teatr v GULAGe: iz kollektsii E. V. Markovoi," Muzei Sakharovskogo tsentra, accessed January 10, 2017, http://museum.sakharov-center.ru/fotodok/index.php?p=141605:141607,141607:142504,142504:150656.

60. Markova, *Vorkutinskie zametki*, 93. Markova followed this note with "This is what the camp theater meant to us!" Guliachenko was imprisoned in Rechlag from 1951 to 1955. After release, Guliachenko returned to Kiev, where she graduated from Kiev State University and later taught English and German. During the war, she was dropped behind enemy lines as a radio operator. She was eventually captured by the Gestapo in Crimea. After escaping back to Red Army lines, she was arrested and sentenced to ten years in corrective labor camps and five years of deprivation of civil rights. For Guliachenko's biography, see Markov, 90–91. See also Virtual'nyi muzei GULAGa, "Vysotskaia (Guliachenko) Larisa Nikolaevna," accessed September 28, 2017, http://www.gulagmuseum.org/showObject.do?object=48578757&language=1.

61. Markova, *Vorkutinskie zametki*, 92–93.

62. Ibid., 161. Ivanov also received letters from his comrades who moved away after release, which he cherished and kept for the rest of his life. See Archive of the Vorkuta Museum–Exhibition Center (VMVTs) f. OF 4262, op. 1, d. 9, l. 2

(K. P. Ivanov to G. V. Trukhina, January 22, 1994); VMVTs f. OF 4262, op. 1, d. 5, ll. 2 (Unidentified former prisoner [Rein] to K. P. Ivanov, December 5, 1955); VMVTs f. NVF 3298, op. 1, d. 3, ll. 2 (K. P. Ivanov to unidentified former prisoner [Volodia], February 8, 1992).

63. Markova, *Vorkutinskie zametki*, 161, 163. See also GBUK MIG f. 5, d. 3, ll. 7–8 (I. Virzhonis to E. V. Markova 1992–1993). On changes in the social composition of Vorkuta's population in the 1950s, see Barenberg, *Gulag Town*, 198–230.

64. Markova, *Vorkutinskie zametki*, 162.

65. Ibid., 162–164. The letter was sent from Edgar Vil'gemovich Shtyrtskober to Markova on his return to Leningrad.

66. Ibid., 214. Markova notes that this was also the experience of their dear friends the Korovins, who were also a family of former political prisoners who spent many years in the camps of Vorkuta and in exile after release.

67. Markova, *Vorkutinskie zametki*, 214. See also Markova, interview, May 17, 2017. On the effect of "having a biography" in Latvia, see Vieda Skultans, *The Testimony of Lives: Narrative and Memory in Post-Soviet Latvia* (London: Routledge, 1998), 67–82. Skultans quotes the biography of a Latvian deportee that echoes the defiance of Markova's proclamation of her biography to would be employers: "Circumstances forced us to relocate to Siberia" (68).

68. Nikolai Ivanovich Korovin (1905–1988) was imprisoned from 1936 to 1939. After release, Korovin remained in Vorkuta. From 1942 to 1950, he worked as the head of the electric station and laboratory TETs-1 but was removed from this post in 1950 when the camp regime and control over former prisoners became more severe. Later, Korovin worked as the senior engineer at Vorkuta Mechanical Factory. From 1944 to 1950, he taught at the Vorkuta Distance Learning Center and the Vorkuta campus of the Leningrad Mining Institute. In 1963, he defended his candidate degree at the Leningrad Mining Institute. His wife, Bronislava Iakovlevna Korovina, was a close friend of Markova and a "Decembrist of the twentieth century." For Korovin's biography, see M. B. Rogachev, *Pokaianie: Martirolog* t. 12, ch. 1 (Syktyvkar: Fond Pokaianie, 2016), 315. For the story of Bronislava Korovina's life in exile in Vorkuta with her husband after his release, see Markova, *Vorkutinskie zametki*, 171–218.

69. Markova, *Vorkutinskie zametki*, 214.

70. Ibid., 216. It is unclear whether or not their wives were former prisoners because Markova does not name them; however, Markova includes them as members of the Vorkuta diaspora. For Volkov's biography, see Rogachev, *Pokaianie: Martirolog*, t. 12, ch. 1, 126–127. For Iasnyi's, Shapiro's, Eisner's, and Raikin's biographies, see Rogachev, *Pokaianie: Martirolog*, t. 12, ch. 2, 159–160, 333, 367, 386–387.

71. Markova, *Vorkutinskie zametki*, 216. Markova writes that she often spoke with other former prisoners about Vorkuta and those engineers and Gulag

"HOW I REMAINED A HUMAN BEING" 173

returnees who built the city of Vorkuta on the permafrost. See also E. V. Markova, *Zhili-byli v XX veke* (Syktyvkar: Fond Pokaianie, 2006), 256.

72. Ibid., 216. See also Markova, interview, October 10, 2017.

73. Ibid.

74. Markova, interview, October 10, 2017. These meetings enabled Markova to collect testimonies for her archive, years before she wrote her memoir. For other examples, see AM f. 2, op. 2, d. 112, l. 164 (Sollertinskii, "Kuda bog smotrit"); AM f. 2, op. 1, d. 77, ll. 54 (Iakov Kuperman, "Piat' desiat let, 1927–1977: Vospominaniia," not dated). Although he was not a prisoner in Komi, Iakov Kuperman worked in Vorkuta as an engineer during the war. He provides an example of how Gulag returnees outside of Komi also met with one another to remember the camps: "They all lived not far from one another, [and] worked together. The great work united them. Not by chance the veterans of BAM [Baikal-Amur Railway], even in the 1960s and 1970s held meetings every year, where (in principle: 'past pain is pleasure') they remembered with pleasure working on the gigantic project under tough, but sensible leadership of Frenkel.'"

75. Markova, *Vorkutinskie zametki*, 106.

76. Ibid., 216.

77. See chap. 2. For letters from children of Gulag returnees and their families, see GU RK NARK f. P-3800, op. 1, d. 39, ll. 33 (Correspondence with the repressed and members of their families regarding the activities of Syktyvkar Memorial, February–December 1993); GU RK NARK f. P-3800, op. 1, d. 56, ll. 69 (Correspondence with the repressed and members of their families on questions of rehabilitation, December 1994–December 1995); GU RK NARK f. P-3800, op. 1, d. 79, ll. 35 (Correspondence with relatives of the repressed on questions of rehabilitation, February–December 1997).

78. Markova, interview, October 10, 2017.

79. Markova's and Virzhonis' letters are organized as two pages in the archival file, which is why the page number repeats. For letters that allude to current events, see GBUK MIG f. 5, d. 3, l. 8 (E. V. Markova to I. Virzhonis, August 10, 1992); GBUK MIG f. 5, d. 3, l. 7 (Virzhonis to Markova, August 19, 1992); GBUK MIG f. 5, d. 3, l. 7 (Virzhonis to Markova, September 25, 1992).

80. GBUK MIG f. 5, d. 3, l. 8–9 (E. V. Markova to I. Virzhonis, July 1, 1992).

81. GBUK MIG f. 5, d. 3, l. 7.

82. Markova, *Vorkutinskie zametki*, 136.

83. Ibid.

5

Local Newspapers and the Production of Cultural Memory in Komi, 1987–2021

On November 26, 1956, the head of the Komi KGB sent a "top secret" report to the secretary of the regional party committee regarding an unprecedented event that had taken place in the subarctic city of Inta. On July 29, 1956, a group of current and former prisoners unveiled the Soviet Union's first monument to the victims of political repression in the village Vostochnyi (figs. 5.1 and 5.2).[1] The memorial was erected at the entrance to the eastern cemetery, which initially served as a graveyard for prisoners. The report described this unprecedented event in full detail and even included a photograph showing flowers that were laid at the foot of the monument with the cemetery in the background:

> Materials received in July-August of this year testified to the fact that Baltic nationalists, living in the city of Inta, Komi ASSR, began to erect monuments to persons who died in the camp and exile.
>
> On the 29 of July of this year at the cemetery in the second district of the city of Inta, the unveiling of a monument to Latvians who died in the camp and exile took place at the entrance to the cemetery. The unveiling occurred with a large crowd of approximately two hundred people with the accompaniment of a brass band.
>
> During the unveiling of the monument, a number of speeches were given; several of them had a nationalist character.
>
> As one speaker, a Latvian [by the name of] Krastins, said:
>
> "... We unveil this monument to the departed daughters and sons, who as victims of arbitrariness will never again see the motherland. The memory of them will forever live in our hearts ..."
>
> After the unveiling of the monument, those present performed the bourgeois Latvian anthem "God save Latvia."

The monument was constructed out of concrete and cement 2.5 meters in height [and] depicts a girl in the national Latvian costume with a branch in her hand, symbolizing Latvia. At the base [of the monument], "to the Motherland" is inscribed in Latvian.

The monument was erected by the sculptor Strazdins, Eduard Teodorovich, born 1902 (released from imprisonment by decision of the Commission of the Presidium of the Supreme Soviet USSR, at present he has left to live in the Latvian Soviet Socialist Republic). The Latvian Puntulis, Adol'f Petrovich, born 1913, who works at the construction-assembly directorate as a technician-builder, lent much aid in the erection of the monument.

At this very cemetery, Lithuanian nationalists intended to erect a monument in honor of Lithuanians buried there. There was already a draft of the monument, and preparatory work had already begun for its construction.

The initiators of the monument were Grigonis, Babrauskas, and Baniunis, the leaders of the mutual aid foundation that exists among the Lithuanians.

Considering that the monument erected at the entrance of the cemetery is not a gravestone monument and was constructed without the permission of the organs of Soviet power, a number of prophylactic measures were conducted by us through the Executive Committee of the Inta city council of workers' deputies with a view to prohibit the construction of new such monuments by Lithuanian and other nationalities and the prevention of nationalistic displays during their unveiling.

In particular, at our request, the active participants in the construction and unveiling of the monument—Puntulis, Krisons, and others—were summoned by the chairman of the city soviet, comrade Petrov, for conversations, during which the illegality of their actions were explained to them [and] that the construction of such monuments are allowed only with the permission of Soviet organs.

The individuals who were summoned to the city soviet stated that in taking part in the construction and unveiling of the monument, they thought that the initiators of the construction had agreed with the city soviet, and they did not knowingly violate any Soviet laws.

As a result of conducting these conversations on the illegal acts of the Latvians, the Lithuanian and Estonian nationalists ceased the construction of similar monuments.[2]

The lack of documentation in this case is curious. Despite an exhaustive search, there is no documentation of local authorities' initial approval of the monument or the KGB's "prophylactic measures."[3] The monument was constructed in a basement studio outside the camp zone, where artists fabricated decorations for Inta's buildings using materials from the camp. Considering

Figure 5.1 The note on the back of the photograph reads, "Photograph of the monument erected by Latvians at the cemetery in Inta. Inscription: 'To the motherland.' Taken in Inta, August 31, 1956. [Signed] Modianov." Source: National Archive of the Komi Republic (GU RK NARK 2 f. P-1, op. 5, d. 461, l. 80).

Figure 5.2 (*above and facing*) Edvard Sidbrabs working on the Dzimtenei monument, Inta, not dated (July 1956?). Source: Inta Local History Museum.

the shifting sands of the party line on the past that followed First Secretary Nikita Khrushchev's denunciation of Stalin's "cult of personality" at the Twentieth Party Congress, just five months before the erection of the monument, it seems that local officials were simply at a loss for what to say or do. Given these circumstances, it is likely that local authorities gave oral consent to the project, which they could deny later if (when) problems arose.[4] Furthermore, the monument's location in a cemetery seems to have given some cover to those who acted as if it would be allowed. Astonishingly, the monument was not destroyed after the KGB and party officials in Syktyvkar learned of its existence. It was left in place and abandoned when the cemetery was closed in 1962.[5] Nevertheless, the monument did not languish and pass on into oblivion.

Thirty-three years after it was first erected, the Dzimtenei monument made headlines in Komi when it once again became the focus of coming to terms with the past. On August 23, 1989, the central Komi newspaper, *Molodezh' Severa*, reported on the restoration and rededication of the monument and the abandoned cemetery in a ceremony attended by local residents, members of the Memorial Society, and former prisoners who first unveiled it in 1956 (fig. 5.3). The newspaper told its readers the history of this forgotten monument, which was the first of its kind in the Soviet Union: "The high relief was done and unveiled in 1956 right after the Twentieth Party Congress and dedicated to the repressed Latvians who died in Minlag during the years of Stalin's lawlessness. . . . Time passed, and after the Thaw, other times arose. The monument was forgotten without a trace; it was overgrown with weeds, just like the old cemetery."[6] Underscoring the highly symbolic presence of survivors, the article continued, "At the meeting that took place here, former repressed [people] said that they believe in the triumph of justice on the Earth and will do everything so that they do not have to unveil this monument a third time."[7] But the episode did not end there. In a subsequent interview in the local newspaper *Iskra*, Al'fred Geidans, the seventy-seven-year-old former prisoner who traveled from Latvia to attend the ceremony, corrected *Molodezh' Severa*'s report and proclaimed the monument "not only a tribute to the memory of Latvians who became victims of Stalin's repressions but also a warning to the future to all people—Russians, Ukrainians, Lithuanians, Germans, Jews—that the fates of the prisoners of the 'GULAG archipelago' must never be repeated."[8]

The story of the Dzimtenei monument is emblematic of a central issue of the late Soviet and early post-Soviet period: How should the victims of political repression be commemorated? Not only the content of memory but also the forms of ceremonies and monuments were major issues, if not *the* issue, debated in Komi newspapers during this period of revolutionary change. This chapter examines the formation of the cultural memory of the Gulag and political repression in the Komi Republic by investigating the ways in which these topics were addressed in the proliferation of articles in Komi newspapers from 1988 to 2021.[9] Reportage on these previously taboo subjects became possible only after President Mikhail Gorbachev relaxed censorship as part of the Communist Party's renewed effort to address the Stalinist past. During this period, the press became the principal forum for debate and source of new information about the past.

Although it initiated reform, the party could not control the process after it started. Former prisoners, exiles, and their children filled the mailbags of local newspapers with testimonies that contradicted the party's claim that the main victims of Stalinist repression were party members. Once these testimonies

Figure 5.3 Rededication of the Dzimtenei monument, August 22, 1989. Source: Inta Local History Museum.

became public, it became increasingly difficult to preserve Lenin's legacy as the country sped toward the precipice. Although stories about Komi's heritage as the "Gulag republic" continue to appear in the local press, they have slowed significantly due to the shrinkage of local newspapers in the region and the shift toward a more nationalist politics of memory that occurred, in part, around the time of President Vladimir Putin's reelection in 2012.

The major themes of the coverage in Komi newspapers over this thirty-three-year period tell us much about the ways in which cultural memory was produced and how people in the Komi Republic came to terms with the past. These themes include the definitions of *victims* and *perpetrators*, the need for a people's archive based on victims' testimonies, and the search for a proper medium to represent the past and commemorate "victims of political repression." What happened, who the perpetrators and the victims were, and how it all should be remembered posed intense dilemmas that played out in the local press: How were people supposed to view those who were once "enemies of the people" and now victims of political repression?

Although it had cast itself as a victim and restorer of justice, the party stood at the center of the mounting evidence of mass death that was literally being unearthed at unmarked mass graves throughout Komi, raising the question: Who was to blame? How the public understood, remembered, and commemorated the past says much about the legacy of the Gulag and Stalinist repression and its place in cultural memory at the end of Soviet history.

The literature on post-Soviet memory has taken two different approaches based on ideas of trauma and transitional justice.[10] Looking through the lens of contemporary politics, these studies overwhelmingly focus on the recycling of Soviet symbols, the partial rehabilitation of Stalin's cult of personality, and the state's contradictory approach to commemorating the victims of political repression. Furthermore, these studies tend to be dismissive of local memory projects aimed at preserving the memory of the Gulag and Stalinist repression, if they consider local memory projects at all.[11] I adopt a different approach. I examine how the cultural memory of the Gulag and political repression developed from *glasnost* forward to the present. Therefore, I am able to illustrate the ways in which cultural memory was produced in Komi while avoiding a teleological examination of the Putin regime's selective use of the past to justify its present authoritarianism and wars of aggression throughout the region of the former Soviet Union.

Building on and moving beyond Alexander Etkind's concept of the "hardware and software" at work in the production of cultural memory, I highlight the development of the "infrastructure" of memory in Komi, which links cultural memory to the lived environment.[12] My examination of Komi newspapers illuminates the transformation of Soviet infrastructure—formerly monuments to socialist achievement—into memorials to the regime's victims.[13] As in previous chapters, this process was initiated by Gulag returnees who were the first to describe the infrastructure they built as monuments to their suffering. This chapter shows the various textual, material, ceremonial, and spatial ways in which memory was produced and the ways in which Gulag returnees' collected memories informed the content of cultural memory.

This chapter is organized into three thematic sections that explore the development of the cultural memory of the Gulag in the Komi Republic; each section develops chronologically from 1988 to 2021. The first section explores the definition of *victim* and *perpetrator* and how these categories changed over time. The second section explores debates about the veracity of memoir testimonies that were published with increasing frequency in the press. The third section examines the most prevalent theme in the coverage on political repressions, which focused on the issue of how to commemorate the "victims of political repression." Starting in the late 1980s, mass graves were discovered throughout Komi and became the primary sites of memory and mourning. The mapping of these gravesites, which in many instances were the only remaining traces of remote camp sections or special settlements, was of great concern to everyone as the sites presented incontrovertible evidence of what survivors described in their memoirs. By marking these grisly sites throughout the region, the people of Komi sought to properly lay the dead to rest while cementing this tragic history in cultural memory. Furthermore, marking gravesites met the minimum demand of the victims' families without requiring formal judgments of perpetrators, which became increasingly difficult as time passed after the collapse of the Soviet Union.

"Restoring Justice": Defining *Victims* and *Perpetrators*

The central theme of early press coverage on Stalin and political repression in Komi focused on identifying the victims and perpetrators. Once this process began, both party officials and members of society realized they needed to define these terms, which led to differences about what they meant. Although the definition of *victim* became clear and comprehensive over time as the full scale of repression was revealed, who exactly was responsible remained vague. This was not a simple question with a straightforward answer. However, defining these categories was essential because they ultimately set the limits of de-Stalinization and, perhaps most importantly, who would be remembered and who would be forgotten.

The opening salvos on this issue in the central press highlighted the Communist Party's renewed efforts to rehabilitate the "innocently repressed victims of Stalin's arbitrariness."[14] Although these articles conceded that some outside the ranks of the party suffered unjustly, they portrayed the party as the primary victim. To support this position, the articles underscored the party's great losses under Stalin's "command administrative system." In many ways, this discourse simply reproduced the language of Khrushchev's attempt to implement "socialist legality," which saw the limited rehabilitation of some party-affiliated Gulag returnees and victims of Stalin's Great Terror.[15]

The first article to address the question of victimhood in the Komi press was an interview with the chairman of the party-led commission, published under the title, "Without a Statute of Limitations," in the September 21, 1988, issue of *Molodezh' Severa*.[16] The Komi ASSR commission was formed in August 1988 in response to the Politburo's formation of its Commission on Additional Studies of Documents Pertaining to Repressive Measures of the 1930s–1940s and early 1950s in 1987.[17] The Komi commission included the general secretary of the regional party committee (Obkom), the head of the Komi Ministry of Justice, the chief justice of the Komi Supreme Court, the chief state prosecutor, the editor-in-chief of the party newspaper *Krasnoe znamia*, and other lower-ranking officials. According to the interview, the commission defined *victims* as "illegally repressed members of the Party," including those sentenced as so-called "Trotskyites," saboteurs, and those who suffered for any "connection with anti-Soviet elements."[18] However, when it came to the perpetrators of these crimes, the chairman was not so clear. Instead, he made a vague statement about the "environment" of the 1930s and 1940s:

> [Question:] Who was subjected to groundless expulsion from the party and for what?

> [Answer:] I want to note that it was impossible to do without strict demands and discipline in those times. But brutality has no justification. There were many false accusations and denunciations made out of a feeling of self-preservation. The rules of behavior were dictated by the environment: things are not going well at the collective farm, the harvesting of grains is dragging on, the plan for lumber production is not being fulfilled—and an order was prepared. All shortcomings were "the work of hands of enemies of the people."[19]

Although the article remained obscure about who the perpetrators of these crimes were, except to blame the environment of "those times," it raised three important issues that demanded readers' attention. First, it laid out the party's narrow definition of *victim*, as a party member who suffered from Stalin's "arbitrariness" during the 1930s and 1940s. Noticeably, it mentioned nothing about those who were shot, sent to the camps, or exiled, although they were certainly among those cited in the figures published in the article. Second, the article reemphasized the current party leadership's role in the restoration of justice, which had been left unfinished following the twenty-second party congress. By taking on the mantle of Khrushchev's reform, the article signaled a break with Brezhnev-era polices of enforced silence and forgetting and initiated a new effort to come to terms with the past in Komi.[20] The third issue, regarding the difficulty of reform raised by the chairman's comment that "there are almost no eyewitnesses left," drew a direct response from those who been left out of the party's narrow definition of *victim*.[21] The "missing" eyewitnesses responded resoundingly in the Komi press.

The definition of *victim* was passionately debated outside the party's ranks, which became the focus of extensive coverage in the Komi press. On November 25, 1988, *Molodezh' Severa* reported that "debates broke out" over the definition of "victims of Stalinism" at Memorial's founding conference.[22] Several members of the audience, which included survivors who were left out of the party's definition, raised questions about the "hangmen" who fell victim themselves after they carried out acts of mass killing during the Red Terror, the Civil War, and the Purges. Another member of the audience responded with the suggestion of "limiting it [the definition] to the years 1925–1953. Otherwise [we will] have to remember the White Terror and the victims of the 1905 revolution."[23] However, the article continued, "He was opposed [by others]: Stalinism has its own roots and continuities, [and] that is why it should not be limited by time, or place. There was even a suggestion to include victims of Maoism and of the Cambodian genocide [*Polpotovshchina*] as inescapable consequences of the *Stalinshchina* [Stalin's mass repressions]. The question was left open."[24]

In addition to the definition of *victim*, the chronology of commemoration was called into question. To get a sense of who else might exist and to help solve these debates, *Molodezh' Severa* opened the issue to all readers in an appeal: "In order to help Memorial, it is not even obligatory to be a member. It would be good even if every reader of *Molodezh' Severa* clarified whether one of their relatives or simply someone they know was repressed and wrote to the editors of the newspaper."[25] This idea of collecting data was a strong central theme from the beginning of *perestroika*. As Kathleen Smith notes, people like Dmitrii Iurasov, who worked in the Central State Archives, used his access to form a card catalog of victims, which he contributed to Memorial's project to identify all victims.[26] Although the question of who was a

184   AFTER THE GULAG

victim and who was to blame was not going to be solved overnight, the editors of *Molodezh' Severa* recognized the debate as the "first step toward national repentance."[27]

Newspapers outside of Komi were also replete with debates about the definition of victim and the timeline of repression as part of the national conversation that began with glasnost and continued through the collapse of the Soviet Union. As former prisoner Lev Razgon wrote about the importance of identifying victims and perpetrators in the newspaper of the International Memorial Society, *Vedomosti Memoriala*, in January 1989: "Yes, it is our moral duty to find out exactly who was who during the tragic years."[28] Although regional newspapers tracked closely with the national conversation, they brought much-needed attention to the local history of Stalinist repression and the concerns of local people. As *Kotlovan*, the newspaper of the Khibin Memorial Society (located on the Kola Peninsula), stated in December 1989, "The goal of our publication is not only to share the activities of the All-Union Memorial Society. We want to bring attention to the issue of special settlers. The problem, in our eyes, is that they remain unrehabilitated to this day. Why are we focusing on this problem? We must not forget that our region was developed primarily by special settlers."[29] The public consumed the new information presented in these publications with voracity in an effort to learn as much as they could as the past changed before their eyes (fig. 5.4); however, the collapse of the Soviet Union brought new concerns to the forefront of people's minds that displaced the issue of political repression. Nevertheless, the coverage of Memorial's ongoing memory project continued in Memorial's newspapers, which closely followed the proliferation of monuments, memory events, and research throughout post-Soviet Russia.[30]

The invitation to share one's experiences as a victim of political repression was not passed over by former prisoners and exiles, their children, and others who lived through the period of the *Stalinshchina*.[31] Survivors' memoirs flooded editors' mailboxes, and newspapers published excerpts in an effort to ground abstract categories in the details of individual lives.[32] In doing so, they humanized the colossal nature of state violence abstractly referred to as "political repression" and contributed to the expansion of the definitions of *victim* and *perpetrator* in public discourse. Furthermore, the narratives that survivors wrote about their lives in Komi and the publication of these testimonies in the local press contributed to the localization of Soviet history. Stalinist repression no longer simply "took place." It happened to people in places in Komi and throughout the Soviet Union.

The December 8, 1989, issue of *Molodezh' Severa* featured a full-page article on the 1953 uprising in Rechlag with testimony from a Gulag returnee

Figure 5.4 This photograph from the newspaper *Ukhta* (1989) identifies the primary perpetrators of repression (left to right): Joseph Stalin, Vyacheslav Molotov, and Kliment Voroshilov. The caption reads, "ASA-KRD-PSh-ChSIR-UPTO-NPG-NIR. Special Board." These were the abbreviations given to those accused of treasonous political crimes. The abbreviations stand for Anti-Soviet Agitation, Counterrevolutionary Activities, Suspicion of Espionage, Counterrevolutionary-Trotskyite Activities, Family Member of a Traitor to the Motherland, Member of an Underground Trotskyite Organization, Illegal Border Crossing, Intention to Betray the Motherland. Source: Ukhta State Technical University Local History Museum (AM UGTU f. Bulychev, A. I. Terent'ev, V. Bulychev, "Khotelos' by vsekh poimenno nazvat,'" *Ukhta*, February 22, 1989, no. 37 [8652]).

who named Stalin personally responsible for the corpses buried in mass graves throughout Komi.[33] He understood the uprising not as an anti-Soviet act of resistance but as an expression of political prisoners' righteous frustration as innocent "victims of Stalin's repression" who remained behind barbed wire while common criminals were set free in the wake of Stalin's death.[34] By featuring the stories of local survivors, the article attempted to provide readers with an understanding of what exactly repression was and who its victims were—ordinary Soviet people from all walks of life.[35]

The relatives of the repressed also shaped public understanding of categories when they wrote to newspapers. On August 7, 1990, for example, *Ukhta* published a "Search Bulletin" for "persons subjected to illegal repressions" who were imprisoned in Ukhta.[36] Listing brief biographical details of repressed people and the families' contact information, the bulletin added to the growing diversity of Stalin's victims.[37] The legacy of the *Stalinshchina* was not some abstract horror that could be compartmentalized and relegated to the past but rather something that continued to resonate in the lives of Soviet families throughout the country.

A growing chorus of voices in the local press asked, "Why was mass lawlessness possible?" This question prompted a response from local party organizations and the Supreme Court of the Komi ASSR. In an article published in *Krasnoe znamia* on March 3, 1989, entitled "To Restore the Good Name of Those Who Were Illegally Repressed," the deputy chairman of the Supreme Court of the Komi ASSR condemned the prior weakness of the courts for having contributed to the "atmosphere of intolerance and enmity" under Stalin.[38] Without naming names, he laid part of the blame for mass violence on the courts themselves. In another unprecedented step, the deputy chair of the Supreme Court shared the case details of former prisoners and victims who were shot during the Great Terror to illustrate how Stalin's "arbitrariness" affected real lives. As the deputy chair wrote, "Lately, the names of honest, innocent people who were crossed out of the history of our country, and sometimes from life itself, on the basis of false denunciations are returning from fifty years ago. These are not only the names of marshals and leaders of industry but also rank-and-file workers, including residents of our republic."[39] Although the article continued to obscure who exactly was guilty of these historical crimes, this self-criticism as part of the state machinery of repression and review of cases—regardless of party affiliation—was a step toward a broader definition of victimhood.

Despite the court's acknowledgment of a growing range of victims, the party's perspective on the issue changed little since 1988. In 1990, *Krasnoe znamia* published two progress reports on the rehabilitation commission's work.[40] Although the focus remained on party members, the second of the two articles entitled "Restoring Justice: For the Sake of Moral Cleansing," published numbers for the first time that revealed the scale of repression:

> During the 1934–1939 period, 3,778,234 were accused of political crimes; of them, 786,098 were shot.[41] The situation of arbitrariness developed in the country during the years of the *Stalinshchina*. In our republic, it touched a thousand people from the Komi oblast' party organization. Seven hundred forty-three members and candidates were expelled from the party. Among those convicted and expelled were leaders of party and Soviet organs, Komsomol and union members, teachers, workers, builders, and transportation workers.... The majority of those expelled were subjected to arrest and trial, and several were taken under arrest straight from the party bureau meeting or as a result of their decisions.[42]

In light of the barrage of survivor testimony, the publication of official numbers seems to have been an attempt to put a tourniquet on the escalation of further revelations in the press. Nevertheless, the juxtaposition of victims who lost their lives alongside those who unjustly lost their party cards read like a half-hearted attempt to convince the public that the party was the real victim. This approach was not enough to evade the question of guilt, which was shifting from resting solely on Stalin's shoulders to the party itself.[43]

The staggering scale of repression revealed on the pages of *Krasnoe znamia* raised questions not only about the party's complicity in mass repression but also about the culpability of ordinary Soviet citizens. Weeks after the publication of the numbers of victims, Komi newspapers struggled to make sense of what Irina Paperno refers to as the "suicidal" nature of Stalinist repression.[44] The search for answers was complicated by the "gray zone" that victims and perpetrators occupied within what Lynn Viola refers to as the "ecosystem of violence" that drove Soviet society to modernity.[45] On September 29, 1990, the newspaper *Ukhta* severely criticized the party's interpretation of the past and its claim to victim status.[46] The article called on its readers to consider tough questions left unanswered by the party:

> Let's better ask ourselves the question, How can it be that the party and the entire Soviet people turned out to be silent witnesses of all the horrors that took place? And they not only silently acquiesced but also wildly welcomed mass punishments of people who were not guilty of anything. How can we understand the faculty of social and party psychology of a person of that time? Why did people who commanded armies for twenty years give themselves, with a lamb's submissiveness, to the tyrant, to be taken to the executioner's block? No one will save the people until each of us is imbued with a consciousness of political and civil responsibility for everything that happened and is happening with the country.[47]

This statement marked an explosive departure from previous efforts to identify victims and perpetrators, which maintained a wall between the party of Stalin and the present. The article is striking not only for its accusation against the party but also for its answer to the question of how to understand the complex legacy of mass repression. The absence of mechanisms through which people could make sense of the past made the struggle to identify perpetrators and victims all the more difficult. The key to this process, it seems, was the development of society's historical consciousness.

Two articles published on October 12, 1990, in the newspaper *Ukhta* illustrate how emerging civil society groups formed a coalition of the repressed and their neighbors and petitioned the party to adopt a broader definition of *victim*. The first article reprinted the speech of Memorial's cochair, Karina Musaelian, which she delivered to the Interregional Deputies Group—the first legal parliamentary opposition in the Soviet Union—at the second Congress of People's Deputies in Moscow. Framing the request for victims' aid as part of building a stronger democracy, her speech cited the examples of other socialist countries (Poland, Hungary) and Germany, which had long since engaged in the process of coming to terms with the dark chapters of the past.[48]

The second of the two articles in *Ukhta* was an open letter to Gorbachev from the participants of Ukhta's "Week of Conscience" hosted by the Ukhta-Pechora Memorial Society from September 30 to October 7, 1990 (which will be examined later).[49] Under the banner of the Ukhta-Pechora Memorial Society, the group of Soviet citizens expressed their "deep anxiety" about the "developing crisis" in Soviet society. They wrote, "Only justice and the whole truth can stabilize this condition."[50] Their petition proposed a comprehensive definition of *victim*, called for the identification and lustration of all perpetrators by stripping them of the honors and privileges they earned working for the secret police, and suggested measures to make "rehabilitated" a status befitting unjustly repressed Soviet citizens:

1. Openly name all those who bravely went through Stalin's camps and exile, and were rehabilitated with the degrading wording "for lack of basis of a crime," *not victims of repression but veterans of unequal struggle with lawlessness* [emphasis added]; to review the formula "rehabilitated for lack of basis of a crime" (article 58), [and] change it to a more just [formula], reflecting the bravery and patriotism of repressed communists and nonparty members who, having served the motherland in the inhumane conditions of the camps and exile, lost their health to hard labor.
2. Condemn the totalitarian system and the ideology it founded in the name of the people at the Congress of Peoples' Deputies of the USSR [by] removing the graves of the hangmen of the people (Stalin, [Vsevolod] Vyshnevskii, [Lev] Mekhlis, and others) from Red Square.
3. Pay compensation to those illegally repressed for [their] slave labor and all the years in the camps and prisons from the budget of the CPSU [Communist Party of the Soviet Union].
4. By state decree, provide privileges to all rehabilitated people at the same level as disabled veterans of the Great Patriotic War [World War II].
5. Revoke all state awards and privileges from those who received them for service in the repressive organs and from their administrators in the party-state who participated in illegal repressions.

6. For complete transparency, open all materials of the archives in connection with those illegally repressed.[51]

This public letter to the Soviet leadership shows not only the most encompassing definition of *victim* but also an attempt to assert the heroism of these long-suffering patriots of the Soviet motherland. This definition of victimhood echoed the voices of former prisoners who sought acknowledgment of their innocence and their contributions to Soviet society but did not wish to be seen as victims.[52] Furthermore, although the letter pointed an accusatory finger at Stalin (and the party by extension), the petition to Gorbachev was an acknowledgment of the party's power not only to affect the restoration of justice in Soviet society but also to punish the perpetrators of crimes against the people.

From 1991 to 1995, the public discourse on victimhood in Komi newspapers shifted from remembering "victims of Stalin's repressions" to victims of "totalitarian" and "communist repression."[53] As a result of the continuing coverage on the "debasement of human dignity" under Soviet rule, the definition of *victim* expanded to include previously excluded children of former prisoners, exiles, and deported nationalities. On October 30, 1992, for example, *Vechernii Syktyvkar* featured an article on "Children of the GULAG," which profiled the life of Nikolai Morozov, Syktyvkar State University professor of history and a founding member of the Syktyvkar Memorial Society. Morozov was born in the camps to two political prisoners and then sent to a home for children of enemies of the people. He was reunited with his mother and stepfather in Inta, where they were forced to live after their release from a strict-regime camp. Addressing the difficult issue of classifying the children of Gulag returnees, Morozov told the interviewer, "And now I ask myself the question, 'Was I guilty of the imaginary sins of my parents?' After all, it turns out that I also had article 58, but for some reason, I am not considered a convict, a repressed person."[54] This same difficulty applied to those repressed during World War II. An article in the November 23, 1991, issue of *Ukhta* argued that those who were repressed as a result of their capture, forced migration, or simply having been in occupied territory during World War II should also be considered victims of political repression: "And do you remember our questionnaires until recently: Were your relatives captured or [taken] abroad? Were you on occupied territory? The answer 'yes' ruined the fates of many people."[55] All of these diverse groups of people fit into an evolving definition of *victim*, as the chairman of Syktyvkar Memorial told *Krasnoe znamia* in 1992: "To us, they are all repressed [*repressirovannye*]."[56]

In 1994, the Ukhta-Pechora Memorial Society published the second volume of its widely lauded book of memory, *In the Bowels of Ukhtpechlag*, which, after years of intense debate, unambiguously proclaimed, "We have come to the conclusion that the victim was the entire people. Before us is the terrible legacy of a genocide never before seen in history."[57] This definition was the product of a long process documented by the Komi press, which was shaped by members of the local community as well as Gulag returnees who wrote to the editors of local newspapers from outside of Komi.

Although there had been some discussion about the need for a "Nuremberg process" during the later years of glasnost, it remained unclear who would stand trial. Memorial argued that a trial of perpetrators was part of the process of restoring the "truth of the past" and a call to "cleanse and improve society" rather than a "call to extract revenge," as conservative critics of Memorial decried the idea.[58] Nevertheless, even after the collapse of the Soviet Union, hesitancy remained among state officials and others to wade further into the issue.[59] In an interview in the February 27, 1995, edition of *Molodezh' Severa*, for example, former KGB officer and historian Veniamin Poleshchikov discussed the idea of prosecuting Stalin's "hangmen."[60] The interviewer asked, "In your book, you imply the need for our own type of 'Nuremburg trial' on the grounds that the genocide against our own people was unleashed by the Soviet state. How do you imagine this process? After all, if there are any of those guilty of this tragedy from those years left alive, they are already very elderly."[61] Despite denouncing the crimes of Stalinism and arguing that the state ought to share their information in the quest to restore dignity and justice to the dead, Poleshchikov ultimately balked at the idea of open archival access and extending retributive justice to lower officials and foot soldiers who carried out these crimes:

> I did not mean [that we should prosecute] specific perpetrators. I think that in the course of this process we must make public the monstrous facts of the heinous crimes of that time. The state should also apologize to those who suffered from these brutalities. Finally, we must somehow mark the places of mass executions. After all, we know where they are. We do not need to go far—take Syktyvkar, for example. There are several of such places here around Verkhnii Chov [and] Dyrnos Kiul'. I even know the person, who carried out the executions. I even know that one day they took people to be shot and drank spirits (they were supposed to drink a glass) until they got down to business. As a result, one person was wounded but not killed. Because they had spent the bullets assigned to them according to the norm set by the bosses, they finished off this person with a shovel. Imagine what would happen to this person if I disclosed his name. The next day, he would be torn to pieces somewhere on Stefanovskaia square.[62]

With the collapse of the Soviet Union fresh in their minds, Poleshchikov's opinion on the possibility of a post-Soviet Nuremberg illustrates how even those who worked to bring the past to light remained hesitant to address the question of complicity at a local level. Identifying the victims of political repression was painful enough. Furthermore, it seems that Poleshchikov and others, such as Human Rights Commissioner Sergei Kovalyov, did not wish to slow the process of democratization and antagonize the new state, which inherited many of its predecessor's former employees.[63]

Although the definition of *victim* became more comprehensive over time, the same was not true for the category of *perpetrator*, which remained ill-defined, vaguely referring to Stalin and the Communist Party. This outcome reflects the intense focus on commemorating victims in the press and the difficulty of unpacking the complex legacy of repression in which perpetrators became victims themselves. These definitions were constantly in flux as citizens of Komi made sense of, commemorated, and mourned the victims of political repression.

New Evidence: Memoirs, Letters, and Memory as Sources of a New History

On September 28, 1989, *Krasnoe znamia* published a full-page editorial that questioned whether the "truth" [*pravda*] about the past could ever be restored in the face of the unimaginably colossal scale and horror of state repression: "Neither fantasy, nor imagination can recreate the cruel pages of that history in full truth. Moreover, even the memory of those who experienced all this refuses to remember. And not because [they] want to forget, but because if they remember everything, [their] heart will break and [their] mind will not endure. Survivors have a right to cross off those years and to forget. But the rest of us do not have this right. [We] have a duty to prevent oblivion. Piece by piece, line by line, [we must] collect history as exhortation and warning."[64] For the memory project to proceed successfully, it required novel sources offering new perspectives. During the late 1980s and 1990s, newspapers turned to survivors as sources with the hope of forming a more complete understanding of the Stalinist past. However, the feeling among many was that time was running short: "We must hurry, time settles accounts with people and memory faster than us. And yet there is still the feeling that, nonetheless, we are too late."[65]

From 1989 to 1992, Komi newspapers saw a peak in the publication of stories about individual lives trampled "under the wheels" of political repression. As one librarian in Ukhta remarked in 1991, "We learned many new things about the camp past of our republic from all the publications in the periodical press."[66] Not only did these stories shed light on Komi's camp past but they also humanized the enormity of mass repression.

One result of featuring survivors' testimonies as a source of history was that it undermined the bias toward state and party archives as the key to the past. This section examines the ways in which survivors' testimonies that were not stored in party archives were discussed in public discourse as the people's "historical memory." It shows how these sources were seen as essential to revising the state's narrative of the past.

Calls for historical revisionism in Komi newspapers highlighted the absence of survivors' voices in the record. The revisionists argued that this previous silence was a product of the attempt to erase all traces of Stalin's crimes. A feature article in the February 22, 1989, issue of *Ukhta* focused on the Ukhta-Pechora Memorial Society's efforts to collect the stories of marginalized groups in Soviet society to build a new archive: "History must not only be built on the evidence of illustrious people or their relatives. Generally, history is understood in simple human fates. But unfortunately, we have never surveyed the surviving witnesses of those times—the dekulakized peasants, repressed workers. Now these people represent a priceless piece of history."[67] Returning the voices of the repressed and writing history "from below" were important on their own, but the local newspaper raised the stakes of this memory project by connecting it to the recovery of the nation's past: "Collecting this material, we will prepare future textbooks of history, we are saving our own national history from oblivion."[68] Consequently, Gulag returnees' testimonies not only shed light on Komi's camp past but also were the basis of an alternate history of the Soviet Union.

Over the course of 1989, denunciations of the party's guarded candor about the past expanded into criticism of the limited archival sources it allowed to pass into circulation. Coupled with the sheer volume and revelatory shock of survivors' testimonies, the incompleteness of official documents led many to question the official version of the past. The May 12, 1989, issue of *Ukhta*, for example, featured a full page of letters to the editor from all over Komi and the Soviet Union. The editor's introduction to this commentary called on readers to reflect on the purported numbers of repressed and to ask oneself how such a thing was possible: "How could such a thing have happened? Where did they find among our people the hundreds and thousands of torturers and murderers of millions of tortured and murdered? After all, if we adhere to the traditional number of losses during the Great Fatherland War—20 million—then the number of victims of Stalinism, the bacchanalia of exiles, arrests, prisons, executions (from 1927 to 1953) [must be] almost two times greater!"[69]

LOCAL NEWSPAPERS AND CULTURAL MEMORY

193

Absent any archival documents on the actual numbers of dead, imprisoned, and exiled persons, the editor cast doubt on the party's repeated claim that Stalin's acts primarily targeted party members. The article concluded with an excerpt from another letter to the editor from the daughter of a Gulag returnee in Kiev. Praising *Ukhta* for publishing the "truth about the past," she underscored the importance of these new sources of information to those left behind: "And, while we still live, we want to extract something more from oblivion than a name and date of birth."[70] Such letters to the editor were an important genre during perestroika as they afforded an opportunity to slip in views that party careerists and editors could not say themselves and were a huge source of emerging pluralism in that era.

The degradation of Stalin's legacy was not welcome by all. In 1990, newspaper editors noted the growing number of anonymous complaints about how such an "obsessed" focus on past tragedies "blackens our glorious history."[71] However, these conservative voices were drowned out by those who saw the total de-Stalinization of Soviet memory as a necessity for the success of reform and the health of Soviet society. This was the position that the Vorkuta newspaper *Zapoliar'e* took in its introduction to a collection of letters from the camp published in the August 2, 1990, issue: "The pernicious legacy of Stalinism still persists in politics, economics, culture, [and] our soul. [It is] like a painful, chronic illness. We must never drive it deep down. Like pus from an abscess, it must come out. Otherwise, the entire organism may be poisoned."[72] For the sake of future generations, the article called for a complete account of the past: "A people that does not know its own past does not have a future. We are obliged, in the name of our own salvation, to tell the whole truth (and not some prescribed part of it!) about what happened to us."[73]

Following the collapse of the Soviet Union, the desire to "extract something more from oblivion" intensified; however, the long sought-after archival documents raised more questions than they answered. As one article in *Krasnoe znamia* lamented, "We search for memory in documents but there is none. Or they lie. Or even more terrible—they tell [us] part of the truth. And what is truth, especially about those times?"[74] As many families came to realize, even the archives of the Ministry of Internal Affairs were incomplete. In many cases, the archives offered little more than a victim's name, date of birth, sentence, place of confinement, and date of death. To the victim's relatives and those who took up the charge to recover the past, such as the Inta Local History Museum, this lack of documentation was evidence of how mass repression continued to obfuscate attempts to overcome it. As the historians at the Inta Local History Museum wrote in an editorial published in the April 22, 1992, issue of *Krasnoe znamia*,

194   AFTER THE GULAG

There are not even the usual photographs in their case file[s]. [The case] was conducted for almost two years. Yellowed and decayed by time, the folder is covered in a multitude of typed numbers and letters. It looks like they set this file aside and then returned to it, but they didn't get around to taking a photo. [This was] precisely because in the 1930s in the provinces, it was difficult [to complete the file] because the investigator would decide it's useless, the case needs to be carried out so that only one person remains in memory: all five—enemies of the people—were sentenced to be shot. The sentence was executed. And forget about them. Yes, happily, we did not forget.[75]

During this new stage in the memory project, the public was confronted with the limitations of archival documents, which were sometimes unable to resolve long-standing questions, nor were they always able to reconstruct the fates of those lost in the camps. Although archival documents (and the lack thereof) raised new questions about the nature and extent of political repression under Soviet rule, a shift had occurred in support of memory as the source of an alternate past. Even after state and party archives became more accessible after the collapse of the Soviet Union, people continued to turn to nonstate archives for insight into how political repression affected individual lives.

Laying the Dead to Rest: Ceremonies and Monuments to the Victims of Political Repression

Commemorations of the victims of political repression focused primarily on laying the dead to rest with monuments and ceremonies designed to restore dignity to those who were denied it in life and to communicate cultural memory of the past. Commemorations of the dead were focused on what Irina Flige refers to as the "necropolis of the Gulag"—the anonymous mass burial sites that hold the remains of those who were shot during the Great Terror, prison and labor camp cemeteries, and cemeteries for deportees, special settlers, and exiles.[76] The ceremonial internment of the dead who lay in unmarked mass graves was an attempt to come to terms with the mounting evidence of the regime's crimes that was literally being unearthed throughout Komi during the late 1980s and 1990s. This process of discovery continues to this day; while I was conducting research for this book in Ukhta in April 2017, a new mass grave was discovered. In June 2021, firefighters discovered another mass grave on the territory of a former camp in the village Emva, 136 kilometers north of Syktyvkar by road.[77] This section explores the ways in which the victims of political repression were commemorated in ceremonies and monuments that formed an infrastructure of memory linking the Komi landscape with the cultural memory of the Gulag.

From the very beginning, the link between memory and space was a central feature of the newspaper coverage on political repression in Komi. In the absence of preserved camp complexes such as Auschwitz in Poland and Perm-36 in Perm oblast', which symbolizes political repression of the 1970s and 1980s rather than the Stalin era, place names in Komi took on new meaning during the collapse of the Soviet Union.[78] By revealing the true origins of many of Komi's towns as sites of repression, newspapers transformed them into monuments to the victims of political repression.[79] Aleksei Terent'ev, the founder of the Ukhta-Pechora Memorial Society and one of the leaders of Komi's environmental movement, underscored this shift in meaning in the September 29, 1989, issue of *Ukhta*: "The camp memory of the village Vetlosian lives by its own name, the concrete and brick buildings: the boiler room, the isolator, the water tower. The wooden buildings still exist—the rotting barracks of the camp guards."[80]

Places associated with Komi's camp past underwent a subsequent transformation into sites of mourning when mass graves were discovered. In addition to confirming the darkest details of survivors' testimonies, these grisly discoveries evoked moral outrage when newspapers reported that many graves were destroyed as camps grew into cities. For many, the lack of respect for the dead was an indicator of the party's moral bankruptcy and another blow to its legitimacy, as a 1990 newspaper article stated: "The industrial use of the areas of former mass graves of the many thousands of prisoners speaks to a deficit of conscience in the leadership. . . . There is no kind memory for the victims of Stalinism."[81]

The return of the dead confronted the public with powerful evidence at a time when it was still working out whom to remember and how to commemorate them. This process was aided by elderly residents who wrote to newspapers to identify the locations of sites missing from the map. A letter to the editor published in the December 9, 1989, issue of the Vorkuta newspaper *Zapoliar'e* read, for example:

I send you a photo of the cemetery as it was in the middle of the 1950s at mine no. 40 (*Vorkutinskaia*). It stood near the fur workshop on the hill. Not a bad place. Then they filled it in with rocks and built over it. Now Kirov Street is there. How many people lie there, having fallen during Stalin's repressions! I myself saw how they hauled off the dead in wagons—pulled by a horse, and behind, two people filled the graves. They did not put the deceased in coffins but simply in wide pits [and] covered them. They drove a stake with a number into the grave mound and that's it.[82]

The unmarked graves covering the vast Komi landscape became the central focus of a nascent civil society's efforts to commemorate Stalin's victims.[83] As one member of Memorial wrote about local residents who aided in the search for the gravesites in *Ukhta* in 1990, "For us *Memorialtsy*, this is not simply help and participation in the search, but also new material, evidence, the truth about what happened to us. For if the people do not know their own past, they will not have a future."[84]

To commemorate the living and the dead victims of political repression, the Ukhta-Pechora Memorial Society developed a ceremony of remembrance. The first, earth-shattering event, organized by the Moscow Memorial Society in 1988, featured a "wall of memory" with documents provided by survivors and their children; inspired, Ukhta's Week of Conscience became an annual memory event starting in 1989 (fig. 5.5).[85] As "ground zero" of the Gulag's colonization of Komi, the choice to hold the Week of Conscience in Ukhta was highly symbolic. As Gulag returnee and local resident Nikolai Volodarksii said in his opening remarks to the 1990 Week of Conscience,

> I remind you, although it is well known without me saying so, that the days of conscience are being held at the very site where, not so long ago, one capital of the GULAG empire was located. Here, more than most, the victims of Stalin's Terror, those who were not guilty of anything, who were sentenced for nothing—people with clean consciences—served sentences. I myself served ten years for the leader of all times and peoples. . . . In Vorkuta, Inta, Abez', Pechora, all throughout Komi, there were thousands of so-called "enemies of the people" behind barbed wire. Stalin's hangmen did not pass over the Poles, western Ukrainians, Belorussians, and Balts—all those to whom the Soviet Army extended a "helping hand" at one time or another. Now, thank God, different times have come. . . . We are gathered here to remember the terrible years, the years of arbitrariness and violence, to remember the names of those who are no longer among us. THE STALINSHCHINA MUST NEVER BE REPEATED.[86]

Noting their diversity, Volodarskii's speech underscored that the purpose of the memory event was to remember all of Stalin's victims rather than selectively remembering the few, as the party or ethnic communities had done. Furthermore, by listing towns and cities that were once camps in Komi, Volodarskii connected the gathering in Ukhta to an expansive infrastructure of memory that connected the region with the rest of the country.

From 1990 to 1993, the Week of Conscience received extensive front-page coverage in the newspaper *Ukhta*. The memory event included seminars on the history of the Gulag and political repression, the opening of a museum exhibit entitled "Memory of the Victims of Illegal Repressions during the Cult of Personality," excursions to former campsites, and an evening of memory featuring the screening of a documentary film and readings of memoirs.[87] However, the main event of the week was the requiem service (*Panikhida*) in memory of the victims of political repression, led by an Orthodox priest from the community. Former prisoners, exiles, and their families came to Ukhta from all over Komi and the rest of the country to remember and mourn their loved ones at gravesites that once belonged to Ukhtpechlag. As *Ukhta* reported on September 29, 1990, "They come to pay their respects to their loved ones, sons, daughters, and grandchildren of those who vanished in these lands. They come for a handful of earth from their parents' graves. And others for whom the search for the graves of the innocent victims of repression has become a matter of debt also come."[88]

As an occasion for coming to terms with the past, the requiem service illuminates the public response to the knowledge that their own government had perpetrated the mass violence they read about; a fact that many others struggled to comprehend throughout the rest of the country.[89] It also shows, as Irina Flige points out, how both the general public and individuals who finally learned the details of their relative's death and the location of their grave experienced these discoveries as "new" deaths that "demanded a funeral."[90] Although many in Komi had first- and second-hand knowledge of state repression, this struggle to comprehend suggests that they did not really know about the massive scale of repression. The requiem also responded to an acute need for closure for those who still did not know the fate of their loved ones decades later. As the son of prisoner wrote in *Ukhta* in 1993, "[My father] died without the right to a burial in a marked grave. And today in Ukhta, there are no traces of the graves of the many thousands of innocently murdered citizens of Russia and other countries in the GULAG.... But the sacred memory of him remains, lives, and will continue to live."[91]

Although Komi is unique in many ways, the focus of memory work on the dead reflects trends that emerged throughout Eastern Europe following the collapse of communism.[92] As Katherine Verdery notes, shifts in the "worlds of meaning" that bind societies together—such as the one that accompanied the collapse of the Soviet Union—are expressed in ceremonies that "set up right relations between living human communities and their ancestors."[93] In this light, the emphasis on mourning the dead can be seen as part of an attempt to cement

Figure 5.5 "Week of Conscience" requiem at Vetlosian. The Orthodox cross was erected by the Ukhta Oil and Gas Geological Trust "in acknowledgment of part of the guilt of their predecessors [the Ministry of Internal Affairs who ran the trust]." Source: For the photo see Bulychev, ed., *V nedrakh Ukhtpechlaga: vypusk vtoroi*, 45. For the quote, see AM UGTU f. Bulychev, V. Bulychev, "A. Akhmatova—'Vsego prochnee na zemle pechal,'" *Ukhta*, October 12, 1991, no. 198 (9063).

the new interpretation of the past in cultural memory by sacralizing it at specific sites throughout Komi, rather than a return of repressed memory or continuity with prerevolutionary religious practices, as other scholars have argued.[94]

While the requiem service at the Week of Conscience drew large crowds and enjoyed broad support among those who could not travel all the way to Ukhta, it did not garner the support of party officials, who refused to attend. The snub did not go unnoticed and resulted in a sharp rebuke of the party's behavior in the October 12, 1990, issue of *Ukhta*: "Wreaths from the city executive committee, Memorial, Ukhta council of veterans of war and labor, and the division of culture were laid on the grave. THERE WAS NO WREATH FROM THE CITY'S COMMUNISTS. Either they forgot in the vanity of vanities (on this day, a party conference was held), or they just did not want to attend. After all, the Vetlosian burial mound was abundantly fertilized with the bones of faithful Leninists."[95]

At a historic moment, when the past was undergoing a radical transformation and the country's future seemed to be at stake, the party's contempt for the new martyrs was unacceptable. In addition to calling out the party's insincerity toward reform, the article placed the blame for the people's suffering squarely on its shoulders: "And generally, who, if not the CPSU, bears responsibility for the situation that has developed in the country? But not only for this? And for collectivization, and for the GULAG, and for the grave consequences and victims of World War II? Although millions of communists were not guilty (they themselves were deceived and became victims), this does not remove responsibility from the 'center' and 'avant-garde,' which has led the country into a dead end."[96]

This scene also played out in other cities. In Krasnodar, for example, the local Memorial Society reported resistance from city and party officials, who denied its application to hold a memorial service for the victims of political repression. Krasnodar Memorial held the event anyway, and a crowd of three hundred people comprising former prisoners, exiles, their children, veterans, and local residents who had not been repressed gathered in front of the former People's Commissariat of Internal Affairs building to hold a memorial service for the dead and missing.[97] Ultimately, however, the riot police who were on the scene did not disperse the peaceful protestors.[98] It was in this context, with the Party discredited by its own actions (both past and present), that the production of a new cultural memory of Soviet repression continued with the erection of a variety of monuments.

An array of monuments to the victims of political repression appeared throughout Komi as the Soviet Union collapsed. As of 2021, there were eighty-three marked gravesites and monuments in Komi.[99] They include simple plaques laying claim to urban infrastructure, memorial stones inspired by the Solovetsky stone in Moscow, and crosses marking the site of mass graves.[100] Despite the existence of gargantuan abstract monuments in places like Magadan and the Levashovo Cemetery in St. Petersburg, no such monuments appeared in Komi.[101] Instead, Komi's monuments primarily resembled grave markers. Local authorities were simply not interested in spending what little money they had on monuments after the collapse of the Soviet Union. It seemed the fate of communism had been decided. Despite the decision of the Supreme Soviet of the (now) Komi Soviet Socialist Republic, for example, to name Vorkuta a "city memorial" and to install a massive monument there—to be sculpted by the émigré sculptor Ernst Neizvestnyi, who completed Magadan's "Mask of Sorrow"—nothing came to fruition.[102] The majority of the monuments that appeared during this period in Komi were erected without financial support from the state.[103]

Smaller-scale monuments primarily funded voluntarily by private individuals began to spring up across Komi in the 1990s. In Ukhta, a statue of Pushkin sculpted by a prisoner of Ukhtpechlag (who was subsequently shot in 1937) was refurbished and moved from the children's garden to the city center in 1993 (fig. 5.6).[104] Although the statue did not depict the camps in any way, it was lauded in *Ukhta* as a "natural symbol and emblem of the city's character" as a site of memory of the Gulag.[105] Other small markers appeared throughout Komi, such as a plaque installed in the city garden of Sosnogorsk in 1993. Perhaps more significant than their appearance, such markers reflected the shift in cultural memory, which commemorated the "victims of the communist regime" instead of just "victims of Stalin's repressions."[106]

Throughout the 1990s, monuments dedicated to particular ethnic groups were installed at camp cemeteries.[107] One year after the restoration of the Dzimtenei monument in Inta, for instance, Lithuanians returned in 1990 to erect the monument dedicated to "the unreturned" in the Lithuanian, Komi, and Russian languages (fig. 5.7).[108] In Vorkuta, several monuments were

Figure 5.6 Pushkin monument to the victims of political repression, Ukhta. (*top left*) Side. (*top center*) Front. Source: Tyler Kirk (personal archive, Spring 2017).

Figure 5.7 (*top right*) Lithuanian monument, "Mourning Savior," to the "unreturned," Inta. Source: Fond Ioffe ("Vostochnoe kladbishche Intalaga: Skorbiashchii spasitel'," Fond Ioffe, accessed August 29, 2018, https://www.mapofmemory.org/11-21).

Figure 5.8 (*bottom left*) In the Rechlag memorial cemetery, where prisoners shot for their role in the 1953 prisoner strike are buried, the Lithuanian monument (est. 1994) looms over the mass grave, Vorkuta. (*bottom center*) Monument to "The Victims of Political Repressions" (est. 1989) overlooking the site of the first camp sections of Ukhtpechlag, with the Polish monument (est. 1997) in the lower right-hand corner, Vorkuta. Source: Fond Pokaianie (AFP f. N. A. Morozov, [photograph of meeting in memory of victims of political repression in Vorkuta, August 3, 2002]; AFP f. N. A. Morozov [photograph of Vorkuta monument 1989]).

Figure 5.9 (*bottom right*) Metal cross erected in 2004 by a former prisoner at the entrance to a series of mass graves of prisoners of Lokchimlag and Ust'vymlag in the village Adzherom. Source: Tyler Kirk (personal archive, Spring 2009).

erected in memory of "The Victims of Political Repressions" (1988, 1990) and repressed Ukrainians (1990), Lithuanians (1994), Germans (1995), and Poles (1997) (fig. 5.8).[109] While many of these monuments of the late 1990s and early 2000s specify whom they mourn, they stand in memory of all who never left Komi (fig. 5.9).

The establishment of Fond Pokaianie in 1998 ushered in a new era in the production of cultural memory in Komi. As the only organization of its kind in Russia, the establishment of Fond Pokaianie formed a partnership between Syktyvkar Memorial and the government of the Komi Republic to "perpetu-ate the memory of the victims of political repression" and to conduct histori-cal research on Komi's Gulag past.[110] This was a major development in the region's politics of memory, which brought state support and financial aid to the memory work that had been done on the initiative of local citizens and Memorial. In May 1998, the official newspaper of the regional government, *Respublika*, printed several decrees from the governor's office that ordered the construction of a monument in Syktyvkar, the development of memorial com-plexes at the camp cemeteries in Ukhta and Inta, and the allocation of funds from the republic's budget to support research projects. These efforts were part of the "year of harmony and reconciliation" in "commemoration of the memory of the victims of mass political repressions in the Komi Republic."[111] Memorial hailed the emergence of Fond Pokaianie and the further develop-ment of Komi's infrastructure of memory as a major achievement and a symbol of progress and hope for the future. Perhaps most significantly, as Memorial wrote in a press release in 1998, the establishment of Fond Pokaianie was the first state-sponsored organization to "officially declare repentance" for Soviet crimes and to act on it.[112] Furthermore, Fond Pokaianie was also engaged in field expeditions that led to the discovery of former campsites, graves, and material objects that had been lost in the taiga and tundra by former prison-ers, which filled the archives of local history museums throughout Komi. Four years later, in 2001, Memorial celebrated Fond Pokaianie again in a featured article in its newspaper, *30 Oktiabria*: "There is nothing like it anywhere else in the Russian Federation."[113]

Fond Pokaianie made two major contributions to Komi's infrastructure of memory: the capital's first monument to the victims of political repression and the publication of the multivolume book of memory, *Martyrology* (*Martiro-log*).[114] Before the 1998 decree, there was no monument to the victims of politi-cal repression in Syktyvkar except for a "foundation stone," which was installed in 1997 to mark the site of the future monument. The form of the monument

202   AFTER THE GULAG

was decided by a committee convened by the governor of the Komi Republic that included representatives of the republican government, members of Fond Pokaianie and Memorial, and the Syktyvkar diocese of the Orthodox Church, which rejected all entries submitted at a competition held in the House of Artists in Syktyvkar in 1998.[115]

A year later the monument was still in the planning stages. As the Day of Memory of Victims of Political Repression approached, no concept had been agreed upon. Although the times had changed, some saw the lack of progress as yet another of the government's broken promises. Gulag returnee Leonid Markizov wrote in an editorial in *Krasnoe znamia* a year after the commission was formed in 1999:

> It is already clear now that the monument in Syktyvkar will not be installed by October 30. That is why some *Syktyvkartsy* [residents of Syktyvkar] think that the project ought to be assigned to one of the studios without any competition and that the city administration should just approve it. To one degree or another, such haste is justified. . . . At Memorial, they think that the inefficacy of the installation of monuments to the victims of groundless repressions is highly characteristic of our country. Take Vorkuta [for example], although they erected monuments to the victims of the GULAG, the main [monument]—designed by the famous sculptor Ernst Neizvestnyi—has still not been installed, even though the celebrated artist made it free of charge. . . . But everything has come to a standstill. When will we finally, honorably, pay homage to the memory of the victims of repression on our island of the GULAG archipelago?[116]

Markizov's editorial in *Krasnoe znamia* shows not only the complicated process of selecting the monument's form but also the growing frustration and lack of faith in the government's pledges of support to such projects.

In the case of the Syktyvkar monument, the two-year stalemate was overcome only when the governor unilaterally assigned the project to local artist Anatolii Neverov.[117] As the artist entrusted with public monuments commemorating topics such as the Soviet-Afghan War and the restoration of the Great Patriotic War memorial, it seems Neverov was a safe choice for the sensitive assignment.[118] However, like others who contributed to the memory project led by Syktyvkar Memorial and now Fond Pokaianie, Neverov felt that addressing this topic and commemorating it with a public memorial was extremely important not only for Komi but also for the health of the country. As he said during an interview, "This topic concerned me as the most tragic fate of our people and all of Russia and the Soviet Union."[119] Despite the false starts, this complicated process of selecting the right artist reveals the diverse interests that shaped the production of cultural memory, which crystallized when the monument was finally erected in 2000.

Continuing traditions established in the late 1980s and early 1990s, the Syktyvkar monument mourns the dead with a mixture of secular and religious iconography (fig. 5.10).[120] Despite its decentralized location, it was chosen for its significance as the former site of Syktyvkar prison no. 1, which served as a transit camp for prisoners on the long road north.[121] Although the monument's facade is that of an Orthodox chapel, oriented east to west and adorned with crucifixes and icons, up close the monument is primarily composed of symbols and imagery representing Komi's camp past.[122] The inner walls of the chapel are lined with the names of those who were sent to Komi (published in vols. 1 and 2 of the *Martirolog*) as a reminder of the diversity of the repressed (fig. 5.12). The outer panels record in bronze the names of the camps, interspersed with scenes from "that world" (fig. 5.12).

The largest outer panel, a triptych entitled "Desecrated Faith—Night Arrest" [Porugannaia vera—Nochnoi arrest], faces east (fig. 5.12).[123] The triptych symbolizes the shattering of communist faith and repentance for past crimes.[124] From eye level looking up, the panel depicts a man standing with a downturned face and outstretched arms reaching out toward the shattered crest of the Order of the Red Banner, indicating that the victim was a distinguished communist. His wife stands next to him, holding a child in her arms; a packed suitcase sits at their feet. Looking upward, above the shattered crest, is the image of the Virgin Mary with the inscription, "To the victims of repression: Our pain, sorrow and repentance." Before the doors to the monument's inner sanctuary, which are made of heavy iron bars to give the appearance and heft of a prison door (fig. 5.12), there is a granite tomb containing earth from the cemeteries of the major camp complexes of Vorkuta, Ukhta, Inta, Sosnogorsk, and Syktyvkar (fig. 5.11).[125] Neverov underscored this tomb as the most important aspect of the monument: "You see, the best message of the chapel is repentance, specifically for the people's eternal sorrow."[126] As a symbolic cemetery for the repressed, the earth from the remote islands of Komi's Gulag archipelago links Syktyvkar with these diffuse sites of memory and mourning.

Fond Pokaianie's multivolume book of memory, *Martirolog* (currently in its twelfth volume), informs the symbolic meaning of the Syktyvkar monument in the cultural memory of political repression and Russia's Far North. Although newspapers continued to serve an important role in keeping the topic of political repression within public historical consciousness during this period, the *Martirolog* became one of the primary sites of what Aleksandr Etkind

Figure 5.10 (*top left*) Syktyvkar Monument to the Victims of Political Repression, Komi Republic, Russian Federation. Source: Tyler Kirk (personal archive, October 30, 2016).

Figure 5.11 (*top right*) Granite tomb at Syktyvkar Monument to the Victims of Political Repression, Komi Republic, Russian Federation. Inscription reads, "Eternal memory to the victims of repression." Source: Tyler Kirk (personal archive, October 30, 2016).

Figure 5.12 Detail of Syktyvkar Monument to the Victims of Political Repression, Komi Republic, Russian Federation. (*bottom left*) Bronze outer paneling. (*bottom center*) Inner sanctuary. (*bottom right*) Triptych panel, "Desecrated Faith—Night Arrest." Source: Tyler Kirk (personal archive, October 30, 2016).

refers to as the "software" of cultural memory.[127] By publishing the names of the dead, archival documents, and survivors' memoirs, the *Martirolog* informs who and what is remembered at the monument, the "hardware" of memory.[128] As the first chairman of Fond Pokaianie, Gennadii Nevskii, wrote in the first volume of the *Martirolog* in 1998, "This is a book of memory and mourning of hundreds of peoples, representatives of those who were thrown into the hell of the GULAG, into one of the islands [of the archipelago] that was on Komi soil. 'Preserve forever' is inscribed on the cover of the *Martirolog*. We must preserve forever the memory of the terrible events of the second quarter of the twentieth century so that this tragedy will never again be repeated. Preserve forever the memory of victims of political repressions—not out of bitterness, not for vengeance, but for repentance."[129] The collected memories contained in the *Martirolog* are anchored to the landscape by the monument, which interrupts daily life to remind passersby that Komi was once the "kingdom of camps." In other words, the *Martirolog* and the monument produce cultural memory that is made part of the landscape and perpetuated by future generations who alter it over time as they remember.

The link between cultural memory and the Komi landscape is also evident in the initiatives of Fond Pokaianie and local history museums. In 2000, for instance, Fond Pokaianie and the Inta Local History Museum partnered to get the Komi government to recognize the Inta water tower as a "protected monument of history, culture and architecture" (fig. 5.13).[130] Built in 1954 by prisoners of Minlag, following the blueprints of imprisoned Swedish architect Artur Tamvelius, the water tower was part of the camp's infrastructure. It continued to serve the needs of the subarctic mining town that emerged after the camp was closed.[131] Its appearance in the 1957 film *Incident at Mine Eight*, written in 1956 by former prisoners Iulii Dunskii and Valerii Frid, was a signal to others who had been to Inta that the film was not only shot onsite but also was about the clash of generations (former prisoners vs. Communist youth) in a northern coal mining town (fig. 5.14).[132] The formal resignification of the water tower into an infrastructural monument to the victims of political repression is documented in the guidebook to the city's "ring of repentance," *Memory of the Gulag: Inta*.[133] The guidebook describes the monument as "representing the boundary between two epochs: life in unfreedom of thousands and thousands of victims of political repression who built the city, and the free development of the toiler-city, born in that very year. It is the embodiment of the link of time: of the tragic fate and deserved glory of the city."[134] The resignification of the water tower as an infrastructural monument led to the 2014 opening of Komi's first museum dedicated solely to the history of the Gulag and political repression

Figure 5.13 Panorama of Inta (not dated) with the water tower visible in the center of town, near the former camp zone. Source: Ukhta Local History Museum (IKMU [f. Ia. Ia. Krems, "Fotografii staroi Inty"]).

Figure 5.14 Screenshot from *Incident at Mine Eight* depicting the Inta water tower, 1957. Source: *Sluchai na shakhte vosem'* [1:02:32], accessed January 18, 2023, https://youtu.be/GCmxSYepuhY.

Figure 5.15 Photo of the museum inside at the base of the Inta water tower (2014). Source: Iaroslava Parkhacheva, "V Inte otkryli pervyi v Komi muzei istorii politicheskikh repressii," *7 x 7*, October 4, 2014, https://7x7-journal.ru/item/48162.

inside the water tower (fig. 5.15).[135] Underscoring that this event was not just symbolic in a small town in the Far North, twelve thousand people visited this museum each year before the COVID-19 pandemic.[136]

By the early 2000s, several Komi newspapers began to express anxiety about the insufficiency of the existing monuments and civil society's declining participation in memory projects dedicated to coming to terms with the past. Local newspapers, such as *NK* in Inta, pointed to the "lack of memory" among local residents.[137] According to the director of the Inta Local History Museum, the biggest indicator of this deficit of memory was that many residents claimed not to know where Inta's sites of memory were located and that no one in the city had "raised one memorial plaque to the Victims of Stalin's repressions with the city limits."[138] What made this situation "shameful" and "painful" was that all the existing monuments, she claimed, "were installed by outsiders, former prisoners of Inta's camps and their relatives."[139] It was not enough that Memorial and others had previously done much to preserve these sites of memory; the director called for the state to officially recognize "these sacred places" and to ensure their continued preservation, which was desperately needed for "the sake of our conscience."[140]

Newspapers of the early 2000s pointed to the disregard for memorial cemeteries, which lay abandoned and littered with trash, as another indicator of the decline in public historical consciousness.[141] In 2002, a Syktyvkar weekly published the comments of residents who expressed outrage about the disrespect for the dead: "Memory of the past, of people, must not only be in museums, memoirs and beautiful speeches. Where in Europe will you find a forsaken and desecrated cemetery? Where would you find such [a thing] in Asia? A cemetery is a sacred place."[142] The rebuke of local authorities for failing to protect the cemetery continued: "After all, far from everyone likes to go to museums, [and] breathe their stale air. But here, it is possible to see works of art, to touch history, to learn about [repressed] peoples' fates directly under the open sky."[143] It is important to note that even during the Soviet period, religious traditions of proper burial and maintaining a family member's grave remained an important part of Soviet culture.[144] Beyond this, the destruction of the cemetery was all the more shameful because it had been hailed publicly in 1990 as a symbol of the triumph of the restoration of justice.[145] Regardless of what one thought about Soviet history and the continuous calls to remember, cemeteries and the monuments that marked them held a special place in cultural memory as "material reminders of the people's past troubles."[146]

Similar outrage was sparked when former Vorkuta mayor Igor Shpektor proposed the construction of a "living" Gulag museum in the tundra. According to the proposal in the July 30, 2010, issue of *Respublika*, tourists would be able to experience the extreme conditions of Stalin's arctic Gulag.[147] Although it was never realized, the plan was vociferously opposed by Fond Pokaianie as making a mockery of human suffering. The arguments in favor of the project expressed dissatisfaction with the absence of museums dedicated wholly to the Gulag (even though almost every museum in Komi features permanent exhibits on the subject) and a desire to recreate the camp experience as a warning that the Gulag could return. As Valerii Budovskii, sitting mayor of Vorkuta and grandson of a former prisoner of Vorkutlag, said of the necessity of such institutions, "Unlike Germany, where Nazi concentration camps such as Dachau or Buchenwald are preserved, or Poland where there is Auschwitz, in Russia there is no such thing. And the memory of the terrible years of the Stalin's repressions must be preserved for [our] descendants."[148] However, unlike his predecessor, Budovskii did not support building a camp as a tourist attraction: "We will exhibit old spades, picks, and dishware in the museum. We will show the conditions in which prisoners lived. But the main thing is this is still history. But I am against people spending the night on bunks in barracks behind barbed wire. I would not stay there one night."[149] The Fond Pokaianie chairman Mikhail Rogachev also opposed the proposal on similar grounds: "Komi needs a Gulag museum. But it should be an actual museum, and not a relaxation center for tourists."[150]

Anxieties about the growing indifference to the past in the early years of the new millennium were met with the introduction of new ceremonies. The Week of Conscience remained a regular event in Ukhta, but it was eventually superseded by the annual celebration of the Day of Memory of the Victims of Political Repression, which is observed throughout Komi and the Russian Federation on October 30.[151] In honor of the holiday, the October 28, 2010, issue of *Krasnoe znamia* featured a brief survey of the recent history of the event that described how it was observed in cities that were once sites of the Gulag throughout Komi.[152] The article underscored the significance of the holiday in Komi's "biography," which was "closely interwoven with the epoch of the GULAG."[153]

Continuing the tradition of blending secular and religious rituals, the Day of Memory of the Victims of Political Repression is observed throughout Komi in candlelight readings of lists of the names of the repressed led by local history museums and Fond Pokaianie at monuments. Such memory events were intended to stabilize what many experienced as the destabilization of cultural memory under Putin, when the state shut down and took over the Perm-36 Museum as it simultaneously passed legislation on the commemoration of the victims of political repression.[154] Echoing earlier appeals to remember the past as an act of ensuring the future, the director of the Inta Local History Museum underscored the importance of remembering in 2010: "[We must] ensure that the link of memory is not broken. People pass away, but we must preserve memory."[155] In addition to the passing of the last generation who directly experienced Stalinist violence, these fears were stoked by the increasing normalcy of justifications of Stalin's repressions found in federal school history textbooks and on state television, despite politicians' posturing speeches to remember the dead.[156] These interpretations of the past frame Stalinist violence within a unifying, patriotic narrative in which the Gulag was essential, rather than detrimental, to industrialization and the war effort.[157] Despite alarming praise for Stalin spreading in public discourse, the politics of memory in Komi remained stable during the first decade of Putin's rule, and Fond Pokaianie was left to continue its work.

Coverage on the topic of political repression slowed considerably over the next decade. This change was not due to a lack of interest in the topic on behalf of the public, Fond Pokaianie, or the local history museums. These organizations continued to uncover Komi's camp past and commemorate it with new monuments, museum exhibits, and publications ranging from self-guided tour pamphlets on Komi's various sites of memory to entire volumes of the *Martirolog*. In 2018, for instance, the National Museum of the Komi Republic celebrated Fond Pokaianie's twentieth anniversary with an exhibit featuring its work over two decades.[158] Nevertheless, the change in coverage in the local press during the period 2012–2021 reflects the overall shift in Putin's politics of memory toward a more nationalist history that emphasizes Russia's role in the Red Army's victory in World War II (referred to by its Soviet-era moniker, the Great Patriotic War) while downplaying the mass repressions of the Soviet regime.

As Nikolai Koposov has written, the cult of the Great Patriotic War was easily "readapted" and adopted as a foundational myth by Putin's regime because it is "deeply rooted in Russian historical memory."[159] Although this myth draws from the Soviet past, it departs from the Soviet cult of the war in important ways. Specifically, Putin's myth has been purified of its communist content. Russian nationalism and the leadership of the state have replaced Soviet associations and the Communist Party that secured the great victory.[160] Putin's myth also emphasizes the unity of the state and its people, who shared in the tragedy and triumph of the war. This message has great mobilizing power. As in other regions throughout Russia, the victory in World War II is celebrated with extreme nationalist fanfare in Syktyvkar, including its own "eternal regiment" in which relatives of those who fought march down the main boulevard—Communist Street—to the main square in a military-type parade. Part of the mobilizing power of this myth is derived from a vague anti-fascism, or, as it has evolved under Putin, anti-Nazism, which Kopsov describes as "one of the key aspects of the USSR's political legacy."[161] As the world has seen in Russia's state-controlled media since its invasion of Crimea in 2014—and with increasing frequency since the invasion of Ukraine on February 24, 2022—Nazism is understood in Russia as "a profoundly anti-Russian force that is absolutely alien to Russia's political tradition," which "implicitly denies the possibility of a fascist movement in Russia."[162] The centrality of the Soviet victory in Russian historical memory is one of the reasons why Moscow remains unwilling to move beyond acknowledging Soviet crimes (albeit on a limited basis) and to try them as Nazi crimes were tried at the postwar Nuremberg Tribunal—something that Memorial and the victims of political repression have lobbied for unsuccessfully since 1989.[163] To do so would be to undermine not only the victory but also a cornerstone of post-Soviet Russia's foundational myth.

Despite the competition between these contradictory memories, the memory of Stalinist repression remains vibrant in Komi thirty years after the collapse of the Soviet Union. Articles continue to regularly appear in the local press highlighting the work of local individuals and organizations who remain dedicated to shining light on the dark chapters of Soviet history. On May 18, 2021, for example, the regional online journal *7x7* released a documentary film, *A Gulag Was Here* [*Zdes' byl GULAG*], which explores the legacy of the Gulag in Komi and the efforts of those who remain in Komi's dying northern cities to preserve this history in memory of the victims of political repression.[164] The film takes us to Syktyvkar, Inta, Pechora, and Vorkuta, where we catch glimpses of the infrastructure of cultural memory that Memorial, Fond Pokaianie, and their allies built, in addition to the landscapes and buildings that Gulag survivors designated as their monuments in their letters and memoirs. The message of *A Gulag Was Here* is that, despite Putin's politics of memory and the difficulties of everyday life in the Far North, the memory of the victims of political repression lives.

The presence of Komi's past was the focus of a 2008 interview with Komi's deputy to the State Duma in Moscow, Rostislav Gol'dshtein, who declared, "All of the Komi Republic is a big monument to the victims of political repression."[165] He elaborated on the importance of historical memory in the present:

> Komi was literally embroiled in camps. The 'zone' stretched for thousands of miles. Most of our northern towns and settlements are former places of exile. At the beginning of the last century, half of Komi's population were "politicals" [political prisoners]. In 1939, the "free" population of the Komi ASSR was 320,300 people, while the "camp" [population was] 112,000. It was the repressed who constructed the coal mines, oil fields, logged and built the railroad on the permafrost, and were even the first in the country to start producing radium. Many of them are heroes—at the very least, the ones who landed in the Gulag without guilt—but they are unknown heroes. We still do not know the exact number of the exiled, or their names. The camp archives have been destroyed and the [last] witnesses are almost gone. *But the memory lives* [emphasis added].[166]

Despite the exhortations of Komi's leaders to remember the past and an infrastructure of memory dedicated to commemorating political repression, new research and efforts to remember outside the proscribed forms are met with resistance from state officials. Moreover, as the collapse of the Soviet Union slides further into the distant past, the turnout in Syktyvkar on October 30 declines. For the most part, the children and relatives of the victims continue to attend, along with the faithful members of Memorial and Fond Pokaianie. While popular historians defend Stalin on national state television and some people see him as an "effective manager," a cohesive cultural memory of the Gulag and political repression remains in Komi. Although memory changes with the context in which it is reproduced, the stability of cultural memory in Komi is the result of a memory project that hás been ongoing since 1987.

Although the party initiated the memory project of coming to terms with the Stalinist past, the production of cultural memory was taken over by the people who published evidence, erected monuments, and invented rituals that ultimately delegitimized the Communist Party and contributed to the collapse of the Soviet Union. Komi, unique in many ways, is emblematic of the memory projects that unfolded during the collapse of the Soviet Union in other parts of the country touched by the Gulag and political repression. Forgetting is a part of every society, and hope remains in the places colonized by forced labor that continuing to commemorate the past will prevent oblivion. Despite the shifting currents of the capital, memory lives in the provinces.

Notes

1. Figure 5.2: It is unclear who took these photographs; however, they were donated to the Inta Local History Museum by Al'fred Iur'evich Puntulis, who was one of the active participants in the monument's construction. Researchers at the museum believe that one of the Latvian exiles took the photos. See N. A. Baranov, email message to the author, February 19, 2019; N. A. Baranov, email message to the author, February 21, 2019. On Edvard Sidrabs, the prisoner who sculpted the monument, see M. B. Rogachev, ed., *Pokaianie: Martirolog*, t. 12, ch. 2 (Syktyvkar: Fond Pokaianie, 2017), 208.

2. National Archive of the Komi Republic (GU RK NARK) 2 f. P-1, op. 5, d. 461, ll. 77–80 (Chairman of the KGB of the Komi ASSR, V. N. Modianov to Secretary of the Komi Obkom KPSS, G. I. Osipov, November 3, 1956).

3. L. A. Kyz"iurov, "Pervyi pamiatnik zhertvam GULAGa v Komi ASSR," in *Politicheskie repressii v Rossii XX vek: Materialy regional'noi nauchnoi konferentsii 7–8 dekabria 2000 g.*, ed. M. B. Rogachev (Syktyvkar: Fond Pokaianie, 2001), 221–222; L. N. Malofeevskaia and M. B. Rogachev, eds., *Pamiat' o GULAGe: Inta. Putevoditel'* (Syktyvkar: Fond Pokaianie, 2012); N. A. Baranov, email message to the author, June 14, 2018; Inta Local History Museum, email message to the author, June 19, 2018. Neither Kyz"iurov's conference paper nor the guide to Inta's sites of memory make any mention of these measures or the initial approval for the monument. Working from a separate report authored by another KGB officer, Alan Barenberg briefly mentions this episode in the context of the crisis of the Gulag after Stalin's death; however, he is also unable to solve this riddle; Barenberg, *Gulag Town, Company Town: Forced Labor and Its Legacy in Vorkuta* (New Haven, CT: Yale University Press, 2014), 210. Thanks to Alan Barenberg

for sharing the report he cites, which was delivered in a speech to the Vorkuta Gorkom by a local KGB official.

4. This is also the conviction shared by archivists, museum staff, and researchers who have been working on the history of the Gulag in Komi since the late 1980s.

5. Starting in 1944, the burial of prisoners in common graves was forbidden by central authorities. The cemetery was opened in the late 1940s, approximately 1.5 km from OLP no. 2 of Minlag. Prisoners were buried here in individual graves until it ceased to be a camp cemetery in the 1950s and started to serve as the Vostochnyi village cemetery. During this time, *vol'nonaemnye*, including those sent to work in Inta as camp staff and exiled former prisoners, were buried alongside the repressed. See M. B. Rogachev, ed., *Pokaianie: Martirolog*, t. 12, ch. 1 (Syktyvkar: Fond Pokaianie, 2016), 142. On Gulag burial practices, see Vladimir Anatol'evich Isupov, *Demograficheskie katastrofy i krizisy v Rossii v pervoi polovine XX veka: istoriko-demograficheskie ocherki* (Novosibirsk: Sibirskii khronograf, 2000), 163.

6. National Library of the Komi Republic (NBRK), L. Kudriashova, "Svechi skorbi i nadezhdy," *Molodezh' Severa*, August 23, 1989. See P. O. Bursian, "V subbotu, v 10 chasov," *Iskra*, September 2, 1989.

7. NBRK, Kudriashova, "Svechi skorbi i nadezhdy."

8. NBRK, L. Kudriashova, "Ty ostalsia zhiv . . . ," *Iskra*, September 2, 1989.

9. I have collected approximately 160 newspaper articles on various topics pertaining to the Gulag and political repression in newspapers with a republic-wide circulation, such as *Krasnoe znamia, Molodezh' Severa, Respublika*, and *Krasnoe znamia Severa* and local city newspapers such as *Ukhta, Zapoliar'e, Iskra, Tvoia gazeta, Vechernii Syktyvkar, Moia Ezhva, Komi mu*, and others.

10. For such studies, see Thomas Sherlock, *Historical Narratives in the Soviet Union and Post-Soviet Russia* (New York: Palgrave Macmillan, 2007); Kathleen E. Smith, "Whither Anti-Stalinism?," *Ab Imperio* 4 (2004): 433–448; Nanci Adler, "The Future of the Soviet Past Remains Unpredictable: The Resurrection of Stalinist Symbols amidst the Exhumation of Mass Graves," *Europe-Asia Studies* 57, no. 8 (December 2005): 1093–1119; Adam Hochschild, *The Unquiet Ghost: Russians Remember Stalin* (Boston: Houghton Mifflin, 2003). For an excellent survey and critique of these approaches to post-Soviet memory, see Antony Kalashnikov, "Stalinist Crimes and the Ethics of Memory," *Kritika: Explorations in Russian and Eurasian History* 19, no. 3 (Summer 2018): 599–626.

11. Alexander Etkind, *Warped Mourning: Stories of the Undead in the Land of the Unburied* (Stanford, CA: Stanford University Press, 2013), 189–192. Etkind is questionably dismissive of local monuments erected by civil society groups. See Zuzanna Bogumił, *Gulag Memories: The Rediscovery and Commemoration of Russia's Repressive Past* (New York: Berghahn, 2018). Curiously, Bogumił's study of

214   AFTER THE GULAG

cultural memory in Solovki, Komi, Perm, and Magadan argues that local memory projects failed to create a cohesive, secular language of commemoration, which left room for the Russian Orthodox Church—supported by the state—to step into the breach. This conclusion overlooks Memorial's and Fond Pokaianie's successes in forming a durable infrastructure of memory in Komi.

12. On the interplay between the two ideas and their usage in studies of Soviet and post-Soviet memory, see Etkind, *Warped Mourning*, 40. On infrastructures of memory, see Iwona Irwin-Zarecka, *Frames of Remembrance: The Dynamics of Collective Memory* (New Brunswick, NJ: Transaction, 1993), 13.

13. Anna Neimark, "The Infrastructural Monument: Stalin's Water Works under Construction and in Representation," *Future Anterior: Journal of Historic Preservation, History, Theory, and Criticism* 9, no. 2 (Winter 2012): 1–14. For an interesting examination of memory and the infrastructural monuments left behind in Spain in the wake of Franco's death, see Jonah S. Rubin, "How Francisco Franco Governs from Beyond the Grave: An Infrastructural Approach to Memory Politics in Contemporary Spain," *American Ethnologist* 45, no. 2 (May 2018): 214–227. Neimark argues that Stalinist infrastructure was meant to be monumental and thus served as the task of "representing memory, sovereignty, and history." I argue the resignification of the railroad to Vorkuta as a road of prisoners' bones in Komi newspapers is not only a reversal of the associated meaning of Stalinist infrastructure but also an essential component of reconstructing the past and producing a new cultural memory of Stalinism.

14. "Torzhestvennoe zasedanie Tsentral'nogo Komiteta KPSS, Verkhovnogo Soveta SSSR i Verkhovnogo Soveta RSFSR: Doklad M. S. Gorbacheva," *Pravda*, November 3, 1987, no. 307 (25294). See also F. A. Karmanov and S. A. Panov, eds., *Reabilitirovan postmertno. Vtoroi vypusk* (Moscow: izd-vo Iuridicheskaia literature, 1988).

15. On the incomplete nature of rehabilitation during the 1950s, see Marc Elie, "Rehabilitation in the Soviet Union, 1953–1964: A Policy Unachieved," in *De-Stalinising Eastern Europe: The Rehabilitation of Stalin's Victims after 1953*, ed. Kevin McDermott and Matthew Stibbe (Baskingstoke: Palgrave Macmillan, 2015), 25–45; Ian Rachinskii, ed., *Reabilitatsiia i pamiat': Otnoshenie k zhertvam sovetskikh politicheskikh repressii v stranakh byvshego SSSR* (Moscow: Memorial-Zven'ia, 2016).

16. NBRK, A. Sivkova, "M. K. Ignatov: Bez sroka davnosti," *Molodezh' Severa*, September 21, 1988. The commission was formed in August 1988 and operated under the authority of the Central Committee of the Politburo. It was composed of V. S. Osipov, Secretary Komi Obkom; V. P. Moskalev, Iu. V. Gavriusov, leaders of the departments of the Party Obkom; V. S. Zhinkin, Chairman of the Supreme Court Komi ASSR; A. I. Bulankov, Procurator Komi ASSR; G. T. Rukavishnikov,

Minister of Justice; V. I. Chistiakov, editor of the newspaper *Krasnoe znamia*; and other heads of district and city party committees throughout Komi.

17. Kathleen E. Smith, *Remembering Stalin's Victims: Popular Memory and the End of the USSR* (Ithaca, NY: Cornell University Press, 2009), 141. In 1988, the Politburo called for the formation of interagency commissions to speed this work up because of the enormity of the task. See Politbiuro KPSS, "O dopolnitel'nykh merakh po zaversheniiu raboty, sviazannoi s reabilitatsiei lits, neobosnovanno repressirovannykh v 30–40-e gody i nachale 50-kh godov, 11 iiulia 1988 g," in *Reabilitatsiia: Politicheskie protsessy 30–50-kh godov*, ed. A. N. Iakovlev (Moscow: Izdatel'stvo politichesoi literatury, 1991), 16.

18. Sivkova, "M. K. Ignatov." The article noted that from April 1988, the commission had reviewed five hundred cases submitted from the village, town, district, and regional party committees.

19. Ibid.

20. For a case study of the politics of memory in Komi under Brezhnev, see, Tyler C. Kirk, "From Enemy to Hero: Andrei Krems and the Legacy of Political Repression in Russia's Far North, 1964–1982," *The Russian Review* 2023 (2023): 1–15, https://doi.org/10.1111/russ.12440.

21. Sivkova, "M. K. Ignatov."

22. NBRK, I. Bobrakov, "Za vsenarodnoe pokaianie," *Molodezh' Severa*, November 25, 1988.

23. Ibid.

24. Ibid.

25. Ibid. For similar coverage and appeals to members of society, see Archive of the Local History Museum at Ukhta State Technical University (AM UGTU) f. Bulychev (A. I. Terent'ev, V. Bulychev "Khotelos' by vsekh poimenno nazvat,'" *Ukhta*, February 22, 1989, no. 37 [8652]). Coverage on the same conference in Moscow in the newspaper *Ukhta* called for the "moral cleansing" of society and the need to recognize "mass illegal repressions a crime against humanity" and to initiate a "social court against Stalin and all those guilty of repression."

26. Smith, *Remembering Stalin's Victims*, 152; Stephen Kotkin, "Terror, Rehabilitation, and Historical Memory: An Interview with Dmitrii Iurasov," *Russian Review* 51 (April 1992): 238–262.

27. Bobrakov, "Za vsenarodnoe pokaianie."

28. Lev Razgon, "Puti k Memorialu," *Vedomosti Memoriala. K uchreditel'noi konferentsii*, January 1989, 4, box 422, Soviet and Post-Soviet Independent Publications, Hoover Institution Library and Archives (hereafter Hoover Institution).

29. *Kotlovan. Khibinskoe obshchestvo "Memorial,"* December 1989, 1, box 163, Soviet and Post-Soviet Independent Publications, Hoover Institution.

30. See, e.g., *30 Oktiabria*, box 2; *Svoboda i Kul'tura: Gazeta Moskovskogo Memoriala*, box 395; and *Memorial: Informatsionnyi biulleten' Pravleniia Mezhdunarodnogo istoriko-prosvetitel'skogo pravozashchitnogo i blagotvoritel'nogo obshchestva "Memorial,"* box 510, Soviet and Post-Soviet Independent Publications, Hoover Institution.

31. Fond Pokaianie Archive (AFP), S. Raevskii, "O nikh vspominaiu vsegda i vezde . . .," *Zapoliar'e*, December 9, 1989; AM UGTU f. Bulychev (A. Balashova, "Po 'delu Alliluevykh,'" *Ukhta*, August 9, 1989, no. 152 [8767]); AM UGTU f. V. Bulychev ("I vnov' Ia posetil . . ." *Ukhta*, July 18, 1991, no. 135 [9250]); AM UGTU f. V. Bulychev ("Ad ili Dos'e na samogo sebia," *Ukhta*, August 7, 1990, no. 151 [9016]); GU RK NARK 2 f. P-3800, op. 1, d. 102, l. 25 (V. Morozova, "Mechenyi GULAGom," *Krasnoe znamia*, January 7, 1992).

32. Catherine Merridale, *Night of Stone: Death and Memory in Twentieth-Century Russia* (New York: Penguin, 2000), 307. On the national impact of survivor's testimonies published in Moscow and Leningrad newspapers, Merridale writes, "Though Brezhnevite negligence and euphemism had robbed the word 'repression' of its human force, no one could read these rediscovered stories of abuse with equanimity. Stalinism—the very word was an ideologized abstract—was detailed for the first time in individual narratives of nerve and muscle" (307).

33. NBRK, I. Gol'ts, "Bunt," *Molodezh' Severa*, December 8, 1989.

34. Ibid.

35. See also AFP, Raevskii, "O nikh vspominaiu vsegda i vezde . . ."; "Zharkoe leto 53-go," *Zapoliar'e*, December 9, 1989; AM UGTU f. Bulychev (S. Volkovinskii, "Nikto ne prosil o poshchade," *Ukhta*, September 29, 1990, no. 139 [9054]).

36. AM UGTU f. Bulychev ("Biulleten' poiska," *Ukhta*, August 7, 1990, no. 151 [9016]).

37. The brief biographies published in this article do not list what these people were arrested for, although it seems they were political prisoners. With the exception of one person, who was arrested in 1939, they were all arrested in 1937–1938 and died in the camps. They included a worker, a diplomat, a teacher, a professor, a priest, a manager of a local branch of the chief administration of supply (Glavsnab), and a translator.

38. NBRK, V. Shishiedin, "Vernut' chestnoe imia tem, kto byl nezakonno repressirovan," *Krasnoe znamia*, March 3, 1989. For similar reports from the Komi party commission, see also NBRK, "V partii vostanovlen posmertno," *Krasnoe znamia*, January 12, 1989; NBRK, "V riadakh partiii vostanovleny," *Krasnoe znamia*, February 4, 1989.

39. Ibid. As the article stated, some of these residents included those who were arrested for committing petty crimes and then charged with counterrevolutionary activities under art. 58.

40. GU RK NARK 2 f. P-3800, d. 102, l. 2 (K. Pavlenko, "Vosstanavlivaia spravedlivost': Radi obshchei pamiati," *Krasnoe znamia*, August 30, 1990).

41. Arch Getty points out that these numbers came from a 1990 KGB press release in *Pravda*. Actual numbers, as far as historians have been able to document, of those shot during 1937–1938 hover around 681,692. Numbers of the repressed vary depending on what categories are used to tally them and what years are considered. See J. Arch Getty and Oleg V. Naumov, *The Road to Terror: Stalin and the Self-Destruction of the Bolsheviks, 1932–1939* (New Haven, CT: Yale University Press, 1999), 590–591.

42. GU RK NARK 2 f. P-3800, d. 102, l. 3 (I. Pavlenko, "Vosstanavlivaia spravedlivost': Radi nravstvennogo ochishcheniia," *Krasnoe znamia*, September 7, 1990). The stakes of this work were highlighted in an interview with a member of the party-led commission in Komi, M. K. Ignatov, who stated: "The process of restoring justice now must go on without haste with the necessary care. Whoever was falsely accused must be reinstated and evaluated by [their] honor, but this does not mean that we must acquit everyone. We should not reinstate in the party those, who intentionally ran down honest, honorable people, [and] Soviet power. The goal of our commission is the restoration of justice"; Ignatov, "Vosstanavlivaia spravedlivost,'" *Krasnoe znamia*, February 10, 1989.

43. GU RK NARK 2 f. P-3800, d. 102, l. 3. See also "Vinovnymi sebia ne priznali," *Krasnoe znamia*, May 12, 1990.

44. Irina Paperno, "Exhuming the Bodies of Soviet Terror," *Representations* 75, no. 1 (Summer 2001): 109. Paperno writes, "For many, the Holocaust is a terror so extreme and unique that it raises the question of the limits of comprehension, interpretation, and representation. Perhaps making sense of the state-perpetrated mass murder that targets its own population is no easier challenge. The difficulty lies in the very nature of the regime that formally came to an end in 1991" (109).

45. Lynn Viola, "The Question of the Perpetrator in Soviet History," *Slavic Review* 72, no. 1 (Spring 2013): 1–23.

46. AM UGTU f. Bulychev (A. Osipov, "Konvoia vernyi strazh," *Ukhta*, September 29, 1990, no. 139 [9054]).

47. Ibid.

48. AM UGTU f. Bulychev (K. Musaelian, "Proshu slova," *Ukhta*, October 12, 1990, no. 198 [9063]). Musaelian condemned the inaction of the party, which made proclamations but did little to realize them in the eyes of Memorial and the people: "A year and a half ago from the lectern of the XIX party conference, the restoration of historical and social justice was declared 'our political and moral responsibility.' However, almost nothing has been actually done to this end. Many have passed away, having not lived to see what was promised."

49. AM UGTU f. Bulychev ("Otkrytoe pis'mo Prezidentu SSSR, General'nomu Sekretariu M. S. Gorbachev ot Uchastnikov Nedeli Sovesti

218   AFTER THE GULAG

provedennoi Ukhto-Pechorskim obshchestvom Memorial," *Ukhta*, October 12, 1990, no. 198 [9063]).

50. Ibid.

51. Ibid.

52. For example, Konstantin Ivanov and Elena Markova thought of themselves in this way.

53. For articles that illustrate this shift in discourse, see GURK NARK 2 f. P-3800, d. 102, l. 16 (V. Poleshchikov, "My zagnany na ledianuiu katorgu: O golodovke zakliuchennykh Vorkutlaga v 1936 godu," *Molodezh' Severa*, October 26, 1991); GU RK NARK 2 f. P-3800, d. 102, p. 45 (I. Bobrakov, "Veniamin Poleshchnikov: Esli Ia nazovu konkretnye imena, etikh liudei rasterzaiut na ploshchadi," *Molodezh' Severa*, April 27, 1995); GU RK NARK 2 f. P-3800, d. 102, l. 46 (T. Roman'kova, "Krovavyi avgust piat'desiat tret'ego," *Molodezh' Severa*, August 31, 1995).

54. GU RK NARK 2 f. P-3800, d. 102, l. 41 (K. Markizov "Deti GULAGa," *Vechernii Syktyvkar*, October 30, 1992). See also GU RK NARK 2 f. P-3800, d. 102, l. 34 (S. Men'shikova, "Suzhdeno li svidet'tsia?," *Krasnoe znamia*, May 7, 1992); GU RK NARK 2 f. P-3800, d. 102, l. 38 (K. Markizov, "Spetspereselentsy," *Vechernii Syktyvkar*, August 27, 1992).

55. AM UGTU f. Bulychev (I. S Chernikov, "U nas plennykh net," *Ukhta*, November 23, 1991, no. 225 [9340]). See also GU RK NARK 2 f. P-3800, d. 102, l. 34 (E. Glok 'byvshii repressirovannyi, nyne reabhilitirovannyi,' "Kopai sebe mogilu! . . ." *Krasnoe znamia*, May 7, 1992).

56. GU RK NARK 2 f. P-3800, op. 1, d. 102, l. 28 (E. Oteva, "Chotb ne propast' poodinochke," *Krasnoe znamia*, April 2, 1992).

57. V. Bulychev, ed., *V nedrakh Ukhtpechlaga: Vypusk vtoroi* (Ukhta: Ukhta-Pechorskoe obshchestvo Memorial, 1994), 44. The address continued, "That is why the human rights work of 'Memorial' was and remains at the center of attention, uniting all strata of society, all generations and aiming at the liquidation of the legacies of genocide. We are not gathered to change one unjust court for another. Memorial was and remains on the side of human law, on guard for the rights of individuals, the rights of the nation, social [and] moral values" (44).

58. P. Besprozvannaia, "Pomogaia—ochishchat,'" *Kotlovan: Spetsial'nyi vypusk otdeleniia obshchestva "Memorial"* December 1989, 1, box 163, Soviet and Post-Soviet Independent Publications, Hoover Institution.

59. Emma Gilligan, *Defending Human Rights in Russia: Sergei Kovalyov, Dissident and Human Rights Commissioner, 1969–2003* (London: RoutledgeCurzon, 2004).

60. GU RK NARK 2 f. P-3800, op. 1, d. 102, l. 45 (I. Bobrakov, "Veniamin Poleshchikov: Esli Ia nazovu konkretnye imena, etikh liudei rasterzaiut na ploshchadi," *Molodezh' Severa*, February 27, 1995). See also V. M. Poleshchikov,

Za sem'iu pechatami: Iz arkhiva KGB (Syktyvkar: Komi knizhnoe izd-vo, 1995), 9. Poleshchikov gained notoriety in Komi when he bucked the commands of his superiors and published an article about the violently suppressed uprising of prisoners in Vorkutlag in 1953 and the location of their mass graves. As a result, Poleshchikov was demoted but not arrested or fired.

61. Ibid.

62. Ibid.

63. AM UGTU f. Bulychev (V. Bulychev, "Veniamin Poleshchikov: Ia vyshel iz partii i poplatilsia za eto," *Ukhta*, October 16, 1991). See also Gilligan, *Defending Human Rights in Russia*, 119.

64. NBRK, T. Boriseevich, "Pole pamiati," *Krasnoe znamia*, September 28, 1989.

65. Ibid. The article noted that the party commission of the Vuktyl district and Memorial were conducting a search "for those once repressed, but now rehabilitated victims of Stalin's tyranny. This search is not very simple—there are few documents, only a handful of eyewitnesses (yes, and how to get them to emerge?). Their relatives have different last names, and more often than not neighbors will not share secret information." However, not every repressed person wanted to participate, illustrating the traumatic nature of remembering and the memory of the thaw followed by the coming of winter and a renewal of repression: "Who needs this? . . . I don't want to remember. You don't understand, but I do. . . . Here is your sermon, a sort of prayer on the radio or television to listen to—nothing more is necessary."

66. AM UGTU f. Bulychev (L. Gechus, "185 let po prigovoram, 36 tiurem i 215 sutok v kamere smertnika," *Ukhta*, September 28, 1991, no. 188 [9303]).

67. AM UGTU f. Bulychev (A. I. Terent'ev, V. Bulychev, "Khotelos' by vsekh poimenno nazvat,'" *Ukhta*, February 22, 1989, no. 37 [8652]).

68. Ibid.

69. AM UGTU f. Bulychev (V. Bulychev, "Trava zabveniia," *Ukhta*, May 12, 1989, no. 90 [8705]).

70. Ibid.

71. NBRK, R. Mirin, "M. V. Kriukov: 'Kak khochetsia zhit'!'" *Zapoliar'e*, August 2, 1990. See also I. Kliamkin "Pochemu trudno govorit' pravdu," *Novy Mir*, no. 2, 1989, cited in AM UGTU f. Bulychev (V. Bulychev, "Trava zabveniia").

72. Ibid.

73. Ibid.

74. GU RK NARK 2 f. P-3800, d. 102, l. 8 (G. Spichak, "Za strokoi A. Solzhenitsyna," *Krasnoe znamia*, November 27, 1990). See also GU RK NARK 2 f. P-3800, d. 102, l. 33 (E. Konstantinova, "Oleg Volkov: My zabyli zhit' po sovesti," *Krasnoe znamia*, May 1, 1992).

75. GU RK NARK 2 f. P-3800, d. 102, l. 31 (N. Kozina, "'Zabud'te o nikh! . . .' Ne zabyli," *Krasnoe znamia*, April 22, 1992).

76. Irina Flige, "The Necropolis of the Gulag as a Historical-Cultural Object: An Overview and Explication of the Problem," in *Rethinking the Gulag: Identities, Sources, Legacies*, ed. Alan Barenberg and Emily D. Johnson (Bloomington: Indiana University Press, 2022), 243.

77. "Na Zabolotnom snova nakhodiat chelovecheskie cherepa i kosti," *Pro Gorod*, May 15, 2018, https://progoroduhta.ru/news/12320; Pavel Vlizkov, "V prigorode Ukhty na meste massovykh rasstrelov zakliuchennykh v gody terrora naideny novye ostanki. Chto ob etom izvestno," *7x7*, June 1, 2018, https://7x7 -journal.ru/item/107749; Ivan Zhuravkov, "V Komi nashli neizvestnoe massovoe zakhoronenie. Ostanki mogut prinadlezhat' zakliuchennym GULAGa," *7x7*, June 8, 2021, https://7x7-journal.ru/news/2021/06/08/v-komi-nashli -neizvestnoe-massovoe-zahoronenie-ostanki-mogut-prinadlezhat -zaklyuchennym-gulaga.

78. Perm-36 is exceptional for Russia and very different from Auschwitz in essence. Once a part of the infrastructure of the Soviet carceral system, it was the last corrective labor camp to be closed in 1987 and subsequently transformed into a museum and made into part of Russia's infrastructure of memory. However, the majority of camps were left to rot, repurposed as part of the towns that sprung up around them, or destroyed after they were closed in the 1950s. See Neimark, "Infrastructural Monument," 1. On Auschwitz as a "warning monument" in the cultural memory of the Holocaust, see Primo Levi, "Revisiting the Camps," in *The Art of Memory: Holocaust Memorials in History*, ed. James Young (New York: Prestel, 1994), 185. Etkind explores the interaction between texts and monuments; *Warped Mourning*, 177–178.

79. On the link between memory and ruins of former camps in Gulag returnees' letters, memoirs, and testimonies, see chap. 1.

80. AM UGTU f. Bulychev (A. Terent'ev, "Vetlosianskaia slabokomanda," *Ukhta*, September 29, 1990, no. 139 [9054]). For Terent'ev's biography, see R. V. Lemzakova, ed., *Aleksei Iosifovich Terent'ev: Liudi Ukhty* (Ukhta: Ukhto-Pechorskoe obshchestvo Memorial, 1994).

81. Ibid.

82. NBRK, Z. V. Petrova, "Tam seichas ulitsa Kirova," *Zapoliar'e*, December 9, 1989. See also Boriseevich, "Pole pamiati."

83. Memorial conducted vast correspondence with victims of political repression (see chap. 1) and their family members. In many cases, their letters shared scraps of information that led to discoveries in the archives or the ground. For Syktyvkar Memorial's correspondence, see GU RK NARK 2 f. P-3800, op. 1, d. 39, ll. 33 1993; f. P-3800, op. 1, d. 56, ll. 69 1994–1995; f. P-3800, op. 1, d. 79, ll. 35 1997 (Correspondence with family members of the repressed regarding

LOCAL NEWSPAPERS AND CULTURAL MEMORY 221

questions of rehabilitation and the activities of the Memorial Society). For an example of correspondence with state institutions (MVD, KGB, FSB) see GU RK NARK 2 f. P-3800, op. 1, d. 105, ll. 134 1994.

84. AM UGTU f. Bulychev (L. Kashanov, "Gorst' zemli s mogily materi," *Ukhta*, August 7, 1990, no. 151 [9016]). On the importance of identifying graves and providing closure to the families who went long years without knowing for certain the fate of their loved ones, see GU RK NARK 2 f. P-3800, d. 102, l. 1–1a (E. Vladimirov, "Ssyl'nym sorok pervogo," *Molodezh' Severa*, August 8, 1990, no. 92 [6354]); AFP, "... Spasi i sokhrani ikh dushi!," *Zapoliar'e*, September 21, 1991.

85. On the first Week of Conscience in Moscow, see Nanci Adler, *Victims of Soviet Terror: The Story of the Memorial Movement* (Westport, CT: Praeger, 1993); Smith, *Remembering Stalin's Victims*, 179–180; Mari Burenkova, Natal'ia Gorlenko, and Ilia Fliarkovskii, dirs., *30 let sovesti* (2018; Moskva: Istoriia Rossii v fotografiiakh i Mezhdunarodnyi Memorial, 2019), streaming, https://www.youtube.com/watch?v=ygpcAaoqM-4&t=106s.

86. Bulychev, *V nedrakh Ukhtpechlaga: Vypusk vtoroi*, 44.

87. AM UGTU f. Bulychev ("Nedelia sovesti' v Ukhte s 30 sentiabria po 7 oktiabria 1990" *Ukhta*, September 29, 1990, no. 139 [9054]). For the 1991 program, see AM UGTU f. Bulychev ("Nedelia sovesti v Ukhte 29, 30 sentiabria, 1 oktiabria," *Ukhta*, September 28, 1991, no. 188 [9303]); V. Bulychev, ed., *V nedrakh Ukhtpechlaga* (Ukhta: Ukhtinskaia tipografiia "Memorial," 1989).

88. AM UGTU f. Bulychev (V. Vladimirov, "Gosti nashei 'nedeli,'" *Ukhta*, September 29, 1990, no. 139 [9054]). A letter addressed to Ukhta-Pechora Memorial in 1991 from a daughter of a former prisoner in Petersburg expressed her desire to participate in the ceremony that year and to bring home a handful of earth from her father's grave. See Bulychev, *V nedrakh Ukhtpechlaga: Vypusk vtoroi*, 26.

89. On the exhumation of purge victims' graves in Ukraine, see Paperno, "Exhuming the Bodies," 108. See also Merridale, *Night of Stone*, 297–324.

90. Flige, "Necropolis of the Gulag," 267.

91. AM UGTU f. Bulychev (Leonid Chizhevskii "Pamiati Chizhevskogo Luki Dmitrievicha," *Ukhta*, June 16, 1993, no. 113 [9728]).

92. Paperno, "Exhuming the Bodies," 106; Catherine Merridale, "Revolution among the Dead: Cemeteries in Twentieth-Century Russia," *Mortality* 8, no. 2 (2003): 176–188; Adler, "Future of the Soviet Past," 1106. This is not unique to post-Soviet countries; it is also the focus of an ongoing memory project on the legacy of fascism in Spain. See Rubin, "How Francisco Franco Governs," 214–227.

93. Katherine Verdery, *The Political Lives of Dead Bodies: Reburial and Postsocialist Change* (New York: Columbia University Press, 1999), 42. See also Svetlana Malysheva, "Soviet Death and Hybrid Soviet Subjectivity: Urban Cemetery as a Metatext," *Ab Imperio* 3 (2018): 351–384.

94. For the argument of the return of repressed memory and the preservation of prerevolutionary religious practices, see Merridale, *Night of Stone*. Zuzanna Bogumił argues the Russian Orthodox Church replaced Memorial in the 1990s as the main shaper of cultural memory. Zuzanna Bogumił, Dominique Moran, and Elly Harrowell, "Sacred or Secular? 'Memorial', the Russian Orthodox Church, and the Contested Commemoration of Soviet Repressions," *Europe-Asia Studies* 67, no. 9 (November 2015): 1416–1444; Bogumił, "Stone, Cross, and Mask: Searching for Language of Commemoration of the Gulag in the Russian Federation," *Polish Sociological Review*, no. 177 (2012): 71–90. For a study of the "iconization" and "veneration" of Russia's "new martyrs" by the Russian Orthodox Church, see Karin Hyldal Christensen, *The Making of the New Martyrs of Russia: Soviet Repression in Orthodox Memory* (New York: Routledge, 2018). While Christensen does not argue that the "new martyrs" are evidence of the continuity of religious practice, she underscores how the church as an institution "icononized" and "venerated" new martyrs as a "traditional" form of producing cultural memory, which focuses on repressed Orthodox clergy and parishioners.

95. AM UGTU f. Bulychev (V. Bulychev, "A. Akhmatova—'Vsego prochnee na zemle pechal,'" *Ukhta*, October 12, 1991, no. 198 [9063]).

96. Ibid.

97. S. Kropachev, "Grazhdanskaia panikhida i sobitiia vokrug nee," *Vestnik "Memoriala": Organ Krasnodarskogo gorodskogo dobrovolnogo obshchestva "Memorial,"* no. 3, May 1990, 15–16, box 557, Soviet and Post-Soviet Independent Publications, Hoover Institution.

98. Ibid.

99. Komi's monuments and mass graves were mapped as part of "Map of Memory: Necropolis of the Terror and Gulag," produced by Fond Ioffe. See "Karta pamiati: Nekropol' terrora i GULAGa," Fond Ioffe, 2015, https://www.mapofmemory.org.

100. On the laying of a memorial stone outside of the Ukhta Local History Museum, which served as the headquarters of Ukhtpechlag, see AM UGTU, f. Bulychev (A. Sorvachev, "Kamen' u muzeiia," *Ukhta*, April 23, 1999). On the choice of a memorial stone, a member of Ukhta-Pechora Memorial said at the opening, "Some ten to twenty thousand years ago, a glacier delivered the boulder from the Kola Peninsula. And in 1929, along a route close to the path of the quartz boulder, moved hundreds and then thousands of *zeks*. This is how the thought arose to use the stone as a monument to the victims of the GULAG."

101. On these monuments, see Etkind, *Warped Mourning*, 186.

102. GU RK NARK 2 f. P-3800, op. 1, d. 102, l. 19 (S. Pystin, "Proekt Neizvestnogo: neizvestno ostaetsia," *Molodezh' Severa*, December 7, 1991). On the controversy surrounding the Vorkuta Neizvestnyi monument, see Bogumił et al., "Sacred or Secular?" It is unclear who paid for the monuments in Komi.

103. The list of Komi's monuments compiled by the Sakharov Center notes where the financial resources for each monument came from. In almost every case, the money came from collections gathered locally or branches of the International Memorial Society. See Sakharov Center, "Pamiatniki zhertvam politicheskikh repressii na territorii byvshego SSSR," accessed August 29, 2018, https://www.sakharov-center.ru/asfcd/pam/pam_place.xtmpl-town=167.htm. According to this list, there are 1,210 monuments and commemorative plaques to the victims of political repression throughout the former Soviet Union, 714 of which are scattered throughout the Russian Federation. The list is updated frequently. For this list, see "Spisok pamiatnikov i pamiatnykh znakov po stranam," Sakharov Center, accessed February 18, 2018, https://www.sakharov-center.ru/asfcd/pam/?t=list.

104. Rogachev, *Pokaianie*, t. 12, ch. 2, 99.

105. AM UGTU f. Bulychev (Vasilii Belykh, "Poet s ottiapannoi desnitsei," *Ukhta*, June 16, 1993, no. 113 [9728]).

106. AFP, "Memorial: Vozdvignut' zhertvam pamiatnik," *Zaria Timana*, November 4, 1993. The article continued, "The fact that *Sosnogortsy*, without any meetings, independently laid flowers on the monument over the weekend speaks to the necessity of such a monument for our city. It must be added that such a thing became possible thanks to the efforts of the administration of the city and the Memorial society." On the installation of other memorial plaques, see NBRK, T. Iurchenko, "Chtoby pomnili," *Pechorskoe vremia*, January 11, 1999.

107. Rogachev, *Pokaianie*, t. 12, ch. 1; Rogachev, *Pokaianie*, t. 12, ch. 2, 99–104; Malofeevskaia and Rogachev, *Pamiat' o GULAGe*; T. G. Afanas'eva and O. I. Azarov, *Pamiat' o GULAGe: Pechora. Putevoditel'* (Syktyvkar: Fond Pokaianie, 2014).

108. Malofeevskaia and Rogachev, *Pamiat' o GULAGe*, 51.

109. Sakharov Center, "Pamiatniki zhertvam."

110. NBRK, "Ob uvekovechenii pamiati zhertv massovykh politicheskikh repressii v Respublike Komi," *Respublika*, February 3, 1998. In his introductory letter to the first volume of Komi's book of memory, *Martirolog*, former governor of the Komi Republic Iurii Spiridonov wrote, "We, the living, owe an unpayable debt to the countless victims of the repressive system. Our fortified memory, our moral repentance for past crimes, for the nightmarish lapse of reason, has given rise to a miracle—a guarantee that reason will never leave us again, that human life is the measure of all value on earth. This is the path to harmony." G. V. Nevskii, ed., *Pokaianie: Martirolog*, t. 1 (Syktyvkar: Komi knizhnoe izd-vo, 1998), 1.

111. NBRK, Iu. Spiridonov, "O respublikanskom memoriale zhertvam massovykh politicheskikh repressii v gorode Syktyvkare: ukaz glavy RK," *Respublika*, May 19, 1998. For the government order, see "Ob uvekovechenii pamiati zhertv massovykh politicheskikh repressii v Respublike Komi," *Respublika*, February 3, 1998.

112. V. A. Kucherenko, "Doroga pokaianiia," *Memorial: Informatsionnyi biulleten' Pravleniia Mezhdunarodnogo istoriko-prosvetitel'skogo pravozashchitnogo i blagotvoritel'nogo obshchestva "Memorial,"* no. 14, December 1999–January 2000, 36, box 510, Soviet and Post-Soviet Independent Publications, Hoover Institution.

113. Viktor Kucherinenko, "Memorial i Fond Pokaianie v Respublike Komi," *30 Oktiabria*, no. 15, 2001, 3, box 2, Soviet and Post-Soviet Independent Publications, Hoover Institution.

114. Nevskii, *Pokaianie*, t. 1.

115. M. B. Rogachev, email message to the author, August 18, 2018. It is unclear why they were all rejected. I found no information about what these entries looked like or who made them.

116. NBRK, Leonid Markizov, "Pamiatnik bez pamiatnika," *Krasnoe znamia*, June 26, 1999.

117. Rogachev, email, August 18, 2018. Although he approved the governor's choice of Nevorov, it seems that the Syktyvkar bishop's concerns over the form and content of the monument may have slowed down the process. The Fond was made aware of the appointment only after the bishop approved it. See M. B. Rogachev, email message to the author, August 24, 2018; Bogumił et al., "Sacred or Secular?," 1439. An article published by *Radio Liberty* does not mention the controversy but notes that the contest lasted for two years before Neverov's design was chosen. See Ol'ga Sergeeva, "Pamiatnik zhertvam politicheskikh repressii v Respublike Komi," *Radio Svoboda*, November 16, 2000, https://www.svoboda .org/a/24198481.html.

118. E. K. Popovtseva, *Izobretatel'noe iskusstvo Respubliki Komi, 1943–2000* (Syktyvkar: Ministerstvo Kul'tury Respubliki Komi, 2011), 132–133.

119. A. I. Neverov, interview with the author by phone, November 4, 2021.

120. Bogumił, *Gulag Memories*, 123. Bogumił writes that the monument did not ruffle feathers with the church because of its "conservatism" in its representation of a burial site.

121. It is also noteworthy that the site is flanked by the current offices of the Komi Ministry of Internal Affairs and the Federal Penitentiary Service.

122. It seems that Bogumił et al. focus on the religious imagery of the monument and miss the mosaic of symbols it is composed of; "Sacred or Secular?," 1439. Rogachev, whom I noted above as having participated in its founding, emphasizes the "eclecticism" of the monument in its commemoration of victims of all faiths and nationalities; Rogachev, email, August 18, 2018.

123. Bogumił, *Gulag Memories*, 123.

124. Ibid.

125. M. B. Rogachev, ed., *Politicheskie repressii v Syktyvkare. Putevoditel'* (Krasnoiarsk: PIK 'Ofset', 2011), 10.

126. Neverov, interview, November 4, 2021.

127. Etkind, *Warped Mourning*, 177. On the *Martirolog* in the press, see "Pokaianie: khranit' vechno," *Krasnoe znamia*, March 5, 1998.

128. Ibid.

129. Nevskii, *Pokaianie*, t. 1, 1. See also "Fond 'Pokaianie' otmetil desiatiletie," *BNK: Informatsionnoe agenstvo*, December 21, 2008, https://www.bnkomi.ru /data/news/1925/.

130. Malofeevskaia and Rogachev, *Pamiat' o GULAGe*, 35.

131. Artur Gustavovich Tamvelius (1907–1959) was a prisoner of Intalag and Minlag from 1946 to 1955. Before arrest, he worked as an architect in Rezh in Sverdlovksia oblast'. Arrested on March 20, 1944, he was sentenced by a NKVD Special Board to twenty years. In addition to the water tower, Tamvelius also designed the Inta polyclinic. He was transferred to Dubrovlag in Mordovia along with other foreign prisoners in 1956 when his case was reviewed and overturned. He returned to Sweden and died in 1959. He was posthumously rehabilitated in Russia in 1991. See Rogachev, *Pokaianie*, t. 12, ch. 2, 243.

132. Kathleen E. Smith, *Moscow 1956: The Silenced Spring* (Cambridge, MA: Harvard University Press, 2017), 210–214; *Sluchai na shakhte vosem'*, dir. Valdimir Basov (1957; Moscow: Mosfilm, 2020), YouTube video, 1:27:00, https://youtu.be /GCmxSYepuhY.

133. Malofeevskaia and Rogachev, *Pamiat' o GULAGe*.

134. Ibid., 35.

135. Viktor Ivanov, "V Inte otkroetsia 'Muzei istorii politicheskikh repressii,'" *7x7*, March 21, 2014, https://7x7-journal.ru/item/39516; Iaroslava Parkhacheva, "V Inte otkryli pervyi v Komi muzei istorii politicheskikh repressii," *7x7*, October 4, 2014, https://7x7-journal.ru/item/48162. In addition, the Virtual Gulag Museum project presents the collections and exhibits of Russia's disperse local history museums in one digital space. Virtual'nyi muzei GULAGa, "Sledy terrora: Vodonapornaia bashnia g. Inta, Respubliki Komi," accessed August 31, 2018, http://www.gulagmuseum.org/showObject.do?object=435503&language=1.

136. N. A. Baranov, email message to the author, February 18, 2019. Baranov, who works at the museum and has been involved in local memory projects since the late 1980s, writes that approximately fifty people travel the Inta "ring of repentance" each year on October 30.

137. AFP, V. Abueva, "Sovest'—poniatie nravstvennoe," *NK*, December 2, 1999, no. 54. See also AFP, "Pamiat': Memorial vedet poisk," *Zaria*, July 9, 2000; AFP, Ol'ga Pleshakova, "V Zapoliar'e poiavilsia eshche odin pamiatnik zhertvam politicheskikh repressii," *Zapoliar'e*, October 21, 2010.

138. Ibid.

139. Ibid.

140. Ibid.

141. AM UGTU f. Bulychev (N. Dukhovskaia, "Krest na kraiu obryva," *Ukhta,* September 5, 2000); AM UGTU f. Bulychev (N. Dukhovskaia, "Programma 'Pokaianie:' god spustia," *Ukhta,* August 26, 2000); AM UGTU f. Bulychev (A. Galkin, "S chego nachinaetsia Rodina? . . .," *Ukhta,* September 6, 2000).

142. AFP, "Zabvenie," *Ogni Vychegdy,* October 11, 2002.

143. Ibid.

144. Malysheva, "Soviet Death," 352. For context, let us also consider for a moment the steady flow of out-migration during this period. From 1990 to 2002, approximately 368,000 people migrated out of Komi due to the declining economy, which led to the shuttering of many of Komi's mines and decaying factories that supported life in the Far North. See V. V. Fauzer, "Migratsionnye protsessy v Respublike Komi: Otsenka i tendentsii protekaniia," in *V Ural'skii demograficheskii forum: Sbornik materialov* (Ekaterinburg: Institute ekonommiki UrO RAN, 2014), 173, http://elar.urfu.ru/bitstream/10995/30048/1/irdso_2014_32.pdf. On the continuing decline of Komi's population, see "Naselenie Komi prodolzhaet sokrashchat'sia iz-za migratsii," *BNK: Informatsionnoe agenstvo,* January 31, 2018, https://www.bnkomi.ru/data/news/73972/.

145. GU RK NARK 2 f. P-3800, d. 102, l. 1–1a (E. Vladimirov, "Ssyl'nym sorok pervogo," *Molodezh' Severa,* August 8, 1990, no. 92 [6354]).

146. AFP, "Nialta: Poslednie v smert,'" *Usinskaia nov',* no. 401–405, November 6, 2008. See also AFP, Nikolai Baranov, "Blagorodnaia missiia," *Iskra,* August 16, 2008; AFP, A. Smingilis, "Poliaki v Komi," *Tvoia gazeta,* no. 16, July 8, 2009. Inta Local History Museum member Nikolai Baranov wrote about the importance of graves as a part of Komi's cultural memory and symbols of its past: "Abez'—it is the historical past of the Inta region, the Komi Republic, [and] the country. To know the historical truth, however bitter it may be, is necessary for the current and future generations, so that it never happens again."

147. NBRK, Artur Arteev, "GULAG dlia turistov: v Vorkute reshili vossozdat' lagernuiu zonu Stalinskoi epokhi," *Respublika,* July 30, 2010. The *New York Times* featured a piece on this story when the idea was first proposed by the then sitting mayor of Vorkuta. See Steven Lee Meyers, "Above the Arctic Circle, a Gulag Nightmare for Tourists?," *New York Times,* June 6, 2005, https://www.nytimes.com/2005/06/06/world/europe/above-the-arctic-circle-a-gulag-nightmare-for-tourists.html.

148. Arteev, "GULAG dlia turistov." Budovskii endorsed the idea of a museum but rejected turning it into a tourist attraction. He said, "I think that even *Vorkutintsy* would be interested to see how and in what conditions our city was built. We don't intend to forget out history, after all Vorkuta was entirely built by prisoners, my grandfather was also a prisoner of the camp."

149. Ibid.

150. Ibid.

151. It remains unclear when exactly this switch occurred. The Day of Memory of the Victims of Political Repression was first celebrated in 1989 by Memorial in Moscow. Originally, it commemorated the Day of Political Prisoners, which began in 1974 when political prisoners launched a mass hunger strike. On October 18, 1991, the Day of Memory of the Victims of Political Repression was added to the calendar of state holidays by decree of the Supreme Soviet RSFSR, "On the establishment of the Day of Memory of the Victims of Political Repression." On the history of the holiday, see Smith, *Remembering Stalin's Victims*, 160–163.

152. AFP, "Iz teni GULAGa: Den' osoboi pamiati," *Krasnoe znamia Severa*, October 28, 2010, no. 126.

153. Ibid.

154. The coverage of the Perm-36 episode was extensive in the West and in Russia; see Anna Dolgov, "Russia's Gulag Museum Shuts Doors amid Mounting State Pressure," *Moscow Times*, March 3, 2015, https://www.themoscowtimes .com/2015/03/03/russias-gulag-museum-shuts-doors-amid-mounting-state -pressure-a44401; Elena Bobrova, "Soviet-Era Gulag Museum NGO Perm-36 Announces Closure," *Russia beyond the Headlines*, March 6, 2015, https://www .rbth.com/society/2015/03/06/soviet-era_gulag_museum_ngo_perm-36 _announces_closure_44297.html; Ivan Kozlov, "'Potok donosov byl bespretsed- entnym' Kak v Permi borolis' s muzeem istorii politicheskikh repressii," *Meduza*, November 10, 2014, https://www.themoscowtimes.com/2015/03/03 /russias-gulag-museum-shuts-doors-amid-mounting-state-pressure-a44401; Irina Tumakova, "'Perm'-36': Muzei GULAGa i Minkul'ta," *Fontanka*, October 30, 2016, https://www.fontanka.ru/2016/10/30/041/. On the state's program to commemorate the victims of political repression under Putin, see Nikolay Koposov, *Memory Laws, Memory Wars: The Politics of the Past in Europe and Rus- sia* (Cambridge: Cambridge University Press, 2018), 238–299. See also J. Paul Goode, "Patriotism without Patriots? Perm'-36 and Patriotic Legitimation in Russia," *Slavic Review* 79, no. 2 (Summer 2020): 390–411.

155. AFP, "Iz teni GULAGa: Den' osoboi pamiati."

156. Thomas Sherlock, "Confronting the Stalinist Past: The Politics of Memory in Russia," *Washington Quarterly*, 34, no. 2 (Spring 2011): 93–109; Nanci Adler, "Reconciliation with—Or Rehabilitation of—The Soviet Past?," *Memory Studies* 5, no. 3 (2012): 327–338.

157. Tyler C. Kirk, "Toward a Settled Past and a Brighter Future: The Creation of a 'Usable Past' in Modern Russia, 2000–2010" (MA thesis, University of Chi- cago, 2011).

158. "V Natsional'nom muzee Komi otkroetsia vystavka, posviashchennaia 20-letiiu fonda 'Pokaianie,'" *Region*, February 15, 2018, https://ourreg .ru/2018/02/15/v-nacionalnom-muzee-komi-otkroetsja-v-2/; "V Komi prezentovali

20-iu knigu martirologa 'Pokaianie,'" *BNK*, February 16, 2018, https://www
.bnkomi.ru/data/news/74775/.

159. Koposov, *Memory Laws*, 248. See David L. Hoffmann, "The Politics of
Commemoration in the Soviet Union and Contemporary Russia," in *The Memory
of the Second World War in Soviet and Post-Soviet Russia*, ed. David L. Hoffmann
(London: Routledge, 2022), 1–15.

160. Koposov, *Memory Laws*, 249.

161. Ibid., 249, 263–264. Koposov writes that this definition abandons the Soviet preference for anti-fascism in favor of anti-Nazism, which is formed "around
a prototypical Nazi Germany to which 'less good examples' (allies, accomplices,
and partisans of Nazism, from Mussolini's Italy to the present-day US) are associated by a sort of 'family resemblance.'"

162. Ibid., 249–250. See Timothy Snyder, "When Stalin Was Hitler's Ally,"
Eurozine, May 8, 2015, https://www.eurozine.com/when-stalin-was-hitlers-ally/;
Tatyana Zhurzhenko, "Russia's Never-Ending War against 'Fascism.' Memory
Politics in the Russian-Ukrainain Conflict," *IMW*, https://www.iwm
.at/transit-online/russias-never-ending-war-against-fascism-memory
-politics-in-the-russian.

163. For the Kremlin's stance on historical revisionism and the Nuremberg
Tribunal as a bulwark of the postwar international order, see Sergei Lavrov,
"65-letie velikoi pobedy," *Dipolmaticheskii Ezhegodnik* (Moscow: Ministerstvo in-
nostrannykh del, 2009), 15.

164. "'Zdes' byl GULAG'. Dokumental'nyi reportazh '7x7' o tom, kak
sokhraniaetsia pamiat' o stalinskikh repressiiakh v Komi," *7x7*, May 18, 2021,
https://7x7-journal.ru/articles/2021/05/18/zdes-byl-gulag-dokumentalnyj
-reportazh-7h7-o-tom-kak-sohranyaetsya-pamyat-o-stalinskih-repressiyah
-v-komi.

165. Olga Repina, "Vsia Respublika Komi—bol'shoi pamiatnik zhertvam politicheskikh repressii ubezhden deputat Gosdumy ot Komi Rostislav
Gol'dshein," *Komiinform*, October 30, 2008, http://www.komiinform.ru
/news/52437/.

166. Ibid.

Epilogue

On October 30, 2016, I joined the crowd of one hundred people gathered around the monument to the victims of political repression in Syktyvkar to observe the twenty-fifth annual ceremony in their honor (fig. 6.1). The temperature hovered well below freezing as snow fell. People of all generations stood in silence during the solemn ceremony, which lasted for more than an hour. The archbishop of the Syktyvkar diocese of the Russian Orthodox Church blessed the ceremony with a prayer before he spoke about the repressed members of his family, some of whom were sent to the camps in the north while others were executed on the outskirts of city.[1] His words were followed by a speech from the chairperson of the State Council of the Komi Republic, Nadezhda Dorofeeva, whose grandfather was executed in 1937. Dorofeeva underscored the importance of preventing history from repeating itself. The memory of the victims of political repression should not just be commemorated on October 30, she stated, but every day so that Komi's children would know "the truth about their ancestors who have come to call Syktyvkar their home."[2] The final speech was delivered by Mikhail Rogachev, chair of Fond Pokaianie and founding member of the Syktyvkar Memorial Society. In the presence of repressed people, their relatives, citizens of Syktyvkar, the archbishop, and representatives of the regional government, Rogachev concluded his speech by questioning the seriousness of those—for example, Komi's governor, who was noticeably absent—who called for remembrance while making it difficult for civic organizations to conduct research:

> We try to tell people about that time, not at all thinking that this exhausts Soviet and Russian history. We should know all chapters of history, and not

Figure 6.1 M. B. Rogachev delivers his speech on Syktyvkar's Day of Political Repression, October 30, 2016, Komi Republic, Russian Federation. Source: Tyler C. Kirk (personal archive).

only those that we have a right to be proud about. Otherwise, our memory will be incomplete. For twenty-five years we have observed this day, but books of memory are published in only a few regions. In several regions, their publication has stopped, and in others, it never even began. On the one hand, we say that we need to name all the names, but on the other, with each passing year, it becomes increasingly difficult to get information about people who vanished in the camps, exile, and the special settlements.[3]

As a participant in the week of events leading up to the October 30 ceremony, I witnessed the continuation of a memory project twenty-nine years in the making. The events of the week included public lectures and evenings of memory, special church services, book releases, documentary film screenings, student essay contests, and the opening of new exhibits at the National Archive, Library, Gallery, and Museum of the Komi Republic.[4] Although fewer people

EPILOGUE   231

participate in these events than they once did, the events were well attended by members of the community, including local government representatives, Russian Orthodox clergy, citizens, and victims of political repression and their families.[5] More than one hundred people filled the large reading room on the second floor of the National Library of the Komi Republic, for example, to hear public lectures led by Fond Pokaianie on the history of the Gulag and political repression.

Although the unifying theme of these events was remembrance, there was another underlying theme. The National Museum of the Komi Republic opened a new exhibit, "The Gorodetskiis: Tragedy of One Family," which told the history of political repression in Komi through the Gorodetskii family's experience. At the opening, Elena Morozova, the museum's curator, and Mikhail Rogachev repeatedly underscored the importance of civil society organizations and private individuals who kept the memory project alive by donating their personal archives to the Fond Pokaianie archive. Without their donations and participation, tightening restrictions on access to state archives containing information broadly construed as "personal and family secrets" would make it virtually impossible to produce new research and exhibits such as the one we were attending.[6] Rogachev noted that these sources were important for another reason as well. The individual lives documented in the Gorodetskii archive represented a "hidden whole" that was obliterated by Stalinist repression. He concluded his speech by noting, "Of these millions, we know the fates of [relatively] few families because of the destructiveness of the regime."[7]

Two days later, another interaction I had with an archivist at the National Archive of the Komi Republic confirmed the continued importance of Fond Pokaianie's archive. During the "Day of Open Doors," archivists at the National Archive of the Komi Republic gave a presentation on Komi's history as a region of exile and imprisonment under tsarist and Soviet rule. Although they acknowledged Komi's tragic past, their narrative struck a remarkably different tone than the one I heard at the national museum. The lecture focused on the contributions of prisoners to the development of the Far North, with little mention of their suffering or the mass death that came at the cost of these achievements. Perhaps to account for the glaring absence of individual prisoners and exiles from the story they told, the archivist invited the audience to examine the individual case files of former prisoners at the end of the lecture. The files covering the long table in the center of the room were the same personal files that are typically off-limits to researchers. As I read several files belonging to the tsar's exiles and Stalin's enemies of the people, one of the archivists approached me and said, "Take a good look and remember what they look like. You will never see them again."[8] Although the archivist acknowledged that these documents were an important piece of Komi's history, they could not allow me to photograph them because they contained "personal data." Despite a decree from the early 1990s mandating that all documents about the mass repressions of the Soviet era be declassified, next to nothing has happened. Data protection has become the standard excuse to withhold inconvenient materials from researchers, as the head of International Memorial Society's research section, Nikita Petrov, has written.[9]

Four years before these events, the Russian State Duma passed a law in 2012 that required all nongovernment organizations that receive funds from foreign sources and engage in "political activities" to register as foreign agents.[10] The law sought to weaken already enfeebled civil society groups following the widespread protests against Putin's election to a third term as president.[11] Branches of the International Memorial Society throughout Russia were threatened with closure and the confiscation of their files when they refused to follow the law, which they unsuccessfully challenged in the Supreme Court as a violation of the constitution of the Russian Federation.[12] Although Memorial was not immediately shut down and its archive was not confiscated, the law was successful in curtailing the activities of smaller branches that did not have the resources of the Moscow and St. Petersburg branches.[13] In the face of increasing pressure, the increased participation that Memorial witnessed during the virtual "Return of the Names" ceremony on October 29, 2021—which lasted twelve hours and resulted in hundreds of letters of support from all over the country—bolstered hope for the future.[14] As Memorial's executive director said during a talk on November 1, 2021, "I look at the future with optimism because just as it was in the beginning thirty-three years ago, when there was a wave of public interest in the memory and restoration of justice and truth, we now see strong interest in the restoration of one's own history, the history of one's family. Just as before, people want the truth about the past. . . . The online format of 'The Return of the Names' this year is a strong confirmation of my optimism."[15]

This optimism has been dashed. On December 28, 2021, the Supreme Court of the Russian Federation ordered the closure of Memorial for its "systematic" breach of the law on foreign agents. As of February 2023, it remains unclear what will become of Memorial's vast archive, library, and small museum. The state prosecutor's lawsuit cited missing labels declaring Memorial's status as a foreign agent on several publications, an allegation that Ian Rachinskii, Memorial's chairperson, refutes as groundless and politically motivated.[16] However, the state prosecutor's testimony at the hearing reveals the state's true motives:

silencing Memorial for "incorrectly interpreting Soviet history" in its "false image of the Soviet Union as a terrorist state" and taking control over the portrayal of Soviet history.[17] This accusation echoes the rhetoric of President Vladimir Putin's former advisor Gleb Pavlovsky and other conservatives who have accused Memorial of reducing "Soviet civilization to a chain of crimes."[18] Fond Pokaianie has also encountered problems because of this law. While it was not forced to register as a foreign agent, its access to the personal files of former prisoners and exiles in the archive of the Komi Ministry of Internal Affairs has been cut off.[19] Despite this blow, Fond Pokaianie's troubles with the state seem to have been resolved for the time being as they continue their work, including the publication of new volumes of the *Martirolog*.

Although the cultural memory of the Gulag has faced direct challenges from the state, which controls access to archives, public space, and funding, it is perpetuated in Komi even as it fades in other parts of the country. Fond Pokaianie's tireless efforts and its historic relationship with the provincial government have been essential to the continued success of the memory project started by Komi's branches of Memorial in 1989. In addition, the vitality of Komi's cultural memory is due in no small part to the efforts of the victims of political repression and their families who, by their participation, form communities of memory that extend far beyond Komi. By continuing to gather to remember outside of the formal contexts designated for commemorating the victims of political repression, these people perpetuate the memory of the Gulag. In turn, this support strengthens Fond Pokaianie, which claims to represent a living memory that has crystallized in the archives, publications, museum exhibits, ceremonies it organized.[20] However, if Fond Pokaianie faces threats in the future, this could very well change. Despite this looming intimidation, Stalinist repression is accepted as part of the region's history and firmly established in cultural memory. The memory of the Gulag cannot be silenced in Komi because it informs the story that its residents tell about themselves.

This is the legacy of the "brotherhood of zeks," who formed a community of Gulag returnees and constructed collected memories of their experiences. These memories formed the basis of an alternate history of the Soviet Union. This alternate history shows that mass repression and the carceral regime were fundamental parts of Soviet society rather than a Stalinist aberration. Although the camps were largely emptied and the penal system was substantively

Figure on following pages Figure 6.2 Wall of Sorrow in Moscow. Source: Kathleen Smith.

reformed after Stalin's death, the industries and cities of Russia's Far North stand as monuments to former prisoners' forced labor. By acknowledging their contributions to Soviet society despite their suffering, this alternate narrative brings those who were excluded back into history, not just as victims to be mourned but also as examples of the country's best people. Although mass repression and its victims became part of the official histories of the Soviet Union after 1991, the victims were presented primarily as helpless and their contributions—if acknowledged at all—were downplayed.[21] Furthermore, the autobiographical narratives that Gulag returnees contributed to this unwritten past illuminate how former "enemies of the people" laid the foundations of the nascent civil society that emerged during the final years of the Soviet regime. Ultimately, their stories reveal how the most vulnerable and marginalized members of Soviet society resisted mass repression through group solidarity and acts of memory, which laid the foundation for future human rights groups such as Memorial and Fond Pokaianie.

The commemoration of the victims of political repression and the memory of the Gulag has continued outside of Komi. Fifty-seven years after Nikita Khrushchev first proposed it and twenty-six years after the collapse of the Soviet Union, the Russian government erected the Wall of Sorrow, dedicated with the participation of human rights groups on October 30, 2017. Although the Solovetsky Stone was the first monument to the victims of political repression erected in Moscow in 1990, the Wall of Sorrow represents the first monument to political repression erected by government decree. Three years in the making, the monument (100 feet long and 20 feet high) depicts human figures in a large wall that forms the shape of a scythe, which represents how people were cut down by political repression (fig. 6.2).[22] At the unveiling of the monument, Putin was joined by Patriarch Kirill and Natalia Solzhenitsyna, the widow of the most famous former resident of the Gulag, Aleksandr Solzhenitsyn. While Putin lauded the monument as an important step toward healing past traumas, he simultaneously highlighted the dangers of dwelling on the past: "Indeed, we and our descendants must remember the tragedy of repression and what caused it. However, this does not mean settling scores. We cannot push society to a dangerous line of confrontation yet again."[23] It is clear that Putin sees Memorial and those who remember Stalin's victims as engaging in a subversive revision of history that threatens the regime's foundations as the heir of the Soviet empire.

While the appearance of new monuments and a revamped state-sponsored Gulag History Museum in Moscow seem to signal victory for human rights groups that fought to bring Stalinist repression to light, they have not occurred

Figure 6.3 Wall of Memory at Kommunarka in Moscow. Source: International Memorial Society (Ian Rachinskii, "O stene pamiati Kommunarka" International Memorial Society, November 2, 2018, https://www.memo.ru/en-us/memorial/departments/intermemorial/news/205).

without controversy.[24] Some activists, including former Soviet dissidents Aleksandr Podrabinek, Pavel Litvinov, and Vladimir Bukovsky, signed a petition published on Facebook in 2017 criticizing the intention behind the Wall of Sorrow when the government continues to persecute and jail human rights activists.[25]

This controversial monument was not the only one erected in recent years. On October 27, 2018, the Wall of Memory was unveiled at the Kommunarka People's Commissariat of Internal Affairs (NKVD) Special Object in Moscow, where 6,609 people who were executed between 1937 and 1941 are buried (fig. 6.3).[26] After years of research, planning, and fundraising, the Wall of Memory was realized as a joint project of Memorial, the State Museum of the History of the Gulag, and the Russian Orthodox Church. The monument drew wide criticism for listing the names of repressed NKVD operatives alongside their victims. Some people accused the project leaders of attempting to "rehabilitate hangmen" with this monument.[27] However, as Rachinskii of the Memorial Society in Moscow wrote, "This wall is a tombstone on a common grave. This is not canonization or rehabilitation. That is why at Kommunarka (as in Butovo), all names are listed on the wall, regardless of presence or absence of rehabilitation. These are all people who lie here. This is not an assessment but a statement."[28] Nearly a year later, the controversy was the topic of a public forum hosted by Memorial where members of various groups who participated in the planning and construction of the monument defended their decisions.[29]

Although debates about the recently erected monuments in Moscow seem to raise new questions about commemorating the past, the issues at the center of these questions are not new. Since the first days of *glasnost* and Khrushchev's reforms before it, members of society and the state have debated whom to mourn, whom to blame, and how to remember them. These debates will continue for the foreseeable future as memory actors throughout Russia—human rights groups, historians, individuals, and the state—produce new knowledge about the past and commemorate it with an ever-expanding infrastructure of memory. The growing queue of participants who wish to read the names of the repressed at the annual "Return of the Names" ceremony, held on October 29 at the Solovetsky stone on Lubyanka Square in Moscow and in thirty-five other Russian cities, illustrates that the memory of the Gulag and political repression is important to more than just the immediate relatives of the repressed.[30] To silence this memory, the state would have to silence these people. Nevertheless, other signs suggest that the state is trying to prevent members of the Memorial Society and sympathetic members of the general public from even informally organizing commemorations on October 29 and 30. The State Gulag History Museum now hosts an event similar to the "Return of the Names" on October 29—called "The Memory Bell"—and members of the liquidated International Memorial Society continue to have difficulties obtaining permission to use the Solovetsky Stone site for the annual event, which—prior to the state's ban on Memorial—was moved online in 2020 and 2021 due to the COVID-19 pandemic. In addition to its permanent exhibits, the State Gulag History Museum conducts important, public historical work such as the "My Gulag" oral history project, traveling exhibits in partnership with local history museums in Russia's regions, and publications of selected memoirs from its growing archive. However, the state's simultaneous repression of civic organizations involved in the memory project since the late 1980s is alarming.

There are signs of these tensions in Komi as well. In December 2019, for example, the Presidential Commission for the Development of Civil Society and Human Rights published its proposal to work with archives and state security services to create a single database of victims of political repression and to partner with local civic organizations and museums in Russia's regions to develop a unified infrastructure of memory.[31] On March 4, 2020, the chair of the Federal Commission, Valerii Fadeev; the director of the State Gulag History Museum in Moscow, Roman Romanov; and other representatives from Moscow met

EPILOGUE 239

with the leaders of regional civic organizations, museum workers, and government officials, such as the Komi Minister of Culture. They discussed a proposal that would direct federal resources to Komi to "help" the region develop a Gulag museum of its own. Komi government officials and members of Fond Pokaianie and the National Museum of the Komi Republic were honored by the praise they received for the infrastructure of memory they built in Komi, including the Komi's monuments and the *Martirolog* (now in its thirteenth volume, with a fourteenth in progress). However, Mikhail Rogachev took the opportunity to highlight the glaring contradiction between the intent of the commission's mission and the government's policies. Specifically, Rogachev once again raised the issue of archival access and underscored the deleterious effect it had on the memory project that the Moscow delegates had praised: "Without a database of names, publishing the *Martirolog* is useless. We publish documents, memoirs, photographs, and much more, but they are only an appendix to the names of the repressed. But according to the law, we cannot to add more names of political prisoners from the various camps. Without these archival sources, we cannot fulfill one of the main theses of the concept of the book of memory."[32]

New memory actors, such as the State Gulag History Museum and the Russian Orthodox Church, are playing active roles in shaping how the past is understood. Nevertheless, the future of the past will be determined by the enduring legacy of those who came forward to testify about the Gulag and political repression in previous decades.[33] The partial opening of the archives has led to greater understanding of how Stalinist terror and the Gulag functioned in Soviet society; however, Gulag returnees' memoirs, letters, artworks, photographs, and other material artifacts are the principal sources that civil society groups and museums draw on to assign meaning to these events. Furthermore, these sources enable the translation of the horror of these events for contemporary audiences, especially those born after the collapse of the Soviet Union, whose personal connection to past repressions grows ever more tenuous with each passing generation. Without these sources that connect the past to real people, history becomes faceless, enabling doubt to creep in about the massive scale and horrible cost of forced labor and the Gulag. Time will tell if society stays interested in these documents, but they are there—at least for now—to be used.

Notes

1. Archbishop Pitirim (Pavel Pavlovich Volochkov) is the archbishop for the Russian Orthodox Church in Komi. See Russkaia Pravoslavnaia Tserkov', "Episkopat RPTs," accessed February 21, 2019, http://www.patriarchia.ru/db/text/31720.html.

2. Nadezhda Dorofeeva, quoted in author's field notes, October 30, 2016.

3. "V Syktyvkare otmetili 25-i Den' pamiati zhertv politicheskikh repressii," *BNK: Informatsionnoe agenstvo*, October 30, 2016; https://www.bnkomi.ru /data/news/55443/. The governor did publish an address to the residents of Komi in a local online newspaper that echoed Dorofeeva's speech; see S. A. Gaplikov, "Obrashcheniie Glavy Respubliki Komi k zhiteliam respubliki v sviazi s Dnem pamiati zhertv politicheskikh repressii," *Komiinform*, October 30, 2016, https:// komiinform.ru/news/140563.

4. Fond Pokaianie Archive (AFP) (schedule of events in observance of the Day of the Memory of Victims of Political Repression, October 20–30, 2016).

5. M. B. Rogachev, noted in the author's field notes, October 31, 2016.

6. For this law, see Federal'noe arkhivnoe agenstvo Rossiskoi Federatsii, "Federal'nyi zakon ot 22.10.2004 No.125-FZ 'Ob arkhivnom dele v Rossiskoi Federatsii," updated June 18, 2017, http://archives.ru/documents/fz/zakon -archivnoe-delo.shtml.

7. M. B. Rogachev, quoted in author's field notes, October 26, 2016. The brochure for the exhibition reads, "The exhibit shows the horror and tragedy of the political repressions of the 1920s-1950s through the personal archive of one family." See Archive of the National Museum of the Komi Republic (NMRK) ("Gorodetskie. Tragediia odnoi sem'i," broshiura, Syktyvkar, 2016).

8. Archivist, quoted in author's field notes, October 28, 2016.

9. "Nikita Petrov: U FSB net videniia svoei istorii," *Agentura.Ru: Spetsluzhby pod kontrolem*, November 9, 2010, https://www.agentura.ru/experts/npetrov/; Elena Shmaraeva, "Istorik Nikita Petrov: pochemu skryvaiut dokumenty o repressiiakh," *Kharkivska pravozakhisa grupa*, January 1, 2017, https://khpg .org/1484053935.

10. "Russia: New 'Foreign Agents' Law Ruling Court Orders Prominent Rights Group to Register," *Human Rights Watch*, December 13, 2013, https://www.hrw .org/news/2013/12/13/russia-new-foreign-agents-law-ruling.

11. The Russian state's attack on human rights organizations under Putin has been widely covered in the Russian and international press. For a recent summary, see "Russia: Government vs. Rights Groups. The Battle Chronicle," *Human Rights Watch*, June 18, 2016, https://www.hrw.org/russia-government -against-rights-groups-battle-chronicle. On the state's takeover of the Perm-36 Museum and the persecution of Memorial as a "foreign agent," see Jeffrey S. Hardy, "The State Museum of Gulag History," in *Museums of Communism: New Memory Sites in Central and Eastern Europe*, ed. Stephen Norris (Bloomington: Indiana University Press, 2020), 275–304.

12. Sarah Rainsford, "Russian Soviet-Era Remembrance Group Memorial Risks Closure," *BBC*, October 30, 2014, https://www.bbc.com/news/world -europe-29831134; "Russia Censures Memorial Rights Group as 'Foreign Agent',"

EPILOGUE 241

BBC, November 9, 2015, https://www.bbc.com/news/world-europe-34767014; "Memorial NGO Fined for Noncompliance with Foreign Agent Law," *Moscow Times*, September 4, 2015, https://www.themoscowtimes.com/2015/09/04/memorial-ngo-fined-for-noncompliance-with-foreign-agent-law-a49353.

13. Kathy Lally, "Putin Pushes NGO Foreign Agent Law," *Washington Post*, April 17, 2013, https://www.washingtonpost.com/world/europe/putin-pushes-ngo-foreign-agent-law/2013/04/15/d9509ec2-a37e-11e2-9c03-6952ff305f35_story.html?utm_term=.21ba04fac380; "Miniust ne vkliuchil NIPTs 'Memorial' v reestr inostrannykh agentov," Memorial Society, February 12, 2019, https://www.memo.ru/ru-ru/memorial/departments/intermemorial/news/235.

14. Irina Shcherbakova, Elena Zhemkova, Steve Barnes, and Isabella Tabarovsky, "Women's Memory of the Gulag and the Future of Memorial," virtual talk hosted by the Kennan Institute, Washington, DC, November 1, 2021, https://www.wilsoncenter.org/event/womens-memory-gulag-and-future-russias-memorial.

15. Ibid.

16. "Genprokuratura potrebovala likvidirovat' 'Memorial' i ego podrazdeleniia," *Novaya Gazeta*, November 11, 2021, https://novayagazeta.ru/articles/2021/11/11/genprokuratura-potrebovala-likvidirovat-mezhdunarodnyi-memorial-news; "Vse pretenzii svodiatsia k otsutstviiu markirovki ob inostrannom agente'. Predsedatel' pravleniia 'Mezhdunarodnogo Memoriala' Ian Rachinskii o trebovanii likvidirovat' organizatsiiu," *7x7*, November 11, 2021, https://7x7-journal.ru/articles/2021/11/11/vse-pretenzii-svodyatsya-k-otsutstviyu-markirovki-ob-inostrannom-agente-predsedatel-pravleniya-mezhdunarodnogo-memoriala-yan-rachinskij-o-trebovanii-likvidirovat-organizaciyu.

17. "Memorial—O likvidatsii Mezhdunarodnogo Memoriala," Mezhdunarodnyi Memorial, December 28, 2021, https://www.memo.ru/ru-ru/memorial/departments/intermemorial/news/667. The prosecutor's words were reproduced on Memorial's website.

18. Quoted in Nikolay Koposov, *Memory Laws, Memory Wars: The Politics of the Past in Europe and Russia* (Cambridge: Cambridge University Press, 2018), 260.

19. On these challenges, particularly battles over archival access in Syktyvkar, see "Izdateli martirologa 'Pokaianie' ne teriaiut nadezhd poluchit' dostup k arkhivam," *BNK: Infromatsionnoe agenstvo*, December 23, 2011, https://www.bnkomi.ru/data/news/11202/; "Predsedatel' pravleniia fonda 'Pokaianie' Mikhail Rogachev: 'Ne iskliucheno, chto izdanie martirologa pridetsia 'svernut,''" *BNK: Informatsionnoe agenstvo*, November 24, 2012, https://www.bnkomi.ru/data/interview/16679/; Valerii Chernitsyn, "Mikhail Rogachev: 'Moia dal'neishaia sud'ba zavisit ot sud'by Martirologa,'" *Krasnoe znamia*, April 2, 2015, https://komikz.ru/news/interview/15295.

20. This illustrates the development of cultural memory, which Aleida Assmann describes as a transition from intergenerational memory to long-term

242 AFTER THE GULAG

transgenerational memory; Assmann, "Transformations between History and Memory," *Social Research* 75, no. 1 (Spring 2008): 56.

21. The controversial state-sponsored history textbooks and teacher's manual published in 2007 are an example of this; see A. A. Danilov, A. I. Utkin, and A. V. Filippov, eds., *Istoriia Rossii, 1945–2008 gg.: 11 klass. Uchebnik dlia uchashchikhsia obshcheobrazovatel' nykh uchrezhdenii* (Moscow: Prosveshchenie, 2008); A. V. Filippov, ed., *Istoriia Rossii, 1945–2008: kniga dlia uchitelia* (Moscow: Prosveshchenie, 2008); Filippov, *Noveishaia Istoriia Rossii, 1945–2007 gg.: kniga dlia uchitelia* (Moscow: Prosveshchenie, 2007).

22. For a description of the monument and its unveiling, see "Putin Orders Memorial to 'Victims of Political Repression,'" *Moscow Times*, September 30, 2015, https://www.themoscowtimes.com/2015/09/30/putin-orders-memorial -to-victims-of-political-repression-a49971. "V Moskve otkryli memorial zhert-vam repressii. Na tseremoniiu otkrytiia 'Steny skorbi' priekhal Putin," *Novaya gazeta*, October 30, 2017, https://www.novayagazeta.ru/news/2017/10/30 /136550-v-moskve-otkryli-memorial-zhertvam-repressiy-na-tseremoniyu -otkrytiya-steny-skorbi-priehal-putin; "Wall of Grief: Putin Opens First Soviet Victims Memorial," *BBC*, October 30, 2017, https://www.bbc.com/news /world-europe-41809659.

23. For Putin's speech see Vladimir Putin, "Opening of Wall of Sorrow Memorial to Victims of Political Repression," President of Russia, October 30, 2017, http://en.kremlin.ru/events/president/news/55948.

24. Andrei Zvadski and Vera Dubina, "Eclipsing Stalin: The GULAG History Museum in Moscow as a Manifestation of Russia's Official Memory of Soviet Repression," *Problems of Post-Communism* (2017): 1–14, https://doi.org/10.1080 /10758216.2021.1983444; Neil MacFarquhar, "Critics Scoff as Kremlin Erects Monument to the Repressed," *New York Times*, October 30, 2017, https://www .nytimes.com/2017/10/30/world/europe/russia-soviet-repression-monument. html. According to this article, most of the $6,000,000 monument was paid for by the city of Moscow, upward of $800,000 was donated from "corporate donors and individuals."

25. Aleksandr Podrabinek, "Podderzhivat' litsemerie vlastei amoral'no," Facebook, October 29, 2017, https://www.facebook.com/alexander.podrabinek /posts/1441353112649712. The petition can also be accessed via the *New York Times* article cited above. For a sympathetic view of Putin's approach to the past and a criticism of Western media coverage of the event, see Stephen F. Cohen, "The Unheralded Putin—Russia's Official Anti-Stalinist No. 1," *The Nation*, November 8, 2017, https://www.thenation.com/article/the-unheralded-putin -russias-official-anti-stalinist-no-1/.

26. Because the killing continued at Kommunarka after 1938, Memorial includes those executed there up until the site was evacuated after the start of the war. Butovo and Kommunarka were two of the largest killing fields of the

EPILOGUE 243

Great Terror discovered in Moscow in 1991. Of the 26,098 executed in Moscow between August 8, 1937, and October 19, 1938, a total of 19,799 were executed at Butovo (15,036) and Kommunarka (4,763). On these killing fields and their excavation in the 1990s, see Karl Schlögel, *Moscow 1937*, trans. Rodney Livingstone (Cambridge: Polity, 2012), 472–504.

27. Ian Rachinskii, "O Stene pamiati v Kommunarke," Memorial Society, November 2, 2018, https://www.memo.ru/en-us/memorial/departments/intermemorial/news/205. See also Ekaterina Vorob'eva, "Tom 3, list 135," *Novaya gazeta*, October 27, 2018, https://www.novayagazeta.ru/articles/2018/10/27/78376-tom-3-list-135.

28. Ibid.

29. The forum took place on February 15, 2019, at the offices of the Memorial Society in Moscow, where the event was live streamed over the internet. Historian and member of Memorial Nikita Petrov agreed with Rachinskii's statement that it would be wrong to divide the victims, as Kommunarka was not only a site of memory but also a mass grave.

30. According to a tweet posted by Memorial, 263 people participated in the first Return of the Names in 2007 and 5,286 people participated in 2018. Names of the repressed are read from 10 a.m. to 10 p.m. See Memorial Moscow (@MemorialMoscow), "Na Vozvrashchenie imen v etom godu prishlo 5286 chelovek (sr: 263 cheloveka na pervoi aktsii v 2007 godu)," Twitter post, October 29, 2018, 12:44 p.m., https://twitter.com/MemorialMoscow/status/924723560337330177. For more on the Return of Names, see "Ob aktsii 'Vozvrashchenie imen,'" Vozvrashchenie imen, accessed February 22, 2019, http://october29.ru/about/. There is even a Return of the Names ceremony in Syktyvkar. This ceremony was added to the schedule of events commemorating the victims of political repression every October in 2014. See "Pravozashchitnik iz Komi Igor' Sazhin o 'Vozvrashchenii imen': U liudei est' zapros na vospriozvedenie proshlogo," *7x7*, October 27, 2018, https://7x7-journal.ru/discuss/113084.

31. "Perechen' poruchenii po itogam zasedaniia Soveta po razvitiiu grazhdanskogo obshchestva i pravam cheloveka i vstrechi s upolnomochennymi po pravam cheloveka," Porucheniia Prezidenta Rossisskoi Federatsii ot 29.01.2020 goda, accessed May 18, 2021, http://www.kremlin.ru/acts/assignments/orders/62700.

32. "Federal'nye eksperty postavili Komi v primer po uvekovechivaniu pamiati politzakliuchennyk," *BNK*, March 5, 2020, https://www.bnkomi.ru/data/news/108008/.

33. For an analysis of this museum and its history, see Hardy, "State Museum of Gulag History," 275–304. For a study of the New Martyrs commemorated by the Russian Orthodox Church, see Karin Hyldal Christensen, *The Making of the New Martyrs of Russia: Soviet Repression in Orthodox Memory* (New York: Routledge, 2018).

BIBLIOGRAPHY

Archives

Archive of the Inta Local History Museum (AIKM), Inta, Russia
Archive of the International Memorial Society (AM), Moscow, Russia
Archive of the Local History Museum at Ukhta State Technical University (AM UGTU), Ukhta, Russia
Archive of the National Gallery of the Komi Republic (NGRK), Syktyvkar, Russia
Archive of the National Museum of the Komi Republic (NMRK), Syktyvkar, Russia
Archive of the State Gulag History Museum (GBUK MIG), Moscow, Russia
Archive of the Ukhta Local History Museum (IKMU), Ukhta, Russia
Archive of the Vorkuta Museum-Exhibition Centre (VMVTs), Vorkuta, Russia
Archive of the Vorkuta Museum of Geology (AVMG), Vorkuta, Russia
Fond Pokaianie Archive (AFP), Syktyvkar, Russia
Hoover Institution Library and Archives (Hoover Institute), Palo Alto, CA
National Archive of the Komi Republic (GU RK NARK), Syktyvkar, Russia
National Library of the Komi Republic (NBRK), Syktyvkar, Russia

Sources

Adler, Nanci. "The Future of the Soviet Past Remains Unpredictable: The Resurrection of Stalinist Symbols amidst the Exhumation of Mass Graves." Europe-Asia Studies 57, no. 8 (December 2005): 1093–1119.
———. *The Gulag Survivor.* New Brunswick, NJ: Transaction, 2002.
———. *Keeping Faith with the Party: Communist Believers Return from the Gulag.* Bloomington: Indiana University Press, 2012.

BIBLIOGRAPHY

———. "Reconciliation with—Or Rehabilitation of—The Soviet Past?" *Memory Studies* 5, no. 3 (2012): 327–338.

———. *Victims of Soviet Terror: The Story of the Memorial Movement.* Westport, CT: Praeger, 1993.

Agamben, Giorgio. *Remnants of Auschwitz: The Witness and the Archive.* Translated by Daniel Heller-Roazen. New York: Zone, 1999.

Agostinho, Daniela, Elisa Antz, and Cátia Ferrira, eds. *Panic and Mourning: The Cultural Work of Trauma.* Berlin: De Gruyter, 2012.

Alexopoulos, Golfo. *Illness and Inhumanity in Stalin's Gulag.* New Haven, CT: Yale University Press, 2017.

Amelang, James S. *The Flight of Icarus: Artisan Autobiography in Early Modern Europe.* Stanford, CA: Stanford University Press, 1998.

Arendt, Hannah. "On the Nature of Totalitarianism." In *Essays in Understanding, 1930–1954. Formation, Exile, and Totalitarianism,* edited by Jerome Kohn, 328–360. New York: Schocken, 1994.

Arteev, Artur. "Nasledie repressirovannykh khudozhnikov." *Respublika,* October 6, 2021. http://respublika11.ru/2021/10/06/nasledie-repressirovannyih-hudozhnikov/.

Artem'eva, Anna, and Elena Rachina, eds. *58-ia. Neiz"iatoe: Istorii liudei, kotorye perezhili to, chego my bol'she vsego boimsia.* Moscow: Izd-vo ACT, 2016.

Artizov, A., A. Kosakovskii, V. Naumov, and I. Shevchuk, eds. *Reabilitatsiia: Kak eto bylo. Dokumenty Prezidiuma TsK KPSS i drugie materialy, t. 1, Mart 1953-fevral' 1956.* Moscow: Mezhdunarodnyi fond "Demokratiia," 2004.

———. *Reabilitatsiia: Kak eto bylo. Dokumenty Prezidiuma TsK KPSS i drugie materialy, t. 3 Seredina 80-kh godov-1991.* Moscow: Mezhdunarodnyi Fond Demokratiia, 2004. http://www.alexanderyakovlev.org/fond/issues/62100.

Assmann, Aleida. "Transformations between History and Memory." *Social Research* 75, no. 1 (Spring 2008): 49–72.

Assmann, Aleida, and John Czaplicka. "Collective Memory and Cultural Identity." *New German Critique,* no. 65 (Spring/Summer 1995): 125–133.

Assmann, Jan. *Moses the Egyptian: The Memory of Egypt in Western Monotheism.* In *The Collective Memory Reader,* edited by Jeffrey K. Olick, Vered Vinitzky-Seroussi, and Daniel Levy, 209–215. Oxford: Oxford University Press, 2011.

Badcock, Sarah. *A Prison without Walls? Eastern Siberian Exile in the Last Years of Tsarism.* Oxford: Oxford University Press, 2016.

Baldaev, D. S., V. K. Belko, and I. M Isupov. *Slovar' tiuremno-lagerno-blatnogo zhargona (rechevoi i graficheskii portret sovetskoi tiur'my).* Moscow: izd-vo "Kraia Moskvy," 1992.

Bardach, Janusz. *Man Is Wolf to Man: Surviving the Gulag.* Translated by Kathleen Gleeson. Berkeley: University of California Press, 1998.

BIBLIOGRAPHY

Barenberg, Alan. "'Discovering' Vorkuta: Science and Colonization in the Early Gulag." *Gulag Studies* 4 (2011): 1–20.

———. "From Prisoners to Citizens? Ex-Prisoners in Vorkuta during the Thaw." In *The Thaw: Soviet Society and Culture in the 1950s and 1960s*, edited by Denis Kozlov and Eleonory Gilburd, 118–144. Toronto: University of Toronto Press, 2013.

———. *Gulag Town, Company Town: Forced Labor and Its Legacy in Vorkuta*. New Haven, CT: Yale University Press, 2014.

———. "Soviet Katorga Reconsidered: Retribution, Punishment, and Social Control in Wartime and the Postwar." In *Social Control under Stalin and Khrushchev: The Phantom of a Well-Ordered State*, edited by Immo Rebitschek and Aaron Retish, 135–160. Toronto: University of Toronto Press, 2023.

Barnes, Steven. *Death and Redemption: The Gulag and the Shaping of Soviet Society*. Princeton, NJ: Princeton University Press, 2011.

Baryshnikova, Natal'ia, Sergei Bondarenko, Kiril Kozhanov, Nikita Lomakin, and Aleksei Makarov. "Pamiat' v proekte." International Memorial Society. Accessed December 9, 2017. http://project.memo.ru.

Beer, Daniel. *House of the Dead: Siberian Exile under the Tsars*. New York: Knopf, 2017.

Bekbulatova, Taisia. "Mezhdunarodnyi 'Memorial' ob"iavili inostrannym agentom." *Kommersant*, October 5, 2016. https://www.kommersant.ru/doc/3107309.

Beliaeva, N. Zh. "Uchastie repressirovannykh khudozhnikov v komi respublikanskikh vystavkakh 1940-kh godov." In *Materialy i issledovaniia*, vypusk 2, 73–98. Syktyvkar: National'naia galereia Respubliki Komi, 2008.

Beliaeva, N. Zh., and L. I. Kochergan, eds. *Khudozhniki Respubliki Komi— uchastniki Velikoi Otechestvennoi voiny*. Syktyvkar: Komi respublikanskaia tipografiia, 2015.

Bell, Duncan, ed. *Memory, Trauma and World Politics: Reflections on the Relationship between Past and Present*. Basingstoke: Palgrave Macmillan, 2006.

Bell, Wilson T. "Sex, Pregnancy, and Power in the Late Stalinist Gulag." *Journal of the History of Sexuality* 24, no. 2 (May 2015): 198–224.

———. *Stalin's Gulag at War: Forced Labor, Mass Death, and Victory in the Second World War*. Toronto: University of Toronto Press, 2018.

———. "Tomsk Regional Identity and the Legacy of the Gulag and Stalinist Repression." In *Russia's Regional Identities: The Power of the Provinces*, edited by Edith W. Clowes, Gisela Erbslöh, and Ani Kokobobo, 206–225. London: Routledge, 2018.

———. "Was the Gulag an Archipelago? De-Convoyed Prisoners and Porous Borders in the Camps of Western Siberia." *Russian Review* 72 (January 2013): 116–141.

Berezina, E. P., V. N. Kazarinova, and I. G. Zhukova, eds. *Politicheskie repressii v Komi krae (20–50-e gody): Bibliograficheskii ukazatel'*. Syktyvkar: Fond Pokaianie, 2006.

Blum, Alain, Marta Kraveri, and Valé Nivelon. *Mir GULAGa i spetsposelenii: Rasskazyvaiut svideteli iz Tsentral'noi i Vostochnoi Evropy.* Moscow: Rosspen, 2016.

Bobrakov, Igor'. "Uchenyi, dissident, deputat." *Region,* June 16, 2021. https://ourreg .ru/2021/06/16/uchenyj-dissident-deputat/?fbclid=IwAR3sBOd12sOczQmHp 5JOKz4uhZs43P-cP4w4WO8z9uO1YeMGN4MbJjWShRY.

Bobrova, Elena. "Soviet-Era Gulag Museum NGO Perm-36 Announces Closure." *Russia beyond the Headlines,* March 6, 2015. https://www.rbth.com/society /2015/03/06/soviet-era_gulag_museum_ngo_perm-36_announces_closure _44297.html.

Bogatkina, Sofiia. "#MyMemorial*. Chetyre voprosa o budushchem pravozash- chitnoi organizatsii." *7x7,* November 19, 2021. https://7x7-journal.ru/articles /2021/11/19/isk-k-memorialu-absurden-predstaviteli-memoriala-rasskazali-o -sudbe-organizacii.

———. "Pochemu likvidirovali 'Mezhdunarodnyi Memorial.' Korotko." *7x7,* December 28, 2021. https://7x7-journal.ru/articles/2021/12/28/pochemu -likvidirovali-mezhdunarodnyj-memorial.

———. "Tsitata dnia. Chlen pravleniia 'Memoriala'* Aleksandra Polivanova— o 'smekhotvornom' sude i budushchem organizatsii." *7x7,* December 28, 2021. https://7x7-journal.ru/news/2021/12/28/citata-dnya.

Bogumił, Zuzanna. *Gulag Memories: The Rediscovery and Commemoration of Rus- sia's Repressive Past.* New York: Berghahn, 2018.

———. "Stone, Cross, and Mask: Searching for Language of Commemoration of the Gulag in the Russian Federation." *Polish Sociological Review,* no. 177 (2012): 71–90.

Bogumił, Zuzanna, Dominique Moran, and Elly Harrowell. "Sacred or Secular? 'Memorial,' the Russian Orthodox Church, and the Contested Commemora- tion of Soviet Repressions." *Europe-Asia Studies* 67, no. 9 (November 2015): 1416–1444.

Borejsza, Jerzy W., and Klaus Ziemer, eds. *Totalitarian and Authoritarian Re- gimes in Europe: Legacies and Lessons from the Twentieth Century.* New York: Berghahn, 2006.

Boym, Svetlana. *The Future of Nostalgia.* New York: Basic, 2001.

———. *Territories of Terror: Mythologies and Memories of the Gulag in Contemporary Russian-American Art.* Seattle: University of Washington Press, 2006.

Bradley, Joseph. *Voluntary Associations in Tsarist Russia: Science, Patriotism, and Civil Society.* Cambridge, MA: Harvard University Press, 2009.

Brown, Kate. A Biography of No Place: From Ethnic Borderland to Soviet Heart- land. Cambridge, MA: Harvard University Press, 2004.

BIBLIOGRAPHY

———. "Out of Solitary Confinement: The History of the Gulag." *Kritika: Explorations in Russian and Eurasian History* 8, no. 1 (Winter 2007): 93–94.

Brown, Matthew Cullerne. *Art under Stalin*. New York: Holmes & Meier, 1991.

Bruner, Jerome. *Acts of Meaning*. Cambridge, MA: Harvard University Press, 1990.

Brunstedt, Jonathan. *The Soviet Myth of World War II: Patriotic Memory and the Russian Question in the USSR*. Cambridge: Cambridge University Press, 2021.

Buber-Neuman, Margarete. *Under Two Dictators: Prisoner of Stalin and Hitler*. Translated by Edward Fitzgerald. London: Pimlico, 2008.

Bulychev, V., ed. *V nedrakh Ukhtpechlaga*. Ukhta: Ukhtinskaia tipografiia "Memorial," 1989.

———. *V nedrakh Ukhtpechlaga: Vypusk vtoroi*. Ukhta: Ukhta-Pechorskoe obshchestvo Memorial, 1994.

Burenkova, Mari, Natal'ia Gorlenko, and Ilia Fliarkovskii, dirs. *30 let sovesti*. 2018. Moscow: Istoriia Rossii v fotografiiakh i Mezhdunarodnyi Memorial, 2019, streaming (in Russian). YouTube video, 43:45. https://www.youtube.com/watch?v=ygpcAaoqM-4&t=106s.

Burke, Peter. "History as a Social Memory." In *Memory: History, Culture and the Mind*, edited by Thomas Butler, 97–113. Oxford: Basil Blackwell, 1989.

Chebankova, Elena. *Civil Society in Putin's Russia*. London: Routledge, 2013.

Chernitsyn, Valerii. "V stolitse Komi otkrylsia 'Revol't Tsentr." *Krasnoe znamia*, June 8, 2019. https://komikz.ru/news/culture/95265.

Christensen, Karin Hyldal. *The Making of the New Martyrs of Russia: Soviet Repression in Orthodox Memory*. New York: Routledge, 2018.

Chuprov, V. I., I. L. Zherebtsov, A. A. Popov, and A. N. Turubanov, eds. *Istoriia Komi s drevneishikh vremen do kontsa XX veka*. t. 1. Syktyvkar: Komi knizhnoe izd-vo, 2004.

Cohen, Stephen F. "The Unheralded Putin—Russia's Official Anti-Stalinist No. 1." *The Nation*, November 8, 2017. https://www.thenation.com/article/archive/the-unheralded-putin-russias-official-anti-stalinist-no-1/.

Corney, Frederick C. *Telling October: Memory and the Making of the Bolshevik Revolution*. Ithaca, NY: Cornell University Press, 2004.

Danilov, A. A., A. I. Utkin, and A. V. Filippov, eds. *Istoriia Rossii, 1945–2008 gg.: 11 klass. Uchebnik dlia uchashchikhsia obshcheobrazovatel 'nykh uchrezhdenii*. 2nd ed. Moscow: Prosveshchenie, 2008.

David-Fox, Michael, ed. *The Soviet Gulag: Evidence Interpretation, and Comparison*. Pittsburgh, PA: University of Pittsburgh Press, 2016.

Davies, R. W. *Soviet History in the Gorbachev Revolution*. London: Macmillan, 1989.

———. *Soviet History in the Yeltsin Era*. London: Macmillan, 1997.

Dobson, Miriam. "Contesting the Paradigms of De-Stalinization: Readers' Responses to 'One Day in the Life of Ivan Denisovich." *Slavic Review* 64, no. 3 (Autumn 2005): 580–600.

———. *Khrushchev's Cold Summer: Gulag Returnees, Crime, and the Fate of Reform after Stalin*. Ithaca, NY: Cornell University Press, 2009.

———. "POWs and Purge Victims: Attitudes toward Party Rehabilitation, 1956–57." *Slavonic and East European Review* 86, no. 2 (April 2008): 328–345.

———. "'Show the Bandits No Mercy!': Amnesty, Criminality, and Public Response in 1953." In *The Dilemmas of De-Stalinisation: A Social and Cultural History of Reform in the Khrushchev Era*, edited by Polly A. Jones, 21–40. Routledge Curzon, 2005.

Dolgov, Anna. "Russia's Gulag Museum Shuts Doors amid Mounting State Pressure." *Moscow Times*, March 3, 2015. https://www.themoscowtimes .com/2015/03/03/russias-gulag-museum-shuts-doors-amid-mounting-state -pressure-a44401.

Dolgun, Alexander. *Alexander Dolgun's Story: An American in the Gulag*. New York: Knopf, 1975.

Domrin, Alexander N. "Ten Years Later: Society, 'Civil Society,' and the Russian State." *Russian Review* 62 (April 2003): 193–211.

Draskoczy, Julie. *Belomor: Criminality and Creativity in Stalin's Gulag*. Boston: Academic Studies, 2014.

Eakin, John Paul. *How Our Lives Become Stories: Making Selves*. Ithaca, NY: Cornell University Press, 1999.

———. *Living Autobiographically: How We Create Identity in Narrative*. Ithaca, NY: Cornell University Press, 2008.

Eastmond, Marita. "Stories as Lived Experience: Narratives in Forced Migration Research." *Journal of Refugee Studies* 20, no. 2 (2007): 248–264.

Edele, Mark. *Soviet Veterans of the Second World War: A Popular Movement in an Authoritarian Society, 1941–1991*. Oxford: Oxford University Press, 2008.

Edkins, Jenny. *Trauma and the Memory of Politics*. Cambridge: Cambridge University Press, 2003.

Edwards, Michael, ed. *The Oxford Handbook of Civil Society*. Oxford: Oxford University Press, 2011.

Elie, Marc. "Rehabilitation in the Soviet Union, 1953–1964: A Policy Unachieved." In *De-Stalinising Eastern Europe: The Rehabilitation of Stalin's Victims after 1953*, edited by Kevin McDermott and Matthew Stibbe, 25–45. Baskingstoke: Palgrave Macmillan, 2015.

Elie, Marc, and Jeff Hardy. "'Letting the Beasts Out of the Cage': Parole in the Post-Stalin Gulag, 1953–1973." *Europe-Asia Studies* 67, no. 4 (June 2015): 579–605.

Erll, Astrid, and Ansgar Nünning, eds. *A Companion to Cultural Memory Studies*. Berlin: De Gruyter, 2010.

Etkind, Alexander. "A Parable of Misrecognition: *Anagnorisis* and the Return of the Repressed from the Gulag." *Russian Review* 68 (October 2009): 623–640.

———. "Sites and Sounds of the Camps: Commentary on the 'Legacies' Section." In *Rethinking the Gulag: Identies, Sources, Legacies*, edited by Alan Barenberg and Emily D. Johnson, 273–283. Bloomington: Indiana University Press, 2022.

———. "Soviet Subjectivity: Torture for the Sake of Salvation?" *Kritika: Explorations in Russian and Eurasian History* 6, no. 1 (Winter 2005): 171–186.

———. *Warped Mourning: Stories of the Undead in the Land of the Unburied*. Stanford, CA: Stanford University Press, 2013.

Evstiunichev, A. P. *Nakazanie bez prestupleniia*. Syktyvkar: Memorial, 1991.

Fauzer, V. V. "Migratsionnye protsessy v Respublike Komi: Otsenka i tendentsii protekaniia." In *V Ural'skii demograficheskii forum: Sbornik materialov*, 170–175. Ekaterinburg: Institute ekonomiki UrO RAN, 2014.

Federal'noe arkhivnoe agentstvo. "Federal'nyi zakon ot 22.10.2004 No.125-FZ 'Ob arkhivnom dele v Rossiskoi Federatsii (v red. ot 18.06.2017 g.).'" Accessed February 21, 2019. http://archives.ru/documents/fz/zakon-archivnoe-delo .shtml.

"Federal'nye eksperty postavili Komi v primer po uvekovechivaniu pamiati polit za-kliuchennyk." *BNK*, March 5, 2020. https://www.bnkomi.ru/data/news/108008/.

Fiedler, Anke, and Michael Meyen. "'The Totalitarian Destruction of the Public Sphere?' Newspapers and Structures of Public Communication in Socialist Countries: The Example of the German Democratic Republic." *Media, Culture, and Society* 37 (2015): 834–849.

Figes, Orlando. *The Whisperers: Private Life in Stalin's Russia*. New York: Picador, 2007.

Filimonova, Kseniia. "Leksikograf rukotvornogo ada." *Gor'kii*, May 20, 2021. https://gorky.media/reviews/leksikograf-rukotvornogo-ada/.

Filippov, A. V. *Istoriia Rossii, 1945–2008: kniga dlia uchitelia*, 2nd ed. Moscow: Prosveshchenie, 2008.

———, ed. *Noveishaia Istoriia Rossii, 1945–2007 gg.: kniga dlia uchitelia*. Moscow: Prosveshchenie, 2007.

Fine, Gary Allen. *Difficult Reputations: Collective Memories of the Evil, Inept, and Controversial*. Chicago: University of Chicago Press, 2001.

Fitzpatrick, Sheila. *Tear Off the Masks! Identity and Imposture in Twentieth-Century Russia*. Princeton, NJ: Princeton University Press, 2005.

Fivush, Robyn, and Catherine A. Haden, eds. *Autobiographical Memory and the Construction of a Narrative Self: Developmental and Cultural Perspectives*. London: Lawrence Erlbaum Associates, 2003.

Flige, Irina. "Mir posle Gulaga: reabilitatsiia i kul'tura pamiati sbornik dokladov 10–11 sentiabria, 2003." In *Vtoroi mezhdunarodnyi simpozium pamiati V.V. Iofe*. St. Petersburg: Memorial, 2004.

———. "The Necropolis of the Gulag as a Historical-Cultural Object: An Overview and Explication of the Problem." In *Rethinking the Gulag: Identities,*

252   BIBLIOGRAPHY

Sources, Legacies, edited by Alan Barenberg and Emily D. Johnson, 243–272. Bloomington: Indiana University Press, 2022.

———. "Visualizations of Soviet Repressions and the Gulag in Museums: Common Exhibition Models." *Problems of Post-Communism* (2021): 1–15. https://doi.org/10.1080/10758216.2021.1987268.

Flige, I., and T. Kosinova. "Vorkuta-Leningrad: istoriia soprotivleniia v zerkale Komi v 1950-kh–1980-kh godakh." Broshiura. Syktyvkar: Natsional'nyi Muzei Republiki Komi, 2003.

Fond Ioffe. "Elektronnyi arkhiv Fonda Ioffe." 2010. https://arch2.iofe.center /person/33276.

Fond Pokaianie. "Komi respublikanskomu blagotvoritel'nomu obshchestven-nomu fondu zhertv politicheskikh repressii 'Pokaianie'—10 let." Broshiura. Syktyvkar: Fond Pokaianie, 2008.

Formakov, Arsenii. *Gulag Letters*. Edited and translated by Emily D. Johnson. New Haven, CT: Yale University Press, 2017.

Forty, Adrian, and Susan Küchler, eds. *The Art of Forgetting*. Oxford: Berg, 1999.

"Fotodokumenty po istorii politicheskikh repressii v SSSR 1930–1950-x godov: teatr v GULAGe." Muzei Sakharovskogo tsentra. Accessed February 18, 2019. http://museum.sakharov-center.ru/fotodok/index.ph p?p=141605:141607,141607:142504,142504:150656.

Foucault, Michel, Luther H. Martin, Huck Gutman, and Patrick H. Hutton, eds. *Technologies of the Self: A Seminar with Michel Foucault*. Amherst: University of Massachusetts Press, 1988.

Fraser, Nancy. "Rethinking the Public Sphere: A Contribution to the Critique of Actually Existing Democracy." *Social Text* 25/26 (1990): 56–80.

Frid, Valerii. *58½. Zapiski lagernogo pridurka*. Moscow: Izdatel'skii Dom Rusanova, 1996.

Frierson, Cathy A. "Russia's Law 'On Rehabilitation of Victims of Political Repression': 1991–2011 an Enduring Artifact of Transitional Justice." Working Paper, National Council for Eurasian and East European Research, February 28, 2014. https://scholars.unh.edu/history_facpub/342/.

Frierson, Cathy A., and Semyon S. Vilensky, eds. *Children of the Gulag*. New Haven, CT: Yale University Press, 2010.

Gaplikov, S. A. "Obrashcheniie Glavy Respubliki Komi k zhiteliam respubliki v sviazi s Dnem pamiati zhertv politicheskikh repressii." *Komiinform*, October 30, 2016. https://komiinform.ru/news/140563.

Garros, Veronique, Natalia Korenevskaya, and Thomas Lahusen, eds. *Intimacy and Terror: Soviet Diaries of the 1930s*. New York: New Press, 1995.

Gavrilova, Sofia. "Regional Memories of the Great Terror: Representation of the Gulag in Russian *Kraevedcheskii* Museums." *Problems of Post-Communism* (2021): 1–16. https://doi.org/10.1080/10758216.2021.1885981.

"Genprokuratura potrebovala likvidirovat' 'Memorial' i ego podrazdeleniia." *Novaya Gazeta*, November 11, 2021. https://novayagazeta.ru/articles/2021/11/11/genprokuratura-potrebovala-likvidirovat-mezhdunarodnyi-memorial-news.

Geraskina, Alla. "Mesto skorbi izmenit' nel'zia." *Novaia gazeta*, October 22, 2019. https://www.novayagazeta.ru/articles/2018/10/22/78295-mesto-skorbi-izmenit-nelzya.

Getty, J. Arch, and Oleg V. Naumov. *The Road to Terror: Stalin and the Self-Destruction of the Bolsheviks, 1932–39.* New Haven, CT: Yale University Press, 1999.

Geyer, Michael, and Sheila Fitzpatrick, eds. *Beyond Totalitarianism: Stalinism and Nazism Compared.* Cambridge: Cambridge University Press, 2009.

Gilligan, Emma. *Defending Human Rights in Russia: Sergei Kovalyov, Dissident and Human Rights Commissioner, 1969–2003.* London: RoutledgeCurzon, 2004.

Ginzburg, Eugenia. *Journey into the Whirlwind.* Translated by Paul Stevenson and Max Hayward. New York: Harcourt, Brace & World, 1967.

———. *Within the Whirlwind.* Translated by Ian Boland. New York: Harcourt Brace Jovanovich, 1981.

"Glava Komi: 'Mikhail Rogachev mnogoe sdelal dlia vosstanovleniia istoricheskoi pravdy'." *BNK*, January 4, 2021. https://www.bnkomi.ru/data/news/122465/.

Goode, J. Paul. "Patriotism without Patriots? Perm'-36 and Patriotic Legitimation in Russia." *Slavic Review* 79, no. 2 (Summer 2020): 390–411.

Gorky, Maxim, ed. *Belomor: An Account of the Construction of the New Canal between the White Sea and the Baltic Sea.* Translated by S. G. Firin. New York: H. Smith and R. Haas, 1935.

Gorodin, Leonid. *Slovar' Russkikh argotizmov: Leksikon katorgi i lagerei imperatorskoi i sovetskoi Rossii.* Svetlana Pukhova, ot. red. Moskva: Izdatel'skaia programma Muzei Istorii Gulaga i Fonda Pamiati, 2021. https://gmig.ru/upload/iblock/17f/17ff966718f1b4bca1d0e918f8e26e1d.pdf.

Gregory, Paul R., and Valery Lazarev, eds. *The Economics of Forced Labor: The Soviet Gulag.* Palo Alto, CA: Hoover Institution Press, 2003.

Grossman, Vasily. *Everything Flows.* Translated by Robert Chandler, Elizabeth Chandler, and Anna Aslanyan. New York: New York Review Books, 2009.

Gullotta, Andrea. *Intellectual Life and Literature at Solovki 1923–1930: The Paris of the Northern Concentration Camps.* Cambridge: Legenda, 2018.

Habermas, Jürgen. *The Structural Transformation of the Public Sphere: An Inquiry into a Category of Bourgeois Society.* Translated by Thomas Burger. Cambridge, MA: MIT Press, 1991.

Halbwachs, Maurice. *On Collective Memory.* Translated by Lewis A. Coser. Chicago: University of Chicago Press, 1992.

Halfin, Igal. *Terror in My Soul: Communist Autobiographies on Trial.* Cambridge, MA: Harvard University Press, 2003.

Hardy, Jeff. *The Gulag after Stalin: Redefining Punishment in Khrushchev's Soviet Union, 1953–1964.* Ithaca, NY: Cornell University Press, 2016.

———. "The State Museum of Gulag History (Moscow, Russia)." In *Museums of Communism: New Memory Sites in Central and Eastern Europe*, edited by Stephen Norris, 275–304. Bloomington: Indiana University Press, 2020.

Harris, James R. *The Great Fear: Stalin's Terror of the 1930s.* Oxford: Oxford University Press, 2016.

Hellbeck, Jochen. *Revolution on My Mind: Writing a Diary under Stalin.* Cambridge, MA: Harvard University Press, 2006.

Hemment, Julie. "Nashi, Youth Voluntarism, and Potemkin NGOs: Making Sense of Civil Society in Post-Soviet Russia." *Slavic Review* 73, no. 2 (Summer 2012): 234–260.

Hochschild, Adam. *The Unquiet Ghost: Russians Remember Stalin.* Boston: Houghton Mifflin, 2003.

Hoffmann, David L., ed. *The Memory of the Second World War in Soviet and Post-Soviet Russia.* New York: Routledge, 2022.

———. "The Politics of Commemoration in the Soviet Union and Contemporary Russia." In *The Memory of the Second World War in Soviet and Post-Soviet Russia*, edited by David L. Hoffmann, 1–15. London: Routledge, 2022.

Holmgren, Beth, ed. *The Russian Memoir: History and Literature.* Evanston, IL: Northwestern University Press, 2003.

Hopkins, Valeri, and Ivan Nechepurenko. "As the Kremlin Revises History, a Human Rights Champion Becomes a Casualty." *New York Times*, December 29, 2021. https://www.nytimes.com/2021/12/29/world/europe/russia-memorial-human-rights-center.html?searchResultPosition=1.

Hosking, Geoffrey A. "Memory in a Totalitarian Society: The Case of the Soviet Union." In *Memory: History, Culture and the Mind*, edited by Thomas Butler, 115–130. Oxford: Basil Blackwell, 1989.

Iakovlev, A. N., ed. *Reabilitatsiia: Politicheskie protsessy 30–50-kh godov.* Moscow: Izdatel'stvo politichesoi literatury, 1991.

Ignatova, N. M., ed. *Pokianie. Martirolog* t. 14. Syktyvkar: Fond Pokaianie, 2021.

———. *Spetspereselentsy v Respublike Komi v 1930–1950-e gg.* Syktyvkar: Institut iazyka, literatury i istorii Komi nauchnogo tsentra UrO RAN, 2009.

International Memorial Society. "Victims of Political Terror in the USSR." Accessed April 1, 2018. http://lists.memo.ru/index18.htm.

Irwin-Zarecka, Iwona. *Frames of Remembrance: The Dynamics of Collective Memory.* New Brunswick, NJ: Transaction, 1993.

Istoginoi, A. Ia., ed. *Intaliia: Stikhi i vospominaniia byvshikh zakliuchennykh Minlaga.* Moscow: Vest', 1995.

BIBLIOGRAPHY

Isupov, Vladimir. Anatol'evich. *Demograficheskie katastrofy i krizisy v Rossii v pervoi polovine XX veka: istoriko-demograficheskie ocherki.* Novosibirsk: Sibirskii khronograf, 2000.

Iusov, Sergei, Veronika Kulakova, and Roman Soldatov. "Plokhaia pamiat': chto privelo k likvidatsii 'Mezhdunarodnogo Memoriala'." *Izvestiia*, December 28, 2021. https://iz.ru/1270870/sergei-iusov-veronika-kulakova-roman-soldatov /plokhaia-pamiat-chto-privelo-k-likvidatcii-mezhdunarodnogo-memorialaю.

Ivanov, K. P. *Leto. Polnoch'. U moego krylechka*, Oil on canvas, 1959–1969. http:// www.kraevidenie.ru/nizhnee_menju/opisanie_kartiny/315?type=125,0.

———. *Ulitsa Usinskaia.* Oil on canvas. Kraevidenie: Respublika Komi glazami khudozhnikov, 1959. Accessed February 18, 2019. http://www.kraevidenie .ru/nizhnee_menju/opisanie_kartiny/317/?type=125,0.

———. *Vid na shaktu 'Kapital'naia' iz okna cherdachnogo pomeshcheniia sgorevshego teatra.* Watercolor on paper. Kraevidenie: Respublika Komi glazami khudozhnikov, 1957. Accessed February 18, 2019. http://www.kraevidenie.ru /nizhnee_menju/opisanie_kartiny/316?type=125,0.

Ivanova, Galina Mikhailovna. *Labor Camp Socialism: The Gulag in the Soviet Totalitarian System.* Edited by Donald J. Raleigh and Translated by Carol Flath. London: M. E. Sharpe, 2000.

"Izdateli martirologa 'Pokaianie' ne teriaiut nadezhd poluchit' dostup k arkhivam." *BNK: Infromatsionnoe agentstvo*, December 23, 2011. https://www .bnkomi.ru/data/news/11202/.

Jelin, Elizabeth. *State Repression and the Labors of Memory.* Translated by Judy Rein and Marcial Godoy-Anativia. Minneapolis: University of Minnesota Press, 2003.

Jones, Polly. "Between Post-Stalinist Legitimacy and Stalin's Authority: Memories of 1941 from Late Socialism to the Post-Soviet Era." *Canadian Slavonic Papers* 54, no. 3–4 (September–December 2012): 357–376.

———. "Memories of Terror or Terrorizing Memories? Terror, Trauma, and Survival in Soviet Culture of the Thaw." *Slavonic and East European Review* 86, no. 2 (April 2008): 346–371.

———. *Myth, Memory, Trauma: Rethinking the Stalinist Past in the Soviet Union, 1953–1970.* New Haven, CT: Yale University Press, 2013.

Joyce, Christopher. "Recycled Victims: The Great Terror in the Komi ASSR." In *Stalin's Terror Revisited*, edited by R. W. Davies, E. A. Rees, M. J. Ilič, and J. R. Smith, 191–220. Basingstoke: Palgrave Macmillan, 2006.

Kadar, Marlene, Jeanne Perreault, and Linda Warley, eds. *Photographs, Histories, and Meanings.* New York: Palgrave Macmillan, 2009.

Kalashnikov, Antony. "Stalinist Crimes and the Ethics of Memory." *Kritika: Explorations in Russian and Eurasian History* 19, no. 3 (Summer 2018): 599–626.

BIBLIOGRAPHY

Kaneva, A. N. *Gulagovskii teatra Ukhty*. Syktyvkar: Komi Knizhnoe izd-vo, 2001.

Karmanov, F. A., and S. A. Panov, eds. *Reabilitirovan posmertno. Vtoroi vypusk*. Moscow: izd-vo Iuridicheskaia literatura, 1988.

Karp, Ivan, Christine Mullen Kreamer, and Steven D. Lavine, eds. *The Politics of Public Culture: Museums and Communities*. Washington, DC: Smithsonian Institution Press, 1992.

"Karta pamiati: Nekropol' terrora i GULAGa." Fond Ioffe, 2015. https://www .mapofmemory.org.

Kenney, Padraic. *A Carnival of Revolution: Central Europe 1989*. Princeton, NJ: Princeton University Press, 2002.

K'eralli, L. "Poeziia GULAGa kak literaturnoe svidetel'stvo: teoreticheskie i epistemologicheskie obosnovaniia." *Studia Litterarum* 3, no. 3 (June 2018): 144–163.

Kersnovskaia, Evfrosiniia. *Naskal'naia zhivopis'*. Moscow: SP Kvadrat, 1991.

Kharkhordin, Oleg. *The Collective and the Individual in Russia: A Study of Practices*. Berkeley: University of California Press, 1999.

Khazanov, Anatoly M. "Whom to Mourn and Whom to Forget? (Re)Constructing Collective Memory in Contemporary Russia." *Totalitarian Movements and Political Religions* 9, no. 2–3 (June–September 2008): 293–310.

Khlevniuk, Oleg. "The GULAG and the Non-GULAG as One Interrelated Whole." In *The Soviet Gulag: Evidence, Interpretation, and Comparison*, edited by Michael David-Fox, 25–41. Pittsburgh: University of Pittsburgh Press, 2016.

———. *The History of the Gulag: From Collectivization to the Great Terror*. New Haven, CT: Yale University Press, 2004.

Khlevnyuk, Daria. "'Silencing' or 'Magnifying' Memories? Stalin's Repressions and the 1990s in Russian Museums." *Problems of Post-Communism* (2021): 1–11. https://doi.org/10.1080/10758216.2021.1983443.

Khlimanova, Alena. "'Kto mozhet nam zapretit' pomnit' nashikh ubitykh?' Chto pishut v sotssetiakh o likvidatsii 'Mezhdunarodnogo Memorial.'*" *7x7*, December 28, 2021. https://7x7-journal.ru/articles/2021/12/28/kto-mozhet -nam-zapretit-pomnit-nashih-ubityh-chto-pishut-v-socsetyah-o-likvidacii -mezhdunarodnogo-memoriala.

Kievelson, Valerie Ann, and Joan Neuberger. "Seeing Into Being: An Introduction." In *Picturing Russia: Explorations in Visual Culture*, edited by Valerie Ann Kievelson and Joan Neuberger, 1–11. New Haven, CT: Yale University Press, 2008.

Kirk, Tyler C. "From Enemy to Hero: Andrei Krems and the Legacy of Political Repression in Russia's Far North, 1964–1982." *The Russian Review* 2023 (2023): 1–15. https://doi.org/10.1111/russ.12440.

———. "Toward a Settled Past and a Brighter Future: The Creation of a 'Usable Past' in Modern Russia, 2000–2010." MA thesis, University of Chicago, 2011.

Kirschenbaum, Lisa A. *The Legacy of the Siege of Leningrad, 1941–1995: Myth, Memories, and Monuments.* Cambridge: Cambridge University Press, 2006.

Kis, Oksana. *Survival as Victory: Ukrainian Women in the Gulag.* Translated by Lidia Wolanskyi. Cambridge, MA: Harvard University Press, 2021.

Klein, Aleksandr Solomonovich. *Moi nomer '2P-904': Avtobiograficheskie stikhi i poemy.* Syktyvkar: Komi respublikanskaia tipografiia, 1992.

———. *Ulybki Nevoli: Nevydumannaia zhizn, sobytiia, sud'by, sluchai.* Syktyvkar: Izdatelstvo Prolog, 1993.

Klein, A. S., and A. A. Popov. "Zapoliarnaia drama . . ." In *Pokaianie: Martirolog* t. 2, ch. 1, edited by G. V. Nevskii, 219–274. Syktyvkar: Komi knizhnoe izd-vo, 1999.

Komaromi, Ann. "Samizdat and Soviet Dissident Publics." *Slavic Review* 71, no. 1 (Spring 2012): 70–90.

"Komissia Soveta Evropy osudila likvidatsiiu 'Memoriala' i zaiavila, chto zakon ob 'inoagentakh' narushaet mezhdunarodnye standarty." *Novaia Gazeta,* December 31, 2021. https://novayagazeta.ru/articles/2021/12/31/komissiia -soveta-evropy-osudila-likvidatsiiu-memoriala-i-zaiavila-chto-zakon-ob -inoagentakh-narushaet-mezhdunarodnye-standarty-news.

Kononov, A. L. "K istorii priniatiia rossiiskogo Zakona 'O reabilitatsii zhertv politicheskikh repressii'." In *Reabilitatsiia i pamiat': Otnoshenie k zhertvam sovetskikh politicheskikh repressii v strankakh byvshevgo SSSR,* edited by Ian Rachinskii, 5–28. Moscow: Memorial-Zven'ia, 2016.

Koposov, Nikolay. *Memory Laws, Memory Wars: The Politics of the Past in Europe and Russia.* Cambridge: Cambridge University Press, 2018.

Korallov, M. M. *Teatr GULAGa: Vospominanie, ocherki.* Moscow: Memorial, 1995.

Kotkin, Stephen. *Armageddon Averted: The Soviet Collapse 1970–2000.* Oxford: Oxford University Press, 2001.

———. *Magnetic Mountain: Stalinism as a Civilization.* Berkeley: University of California Press, 1995.

———. "Terror, Rehabilitation, and Historical Memory: An Interview with Dimitrii Iurasov." *Russian Review* 51, no. 2 (April 1992): 238–262.

Kozlov, Denis. *The Readers of Novy Mir: Coming to Terms with the Stalinist Past.* Cambridge, MA: Harvard University Press, 2013.

Kozlov, Denis, and Eleonory Gilburd, eds. *The Thaw: Soviet Society and Culture in the 1950s and 1960s.* Toronto: University of Toronto Press, 2013.

Kozlov, Ivan. "'Potok donosov byl bespretsedentnym' Kak v Permi borolis' s muzeem istorii politicheskikh repressii." *Meduza,* November 10, 2014. https://www.themoscowtimes.com/2015/03/03/russias-gulag-museum-shuts -doors-amid-mounting-state-pressure-a44401.

Kozlov, Vladimir, ed. *Istoriia Stalinskogo GULAGa*, t. 6. Moscow: ROSSPEN, 2004.

Kozlova, Alena, Nikolai Mikhialov, Irina Ostrovskaia, and Svetlana Fadeeva, eds. *Papiny pis'ma: Pis'ma otsov iz GULAGa k detiam*. Moscow: WAM, 2015.

Kulakov, I. E., and I. L. Zherebtsov, eds. *Politicheskii repressii v Rossii v XX veke: Materialy regional'noi nauchnoi konferentsii Syktyvkar, 7–8 dek. 2000 g.* Syktyvkar: Fond Pokaianie, 2001.

Kulikova, Iuliia. "'Ukrepliali nasyp' trupami.' Kak stroili zheleznuiu dorogu do Vorkuty." *RFE/RL*, December 28, 2020. https://www.severreal.org/a/31021591.html.

Kuntsman, Adi. "'With a Shade of Disgust': Affective Politics of Sexuality and Class in Memoirs of the Stalinist Gulag." *Slavic Review* 68, no. 2 (Summer 2009): 308–328.

Kurilova, Anastasiia. "Istoricheski dokazannyi metod. Na spetspoligone 'Kommunarka' obnaruzheny novye zakhoroneniia." *Kommersant*, May 20, 2021. https://www.kommersant.ru/doc/4817849?query=Коммунарка#id2057236.

Kuromiya, Hiroaki. *The Voices of the Dead: Stalin's Great Terror in the 1930s*. New Haven, CT: Yale University Press, 2007.

Kustyshev, A. N. *Evropeiskii sever Rossii v repressivnoi politike XX v. Uchebnoe posobie*. Ukhta: Ukhtinskii gosudarstvennyi tekhnicheskii universitet, 2003.

———. *Ukhtizhemlag. 1938–1955*. Ukhta: Ukhtinskii gosudarstvennyi tekhnicheskii universitet, 2010.

Kuznetsov, Daniil, and Irina Shabalina. "'Vpolne ozhidaemoe iavlenie'. Chto proiskhodit v Rossii s pamiatnikami Stalinu i memorialami zhertvami politicheskikh repressii." *7x7*, May 22, 2019. https://7x7-journal.ru/articles/2019/05/22/stalin-zhertvy.

Kuznetsov, I. L., ed. *Pechal'naia pristan'*. Syktyvkar: Komi Knizhnoe izd-vo, 1991.

Kyz"iurov, L. A. "Pervyi pamiatnik zhertvam GULAGa v Komi ASSR." In *Politicheskie repressii v Rossii XX vek: Materialy regional'noi nauchnoi konferentsii 7–8 dekabria 2000 g.*, edited by M. B. Rogachev, 221–222. Syktyvkar: Fond Pokaianie, 2001.

Kyz"iurov, L. A., and M. M. Sel'kova. *Severnyi zheleznodorozhnyi ispravitel'no-trudovoi lager' (Sevzheldorlag). 1938–1951*. Syktyvkar: GU RK Natsional'nyi arkhiv RK, 2014.

Kyz"iurov, L. A., M. M. Sel'kova, and G. V. Khudiaeva. *Lokchimskii ispravitel'no-trudovoi lager' NKVD SSSR (Lokchimlag). 1937–1940*. Syktyvkar: GU RK Natsional'nyi Arkhiv Respubliki Komi, 2015.

Lahusen, Thomas. *How Life Writes the Book: Real Socialism and Socialist Realism in Stalin's Russia*. Ithaca, NY: Cornell University Press, 1997.

Lally, Kathy. "Putin Pushes NGO Foreign Agent Law." *Washington Post*, April 17, 2013. https://www.washingtonpost.com/world/europe/putin-pushes-ngo

-foreign-agent-law/2013/04/15/d9509ec2-a37e-11e2-9c03-6952ff305f35_story
.html?utm_term=.21ba04fac380.

Lass, Andrew. "From Memory to History: The Events of November 17 Dis/membered." In *Memory, History, and Opposition under Socialism*, edited by Rubie S. Watson, 87–104. Santa Fe, NM: School of American Research Press, 1994.

Lebow, Richard, Wulf Kansteiner, and Claudio Fogu, eds. *The Politics of Memory in Postwar Europe*. Durham, NC: Duke University Press, 2006.

Le Goff, Jacques. *History and Memory*. Translated by Steven Rendall and Elizabeth Claman. New York: Columbia University Press, 1992.

Levi, Primo. *The Drowned and the Saved*. New York: Summit, 1988.

———. "Revisiting the Camps." In *The Art of Memory: Holocaust Memorials in History*, edited by James Young, 185. New York: Prestel, 1994.

Lisova, I., ed. *'Ia tot, chei dukh ne pokorilsia . . .' sbornik Ukrainskikh poetov – politicheskikh uznikov Vorkutinskikh i Intininskikh lagerei*. Translated by Mark Kagantsov. Syktyvkar: Komi respublikanskaia tipografiia, 2011.

MacFarquhar, Neil. "Critics Scoff as Kremlin Erects Monument to the Repressed." *New York Times*, October 30, 2017. https://www.nytimes.com /2017/10/30/world/europe/russia-soviet-repression-monument.html.

MacKinnon, Elaine. "Motherhood and Survival in the Stalinist Gulag." *Aspasia* 13, no. 1 (2019): 65–94.

Makarets, Vera, and M. B. Rogachev, eds. *Politicheskii repressii v Syktyvkare: Putevoditel'*. Syktyvkar: Fond Pokaianie, 2011.

Maksimova, L. A., and L. V. Liamtseva. *GULAG kak factor modernizatsii na Evropeiskoi Severo-Vostoke*. Moscow: Izd-vo MGOU, 2011.

Malofeevskaia, L. N. *Narekli nas vragami*. Syktyvkar: Komi respublikanskaia tipografiia, 2008.

———. *Na ugol'nom meridiane*. Syktyvkar: Komi respublikanskaia tipografiia, 2012.

Malofeevskaia, L. N., and M. B. Rogachev, eds. *Pamiat' o GULAGe: Inta. Putevoditel'*. Syktyvkar: Fond Pokaianie, 2012.

Malyshev, Evgenii, Ekaterina Vulikh, Sergei Markelov, Aleksei Ukhankov, Aleksandra Iasharkina, and Ivan Zhuravkov. "'Ottogo chto my prishli malym sostavom, pamiat' o zhertvakh ne ischeznet.' Kak v pandemiiu pochtili pamiat' repressirovannykh." *7x7*, October 30, 2020. https://7x7-journal.ru /articles/2020/10/30/ot-togo-chto-my-prishli-malym-sostavom-pamyat-o -zhertvah-ne-ischeznet-kak-v-pandemiyu-pochtili-pamyat-repressirovannyh.

Malysheva, Svetlana. "Soviet Death and Hybrid Soviet Subjectivity: Urban Cemetery as a Metatext." *Ab Imperio* 3 (2018): 351–384.

Manchester, Laurie. *Holy Fathers, Secular Sons: Clergy, Intelligentsia, and the Modern Self in Revolutionary Russia*. DeKalb: Northern Illinois University Press, 2008.

Markizov, Leonid P. *Do i posle 1945 goda: Glazami ochevidtsa*. Edited by M. B. Rogachev. Syktyvkar: Pokaianie, 2003.

Markova, E. V. "Doroga, kotoruiu ia ne vybirala." *Radost'* 3–4 (1995): 126–133. http://www.sakharov-center.ru/asfcd/auth/?t=page&num=2793.

———. "Lektsiia: Dukhovnoe soprotivlenie v GULAGe." Sakharov Center, April 20, 2017. YouTube video, 2:31:54. https://www.youtube.com/watch?v=rHk-j2t3Cyg.

———. *Vorkutinskie zametki katorzhanki "E-105."* Syktyvkar: Fond Pokaianie, 2005.

———. *Zhili-byli v XX veke*. Syktyvkar: Fond Pokaianie, 2006.

Markova, E. V., and K. K. Voinovskaia. *Konstantin Genrikhovich Voinovskii-Kriger 1894–1979*. Edited by I. S. Pashkovskii. Moscow: Nauka, 2001.

Markova, E. V., V. A. Volkov, A. N. Rodnyi, and V. K. Iasnyi. *Gulagovskie tainy osvoeniia severa*. Moscow: Stroiizdat, 2001.

Martin, Barbara. *Dissident Histories in the Soviet Union: From De-Stalinization to Perestroika*. London: Bloomsbury, 2021.

Masliukova, Margarita, Ekaterina Mel'nikova, and Ekaterina Pavlenko. "Memorial: Epizod I." International Memorial Society. Accessed February 12, 2019. http://prequel.memo.ru/about.

Massino, Jill. "Gender as Survival: Women's Experiences of Deportation from Romania to the Soviet Union, 1945–1950." *Nationalities Papers* 36, no. 1 (March 2008): 55–83.

McDermott, Kevin, and Matthew Stibbe, eds. *De-Stalinising Eastern Europe. The Rehabilitation of Stalin's Victims after 1953*. New York: Palgrave Macmillan, 2015.

Memorial Moscow (@Memorial Moscow). "Na Vozvrashchenie imen v etom godu prishlo 5286 chelovek (sr: 263 cheloveka na pervoi aktsii v 2007 godu)." Twitter post, October 29, 2018, 12:44 p.m. https://twitter.com/MemorialMoscow/status/924723560337330177.

"Memorial NGO Fined for Noncompliance with Foreign Agent Law." *Moscow Times*, September 4, 2015. https://www.themoscowtimes.com/2015/09/04/memorial-ngo-fined-for-noncompliance-with-foreign-agent-law-a49353.

"Memorial—O likvidatsii Mezhdunarodnogo Memoriala." Mezhdunarodnyi Memorial, December 28, 2021. https://www.memo.ru/ru-ru/memorial/departments/intermemorial/news/667.

Merridale, Catherine. *Night of Stone: Death and Memory in Twentieth-Century Russia*. New York: Penguin, 2000.

———. "Revolution among the Dead: Cemeteries in Twentieth-Century Russia." *Mortality* 8, no. 2 (2003): 176–188.

"Mikhail Rogachev: 'Istoriia Komi kraia: eto interesno?'" *BNK*, January 5, 2021. https://www.bnkomi.ru/data/news/122470/.

"Mikhail Rogachev: 'Istoriia Komi kraia: eto interesno?'" *BNK*, 2011. YouTube video, 40:00. https://www.youtube.com/watch?v=IbI4AowCGIU&t=1s.

"Miniust ne vkliuchil NIPTs 'Memorial' v reestr inostrannykh agentov." International Memorial Society, February 12, 2019. https://www.memo.ru/ru-ru/memorial/departments/intermemorial/news/235.

Minkin, A., dir. *Po Pechorskoi doroge*. Film. Leningradkoe proizvodstvo, studiia Kinokhronika, 1955.

Mitlander, Conny, John Sundholm, and Adrian Velicu, eds. *European Cultural Memory Post-89*. Amsterdam: Rodopi, 2013.

Mochulsky, Fyodor Vasilevich. *Gulag Boss: A Soviet Memoir*. Translated by Deborah Kaple. Oxford: Oxford University Press, 2011.

Morozov, Nikolai A. *Gulag v Komi krae, 1929–1956*. Syktyvkar: Syktyvkarskii Gosudarstvennyi Universitet, 1997.

―――― . "Istrebiteil'no-trudovye gody: Komi - krai politicheskoi ssylki." In *Pokaianie: Martirolog*, t.1, edited by G. V. Nevskii, 15–237. Syktyvkar: Fond Pokaianie, 1998.

―――― . "Mnogonatsional'nyi GULAG." In *Pokaianie: Martirolog*, t.1, edited by G. V. Nevskii, 15–237. Syktyvkar: Fond Pokaianie, 1998.

―――― . *Osobye lageria MVD SSSR v Komi ASSR (1948—1954 gody)*. Syktyvkar: Syktyvkarskii Gosudarstvennyi Universitet, 1998.

Morozova, E. I. "Kara, podvig i nagrada: Sud'by uchenykh—laureatov Stalinskoi premii." Katalog vystavki. Syktyvkar: Natsional'nyi Muzei Respubliki Komi, n.d.

―――― . "My deti strashnykh let Rossii . . . (Deti GULAGa)." Katalog vystavki. Syktyvkar: Natsional'nyi Muzei Respubliki Komi, 2007.

―――― . "Repressirovannyi Pushkin." Katalog vystavki. Syktyvkar: Natsional'nyi Muzei Respubliki Komi, 2012.

Nakonechnyi, Mikhail. "'Factory of Invalids': Mortality, Disability, and Early Release on Medical Grounds in GULAG, 1930–1955." PhD diss., University of Oxford, 2020.

―――― . "'They Won't Survive for Long': Soviet Officials on Medical Release Procedure." In *Rethinking the Gulag: Identies, Sources, Legacies*, edited by Alan Barenberg and Emily D. Johnson. Bloomington: Indiana University Press, 2022.

Nathans, Benjamin. "Talking Fish: On Soviet Dissident Memoirs." *Journal of Modern History* 87 (September 2015): 579–614.

Nechepurenko, Ivan, and Andre Kramer. "Russian Court Orders Prominent Human Rights Group to Shut." *New York Times*, December 28, 2021. https://www.nytimes.com/2021/12/28/world/europe/russia-memorial-human-rights.html?searchResultPosition=2.

Neimark, Anna. "The Infrastructural Monument: Stalin's Water Works under Construction and in Representation." *Future Anterior: Journal of Historic Preservation, History, Theory, and Criticism* 9, no. 2 (Winter 2012): 1–14.

Nevskii, G. V., ed. *Pokaianie: Martirolog.* Syktyvkar: Fond Pokaianie, 1999.

"Nikita Petrov: U FSB net videniia svoei istorii." *Agentura.Ru: Spetsluzhby pod kontrolem,* November 9, 2010. https://www.agentura.ru/experts/npetrov/.

Nora, Pierre. "Between Memory and History: *Les Lieux de Mémoire.*" *Representations* 26 (Spring 1989): 7–24.

———. *Realms of Memory: The Construction of the French Past.* Translated by Arthur Goldhammer. New York: Columbia University Press, 1992.

"Novosti partnerov: '20 let raboty istorikov v szhatom vide." *BNK,* February 20, 2018. https://www.bnkomi.ru/data/news/74931/.

"Novosti partnerov: '20 let raboty istorikov v szhatom vide." *BNK,* February 20, 2018. YouTube video, 3:31. https://www.youtube.com/watch?v=IbI4AowCGIU&t=1s.

Olick, Jeffrey K. *The Politics of Regret: On Collective Memory and Historical Responsibility.* New York: Routledge, 2007.

———, ed. *States of Memory: Continuities, Conflicts, and Transformations in National Retrospection.* Durham, NC: Duke University Press, 2003.

Ol'shevskii, Vitallii. "Vyzhit!" In *Pechal'naia pristan'.* Edited by I. L. Kuznetsov, 257–267. Syktyvkar: Komi Knizhnoe izd-vo, 1991.

Orlov, V. P. *Repressirovannye geologi: Biograficheskie materialy.* Moscow: Roskomnedra, 1995.

Oushakine, Sergei Alex. *The Patriotism of Despair: Nation, War, and Loss in Russia.* Ithaca, NY: Cornell University Press, 2009.

———. "'We're Nostalgic, but We're Not Crazy': Retrofitting the Past in Russia." *Russian Review* 66 (July 2007): 451–482.

Pallot, Judith. "Forced Labour for Forestry: The Twentieth-Century History of Colonisation and Settlement in the North of Perm' Oblast'." *Europe-Asia Studies* 54, no. 7 (2002): 1055–1084.

Pal'veleva, Liliia. "Slovar' [ne]svobody. Lagernoe naslediie russkogo iazyka." *Radio Svoboda,* February 10, 2021. https://www.svoboda.org/a/31092341.html.

Paperno, Irina. "Exhuming the Bodies of Soviet Terror." *Representations* 75, no. 1 (Summer 2001): 89–118.

———. *Stories of the Soviet Experience.* Ithaca, NY: Cornell University Press, 2009.

———. "What Can Be Done with Diaries?" *Russian Review* 63 (October 2004): 561–573.

Passerini, Luisa. *Fascism in Popular Memory: The Cultural Experience of the Turin Working Class.* Translated by Robert Lumley and Jude Bloomfield. Cambridge: Cambridge University Press, 1987.

———, ed. *International Yearbook of Oral History and Life Stories,* vol. 1. *Memory and Totalitarianism.* Oxford: Oxford University Press, 1992.

"Perechen' poruchenii po itogam zasedaniia Soveta po razvitiiu grazhdanskogo obshchestva i pravam cheloveka i vstrechi s upolnomochennymi po pravam

BIBLIOGRAPHY 263

cheloveka." Porucheniia Prezidenta Rossisskoi Federatsii, January 29, 2020. http://www.kremlin.ru/acts/assignments/orders/62700.

Pereyaslavska, Katya. "Gulag Art: Elusive Evidence from the Forbidden Territories." *Art Documentation* 30, no. 1 (2011): 33–42.

Petkevich, Tamara. *Memoir of a Gulag Actress*. Translated by Yasha Klots and Ross Ufberg. DeKalb: Northern Illinois University Press, 2010.

Petrov, N. V., ed. *Istoriia Stalinskogo GULAGa*. t. 2. Moscow: ROSSPEN, 2004.

Platonova, Anastasiia. "Smert', rastianutaia na desiatiletiia." *Takie Dela*, February 25, 2019. https://takiedela.ru/2019/02/smert-rastyanutaya-na -desyatiletiya/.

"'Pokaianie' okazalos' pod ugrozoi." *Nevskoe Vremia*, December 27, 2012. https:// nvspb.ru/2012/12/27/pokayanie-okazalos-pod-ugrozoy-50208.

Poleshchikov, V. M. *Ot Vorkuty do Syktyvkara. Sud'by evreev v Respublike Komi: Sbornik*. Syktyvkar: Izd-vo "Eskom," 2003.

———. *Za sem'iu pechatami. Iz arkhiva KGB*. Syktyvkar: Komi knizhnoe izd-vo, 1995.

Poliakov, V. V., ed. *Ministerstvo Kul'tury Komi ASSR XI-ia Vystavka rabot khu-dozhnikov Komi ASSR: Katalog*. Syktyvkar: Ministerstvo Kul'tury Komi ASSR, 1955.

Polian, Pavel. *Against Their Will: The History and Geography of Forced Migrations in the USSR*. Budapest: Central European University Press, 2004.

Pollack, Deflef, and Jan Wielgohs, eds. *Dissent and Opposition in Communist Eastern Europe: Origins of Civil Society and Democratic Transition*. Burlington, VT: Ashgate, 2004.

Polushina, Iuliia, Ivan Zhurakov, Evgenii Malyshev, Aleksandra Iasharkina, and Aleksei Ukhankov. "Samoe plokhoe, chto mozhet proizoiti s politzakliuchen-nym, – ego mogut zabyt'. Kak v regionakh proshli aktsii pamiati repres-sirovannykh." *7x7*, October 30, 2021. https://7x7-journal.ru/articles/2021/10/30 /samoe-plohoe-chto-mozhet-proizojti-s-politzaklyuchennym-ego-mogut-zabyt -kak-v-regionah-proshli-akcii-pamyati-repressirovannyh.

Popovtseva, E. K. *Izobretatel'noe iskusstvo Respubliki Komi, 1943–2000*. Syk-tyvkar: Ministerstvo Kul'tury Respubliki Komi, 2011.

Portelli, Alessandro. *The Death of Luigi Trastulli and Other Stories: Form and Meaning in Oral History*. Albany, NY: SUNY Press, 1991.

Pouligny, Béatrice, Simon Chesterman, and Albrecht Schnabel, eds. *After Mass Crime: Rebuilding States and Communities*. Tokyo: United Nations University Press, 2007.

"Pravozashchitnik iz Komi Igor' Sazhin o 'Vozvrashchenii imen': U liudei est' za-pros na vosproizvedenie proshlogo." *7x7*, October 27, 2018. https://7x7-journal .ru/discuss/113084.

BIBLIOGRAPHY

"Predsedatel' pravleniia fonda 'Pokaianie' Mikhail Rogachev: 'Ne iskliucheno, chto izdanie martirologa pridetsia svernut'." *BNK: Informatsionnoe agenstvo*, November 24, 2012. https://www.bnkomi.ru/data/interview/16679/.

"Prezentatsiia 1-go toma Marirologa 'Pokaianie,' Anna Nevskaia i Igor' Sazhin, 30.04.2021." Peshkom po Ust'-Sysol'sku i Komi Memorial, May 1, 2021. YouTube video, 30:27. https://www.youtube.com/watch?v=uRilHFqdo9c.

Prilutskaia, L. *Komi ASSR k 50-letiiu Sovetskoi vlasti: Statisticheskii sbornik*. Syktyvkar: Komi knizhnoe izd-vo, 1967.

"Prokuror poprosil Verkhovnyi sud likvidirovat' 'Memorial.'" *Izvestiia*, December 28, 2021. https://iz.ru/1270733/2021-12-28/prokuror-poprosil-verkhovnyi -sud-likvidirovat-memorial.

Purdue, Derrick, ed. *Civil Societies and Social Movements: Potentials and Problems*. London: Routledge, 2007.

"Putin Orders Memorial to 'Victims of Political Repression.'" *Moscow Times*, September 30, 2015. https://www.themoscowtimes.com/2015/09/30/putin -orders-memorial-to-victims-of-political-repression-a49971.

Putin, Vladimir. "Opening of Wall of Sorrow Memorial to Victims of Political Repression." President of Russia, October 30, 2017. http://en.kremlin.ru /events/president/news/55948.

Rachinskii, Ian. "O Stene pamiati v Kommunarke." International Memorial Society, November 2, 2018. https://www.memo.ru/en-us/memorial /departments/intermemorial/news/205.

―――, ed. *Reabilitatsiia i pamiat': Otnoshenie k zhertvam sovetskikh politicheskikh repressii v stranakh byvshego SSSR*. Moskva: Memorial-Zven'ia, 2016.

―――. "Zhertvy politicheskogo terrora v SSSR." Moscow: International Memorial Society, 2016. http://lists.memo.ru.

Rachkov, Pavel. "Kak my tam zhili (zapiski ssylnogo)." In *Pechal'naia pristan'*, edited by I. L. Kuznetsov, 18–98. Syktyvkar: Komi Knizhnoe izd-vo, 1991.

Rainsford, Sarah. "Russian Soviet-Era Remembrance Group Memorial Risks Closure." *BBC*, October 30, 2014. https://www.bbc.com/news/world -europe-29831134.

Ranitskaia, O. M. *Meteo-chertik. Trudy i dni*. Edited by Alena Skhanova. Moscow: Avgust Borg, 2017.

Rasport, Iu. M. *Stratifikatsiia v Rossii: istoriia i sovremennost' sbornik nauchnykh trudov*. Syktyvkar: Syktyvkarskii gosudarstvennyi universitet, 1999.

Riekstins, Maris. "Ne zakhoronit' otnosheniia: Posol Latvii Maris Riekstin'sh o vazhnosti sokhraneniia istoricheskoi pamiati mezhdu Rossiei i Latviei." *Novaia Gazeta*, June 11, 2021. https://novayagazeta.ru/articles/2021/07/11/ne -zakhoronit-otnosheniia?fbclid=IwAR2DytuW3PDprT1MLYI8ChXoZDEuD OfSQP4gghjWIhTqAy-to1756MFIPB8.

Rimvidas, Ratsenas. *Litva—Komi—Litva: Zapiski spetspereselentsa.* Syktyvkar: Fond Pokaianie, 2006.

Robertson, Graeme B. "Managing Society: Protest, Civil Society, and Regime in Putin's Russia." *Slavic Review* 68, no. 3 (Fall 2009): 528–547.

Rogachev, M. B., ed. *Pokaianie: Martirolog.* t. 12, ch. 1. Syktyvkar: Fond Pokaianie, 2016.

———, ed. *Pokaianie: Martirolog.* t. 12, ch. 2. Syktyvkar: Fond Pokaianie, 2017.

———, ed. *Politicheskie repressii v Syktyvkare. Putevoditel'.* Krasnoiarsk: PIK 'Ofset', 2011.

Roginskii, A. B., ed. *Tvorchestvo i byt GULAGa: Katalog muzeinogo sobraniia Obshchestvo "Memorial."* Moscow: Izd-vo Zven'ia, 1998.

Rossi, Jacques. *The Gulag Handbook: An Encyclopedia Dictionary of Soviet Penitentiary Institutions and Terms Related to the Forced Labor Camps.* Translated by William A. Burhans. New York: Paragon House, 1989.

Round, John. "Marginalized for a Lifetime: The Everyday Experiences of Gulag Survivors in Post-Soviet Magadan." *Geografiska Annaler, Series B, Human Geography* 88, no. 1 (2006): 15–34.

Rozhina, Tat'iana, dir. "Oni spasut Rossiu." Nezavisimaia studiia dokumental'nykh fil'mov "ASTI." 1995 (2019). YouTube video, 45:54. https://www.youtube.com/watch?v=XuUv5xixWxE&t=289s.

Rubin, Jonah S. "How Francisco Franco Governs from Beyond the Grave: An Infrastructural Approach to Memory Politics in Contemporary Spain." *American Ethnologist* 45, no. 2 (May 2018): 214–227.

Ruder, Cynthia. *Building Stalinism: The Moscow Canal and the Creation of Soviet Space.* New York: I. B. Taurus, 2018.

———. *Making History for Stalin: The Story of the Belomor Canal.* Gainsville: University Press of Florida, 1998.

Rusanova, Natal'ia Vasil'evna. "Komi krai—odin iz 'ostrovov' chudovishchnogo 'Arkhipelaga GULAG.'" *III mezhraionnye listeraturno-kraevedcheskie chteniia, posviashchennye 105-letiiu so dnia rozhdeniia M. D. Puzyreva,* October 29, 2020. https://vilcbs.arkh.muzkult.ru/media/2020/10/29/1241682795/Comi_krayi.pdf.

"Russia Censures Memorial Rights Group as 'Foreign Agent.'" *BBC,* November 9, 2015. https://www.bbc.com/news/world-europe-34767014.

"Russia: Government vs. Rights Groups. The Battle Chronicle." *Human Rights Watch,* June 18, 2016. https://www.hrw.org/russia-government-against-rights-groups-battle-chronicle.

"Russia: New 'Foreign Agents' Law Ruling Court Orders Prominent Rights Group to Register." *Human Rights Watch,* December 13, 2013. https://www.hrw.org/news/2013/12/13/russia-new-foreign-agents-law-ruling.

Russkaia Pravoslavnaia Tserkov'. "Episkopat RPTs." Accessed February 21, 2019. http://www.patriarchia.ru/db/text/31720.html.

Sakharov Center. "Markova Elena Vladimirovna (urozhd. Ivanova)." Accessed March 27, 2019. https://www.sakharov-center.ru/asfcd/auth/?t=author&i=593.

———. "Pamiatniki zhertvam politicheskikh repressii na territorii byvshego SSSR." Accessed August 29, 2018. https://www.sakharov-center.ru/asfcd /pam/pam_place.xtmpl-town=167.htm.

Sanford, Rhonda Lemke. *Maps and Memory in Early Modern England: A Sense of Place*. New York: Palgrave, 2002.

Savenkova, Valentina. "VYZhIVShIE: Fil'm-rassledovanie o zhertvakh GU-LAGa." *Dozhd'*, May 27, 2021. YouTube video, 1:36:55. https://www.youtube .com/watch?v=uP2CZFYimdI.

Sazhin, Igor'. "Gulagovskoe proshloe Emvy." *7x7*, November 3, 2021. https://7x7 -journal.ru/posts/2021/11/03/gulagovskoe-proshloe-emvy.

———. "Kolonii Respubliki Komi." *7x7*. May 7, 2011. https://7x7-journal.ru /opinion/13939.

Schama, Simon. *Landscape and Memory*. New York: Alfred A Knopf, 1995.

Schlögel, Karl. *Moscow, 1937*. Translated by Rodney Livingstone. Cambridge: Polity, 2012.

Scholmer, Joseph. *Vorkuta*. Translated by Robert Kee. New York: Henry Holt, 1955.

Schrek, Karl, and Nikita Tatarsky. "Tortured Past: On Russian Memorial, Victims and Perpetrators Side by Side." *Radio Free Europe/Radio Liberty*, December 27, 2018. https://www.rferl.org/a/russian-memorial-victims-and -perpetrators-of-stalin-s-purges-stand-side-by-side/29679174.html.

Sergeeva, Ol'ga. "Pamiatnik zhertvam politicheskikh repressii v Respublike Komi." *Radio Svoboda*, November 16, 2000. https://www.svoboda.org/a /24198481.html.

"Sergei Gaplikov i sovetnik prezidenta Rossii Valerii Fadeev obsudili voprosy sokhraneniia pamiati zhertv politicheskikh repressii." *BNK*, March 4, 2020. https://www.bnkomi.ru/data/news/107971/.

Sgovio, Thomas. *Dear America! Why I Turned against Communism*. New York: Partners, 1979.

Shalamov, Varlam. *Kolyma Tales*. Translated by John Glad. New York: Norton, 1980.

Shcherbakova, Irina, Elena Zhemkova, Steven Barnes, and Isabella Tabarovsky. "Women's Memory of the Gulag and the Future of Memorial." Virtual talk hosted by the Kennan Institute, Washington, DC, November 1, 2021. https://www.wilsoncenter.org/event/womens-memory-gulag-and -future-russias-memorial.

Sherenas, Al'girdas Iono. *Zapiski ssyl'nogo, ili Ne znaem svoei viny*. Syktyvkar: Fond Pokaianie, 2006.

Sherlock, Thomas. "Confronting the Stalinist Past: The Politics of Memory in Russia." *Washington Quarterly*, 34, no. 2 (Spring 2011): 93–109.

BIBLIOGRAPHY

267

———. *Historical Narratives in the Soviet Union and Post-Soviet Russia: Destroying the Settled Past, Creating an Uncertain Future.* New York: Palgrave Macmillan, 2007.

Shevchenko, Olga. *Crisis and Everyday Life in Postsocialist Moscow.* Bloomington: Indiana University Press, 2009.

Shilin, Andrei, and Sofiia Bogatkina. "V Syktyvkare pensioner vyshel na odinochnyi piket v podderzhku 'Memoriala.'*" 7x7, November 14, 2021. https://7x7-journal.ru/news/2021/11/14/v-syktyvkare-pensioner-vyshel-na -odinochnyj-piket-v-podderzhku-mermoriala.

Shmaraeva, Elena. "Istorik Nikita Petrov: pochemu skryvaiut dokumenty o repressiiakh." *Kharkivska pravozakhisa grupa,* January 1, 2017. https://khpg .org/1484053935.

Sitko, L., B. Leviatov-Seliverstov, A. Turkov, and A. Istogina. *Intaliia: Stikhi i vospominaniia byvshikh zakliuchennykh Minlaga (g. Inta Komi ASSR).* Edited by A. Ia. Istoginoi. Moskva: Vest', 1995.

Sivkova, K. V., A. A. Zimina, and L. I. Surinoi, eds. *Ocherki po istorii Komi ASSR,* tom 1. Syktyvkar: Komi knizhnoe izd-vo, 1955.

"Skonchalsia istorik Mikhail Rogachev." *BNK,* January 4, 2021. https://www .bnkomi.ru/data/news/122447/.

Skultans, Veida. *The Testimony of Lives: Narrative and Memory in Post-Soviet Latvia.* London: Routledge, 1998.

"Slova ne stol' otdalennye." *Diletant,* February 13, 2021. https://diletant.media /articles/45304383/#.

Smith, Kathleen E. *Moscow 1956: The Silenced Spring.* Cambridge, MA: Harvard University Press, 2017.

———. *Remembering Stalin's Victims: Popular Memory and the End of the USSR.* Ithaca, NY: Cornell University Press, 2009.

———. "Whither Anti-Stalinism?" *Ab Imperio* 4 (2004): 433–448.

Smolev, Dmitrii. "Roman Romanov: 'Mezhdu nami propast', i muzei—. nekii most'." *Novosti Iskusstva,* July 22, 2021. https://www.theartnewspaper.ru /posts/20210722-WRdR/?fbclid=IwAR1KVsZPPU-WRKFKSuDB9iOtiJQ-CAJEoDqCjz6-f-_rdDJqdh7DbXsOCEag.

Sniegon, Tomas. "Dying in the Soviet Gulag for the Future Glory of Mother Russia? Making 'Patriotic' Sense of the Gulag in Present-Day Russia." In *Cultural and Political Imaginaries in Putin's Russia,* edited by Niklas Bernsand and Barbara Törnquist-Plewa, 105–140. Boston: Brill, 2018.

Solzhenitsyn, Aleksandr I. *The Gulag Archipelago: An Experiment in Literary Investigation,* vols. 1–3. New York: Harper & Row, 1975.

———. *One Day in the Life of Ivan Denisovich.* Translated by Ralph Parker. New York: Signet Classic, 1998.

Stibbe, Matthew, and Kevin McDermott. "De-Stalinising Eastern Europe: The Dilemmas of Rehabilitation." In *De-Stalinising Eastern Europe: The Rehabilitation of Stalin's Victims after 1953*, edited by Kevin McDermott and Matthew Stibbe, 1–24. Baskingstoke: Palgrave Macmillan, 2015.'

Stolpovskii, P. M., ed. *Tam gde techet Pechora*. Moscow: Sovremennik, 1988.

Suvorov, Evgenii. "'Treugol'niki' iz lagernogo detstva." *Vera: Pravoslavnaia gazeta Severa Rossii*. Accessed January 17, 2023. http://www.rusvera.mrezha.ru/674/4.htm.

Taylor, Brian D. "Law Enforcement and Civil Society in Russia." *Europe-Asia Studies* 58, no. 2 (March 2006): 193–213.

Teplov, E. L., N. A. Kostygov, N. N. Murygina, L. A. Nekrasov, and I. D. Chudinova, eds. *Dorogami nadezhd i somnenii. Istoriia poiskov mestorozhdenii nefti i gaza v Timano-Pechorskoi neftegazonosnoi provintsii*. Syktyvkar: Komi respublikanskaia tipografiia, 2000.

Tester, Keith. *Civil Society*. London: Routledge, 1992.

Tismaneanu, Vladimir, and Iacob, Bogdan C., eds. *End and the Beginning: The Revolutions of 1989 and the Resurgence of History*. Budapest: Central European University Press, 2012.

Todorov, Tzvetan. *Memory as a Remedy for Evil*. Translated by Gila Walker. London: Seagull, 2010.

Toker, Leona. *Return from the Archipelago: Narratives of Gulag Survivors*. Bloomington: Indiana University Press, 2000.

Tolczyk, Dariusz. *See No Evil: Literary Cover-ups and Discoveries of the Soviet Camp Experience*. New Haven, CT: Yale University Press, 1999.

Tonkin, Elizabeth. *Narrating Our Pasts: The Social Construction of Oral History*. Cambridge: Cambridge University Press, 1992.

Troitskii, Artemii. "NKVDemokratiia: Artemii Troitskii o likvidatsii 'Memoriala.'*" *Novaia Gazeta*, December 30, 2021. https://novayagazeta.ru/articles/2021/12/30/nkvdemokratiia.

Tromly, Benjamin. "Intelligentsia Self-Fashioning in the Postwar Soviet Union: Revol't Pimenov's Political Struggle, 1949–57." *Kritika: Explorations in Russian and Eurasian History* 13, no. 1 (Winter 2012): 151–176.

Trukhina, G. V. "Pamiati Iakova Vundera: Zhivopis', grafika, dokumenty, fotografii" (brochure). Vorkuta: Vorkuta Muzei-Vystavochnyi Tsentr, 2010.

Tumakova, Irina. "'Perm'-36': Muzei GULAGa i Minkul'ta." *Fontanka*, October 30, 2016. https://www.fontanka.ru/2016/10/30/041/.

Tumarkin, Nina. *The Living and the Dead: The Rise and Fall of the Cult of World War II in Russia*. New York: Basic, 1994.

Upravlenie Federal'noi sluzhby ispoleneniia nakazaniia (UFSIN) Rossii po Respublike Komi. "Istoriia UIS Komi." Updated December 12, 2017. http://www.11.fsin.su/istoriya-uis-komi/.

"V Komi prezentovali 20-iu knigu martirologa 'Pokaianie'." *BNK*, February 16, 2018. https://www.bnkomi.ru/data/news/74775/.

"V Komi vyidet novaia chast' martirologa zhertv politicheskikh repressii 'Po-kaianie.'" *BNK*, February 27, 2020. https://www.bnkomi.ru/data/news/107695/.

"V Mikune otkyrly pamiatnyi znak repressirovannym." *BNK Komi*, October 30, 2021. https://www.bnkomi.ru/data/news/135722/.

"V Moskve otkryli memorial zhertvam repressii. Na tseremoniiu otkrytiia 'Steny skorbi' priekhal Putin." *Novaia gazeta*, October 30, 2017. https://www.novayagazeta.ru/news/2017/10/30/136550-v-moskve-otkryli-memorial-zhertvam-repressiy-na-tseremoniyu-otkrytiya-steny-skorbi-priehal-putin.

"V severnoi 'stolitse' GULaga vorkutinskie kommunisty vspomnili Stalina." *BNK*, December 24, 2019. https://www.bnkomi.ru/data/news/104763/.

"V stolitse Komi pochtili pamiat' zhertv politicheskikh repressii." *BNK*, March 3, 2020. https://www.bnkomi.ru/data/news/107924/.

"V Syktyvkare otmetili 25-i Den' pamiati zhertv politicheskikh repressii." *BNK: Informatsionnoe agenstvo*, October 30, 2016, https://www.bnkomi.ru/data/news/55443/.

"V Syktyvkare pochtili pamiat' o zhertv politicheskikh repressii." *BNK*, October 30, 2019. https://www.bnkomi.ru/data/news/102072/.

"V Syktyvkare pochtili pamiat' zhertv politicheskikh repressii." *Komiinform*, October 30, 2021. https://komiinform.ru/news/224083/.

"V Syktyvkare prostilis' s Mikhailom Rogachevym." *BNK*, January 8, 2021. https://www.bnkomi.ru/data/news/122542/.

Varese, Federico. "The Society of the *vory-v-zakone*, 1930–1950s." *Cahiers du Monde russe* 39, no. 4 (1998): 515–538.

Vasil'ev, Veniamin. "V'iugi Vorkutlaga." In *Pechal'naia pristan'*. Edited by I. L. Kuznetsov, 145–203. Syktyvkar: Komi Knizhnoe izd-vo, 1991.

Vekshina, T. A., A. I. Fomenko, R. N. Fedorovich, and T. L. Kornilova. *Khudozhniki Ukhty. Period GULAGa (1929–1955 gg.)*. Ukhta: MU 'Tsentral'naia biblioteka MOGO 'Ukhta', 2017.

Vekshina, T. A., A. Skorniakova, O. Sizonenko, and N. Filippovoi, eds. *Ukhta Internatsional'naia*. Ukhta: Munitsipal'noe uchrezhdenie Tsentral'naia biblioteka Ukhta, 2014.

Verdery, Katherine. *The Political Lives of Dead Bodies: Reburial and Postsocialist Change*. New York: Columbia University Press, 1999.

"Verkhovnyi sud RF likvidiroval 'Memorial.'" *Izvestiia*, December 28, 2021. https://iz.ru/1270753/2021-12-28/verkhovnyi-sud-rf-likvidiroval-memorial.

Viola, Lynne. "The Question of the Perpetrator in Soviet History." *Slavic Review* 72, no. 1 (Spring 2013): 14.

———. *The Unknown Gulag: The Lost World of Stalin's Special Settlements*. New York: Oxford University Press, 2007.

Virtual'nyi muzei GULAGa. "Sledy terrora: Vodonapornaia bashnia g. Inta, Respubliki Komi." Accessed August 31, 2018. http://www.gulagmuseum.org/showObject.do?object=435503&language=1.

———. "Vysotskaia (Guliachenko) Larisa Nikolaevna." Accessed September 28, 2017. http://www.gulagmuseum.org/showObject.do?object=48578757&language=1.

"Vladimir Uiba vozlozhil tsvety k memorial'noi doske Ivanu Kulakovu v Pechore." *BNK*, July 20, 2020. https://www.bnkomi.ru/data/news/115123/.

Vladis, Galina. "Repressirovannyi arkhitektor Reinval'd Bartolomei." *Respublika*, September 24, 2021. http://respublika11.ru/2021/09/24/repressirovannyiy-arhitektor-reynvald-bartolomey/.

Vlasova, Liudmila. "Memorial stal inostrannym agentom." *Respublika*, July 24, 2015. http://respublika11.ru/2015/07/24/memorial-stal-inostrannyim-agentom/.

"Vlasti Moskvy otozvali soglasovanie aktsii 'Vozvrashchenie imen.'" *Novaia gazeta*, October 19, 2019. https://www.novayagazeta.ru/news/2018/10/19/146098-vlasti-moskvy-otozvali-soglasovanie-aktsii-vozvraschenie-imen.

Voitolovskaia, A. *Po sledam sud'by moego pokoleniia*. Syktyvkar: Komi knizhnoe izd-vo, 1991.

Volkov, Vadim. *"Obshchestvennost'*: Russia's Lost Concept of Civil Society." In *Civil Society in the Baltic Sea Region*, edited by Norbert Götz and Jörg Hackmann, 63–72. Burlington, VT: Ashgate, 2003.

Von Weikersthal, Felicitas Fischer, and Karoline Thaidsigsmann, eds. *(Hi-)Stories of the Gulag: Fiction and Reality*. Heidelberg: Universitätsverlag Winter, 2016.

Von Zitzewitz, Josephine. "The Role of Nature in Gulag Poetry: Shalamov and Zabolotsky." In *Rethinking the Gulag: Identies, Sources, Legacies*, edited by Alan Barenberg and Emily D. Johnson, 243–272. Bloomington: Indiana University Press, 2022.

Vorob'eva, Ekaterina. "Tom 3, list 135." *Novaia gazeta*, October 27, 2018. https://www.novayagazeta.ru/articles/2018/10/27/78376-tom-3-list-135.

Vozvrashchenie imen. "Ob aktsii 'Vozvrashchenie imen.'" Accessed February 22, 2019. http://october29.ru/about/.

"Vse pretenzii svodiatsia k otsutstviiu markirovki ob inostrannom agente'. Predsedatel' pravleniia 'Mezhdunarodnogo Memoriala' Ian Rachinskii o trebovanii likvidirovat' organizatsiiu." *7x7*, November 11, 2021. https://7x7-journal.ru/articles/2021/11/11/vse-pretenzii-svodyatsya-k-otsutstviyu-markirovki-ob-inostrannom-agente-predsedatel-pravleniya-mezhdunarodnogo-memoriala-yan-rachinskij-o-trebovanii-likvidirovat-organizaciyu.

"Vyslany, no ne zabyty: kak zhiteli Trekhozerki vozrozhdaiut zabroshennoe kladbishche spetspereselentsev." Moi Syktyvkar, October 5, 2021. https://

mysyktyvkar.ru/новости/Высланы__но_не_забыты__как_жители
_Трехозерки_возрождают_заброшенное_кладбище_спецпереселенцев.

"Vystavka grafiki i zhivopisi iz fondov Vorkutinskogo muzeino-vystavochnogo tsentra otkrylas' v Gorodskom vystavochnom zale Vorkuty." Vorkutinskii Muzeino-Vystavochnyi Tsentr, October 5, 2021. http://museumworkuta.ru /novosti_809/vystavka-grafiki-i-zhivopisi-iz-fondov-vorkutinskogo-muzejno -vystavochnogo-centra-otkrylas-v-gorodsk/.

"Vystavka: Iazyk [ne]svobody." Muzei istorii GULAGa, June 10–July 25, 2021, El'tsyn Tsentr. https://gmig.ru/museum/exhibitions/yazyk-ne-svobody/.

Walker, Barbara. "On Reading Soviet Memoirs: A History of the 'Contemporaries' Genre as an Institution of Russian Intelligentsia Culture from the 1790s to the 1970s." *Russian Review* 59 (July 2000): 327–352.

"Wall of Grief: Putin Opens First Soviet Victims Memorial." *BBC*, October 30, 2017. https://www.bbc.com/news/world-europe-41809659.

Warner, Michael. *Publics and Counterpublics.* New York: Zone, 2005.

Watson, Rubie S., ed. *Memory, History, and Opposition under Socialism.* Santa Fe, NM: School of American Research Press, 1994.

Weiner, Amir. "The Empire Pays a Visit: Gulag Returnees, East European Rebellions, and Soviet Frontier Politics." *Journal of Modern History* 78, no. 2 (June 2006): 333–376.

Werth, Nicolas. "A State against Its People: Violence, Repression, and Terror in the Soviet Union." In *The Black Book of Communism: Crimes, Terror, Repression*, edited by Mark Kramer, 33–39. Cambridge, MA: Harvard University Press, 1999.

White, Anne. "The Memorial Society in the Russian Provinces." *Europe-Asia Studies* 47, no. 8 (1995): 1343–1366.

Winter, Jay. *Sites of Memory, Sites of Mourning: The Great War in European Cultural History.* Cambridge: Cambridge University Press, 1995.

Wolf, Erika. "The Visual Economy of Forced Labor: Alexander Rodchenko and the White Sea-Baltic Canal." In *Picturing Russia: Explorations in Visual Culture*, edited by Valerie Ann Kievelson and Joan Neuberger, 168–174. New Haven, CT: Yale University Press, 2008.

Worton, Michael, and Judith Still, eds. *Intertextuality: Theories and Practices.* Manchester: Manchester University Press, 1990.

Yasuhiro, Matsui, ed. *Obshchestvennost' and Civic Agency in Late Imperial and Soviet Russia: Interface between State and Society.* Baskingstoke: Palgrave Macmillan 2015.

Young, James. *The Texture of Memory: Holocaust Memorials and Meaning.* New Haven, CT: Yale University Press, 1993.

Young, Sarah J. "Recalling the Dead: Repetition, Identity, and the Witness in Varlam Shalamov's *Kolymskie rassazy*." *Slavic Review* 70, no. 2 (Summer 2011): 353–372.

Yurchak, Alexei. *Everything Was Forever, until It Was No More: The Last Soviet Generation*. Princeton, NJ: Princeton University Press, 2006.

Zakon Rossiiskoi Sovetskoi Federativnoi Sotsialisticheskoi Respubliki. "O reabilitatsii zhertv politicheskoi repressii ot 18 oktiabria 1991 g." In *Sbornik zakondatel'nykh i normativnykh aktov o repressiiakh i reabilitatsii zhertv politicheskikh repressii*, edited by V. Ia. Gribenko, 194–204. Moscow: Izd-vo Respublika, 1993.

Zaretskiy, Yury. "Confessing to Leviathan: The Mass Practice of Writing Autobiographies in the USSR." *Slavic Review* 76, no. 4 (Winter 2017): 1027–1047.

"'Zdes' byl GULAG.' Dokumental'nyi reportazh 7x7 o tom, kak sokhraniaetsia pamiat' o stalinskikh repressiiakh v Komi." *7x7*, May 18, 2021. https://7x7 -journal.ru/articles/2021/05/18/zdes-byl-gulag-dokumentalnyj-reportazh -7h7-o-tom-kak-sohranyaetsya-pamyat-o-stalinskih-repressiyah-v-komi.

Zelenskaia, E. A., and M. B. Rogachev, eds. *Pokaianie: Martirolog. Komi respublikanskii matirolog zhertv massovykh politicheskikh represii*, t. 1–10. Syktyvkar: Komi knizhnoe izd-vo, 1998–2010.

Zelenskaia-Zysman, E. A. *Lagernoe proshloe Komi kraia (1929–1955 gg.) v sud'bakh i vospominaniiakh sovremennikov*. Ukhta: UPOO Memorial, 2016.

Zemskov, V. N. *Spetsposelentsy v SSSR, 1930–1960*. Moscow: "Nauka," 2003.

Zherebtsov, I. L., L. A. Maksimova, N. M. Ignatova, A. F. Smetanin, and M. V. Taskaev. *Ocherki po istorii politicheskikh repressii v Komi*. Syktyvkar: Fond Pokaianie, 2006.

"Zhit'-chtoby pomnit'. Pomnit' chtoby zhit'!" Upravlenie kul'tury administratsii MO GO "Syktyvkar," October 30, 2021. YouTube video, 41:31. https://www .youtube.com/watch?v=7QHVOwUa9tw.

Zhurakov, Ivan. "Istorika i pravozashchitnika is Komi Mikhaila Rogacheva posmertno priznali pochetnym grazhdaninom Syktyvkara." *7x7*, March 13, 2021. https://7x7-journal.ru/news/2021/05/13/istorika-i-pravozashitnika -iz-komi-mihaila-rogachyova-posmertno-priznali-pochetnym-grazhdaninom -syktyvkara?fbclid=IwAR12qnFehG6zptBI9mf_zlMshT7LVp4hNQZSrlYDO dPbchbIZyTiRQ62Mi4.

———. "V Komi nashli neizvestnoe massovoe zakhoronenie. Ostanki mogut prinadlezhat' zakliuchennym GULAGa." *7x7*, June 8, 2021. https://7x7 -journal.ru/news/2021/06/08/v-komi-nashli-neizvestnoe-massovoe -zahoronenie-ostanki-mogut-prinadlezhat-zaklyuchennym-gulaga.

Zvadski, Andrei, and Vera Dubina. "Eclipsing Stalin: The GULAG History Museum in Moscow as a Manifestation of Russia's Official Memory of Soviet Repression." *Problems of Post-Communism* (2017): 1–14. https://doi.org/10 .1080/10758216.2021.1983444.

INDEX

Abez' camp, 11, 25, 226n146
Adak camp, 79, 93n45
Adler, Nanci, 7–8, 16n10, 19n33
agency, 9, 14
Akhmatova, Anna, 153
Alexopoulos, Golfo, 91n29, 105, 106
All-Union Memorial Society, 33
Amdera, 42
anthropologists, 25
"anti-Soviet organizations," 52n14
anti-Stalinism, 50, 81–82
archaeologists, 25
"Architectural Forms of Stalinist Prosperity" (Ivanov), *129*
archives, 25, 36, 41, 48, 189, 238; absence of, 52n12; alternate history of Soviet Union and, 24; call for opening of, 189, 190; control over access to, 233; destroyed, 211; dispersed, 11; FSB (Federal Security Service), 16n10; KGB (Committee for State Security), 98n86; limitations of, 194; of local history museums, 11, 201; of Memorial local branches, 52n10; MVD (Ministry of Internal

Affairs), 5, 16n10, 193; nonstate, 2, 11; partial opening of, 18n25, 28, 239; personal, 8, 39, 231; state and party, 28, 32, 92n35, 168n14, 192, 194, 231; survivors' archives as threat to Putin regime, 3
Arkhipov, Ivan Andreevich, 39
Armenians, 4
article 58 (anti-Soviet groups/activities), 45, 61n90, 87n1, 90n25, 103
Assmann, Aleida, 10, 16n12, 241n20
Auschwitz, 195, 208, 220n78
"authentic realism," of Gulag art, 124, 145n101
autobiographical narratives, 1, 26, 236; authority to testify and, 39; commemoration of victims and, 36; defined, 8; first days of release recorded in, 76; Gulag returnees as community and, 64; identities constructed in, 12; identity constructed in, 136n3; individual and collective merged in, 64; Ivanov's artwork as, 103; spaces documented in, 11; as textual monuments to fallen com-

273

INDEX

autobiographical narratives (*Cont.*)
rades, 74, 93n45; visual art as autobiographical testimony, 8. *See also*
memoirs

Babrauskas, Lithuanian monument
and, 175
Baital'skii, M. D., 89n14, 93n44
Baltic countries, 77, 163, 196
Bandera, Stepan, 54n25
"Banderites," 28, 54n25
Baniunis, Lithuanian monument
and, 175
Baranov, Nikolai, 225n136,
226n146
Barenberg, Alan, 4, 7, 16n10, 91n29;
on Dzimtenei monument, 212n3; on
former prisoners living in Vorkuta,
92n34, 140n41; on *katorga*, 105; on
prisoner population of Vorkutlag,
18n26, 137n8; on social networks
in Vorkuta, 112; on systematic dis-
crimination against former prison-
ers, 97n76
Barnes, Steven, 90n23, 105
Belarus/Belorussians, 4, 49,
58n69, 196
Bell, Wilson, 132
Belomor Canal, 67
Bendel,' Petr, 138n16
Bobrakov, Igor,' 28
Bogumil, Zuzanna, 213–14n11,
222n94, 224n122
Bokal, Anna, 74, 94n48
Bolsheviks, 4, 57n63, 138n22
bratia 58 ("brother 58-ers"), 64
Bratsk, 42
Brezhnev, Leonid, 6
Brunstedt, Jonathan, 15n5
Budovskii, Valerii, 208, 226n148
Bukovsky, Vladimir, 237

Bulankov, A. I., 214n16
Butovo (Moscow) executions, 237,
242–43n26

camp brotherhood (brotherhood of
zeks), 4, 12, 64, 104, 233; attitudes
toward work, 72–74, 91n32; defined
in opposition to criminals, 69–71;
ethnicity of, 71, 91n29, 142n69;
formation of, 9; friendship bonds
as foundation of, 69, 90nn21–22;
life after release, 75–80, 95n60; in
Markova's memoir, 149; origins of,
65–75; shaped by discrimination,
136; writing of memoirs and,
80–87
camp guards, 23, 41, 65; corrupt,
154; criminals as, 90n25; liquidation of Stalin's prison camps and,
23; oral histories of former guards,
60n82; ruins of guard barracks, 195;
women, 107
camp officials, 11, 80, 92n39
capitalism, transition to, 42
cemeteries, prisoners,' 23, 194, 208;
earth from parents' graves, 197,
221n88; monuments to particular
ethnic groups in, 199, *200*, 201
censorship: evasion of, 125, 153,
170n39; relaxation of, 1, 178; self-
censorship of former prisoners, 113
"Check of the Correctness of the
Number on My Padded Jacket, A"
(Ivanov), *132*
children, born in the camps, 7, 27, 38,
48, 52n14
"children of the Gulag," 26, 47–48
Chinese prisoners, 4
Chistiakov, V. I., 215n16
Christensen, Karin Hyldal, 222n94
Chuvash Republic, 38, 39

civil society, 50, 187–88, 196, 207, 231, 236, 239
Civil War, Russian, 4, 6, 183
class divisions, 64
class enemies, 7, 27
coal mines, 114, 128, 132, 151, 211
Cold War, 3
collected memories, 10, 21n57, 166, 233; content of cultural memory and, 181; individual identity and, 149; institutionalization of, 12, 24
colony-settlements, 17n23
communism: art under, 110–11; collapse of, 3, 197
Communist Party, Soviet, 3, 26, 82; delegitimization of, 212; de-Stalinization and, 6, 182; former prisoners as members of, 73, 92n36; guilt for the repressions and, 187; Gulag prisoners as members of, 7–8, 15n3; Ivanov's theater work noticed by, 109; Komi commission on repression (1988), 182, 214–15n16, 215n18; loss of control over reform process, 178, 180; Twentieth Party Congress (1956), 1, 6, 98n80, 177, 178; Twenty-Second Party Congress, 6
"community of memory," 4, 16n12
Congress of People's Deputies, 29
"Conversation by the Stove" (Ivanov), 120
corrective colonies, 17n23
"counterrevolutionary" (political) crimes, 5
criminals, 64, 82; brotherhood of zeks defined in resistance to, 69–71; camps run by, 90n25; "everyday life crimes" (bytoviki), 88n11, 93n44; as majority of Gulag prisoners, 15n3; memoirs unlikely to be written by,

88n11; reeducation of, 93n44; ugolovniki (seasoned criminals), 68
cultural memory, 8, 21n58, 87, 195, 224n117, 233; destabilized under Putin, 209; formation of, 178; "hardware" and "software" of, 10, 180, 203–4; individual and group identities in, 16n12; infrastructure of, 211; Komi landscape linked to, 205, 206; monuments and, 199; mourning of the dead and, 197–98; Orthodox Church and, 222n94; shifts in, 199; stability of, 212; transition from intergenerational to transgenerational, 241–42n20; transmission of the past to future generations and, 10; in Western and Eastern Europe, 3

Day of Memory of Victims of Political Repression (annual event on October 30), 16n14, 209, 211, 227n151, 229–30, 230
Deineka, Boris, 138n16
dekulakization, 7, 86, 192
deportation and deportees, 7, 16, 194
"Despair" (Ivanov), 128, 134
de-Stalinization, 3, 4, 6, 181, 193
D'iakov, Boris, 99n98
diseases, 39
Dobson, Miriam, 7
Dorofeeva, Nedezhda, 229, 240n3
"dry execution," 105, 139n25
Dunskii, Iulii, 205
Dzimtenei monument (Inta, 1956), 176, 177, 199, 212n1; KGB report on, 174–75; rededication of (1989), 177, 178

Eakins, John Paul, 9, 136n3
Eisner, Aleksei, 162
Emva, village of, 194

276 INDEX

"enemies of the people," 14, 39, 40, 81, 231; changing views of, 180; children of, 47, 61n94; criminals as persecutors of, 91n26; family members of, 27, 150; former prisoners still perceived as, 108; foundations of civil society and, 236

"En Route, 1944" (Ivanov), *120*

Erll, Astrid, 21–22n60

Estonians, 4, 175

Etkind, Alexander, 8, 64; on hardware and software of cultural memory, 10, 180, 203–4; local monuments dismissed by, 213n11; on the "parable of misrecognition," 78; on surrealist images in Gulag art, 132, 145n106

Everything Flows (Grossman), 98n84

Evstiunichev, Andrei, 69–70, 75–76

"Exhibition of Komi Artists," 142n71

exile/exiles, 6, 13, 23, 79, 103, 114; as category of victim, 19n42; children born in exile, 7; death in exile, 174; described in letters, 79–80, 161; eternal, 76, 93n43; family members of "enemies of the people" and, 75; Komi Republic's history as place of, 4, 211, 231; memory of, 48; relationships formed in, 94n47; release from, 151; treatment of former prisoners, 79; as "victims," 27; work as means of surviving, 109

eyewitnesses, 24, 62n96

Fadeev, Valerii, 238

"file autobiography" genre, 26, 53n19

Flige, Irina, 194, 197

Flug, Konstantin, 42, 78–79; comparison with Solzhenitsyn's account of Gulag, 85–86; pride and attachment to city of Vorkuta, 140–41n53

Fond Pamiati, 40

Fond Pokaianie (Repentance Foundation), 5–6, 7, 14, 208–9, 214n11; archive of, 231; Day of Memory events and, 229, 231; founding of (1998), 25, 30, 201. See also *Martirolog*

food rations, in camps, 39

"formers" (*byvshie*), 64, 79, 112, 135

Frenkel,' Naftalii, 92n39, 173n74

Frid, Valerii, 205

friendship, 9, 68–69, 102, 128; importance to life after release, 111; importance to survival, 66; in Markova's memoir, 149

Frierson, Cathy A., 7, 19n41

FSB (Federal Security Service), 16n10

Gavriusov, Iu. V., 214n16

Geidans, Al'fred, 178

Georgians, 4

Germans, ethnic, 4, 150, 168n17, 178

Germany, concentration camps preserved in, 208

Ginzburg, Evgeniia, 66, 141n53

glasnost (openness) policy, 1, 9, 12, 13, 85, 162; cultural memory of the Gulag and, 180; debates over definition of victim and, 184; flood of testimonies from Gulag returnees and, 86; formation of Memorial and, 24, 25, 27; as period of interest in political repression, 102, 122; reckoning with Stalinist past and, 64

"Godfathers Play Cards/Criminal Group" (Ivanov), *123*

Gol'dshtein, Rostislav, 211

"Goner" (Ivanov), 126, *127*

Gorbachev, Mikhail, 1, 3, 64, 85, 178; de-Stalinization supported by, 31; rehabilitation decree and, 6; *Ukhta* newspaper open letter to, 187–89. See also *glasnost*

INDEX

Gorky, Maxim, 67

Gorodetskii family, 231

"Gorodetskiis, The: Tragedy of One Family" (Komi National Museum exhibit, 2016), 231, 240n7

Gorodin, Leonid: on camp brotherhood and survival, 90n22; on destruction of work ethic, 73–74; encyclopedic dictionary of the Gulag, 39–40, 58n71, 59nn72–73, 166n2; mugshots of, 75; releases and rehabilitation of, 73, 93n43

Great Terror (1936–1938), 97n80, 150, 168n14, 182, 186, 194, 243n26

Grigonis, Lithuanian monument and, 175

Grossman, Vasily, 98n84

Gulag Archipelago, The (Solzhenitsyn), 66, 89n19, 98n89

Gulag camps: conditions in, 67–68; cultural memory of, 12; death as "early release," 106, 124, 126, 139n29; dictionary of the Gulag, 39–40, 58n71, 59nn72–73; formation of cultural memory of, 178; locations in Komi Republic (map), *xiv*; mass burial sites, 194; mortality in, 39, 67, 105, 137n8; prisoners with medical experience/training, 151, 168n24; proposed Gulag museum as tourist attraction, 208–9; spiritual resistance in, 152–59. *See also specific camps*

Gulag returnees, 3, 9, 15n3, 32, 190, 239; as "Adakovtsy," 79, 97n74; attachment to places of former imprisonment, 26; children of, 50; community of, 3, 88n7; as "community of memory," 4; correspondence with Syktyvkar Memorial, 24; discrimination faced by, 108, 112,

136, 148; as "ethnographers," 24, 51n5; life after release, 66; marriages after release, 79, 96n71; Memorial's relationship with, 25; motivations to write after decades of silence, 24; numbers of, 16n10; passing away of, 50; reintegration into Soviet society after release, 7; relations of "formers" with "civilians," 79; self and community of, 10; stigma attached to, 72; World War II veterans compared with, 16n11. *See also* camp brotherhood; "formers"; victims of political repression

Gulag Was Here, A [*Zdes' bl GULAG*] (film, 2021), 211

Guliachenko, Larisa, 159, *160*, 171n60

Gumilev, Nicolai, 153

Gurevitch, Aleksandr, 67–68, 78, 89n19

Gusev, Konstantin, 108, 113

Halbwach, Maurice, 10

Hardy, Jeff, 18n26, 138n22

historians, 19n33, 25, 59n73; autobiographical narratives and, 65; defense of Stalin by popular historians, 211; infrastructure of memory and, 238; on lack of documentation, 193–94; on numbers of repressed victims, 168n14, 217n41

Historical Enlightenment Society "Memorial," 24

history museums, local, 8, 11, 209; autobiographical narratives sent to, 65, 71, 81; Inta Local History Museum, 193, 205, 207, 209, 212n1; memoirs sent to, 50; Memorial archive in, 22n66; Vorkuta Regional History Museum, 113

Holocaust, 3, 217n44

INDEX

"Hope Dies Last" [*Nadezhda umiraet poslednei*] (Ivanov), 103, 118, 124. *See also* Ivanov, Konstantin Petrovich, artworks of

human rights, 3, 75, 218n57, 236, 240n11

Iasnyi, Vadim, 162

identity, 10, 102; collected memories and, 149, 168n12; constructed in autobiographical narrative, 136n3; individual and group identities intertwined, 64; loss of, 78; survival and sense of self, 103

Ignatov, M. K., 217n42

incarceration rate, 18n26

Incident at Mine Eight (film, 1957), 205, *206*

infrastructure, Soviet/Stalinist, 60n81, 181

Inta, 11, 42, 46, 211; artists from, 113; Dzimtenei monument (1956), 174–75, *176*, 177, *177*, 199, 212n1; life after release from, 95n60; Memorial branch in, 25; "Mourning Savior" monument, *200*; strict-regime camp in, 69; Syktyvkar monument and, 203; water tower monument, 205, *206*, 207, *207*, 225n131

intellectuals/intelligentsia, 59n73, 104; as "lay ethnographers," 51n5; Solzhenitsyn's definition of, 138n18

In the Bowels of Ukhtpechlag (book of memory), 189–90

In the First Circle (Solzhenitsyn), 99n91

In the Steps of the Fate of My Generation (Voitalovskaia), 48

investigative isolators, 17n23

Irwin-Zarecka, Iwona, 16n12, 47; on communities of memory, 62n96,

88n7; on infrastructure of cultural memory, 10, 22n63

"Iun'Iaga Under Construction" (Ivanov, 1958), 115, *117*

Iurasov, Dmitrii, 183

Ivanov, Konstantin Petrovich, 13, 77, 84, 148, 154; art of survival learned by, 104, 105–6; attachment to Vorkuta, 102; correspondence from camp comrades, 171n62; death of, 135, 146n110; on incompleteness of memory, 106, 118, 143n84; life in Vorkuta after release, 107–18; "memoir-letters" of, 101, 103, 104, 111, 117, 122, 132, 135, 136n2; narration of life in the Gulag, 104–6; personal archive donated to Vorkuta Museum, 102–3; photograph of, *108*; postcard sent by Polish friends to, 113, *114–15*; as prisoner in Vorkutlag and Rechlag, 103, 119, 124, 137n12; on purpose of art, 118–19; rehabilitation of, 137n11; tax-evasion case and, 109–10; at Vorkuta Theater, 103, 108–9, *111*, 140n47; wife and children of, 103, 118, 137n10, 139–40n38

Ivanov, Konstantin Petrovich, artworks of, 135; "Architectural Forms of Stalinist Prosperity," *129*; "A Check of the Correctness of the Number on My Padded Jacket," *132*; "Conversation by the Stove," *120*; "Despair," 128, *134*; "En Route, 1944," *120*; "Godfathers Play Cards/Criminal Group," *123*; "Goner," 126, *127*; "Iun'Iaga Under Construction" (1958), 115, *117*; literary comparisons to, 145n100; lost or given away, *122*, 144n95; "Love in the Mine," 128, *134*; "A Man Passes

INDEX   279

By Like a Master," *124*, 125–26; "Memory of Vorkuta," 128, 132, *134*; "Miners-*katorzhanki* '45–'46," *131*; "Miners KTR '45–'46" (1987), 124, *130*; natural environment of Arctic and, 113; "The Path to Early Release," 124, 126, *128*; "Plank Beds," *121*, 126; "Polar Stokehold of the Country," *126*; "Prayer-Roll Call," *121*, 126; "Prisoner Selection," *120*; "Step to the Left, Step to the Righ, I Shoot," *120*; "Summer. Midnight. On My Roof." (1959–1969), 114, *116*; "Untitled," *125*, 144n98; "Untitled" or "Miners of the Polar Stokehold," *129*; "Usinsk Street" (1959), 113–14, *116*; "View of the Mine 'Kaptial'naia'" (1957), 114, *116*; in Vorkuta Union of Artists exhibitions, 113, 142n72; "Without a Last One," *122*, 126; "Women Miners Hauling Coal at Mine no. 2," *133*
Izhma, 37

Jews, 4, 178
Johnson, Emily, 170n39
Jones, Polly, 8

Kapler, Aleksei, 138n16
katorga [KTR] (penal labor system), 40, 99n98, 103, 147, 149, 151, 166; mortality rates and, 105, 167n5; as protracted murder, 138n20; reintroduced (1943), 137n9
katorzhane (prisoners sentenced to *katorga*), 91n31, 148; in Ivanov's artworks, 125, 128, *131*; numbers on clothing worn by, 104, 105, 128, 145n104; spiritual resistance of, 153, 155, 157
Kersnovskaia, Evfrosiniia, 143n90

KGB (Committee for State Security), 24, 51n7, 217n41; archives of, 98n86; cautious tolerance of Memorial, 28; Dzimtenei monument and, 174–75, 177; Sollertinskii's encounter with, 74, 94n50
Khazanov, Anatoly M., 20n49
Khokhlov, Aleksandr Vasil'evich, 165
Khrushchev, Nikita, 1, 3, 31, 183; denunciation of Stalin's cult of personality by, 6, 80–81, 177; "socialist legality" and, 182; "Thaw" of, 7; Wall of Sorrow proposed by, 236
Klein, Aleksandr, 25, *34*, 35
Kolyma camp, 78, 106
Kolyma Tales (Shalamov), 145n100
Kolymsk, 42
Komi Autonomous Soviet Socialist Republic, 1, 17n16, 31, 81; Central State Archive of, 28; "free" and prisoner population of, 211; Regional Party Committee Archive (Komi Obkom), 28, 109, 182; Supreme Court of, 186; Syktyvkar Television Studio, 103; Union of Soviet Artists of, 110, 112, 141n62
Komi people, 4, 41, 65
Komi Republic, 2, 24, 214n11; alternate history of, 50; cultural memory of the Gulag in, 87, 201; discovery of mass graves in, 181, 195; as the "Gulag Republic," 5, 180; as home for Gulag returnees, 77; map, *xiv*; memory of Gulag anchored to landscape of, 42; monuments and gravesites in, 199–200, 223n103; National Archive of, 11, 231; National Museum of, 231, 239; numbers and categories of prisoners, 5, 18n25; outmigration from, 226n144; Poles in, 142n68; population of, 4, 16n13,

INDEX

Komi Republic (*Cont.*)
17n16; Presidential Commission for the Development of Civil Society and Human Rights, 238; Syktyvkar monument to victims of political repression, *200*, 201–3, *204*, 224n117, 224nn120–122
Komi Scientific Center archives, 32
Komsomol activists, 27
kontriki (counterrevolutionaries, political prisoners), 64
Koposov, Nikolai, 210, 228n161
Koreans, 4
Korovin, Nikolai Ivanovich, 162, 172n68
Korovina, Bronislava Iakovlevna, 172n68
Korovin family, 162, 163, 172n66, 172n68
Kossior, Stanislav, 81, 97–98n80
Kotlovan (newspaper), 184
Kotov, Petr, 23, 29, 86, 90n21, 97n74; criticism of Solzhenitsyn, 84, 85; on ethnicity of prisoners, 71; on remembrance of fallen comrades, 93n45; on solidarity of former prisoners, 97n78; on treatment of former prisoners, 79
Kotvitskii, Anton, 60n84, 71, 80–81
Kovalyov, Sergei, 191
Krasnoe znamia (newspaper), 28, 36, 45, 56n53, 187, 189, 215n16; Day of Memory of Victims of Political Repression and, 209; editorial on duty to collect history, 191, 219n65; Komi commission on repression and, 182; on lack of documentation, 193–94; "To Restore the Good Name of Those Who Were Illegally Repressed" (1989), 186; "Restoring Justice: For the Sake of Moral

Cleansing," 186; on search for memory and the truth, 193; on the Syktyvkar monument, 202
Krasnye Chetai (Chuvash ASSR), 39
KRD (counterrevolutionary activities), 38, *185*
Krems, Andrei, 92–93n39
Krisons, Lithuanian monument and, 175
kulaks, 27, 49
Kuperman, Iakov, 92n39, 99n91, 173n74
Kyz'iurov, L. A., 212n3

lagerniki (camp inmates), 64
Lass, Andrew, 57n60
Latvia/Latvians, 4, 77; death in Minlag camp, 178; Dzimtenei monument and, 212n1; Latvian Soviet Socialist Republic, 175; Soviet annexation of Latvia, 95n56
Lenin, Vladimir, 180
Levashovo Cemetery (St. Petersburg), 199·
Likhtenshtein, T., 96n71
Lipilin, V. G., 60n82
Lithuanians, 4, 178, 199, 200; Rechlag Lithuanian monument, *200*, 201
Litvinov, Pavel, 236
lived environment, 10, 22n63, 181
Lokchim, 42
Lokchimlag (camp in Komi ASSR), 38, *200*
"Love in the Mine" (Ivanov), 128, *134*

Magadan, 42, 141n53, 214n11; "Mask of Sorrow" monument, 199
Mandelshtam, Osip, 153
"Man Passes By Like a Master, in Vorkuta Everything Is Alright, A" (Ivanov), *124*, 125–26

Markizov, Leonid, 202
Markov, Aleksei Alekseevich, 151, 169n26
Markova, Elena Vladimirovna, 13, 91n31, *160*, *164*; bond with fellow Gulag survivors, 148; camp poems of, 153, 154, 170n39; correspondence in Gulag, 154–55, *156*, 157, *158–59*, 170n50, 171n55; on imprisonment as time of development, 148–49; life after release, 149, 167n10; life history of, 150–52; rehabilitation of, 151–52; spiritual resistance and, 147, 148, 149, 152–59, 166; splitting of autobiographical self, 169n33; survivor status emphasized by, 148; "Vorkuta diaspora" and, 149, 159, *160*, 161–63, *164*, 165–66, 172n70; on waiting to write memoir, 148, 167n8
Markova, Inna, 151, 163
Martin, Barbara, 8, 65
Martirolog (book of memory), of Fond Pokainie, 7, 19n41, 133, 135, 145n108, 201, 210, 223n110; database of names and, 239; Ivanov's artwork in, 133; as ongoing project, 233; Syktyvkar Memorial questionnaire and, 34; Syktyvkar monument and, 203, 205
Marushchiak, Konstantin, 72–73, 81–82, 91n32
medical clinics, 17n23
Medvezhegorsk, 42
Mekhlis, Lev, 188
memoirs, 2, 11, 53n16, 65, 136, 239; autobiography distinguished from, 8; ethnicity omitted from, 71; "evenings of memory" gatherings and, 4; of Evstiunichev, 75; of Flug, 85; as genre hybrid, 9, 20n51; Gulag

memoir as genre, 20n51, 102, 107; of Kotov, 23, 79–80; of Markova, 147, 166n3; memorialization of camp comrades in, 111, 141n59; "parable of misrecognition" trope in, 78; reasons for writing of, 80–87; of Serov, 63; tension between past and present in, 111, 141n58; unpublished, 12. *See also* autobiographical narratives
Memorial (International Memorial Society), 1, 2, 214n11, 218n57, 237; branches of, 5, 6; breach of law on foreign agents, 232–33; closure of (2021), 12, 14; conservative critics of, 190; formation of, 24, 51n6, 58n69; historic mission of, 27; Komi branches of, 25, 52n10; Krasnodar branch, 198–99; personal archives donated to, 8, 11; research section, 232; *Vedomosti Memoriala* newspaper, 184. *See also* Syktyvkar Memorial Society
memory: actualization of, 21–22n60; anchored to landscape, 42; chronological shifts in narrative and, 136n4; communities of, 62n96; duty to remember, 23; incompleteness of, 106; infrastructure of, 14, 180–81, 196, 201, 220n78, 238; Ivanov's artworks and, 119; lifelong process of remembering, 149; nationalist politics and, 180; of Ol'shevskii, 68, 89–90n20; plurality of, 10; in provinces, 3; relationships and, 15n3; reliability after passage of time, 38; silences ("blank spots") in, 38; space linked to, 195; state-friendly agents of, 11. *See also* collected memories; cultural memory
"Memory Bell" ceremony, 238

INDEX

Memory of the Gulag: Inta (guidebook), 205

"Memory of Vorkuta" (Ivanov), 128, 132, *134*

Merridale, Catherine, 216n32

Meshcheriakova, Evdokiia, 46, 61n91

migration, internal, 152, 169n34, 189

Mikhail'chenkov, A. A., 46

Mikhailovna, Nina, 80, 84, 90n21, 97n73

Miller, Nikolai, 144n90

"Miners-*katorzhanki* '45–'46" (Ivanov), *131*

"Miners KTR '45–'46" (Ivanov, 1987), 124, *130*

mining-metallurgical industry, 42

Minlag camp, 178, 205, 213n5, 225n131

Molodezh' Severa (newspaper), 27, 29, 45, 54n20; on call for "Nuremberg process," 190; on debates over definition of "victims," 183–84; on Dzimtenei monument, 178; letters to, 47–48; on Rechlag uprising (1953), 184–85; "Without a Statute of Limitations" (1988), 182

Molotov, Vyacheslav, *185*

monuments, 2, 6, 14, 202, 210; collapse of Soviet Union and, 199, 212; conservative backlash and, 54n25; controversy over, 237, 238; cultural memory and, 208; to ethnic groups, 50, 175, 199, *200*; as "hardware" of cultural memory, 10; infrastructure of memory and, 194–95, 239; insufficiency of, 207; memory actualization and, 22n60; number of, 223n103; proliferation of, in post-Soviet Russia, 184; Socialist monuments transformed into monuments of repression, 10, 22n63, 41, 181;

textual, 74. *See also* victims of political repression, commemoration of; *specific monuments by name*

Morozov, Nikolai, 25, 61n94, 189

Morozova, Elena, 231

Moscow, 147, 232; Memorial formed in (1989), 24, 51n6; regional influences on, 2; Solovetsky Stone, 236, 238; State Gulag History Museum, 236, 237, 239; Wall of Memory (Kommunarka), 237–38, *237*, 243n29; Wall of Sorrow monument, *234–35*, 236–37, 242n24

Moskalev, V. P., 214n16

"Mourning Savior" monument (Inta), *200*

Murav'eva, A. K., 45

Musaelian, Karina, 188, 217n48

mutual aid, 3, 76, 95n59, 105

MVD (Ministry of Internal Affairs), 5, 16n10, 28; archive of, 46, 165; difficulty of access to archives of, 18n25; former prisoners as members of, 72, 92n39; rehabilitation of former prisoners and, 6, 51n7; special boards of, 6

"My Gulag" oral history project, 238

Nakonechnyi, Mikhail, 105

nashi (ours), 64, 112, 113

Nathans, Benjamin, 65

nationalism, Russian, 3, 210

Neimark, Anna, 60n81, 214n13

Neizvestnyi, Ernst, 199, 202

Neverov, Anatolii, 202, 224n117

Nevskii, Gennadii, 205

"New Soviet Man," 64

newspapers, 36, 178, 213n9; coverage of political repression, 13; identification of prisoner cemeteries and, 195–96; on local disregard for memorials, 207–8; of Moscow Memorial, 53n17; sources for new history of Gulag repression, 191–94. *See also specific titles*

NKVD (Peoples Commissariat of Internal Affairs), 4, 37, 38, 39, 63, 150; evenings of memory held by, 57n63; Gulag and, 86; Kommunarka executions by, 237, 242–43n26, 243n29; in World War II, 103, 151

Nora, Pierre, 22n63

Noril'sk, 42

Novaya Gazeta (newspaper), 58n66

Novokhatskii, Vladimir, 76–77, 78

"Nuremberg process," calls for, 190, 191, 210

October Revolution (1917), 4, 57n63

odnoetapnik (fellow prisoner from same transport), 40, 59n76

OGPU (Joint State Political Directorate), 4, 57n63

Old Bolsheviks, 81

Oliger, Valentin Viktorovich, 163, *164*, 165

Ol'shevskii, Vitalii, 68, 89–90n20; letter to Syktyvkar Memorial (1990), 37–38; memoir of, 1–2; on preservation of personal integrity, 90n24

One Day in the Life of Ivan Denisovich (Solzhenitsyn), 66, 84, 89n17, 145n100

Oni spasut Rossiiu (documentary film, dir. Rozhina, 1995), 119, 144n91

"On the Rehabilitation of Victims of Political Repression" (law, 1991), 7, 19n41

oral histories, 57n63, 60n82, 136n4, 149, 238

Orthodox Church, Russian, 197, 202, 231; Archbishop of Syktyvkar

diocese, 229, 239n1; nationalist politics of memory and, 11, 214n11; Patriarch Kirill, 236; as shaper of cultural memory, 222n94, 239; Wall of Memory project and, 237

Osipov, V. S., 214n16

Paperno, Irina, 8, 9, 65, 141n58; on distinction between memoirs and autobiographies, 20–21n51; on "suicidal" nature of Stalinist repression, 187, 217n44

"parable of misrecognition," 78

Passerini, Luissa, 10

passport restrictions, 76, 97n73, 168n11

"Path to Early Release, The" (Ivanov), 124, 126, *128*

Pavlovsky, Gleb, 233

peasants, 7, 65, 192

Pechora, 11, 25, 63, 211

Pechorlag, 25

Pechuro, Susana, 69, 86, 90n21; on nationality/ethnicity of prisoners, 71; photograph of, *70*

perestroika policy, 183

Pereyaslavska, Katya, 124–25, 145n101

Perm, 214n11

Perm-36 camp, 195, 209, 220n78

Pervina, Raisa, 107

petitions, by former prisoners, 6, 7, 46, 49, 119

Petrov, Nikita, 232, 243n29

Pimenov, Revol't, 25, 28, 31, 37, 52n14; death of, 30; election to Congress of People's Deputies, 29; on memories of living victims, 33; on origins of Memorial, 27

Pitirim, Archbishop (Pavel Pavlovich Volochkov), 229, 239n1

284 INDEX

place, sense of, 26, 37
"Plank Beds" (Ivanov), *121*, 126
Podobedov, Nikolai Vladimirovich, 84
Podrabinek, Aleksandr, 237
Podval'nyi, Boris Petrovich, 41
poetry, 13, 147, 157; as autobiographical testimony, 8; as resistance, 153–54
Poland/Poles, 4, 41, 71, 80, 196; Polish monument in Vorkuta, *200*, 201; preserved Auschwitz complex, 195, 208; wartime deportations to USSR, 113, 142n68
"Polar Stokehold of the Country" (Ivanov), *126*
Poleshchikov, Veniamin, 190, 191, 219n9
Poliakov, Valentin, 141n62
Polian, Pavel, 168n17
political prisoners, 70, 216n37; brief biographies published in newspaper, 185, 216n37; broken spirit of, 67, 89n17; burial in camp cemetery, 177, 213n5; contribution to development of the Russian Far North, 37, 82, 231, 236; gender of, 4–5; generational differences among, 20n48; letters written by, 53n18; life after release, 2; national and ethnic composition of, 4; nondisclosure agreements signed upon release, 142n71, 167n8; slang language of, 40, 59n72, 64, 143n79; subgroups of, 64; unmarked graves of, *43*, 60n84, 180, 194, 195–96; uprisings of, 62n97, 185. *See also* zeks
Portelli, Alessandro, 136n4, 168n12
"Prayer-Roll Call" (Ivanov), *121*, 126
pridurki (camp "stooges"), 84, 99n94
"Prisoner Selection" (Ivanov), *120*
Procuracy, 24, 51n7, 52n8

production quotas, 72, 105, 139n25
psychiatric facilities, forced internment in, 7
Puntulis, Al'fred Iur'evich, 175, 212n1
Putin, Vladimir, 3, 11, 180, 233; elected to third term as president, 14, 232; human rights organizations attacked under, 240n11; politics of memory and, 209, 211; speech at unveiling of Wall of Sorrow monument, 236
Putriu, Aleksei, 68

questionnaires, 8, 11, 24, 53n16, 102; breakdown by categories, 33, 55n45; as template of autobiography, *34, 35*

Rachinskii, Ian, 237, 243n29
Raikin, Leonid, 162
railroads, 37, 40, 151, 211; BAM (Baikal-Amur Railway), 37, 173n74; as graveyard for prisoners, 41, 60n82; GULZhDS (Directorate of Railroad Construction), 92n39; Northern Pechora Mainline, *xiv*, 37; Vorkuta-Pechora railroad, 40–41, 42
Razgon, Lev, 184
Rechlag (Special Camp No. 6), 25, 103, 113, 118, 133, 135; ethnic composition of, 91n29; Lithuanian monument in cemetery, *200*; prisoner population of, 137n8; as strict-regime camp, 104, 151; uprising in (1953), 184–85
Red Army, 28, 54, 105, 150
reeducation, 67, 93n44, 105
rehabilitation, 6, 18n31, 151–52; certificates of, 11, 45, 49, 53n16, 78, 82; collapse of Soviet Union and, 46–47; complete rehabilitation as rarity, 149, 168n11; as complicated

process, 35; decrees issued by Communist Party, 24, 51n7; definitions of, 12; denial of, 61n90; difficulties in application for, 45; false convictions and, 9; numbers of people eligible for, 51n7, 52n8; numbers of rehabilitated prisoners, 19n33, 19n37, 36, 52–53n15; opponents of, 28, 54n25; performance of, 109, 140n49; removal of stigma and, 49; "Week of Conscience" (1990) and, 188

resistance, 4, 9, 70; collecting data in camps as, 51n5, 66, 88n13; sex as form of, 128, 132. *See also* spiritual resistance

Respublika (Komi regional newspaper), 201, 208

"Return of the Names" ceremony, 232, 238, 243n30

Rivkin, Grigorii, *70*

Rogachev, Mikhail, 29–31, 40, 61n91, 209; "Book of Memory" and, 32; on the Gorodetskii exhibit, 231, 240n7; as "guardian angel" to Ivanov, 119; on importance of name database, 239; on Ivanov's artworks, 135; on number of rehabilitated former prisoners, 36; on Polish prisoners in Komi, 142n68; on questionnaires, 33; speech at Day of Memory (30 Oct. 2016), 229–30, *230*; on Syktyvkar monument, 224n122

Romanov, Roman, 238

Rontal,' Georgii M., correspondence with Markova, 155, *155*, *156*, *158–59*, 171n57

Rossi, Jacques,' 58n71

Rozhina, Tat'iana, 144n91

Rukavishnikov, G. T., 214n16

Russian Empire, 4, 231

Russian Far North, 1, 2, 79, 103, 166, 203; civil associations in, 2; contribution of prisoners to development of, 37, 82, 231, 236; cultural memory of political repression in, 203; declining economy of, 226n144; harsh climate of, 67; transformed into site of memory, 37; transportation by cattle car to, 151

Russian Federation, 2, 14, 58n66, 201; constitution of, 232; Day of Memory of Victims of Political Repression observed throughout, 209; monuments in, 223n103; Supreme Court of, 232

Russian Soviet Federative Socialist Republic (RSFSR), 29, 103, 227n151

Safronov, Leonid, 65

Safronov, Lev, 40–41, 59n78, 95n62; camp brotherhood as adopted family, 77; on former prisoners' fears for the future, 82–83, 98n86

Sakharov, Andrei, 25

Sakharov Center, 168n13, 171n59, 223n103

samizdat, 52n14, 66

Sapozhnikova, A. I., 92n36

Serov, Boris, 61n90, 63–64, 87n1

7x7 (online journal), 211

sex, as resistance, 128, 132

Sgovio, Thomas, 106, 143n90

Shalamov, Varlam, 66, 143n84, 154

Shapiro, Pavel, 162

Shepletto, Iurii, 113

Shlezhkova, Liubov,' 47–48, 62n97

Shmatov, E. L., 53n19

Shpektor, Igor, 208

Shtyrtskober, Edgar, 161–62, 172n65

Shur, S. P., 95n60

Sidbrabs, Edvard, *176*

Siderskii, Vladimir, 37, 38
Skakovskaia, Irina, 74, 86, 94n47
Smith, Kathleen, 183
Sobinova, Nina, 79, 84, 86
Socialist Realism, 126, 145n101
social networks, 4, 7, 24
Sollertinskii, Vladimir E., 57n64, 67, 74–75, 86, 89n17; on criminals as "genuine citizens of the USSR," 91n26; on friendships in post-Gulag life, 141n60; KGB attention to autobiography of, 74, 94n50; life after release, 79, 95n57; photograph of, 70
Solovetsky Islands, 11
Solovetsky Stone (Moscow), 236, 238
Solov'eva, Kaleria Anatol'evna, 53n19
Solovki, 214n11
Solzhenitsyn, Aleksandr, 42, 47, 83, 84–85, 98n89, 236; on death as "early release," 139n29; on "dry execution," 139n25; on the intelligentsia, 138n18; on *katorga* as protracted murder, 105, 138n20. See also *Gulag Archipelago, The*; *One Day in the Life of Ivan Denisovich*
Solzhenitsyna, Natalia, 236
Soobtskov, Madinat Garunovich, 46
Sorrowful Pier (memoirs of Komi camps), 106
Sosnogorsk, 11, 79, 199; Memorial branch in, 25; Syktyvkar monument and, 203
Soviet Union (USSR): alternate history of, 24, 50, 192, 233; anti-Nazism and political legacy of, 210, 228n161; first civic organizations in, 1, 24; former Soviet officials in new Russian state, 191; last years of, 102; Nazi invasion of (1941), 150; religious traditions of burial in, 208; Supreme Court of, 151

Soviet Union (USSR), collapse of, 7, 12, 13, 26, 35, 83, 101, 211; accessibility of state/party archives and, 194; chance to write about camps presented by, 148, 149; cultural memory and, 212; debates over definition of victim and, 184; emergence of civil society and, 50; flood of testimonies from Gulag returnees and, 86; generations born after, 239; Gulag returnees' experiences of, 135; increase of time since, 211; monuments erected after, 199; as periof of interest in political repression, 102; rehabilitation on basis of citizenship and, 46; shift in "worlds of meaning" and, 197; tension between past and present in wake of, 111
Sovnarkom, 142n68
spaces: camp ruins as sacred spaces, 42; carceral, 66; cultural memory and, 10; documented in autobiographical narratives, 11; Gulag returnees' letters and, 37; infrastructure of cultural memory and, 22n63; living in two temporal spaces simultaneously, 149; private, 80
special settlements/settlers, 7, 26, 49, 50, 81; cemeteries for, 194; people who vanished in, 229; Polish citizens deported to USSR, 113, 142n68; rehabilitation denied to, 184
Spiridinov, Iurii, 223n110
Spiridov, Sergei Nikoforovich, 39
spiritual resistance, 147, 152–59, 166; internal migration and, 152, 169n34; "public" of zeks and, 148, 149
Stalin, Joseph, 3, 29, 82, 126, 236; "arbitrariness" of, 182–83, 186; col-

INDEX 287

lectivization of agriculture under, 7; cult of personality, 1, 6, 177, 180; death of, 6, 8, 15n3, 137, 185, 236; face of Stalin in sketches by Ivanov, *123*, *128*, 132, *134*; favorably viewed in post-Soviet Russia, 180, 209, 211–12; identified as perpetrator, 181, *185*, 188, 189, 191; Khrushchev's denunciation of, 80–81, 177; lawlessness of, 178; roots of repression predating rule of, 38

Stalinism, 1, 8, 27, 63, 76, 216n32; artworks and memory of, 122; claim of Party members as main victims of, 180, 182–83, 187, 193; coming to terms with the past of, 86; confrontation with crimes of, 64; cultural memory and, 233; feared return of, 82; Maoism and Cambodian genocide as consequences of, 183; number of victims of, 192; prisoners' memoirs written to combat legacy of, 87; Stalinist infrastructure, 60n81, 214n13; violence of, 2, 13, 102, 209

State Gulag History Museum (Moscow), 14, 40, 168n13, 236, 237, 239

"Step to the Left, Step to the Righ, I Shoot" (Ivanov), *120*

Strazdins, Eduard Teodorovich, 175

Subokov, Tikhon, 165

"Summer. Midnight. On My Roof." (Ivanov, 1959–1969), 114, *116*

Supreme Court, of Russia, 14

Supreme Soviet, 51n7

survival: art of, 104, 105–6; camp brotherhood and, 68, 70, 105; economic crisis of 1990s and, 50; friendship and, 66; loss of identity as cost of, 78; psychological, 148; sense

of self and, 103; solidarity and, 72; spiritual, 149

survivor testimonies, 1, 187, 195, 216n32; reconstruction of the past and, 32; state and party archives undermined by, 192; transformation of infrastructure and, 10

svoi ("our own"), 12, 64, 87, 142n69; ability to identify at a glance, 78; camp brotherhood and, 112, 148, 167n4; publics of *svoi*, 87n3; spiritual resistance and, 167n4. *See also* zeks (prisoners), brotherhood of

Syktyvkar, 5, 11, 113, 211; as "capital of the camp republic," 5, 17n23, 35; former prisoners as residents of, 77; monument to victims of political repression, *200*, 201–3, *204*, 224n117, 224nn120–122, 229, *230*; police files on exiles in, 16n14; World War II victory celebrated in, 210

Syktyvkar Department of Social Security, 36, 56n55

Syktyvkar Executive Committee (Gorispolkom), 25, 27

Syktyvkar Memorial Society, 1, 6, 7, 63, 135, 189, 229; archive of, 31, 32, 59n78; documentary film about (1995), 119, 144n91; emergence of, 12; founding of (1998), 27–36; volunteer members of, 29–30

Syktyvkar Memorial Society, letters to, 23–26, 220n83; desire for rehabilitation and, 45–50; reconstruction of the past and, 36–45; sense of place/space and, 37; setting record straight as aim of, 38; "Vorkuta diaspora" and, 163

Tamvelius, Artur, 205, 225n131

Tatars, 4

Terent'ev, Aleksei, 195
"Thaw" (de-Stalinization period), 3, 7, 15n4, 107, 153
30 Oktiabria (Memorial newspaper), 201
Toker, Leona, 8, 9, 20n51, 83, 139n27; on data collection as resistance, 51n5, 66, 88–89n13; on The Gulag Archipelago, 98n89; on highlighted portraits in memoirs, 93n46; on homecoming in Gulag memoirs, 107
Tonkin, Elizabeth, 36–37
totalitarianism, 188, 189
trauma, post-Soviet memory and, 180
"troikas," 6, 39
"Trotskyites," 182, 185
Tsidzik, Cheslava ("Chesia"), 107, 113, 114, 144n95
Tsvetaeva, Marina, 153

Ukhnalev, Evgenii, 144n93
Ukhta, 4, 11, 36, 42, 185; artists from, 113; Khrushchev's speech read in, 80–81; Memorial branch in, 25, 28–29; memorial stone outside local history museum, 222n100; MVD archive in, 46; Pushkin monument, 198, 199; Syktyvkar monument and, 203
Ukhta (newspaper), 185, 187, 192, 215n25; on camp memory of Vetlosian, 195; emergence of civil society and, 187–88; open letter to Gorbachev (1990), 188–89; search for gravesites and, 196; "Week of Conscience" covered in, 197
Ukhta-Pechora Memorial Society, 29, 71, 81, 192, 195; In the Bowels of Ukhtpechlag, 189–90; mission and platform of, 30; "Week of Conscience," 188, 196–97, 209, 221n88

Ukhtizhemlag corrective labor camp, 5, 29, 53n19
Ukhtizhemstroi camp, 5
Ukhtpechlag camp, 5, 29, 65, 93n43, 197, 200
Ukraine/Ukrainians, 4, 76, 178, 196; German advance into Ukraine, 150, 168n17; "Holodomor" famine, 97n80; Soviet annexation of western Ukraine, 41
Ul'ianov, A. N., 150–51
"union of outcasts," 102, 109, 112, 133, 136, 143n79
"Untitled" (Ivanov), 125, 144n98
"Untitled" or "Miners of the Polar Stokehold" (Ivanov), 129
Ural Mountains, 4, 103
Usa River camp, 159, 161
"Usinsk Street" (Ivanov, 1959), 113–14, 116
Ustilovskii, Georgii, 42, 83
Ust'vymlag: Department of Major Construction, 72; marker of mass graves in, 200; remnants of, 44

Vechernii Syktyvkar (newspaper), 189
Vedomosti Memoriala (newspaper), 184
Verdery, Katherine, 197
Veselova, L., 38
Vet'iu, village of, 49, 62n100
Vetlosian camp, 53, 195, 198; "Week of Conscience" requiem at, 179
victims of political repression, 1, 37, 65, 71; categories of, 19n42; children born in camps as, 47; children of former prisoners as, 7, 189; cultural memory and, 8; definition of victims and perpetrators, 12, 26, 180, 181–91; erased from history, 9; expanded definition of "victim," 6, 26,

27, 186, 188; as former "enemies of the people," 14; "gray zone" of victims and perpetrators, 187; number of executions, 186; rehabilitation of, 6, 35, 45, 46, 82; Syktyvkar Memorial Society and, 50; victim versus survivor identity, 85; whole of Soviet society as, 190

victims of political repression, commemoration of, 24, 25, 36, 42, 178, 181; ceremonies and monuments, 194–212; Day of Victims of Political Repression (1993), 165, 202; outside the Komi Republic, 236; Pushkin monument (Ukhta), 198, 199; Sosnogorsk city garden plaque, 199, 223n106; Ukhta "Week of Conscience," 188, 196–97, 221n88; "wall of memory" (Moscow), 196

"View of the Mine 'Kaptial'naia' from the Attic of the Burned Theater" (Ivanov, 1957), 114, 116

Viola, Lynn, 187

Virtual Gulag Museum, 225n135

Virzhonis, Iosif, 163, 164, 165, 173n79

Visvaldis, Kraulis, 77, 113, 118, 143n83

Vlasov, Andrei, 54n25

"Vlasovites," 28, 54n25

Voitalovskaia, A., 48

Volkov, Iurii, 162

Volkov, Nikolai, 73, 80, 82

vol'nonaemnye (civilians), 5, 79, 80, 96n68, 213n5

Volodarskii, Nikolai, 196

Vorkuta, 7, 11, 42, 77, 102, 211; coal mines of, 132, 151; development of culture in, 109, 117; former prisoners as residents of, 16n10, 92n34, 108, 140n41; founding of, 85; Memorial branch in, 25; Polish monument in, 200; railroads and,

37; Syktyvkar monument and, 203; transformation from prison camp to city, 101; "Union of Artists," 111–12, 113, 133; "Vorkuta diaspora" after release, 149, 159, 161–63, 165–66; Vorkutiane (natives/veterans of Vorkuta), 74; "Vorkutinets" (veteran of Vorkuta), 39

Vorkuta Art School and Studio, 118

Vorkuta Museum–Exhibition Center, 13, 84, 101, 102, 119; Ivanov's donation to, 110; questionnaires submitted to, 102

Vorkuta Party Committee (Gorkom), 85

Vorkuta State Drama Theater, 103, 108, 113, 169n26

Vorkutiane (natives/veterans of Vorkuta), 148, 163

Vorkutlag camp, 4, 103; criminals released in amnesty (1953), 108; ethnic composition of, 91n29; gender of prisoners in, 5; mortality rate in, 167n5; prisoner population of, 18n26, 137n8; uprising in (1953), 219n9

Voroshilov, Kliment, 185

Vostochnyi, village of, 213n5

Vunder, Iakov, 111, 112, 138n16, 154

Vunder, Maria Grigor'evna, 112

Vyshnevskii, Vsevolod, 188

Walker, Barbara, 65

Wall of Memory (Kommunarka, Moscow), 237–38, 237, 243n29

Wall of Sorrow (Moscow), 234–35, 236–37, 242n24

"Week of Conscience" (Ukhta), 188, 196–97, 209, 221n88

"Without a Last One" (Ivanov), 122, 126

"Women Miners Hauling Coal at Mine no. 2" (Ivanov), *133*

World War II ("Great Patriotic War"), 3, 35, 54n25, 86, 103, 198; German invasion of the Soviet Union, 150–51; invasion of Ukraine (2022) and memory of, 15n5; patriotic play set during, 140n47; politics of memory under Putin and, 210; prisoners of war punished by Soviet authorities, 45–46, 78, 105, 171n60; Soviet losses in, 192; veterans of, 16n11, 97n79, 188

Yeltsin, Boris, 7

Young, James, 21n57

Young, Sarah J., 64

Yurchak, Alexei, 87n3, 148, 169n34

Zabolotsky, Nikolai, 154

Zapoliar'e (Vorkuta newspaper), 89n14, 193, 195–96

zeks (prisoners), 40, 101; civilian relations with, 41; community of, 161; "public" of, 148, 149, 166. *See also* camp brotherhood (brotherhood of *zeks*); political prisoners

Zhinkin, V. S., 214n16

Zil'berg, 28

Zitzewitz, Josephine von, 154

Zvezda (journal), 99n98

Tyler C. Kirk is Assistant Professor of History and Arctic and Northern Studies at the University of Alaska Fairbanks.

For Indiana University Press

Lesley Bolton, Project Manager/Editor
Brian Carroll, Rights Manager
Sophia Hebert, Assistant Acquisitions Editor
Brenna Hosman, Production Coordinator
Katie Huggins, Production Manager
Bethany Mowry, Acquisitions Editor
Dan Pyle, Online Publishing Manager
Samantha Heffner, Marketing and Publicity Manager
Pamela Rude, Senior Artist and Book Designer